To: Winston & Doreen

Love

Bill & Maureen

II Timothy 1:13

March 24, 1992

A Quest for Godliness

A QUEST FOR GODLINESS

The Puritan Vision of the Christian Life

J. I. PACKER

CROSSWAY BOOKS • WHEATON, ILLINOIS
A DIVISION OF GOOD NEWS PUBLISHERS

Printed in the United States of America

Library of Congress Catalog Card Number 90-80620

ISBN 0-89107-579-8

99	98	97	96	95	94	93	92	91
15	14	13	12	11	10	9	8	7	6	5	4	3

In memory of two friends

John Gywn-Thomas
preacher of grace,
shepherd of souls

and

Raymond Johnston
champion of truth
campaigner for righteousness,

both of whom knew what the Puritans were about
and shared their wisdom with me.

He was . . . [a man foursquare],
immoveable in all times, so that they
who in the midst of many opinions
have lost the view of true religion,
may return to him and there find it.

John Geree,

*The Character of
an Old English Puritane,
or Nonconformist*

Contents

CHAPTER 1:   Introduction   11

THE PURITANS IN PROFILE

CHAPTER 2:   Why We Need the Puritans   21
CHAPTER 3:   Puritanism as a Movement of Revival   35
CHAPTER 4:   The Practical Writings of the English Puritans   49

THE PURITANS AND THE BIBLE

CHAPTER 5:   John Owen on Communication from God   81
CHAPTER 6:   The Puritans as Interpreters of Scripture   97
CHAPTER 7:   The Puritan Conscience   107

THE PURITANS AND THE GOSPEL

CHAPTER 8:   'Saved by His Precious Blood': An Introduction to
               John Owen's *The Death of Death
               in the Death of Christ*   125
CHAPTER 9:   The Doctrine of Justification in Development and
               Decline Among the Puritans   149
CHAPTER 10:   The Puritan View of Preaching the Gospel   163

THE PURITANS AND THE HOLY SPIRIT

CHAPTER 11:   The Witness of the Spirit in Puritan Thought   179
CHAPTER 12:   The Spirituality of John Owen   191
CHAPTER 13:   John Owen on Spiritual Gifts   219

THE PURITAN CHRISTIAN LIFE

CHAPTER 14:   The Puritans and the Lord's Day   233
CHAPTER 15:   The Puritan Approach to Worship   245
CHAPTER 16:   Marriage and Family in Puritan Thought   259

THE PURITANS IN MINISTRY

CHAPTER 17:   Puritan Preaching   277
CHAPTER 18:   Puritan Evangelism   291
CHAPTER 19:   Jonathan Edwards and Revival   309
CHAPTER 20:   Afterword   329
NOTES   337
INDEX   361

Introduction

On a narrow strip of the northern California coastline grow the giant Redwoods, the biggest living things on earth. Some are over 360 feet tall, and some trunks are more than 60 feet round. They do not have much foliage for their size; all their strength is in those huge trunks, with foot-thick bark, that rise sheer for almost half their height before branching out. Some have actually been burned, but are still alive and growing. Many hundreds of years old, over a thousand in some cases, the Redwoods are (to use a much-cheapened word in its old, strict, strong sense) awesome. They dwarf you, making you feel your smallness as scarcely anything else does. Great numbers of Redwoods were thoughtlessly felled in California's logging days, but more recently they have come to be appreciated and preserved, and Redwood parks are today invested with a kind of sanctity. A 33-mile road winding through Redwood groves is fittingly called the Avenue of the Giants.

California's Redwoods make me think of England's Puritans, another breed of giants who in our time have begun to be newly appreciated. Between 1550 and 1700 they too lived unfrilled lives in which, speaking spiritually, strong growth and resistance to fire and storm were what counted. As Redwoods attract the eye, because they overtop other trees, so the mature holiness and seasoned fortitude of the great Puritans shine before us as a kind of beacon light, overtopping the stature of the majority of Christians in most eras, and certainly so in this age of crushing urban collectivism, when Western Christians sometimes feel and often look like

11

ants in an anthill and puppets on a string. Behind the Iron Curtain and in the starving, war-torn lands of Africa the story may well have been different, but in Britain and America, the parts of the world that I know best, affluence seems for the past generation to have been making dwarfs and deadheads of us all. In this situation, the teaching and example of the Puritan giants have much to say to us.

The ecclesiology and politics of the Puritans, their conscience-bound but reluctant and stumbling transitions from medieval solidarities to the individualism of their nonconformist and republican stances, have often been studied, but only recently have Puritan theology and spirituality (that is, to use their own word, godliness) begun to receive serious scholarly attention. Only recently has it been noted that a devotional quickening occurred throughout the divided Western church during the century after the Reformation and that Puritanism was a foremost expression (the foremost expression, I would contend) of this stirring. My own interest in the Puritans has, however, always centred here, and the essays in this book are the fruit of more than forty years' pursuit of it. Nor is my interest merely academic, though it is not, I hope, less than academic. The Puritan giants have shaped me in at least seven ways, and the thrust of the following chapters may be clearer if I list at the outset these items of conscious debt. (Any reader whom this personal stuff wearies may of course skip it; I do not claim for it any intrinsic importance.)

First, at something of a crisis time soon after my conversion, John Owen helped me to be realistic (that is, neither myopic or despairing) about my continuing sinfulness and the discipline of self-suspicion and mortification to which, with all Christians, I am called. I have written about this elsewhere,[1] and shall not rehash the matter here. Suffice it to say that without Owen I might well have gone off my head or got bogged down in mystical fanaticism, and certainly my view of the Christian life would not be what it is today.

Second, some years after that, Owen, under God, enabled me to see how consistent and unambiguous is the biblical witness to the sovereignty and particularity of Christ's redeeming love (which is also, of course, the love of the Father and the Holy Spirit: the Persons of the Godhead are always at one). The theological implications of 'he loved *me* and gave himself for *me*' (Gal 2:20), 'Christ loved *the church* and gave himself up *for her*' (Eph 5:25), 'God shows his love *for us* in that while we were yet sinners Christ died *for us*' (Rom 5:8), and many other passages came clear to me, after some years of dalliance with what I now know to call Amyraldism, through a study of Owen's *The Death of Death in the Death of Christ*, out of which five years later grew the essay on that title in this book. I have found since that I could have learned the same lesson in substance from Spurgeon's sermons or Toplady's hymns or Bernard's discourses on Canticles; but in fact it was Owen who taught it to me, and it has marked my Christianity ever since, as decisively as did the kindred realization, which came to me some years earlier, that biblical religion is God-centered, not man-centered. To get the love of Christ in focus changes one's whole existence.

Third, Richard Baxter convinced me long ago that regular discursive meditation, in which as he quaintly put it you 'imitate the most powerful preacher you ever heard' in applying spiritual truth to yourself, as well as turning that truth into praise, is a vital discipline for spiritual health. This was the unanimous Puritan view, and it is now mine too. God knows, I am a poor practitioner of this wisdom, but when my heart is cold I do at least know what I need. In much current teaching about prayer, contemplation is 'in' and talking to yourself before God is 'out.' I am Puritan enough to think that this contemplative fashion is largely a reaction against devotional formalism, and that it owes as much to twentieth-century anti-intellectualism and interest in non-Christian mysticism as it does to Scripture, and that in cutting loose from the meditative manner of the Psalms, the Fathers, and specifically the Augustinian heritage of which the Puritans are part, it loses without gaining. The contemplative style is not the whole of biblical prayer. At this point Puritan influence puts me out of step with my time, but much, I think, to my advantage.

Fourth, Baxter also focused my vision of the ordained minister's pastoral office. As Warfield said of Luther's *Bondage of the Will*, so do I say of Baxter's *Reformed Pastor*: its words have hands and feet. They climb all over you; they work their way into your heart and conscience, and will not be dislodged. My sense of being called to preach the gospel, teach the Bible, and shepherd souls could have been learned from the Anglican ordinal that was used to ordain me, but in fact it crystallised out through my study of Baxter's own ministry and his *Reformed* (we would say, *Revived*) *Pastor*. From student days I have known that I was called to be a pastor according to Baxter's specifications, and my subsequent commitments to lecturing and writing have simply defined for me aspects of the way in which I should fulfil that role. I wish I had done better at it.

Fifth, the Puritans have taught me to see and feel the transitoriness of this life, to think of it, with all its richness, as essentially the gymnasium and dressing-room where we are prepared for heaven, and to regard readiness to die as the first step in learning to live. Here again is an historic Christian emphasis—Patristic, Medieval, Reformational, Puritan, Evangelical—with which the Protestantism that I know has largely lost touch. The Puritans experienced systematic persecution for their faith; what we today think of as the comforts of home were unknown to them; their medicine and surgery were rudimentary; they had no aspirins, tranquillisers, sleeping tablets or anti-depressant pills, just as they had no social security or insurance; in a world in which more than half the adult population died young and more than half the children born died in infancy, disease, distress, discomfort, pain and death were their constant companions. They would have been lost had they not kept their eyes on heaven and known themselves as pilgrims travelling home to the Celestial City. Dr. Johnson is credited with the remark that when a man knows he is going to be hanged in a fortnight it concentrates his mind wonderfully, and in the same way the Puritans' awareness that in the midst of life we are in death, just one step from eternity, gave them a deep seriousness, calm yet passionate, with regard to the business of living that Christians in today's opulent, mollycoddled, earthbound Western world rarely manage to match. Few of us, I think, live daily on the edge of eternity in the conscious way that the Puritans did, and we lose out as a result. For the extraordinary vivacity, even hilarity (yes, hilarity; you will find it in the sources), with which the Puritans lived stemmed directly, I believe, from the unflinching, matter-of-fact realism with which they prepared themselves for death, so as always to be found, as it were, packed up and ready to go. Reckoning with death brought appreciation of each day's continued life, and the knowledge that God would eventually decide, without consulting them, when their work on earth was done brought energy for the work itself while they were still being given time to get on with it. As I move through my own seventh decade, in better health than can possibly last, I am more glad than I can say for what Puritans like Bunyan and Baxter have taught me about dying; I needed it, and the preachers I hear these days never get to it, and modern Christian writers seem quite clueless about it—save for C. S. Lewis and Charles Williams, whose insight on this as on so much else is surely unique in the twentieth century.

Sixth, the Puritans shaped my churchly identity, by imparting to me their vision of the wholeness of the work of God that they called reformation, and that we would more likely nowadays call renewal. Today, as in my youth, some conservative Anglicans (I speak as one of them) care about orthodoxy, some about liturgy and corporate life, some about individual conversion and nurture, some about aspects of personal sanctity, some about central and congregational structures, some about national moral standards, some about compassionate social witness, some about the reviving of piety amid our Laodiceanism. But each of these concerns gets outflanked, undermined, and ultimately trivialised if it is not linked with all the others. Divided, they fall and run into the sand. I have seen this happen across the board, both in and outside Anglicanism, in my own lifetime. The Puritans gave me a concern for all these things together, as all sustaining each other, and all bearing on the honour and glory of God in his church, and I am thankful to be able to say that inside me they are together still.

I could have learned this ideal of overall evangelical renewal from England's still unappreciated reforming genius Thomas Cranmer or from the nineteenth-century colossus J. C. Ryle (hardly from any more recent Anglican, I think); but, in fact, I got most of it from the Puritans, and principally from the would-be Anglican and reluctant nonconformist Richard Baxter, to whom I owe so much in other areas, as I have already said. Following this gleam as a reforming Anglican has sometimes put me in places where I seemed not to be in step with anyone, and I do not suppose that my judgement on specific questions was always faultless, but looking back I am sure that the comprehensive, non-sectarian lead that Baxter gave me was the right one. I continue to be grateful for it, and expect that gratitude to last for eternity.

Seventh, the Puritans made me aware that all theology is also spirituality, in the sense that it has an influence, good or bad, positive or negative, on its recipients' relationship or lack of relationship to God. If our theology does not quicken the conscience and soften the heart, it actually hardens both; if it does not encourage the commitment of faith, it reinforces the detachment of unbelief; if it fails to promote humility, it inevitably feeds pride. So one who theologises in public, whether formally in the pulpit, on the podium or in print, or informally from the armchair, must think hard about the effect his thoughts will have on people—God's people, and other people. Theologians are called to be the church's water engineers and sewage officers; it is their job to see that God's pure truth flows abundantly where it is needed, and to filter out any intrusive pollution that might damage health. The sociological remoteness of theological colleges, seminaries, and university faculties of theology from the true life of the church makes it easy to forget this, and the track record of professional teachers in these units has in my time been distinctly spotty so far as concerns their responsibility to the church and to the world. In fact, anyone could learn the nature of this responsibility from the Fathers, or Luther, or Calvin, or even, in his own funny fashion, Karl Barth, but it was given to me to learn it through watching the Puritans put every 'doctrine' (truth) they knew to its proper 'use' (application) as a basis for life. It seems to me in retrospect that by virtue of this Puritan influence on me all my theological utterances from the start, on whatever theme, have really been spirituality (i.e., teaching for Christian living), and that I cannot now speak or write any other way. Am I glad? Frankly, yes. It is a happy inability to suffer from.

C.S. Lewis' first and, for my money, most dazzling Christian book was his Bunyanesque allegory, *The Pilgrim's Regress* (1933). There he traced the lure of what he called Sweet Desire, and Joy: namely, that tang of the transcendent in the everyday that hits the heart like a blow as one experiences and enjoys things, revealing itself ultimately as a longing not satisfied by any created realities or relationships, but assuaged only in self-abandonment to the Creator's love in Christ. As Lewis knew, different stimuli trigger this desire in different people; for himself, he talks of 'the smell of a bonfire, the sound of wild ducks flying overhead, the title of *The Well at the World's End*, the opening lines of *Kubla Khan*, the morning cobwebs in late summer, the noise of falling waves'.[2] None of those items produces the full effect for me, though I understand how they could do so for Lewis and others; but I can speak of the sight of trees, waterfalls, and steam locomotives, the taste of curry and crab, bits of Bach, Beethoven, Brahms, Bruckner, and Wagner, some improvisatory moments and architectural marvels on my records of performances by Wilhelm Furtwängler, Edwin Fischer, and Otto Klemperer, and occasional sublimities by Jelly-Roll Morton, Bubber Miley, and Louis Armstrong, plus—and this is why I bring the matter up—some touches of rhetoric which for me are recurrently numinous in the five writers I have already named: Lewis himself, and Williams, and (you saw it coming) seraphic Baxter, dreamer Bunyan, and elephantine Owen. Form and content though distinct are connected, and here I connect them, saying that by writing *as* they do, no less than *what* they do, these authors fill their books with God for me, making me want him more as they bring him closer. That this material should be as significant for me in its style as it is in its substance seems to me peculiarly happy. Your experience here may not match mine (Owen's lumbering Latinised idiom, in particular, delights very few); however, there will be that in your experience which enables you to understand mine, and I wanted you fully to know where, as the Americans say, I am coming from when I celebrate the Puritan giants.

I hope these chapters will excite you, for in them I share discoveries that for forty years have been exciting me. The essays are not just history and historical theology; they are themselves, in aim at least, spirituality, as much as anything else I have written; they focus on ways in which, as I see it, the Puritans are giants compared with us, giants whose help we need if ever we are to grow. Learning from the heroes of the Christian past is in any case an important dimension of that edifying fellowship for which the proper name is the communion of saints. The great Puritans, though dead, still speak to us through their writings, and say things to us that we badly need to hear at this present time. I shall try to set some of these before you, in the chapters that follow.

Sources

Much of the material in this book is reproduction or revision of items that have appeared in print before: hence the occasional repetition.

'Why We Need the Puritans' is partly based on a chapter contributed to Leland Ryken, *Worldly Saints* (Zondervan: Grand Rapids, 1986), pp ix-xvi.

'Puritanism as a Movement of Revival' was published in *The Evangelical Quarterly*, LII:i (January 1980), pp 2-16.

'The Practical Writings of the English Puritans' began life as the Evangelical Library Lecture for 1951.

From the privately printed and now out of print annual reports of the Puritan and Reformed Studies Conference come 'John Owen on Communication from God' (*One Steadfast High Intent*, 1966, pp 17-30); 'The

Puritans as Interpreters of Scripture' (*A Goodly Heritage*, 1958, pp 18-26); 'The Puritan Conscience' (*Faith and a Good Conscience*, 1962, pp 18-26); 'The Doctrine of Justification in Development and Decline among the Puritans' (*By Schisms Rent Asunder*, 1969, pp 18-30); 'The Puritan View of Preaching the Gospel' (*How Shall they Hear?*, 1959, pp 11-21); 'The Witness of the Spirit in Puritan Thought' (*The Wisdom of our Fathers*, 1956), pp. 14-25; 'John Owen on Spiritual Gifts' (*Profitable for Doctrine and Reproof*, 1967, pp 15-27); 'The Puritans and the Lord's Day' (*Servants of the Word*, 1957, pp 1-12); 'The Puritan Approach to Worship' (*Diversity in Unity*, 1963, pp 3-14); 'Jonathan Edwards and Revival' (*Increasing in the Knowledge of God*, 1960, pp 13-28).

Some of the material in 'The Spirituality of John Owen' was printed in my introduction to *Sin and Temptation*, by John Owen, abridged and edited by James M. Houston (Multnomah Press: Portland, 1983), pp xvii-xxix, and some is taken from 'The Puritan Idea of Communion with God' (*Press Toward the Mark*, Puritan and Reformed Studies Conference report, 1961, pp 5-15).

'Puritan Preaching' in its original form was written for *The Johnian* (Lent 1956), pp 4-9.

'Puritan Evangelism' broke surface in *The Banner of Truth*, 4 (1957), pp 4-13. Some of the material in the chapter comes from my introduction to Richard Baxter, *The Reformed Pastor*, edited by William Brown (Banner of Truth: London, 1974), pp 9-19.

'"Saved by his Precious Blood"' is my introduction to a 1958 reprint of John Owen's *The Death of Death in the Death of Christ* (Banner of Truth: London).

Quotations

Absolute consistency in reproducing sixteenth- and seventeenth-century material has not been aimed at, nor achieved. Materials are cited as they appear in whatever printed books I was using as I wrote each item. Where reprints of Puritan material exist I usually cite them, but not invariably.

THE PURITANS IN PROFILE

CHAPTER TWO

Why We Need the Puritans

1

Horse racing is said to be the sport of kings. The sport of slinging mud has, however, a wider following. Pillorying the Puritans, in particular, has long been a popular pastime both sides of the Atlantic, and most people's image of Puritanism still has on it much disfiguring dirt that needs to be scraped off.

'Puritan' as a name was, in fact, mud from the start. Coined in the early 1560s, it was always a satirical smear word implying peevishness, censoriousness, conceit, and a measure of hypocrisy, over and above its basic implication of religiously motivated discontent with what was seen as Elizabeth's Laodicean and compromising Church of England. Later, the word gained the further, political connotation of being against the Stuart monarchy and for some sort of republicanism; its primary reference, however, was still to what was seen as an odd, furious, and ugly form of Protestant religion.

In England, anti-Puritan feeling was let loose at the time of the Restoration and has flowed freely ever since. In North America it built up slowly after the days of Jonathan Edwards to reach its zenith a hundred years ago in post-Puritan New England. For the past half-century, however, scholars have been meticulously wiping away the mud, and as Michelangelo's frescoes in the Sistine Chapel have unfamiliar colours today now that restorers have removed the dark varnish, so the conventional image of the Puritans has been radically revamped, at least for those in the know. (Knowledge, alas, travels slowly in some quarters.) Taught by Perry Miller, William Haller, Marshall Knappen, Percy Scholes, Edmund Morgan, and a host of more recent researchers, informed folk now acknowledge that the typical Puritans were not wild men, fierce and freaky, religious fanatics and social extremists, but sober, conscientious, and cultured citizens: persons of principle, devoted, determined, and disciplined, excelling in the domestic virtues, and with no obvious shortcomings save a tendency to run to words when saying anything important, whether to God or to man. At last the record has been put straight.

But even so, the suggestion that we *need* the Puritans—we late twentieth-century Westerners, with all our sophistication and mastery of technique in both secular and sacred fields—may prompt some lifting of eyebrows. The belief that the Puritans, even if they were in fact responsible citizens, were comic and pathetic in equal degree, being naive and superstitious, primitive and gullible, superserious, overscrupulous, majoring in minors, and unable or unwilling to relax, dies hard. What could these zealots give us that we need, it is asked.

The answer, in one word, is maturity. Maturity is a compound of wisdom, goodwill, resilience, and creativity. The Puritans exemplified maturity; we don't. We are spiritual dwarfs. A much-travelled leader, a native American (be it said), has declared that he finds North American Protestantism, man-centered, manipulative, success-oriented, self-indulgent and sentimental, as it blatantly is, to be 3,000 miles wide and half an inch deep. The Puritans, by contrast, as a body were giants. They were great souls serving a great God. In them clear-headed passion and warm-hearted compassion combined. Visionary and practical, idealistic and realistic too, goal-oriented and methodical, they were great believers, great hopers, great doers, and great sufferers. But their sufferings, both sides of the ocean (in old England from the authorities and in New England from the elements), seasoned and ripened them till they gained a stature that was nothing short of heroic. Ease and luxury, such as our affluence brings us today, do not make for maturity; hardship and struggle however do, and the Puritans' battles against the spiritual and climatic wildernesses in which God set them produced a virility of character, undaunted and unsinkable, rising above discouragement and fears, for which the true precedents and models are men like Moses, and Nehemiah, and Peter after Pentecost, and the apostle Paul.

Spiritual warfare made the Puritans what they were. They accepted conflict as their calling, seeing themselves as their Lord's soldier-pilgrims, just as in Bunyan's allegory, and not expecting to be able to advance a single step without opposition of one sort or another. Wrote John Geree, in his tract *The Character of an Old English Puritane or Nonconformist* (1646): 'His whole life he accounted a warfare, wherein Christ was his captain, his arms, praiers and tears. The Crosse his Banner and his word [motto] *Vincit qui patitur* [he who suffers conquers].'[1]

The Puritans lost, more or less, every public battle that they fought. Those who stayed in England did not change the Church of England as they hoped to do, nor did they revive more than a minority of its adherents, and eventually they were driven out of Anglicanism by calculated pressure on their consciences. Those who crossed the Atlantic failed to establish new Jerusalem in New England; for the first fifty years their little colonies barely survived. They hung on by the skin of their teeth. But the moral and spiritual victories that the Puritans won by keeping sweet, peaceful, patient, obedient, and hopeful under sustained and seemingly intolerable pressures and frustrations give them a place of high honour in the believers' hall of fame, where Hebrews 11 is the first gallery. It was out of this constant furnace-experience that their maturity was wrought and their wisdom concerning discipleship was refined. George Whitefield, the evangelist, wrote of them as follows:

> Ministers never write or preach so well as when under the cross; the Spirit of Christ and of glory then rests upon them. It was this, no doubt, that made the Puritans . . . such burning and shining lights. When cast out by the black Bartholomew-act [the 1662 Act of Uniformity] and driven from their respective charges to preach in barns and fields, in the highways and hedges, they in an especial manner wrote and preached as men having authority. Though dead, by their writings they yet speak; a peculiar unction attends them to this very hour. . . .[2]

Those words come from a preface to a reprint of Bunyan's works that appeared in 1767; but the unction continues, the authority is still felt, and the mature wisdom still remains breathtaking, as all modern Puritan-readers soon discover for themselves. Through the legacy of this literature the Puritans can help us today towards the maturity that they knew, and that we need.

2

In what ways can they do this? Let me suggest some specifics. First, there are lessons for us in *the integration of their daily lives*. As their Christianity was all-embracing, so their living was all of a piece. Nowadays we would call their lifestyle holistic: all awareness, activity, and enjoyment, all 'use of the creatures' and development of personal powers and creativity, was integrated in the single purpose of honouring God by appreciating all his gifts and making everything 'holiness to the Lord'. There was for them no disjunction between sacred and secular; all creation, so far as they were concerned, was sacred, and all activities, of whatever kind, must be sanctified, that is, done to the glory of God. So, in their heavenly-minded ardour, the Puritans became men and women of order, matter-of-fact and down-to-earth, prayerful, purposeful, practical. Seeing life whole, they integrated contemplation with action, worship with work, labour with rest, love of God with love of neighbour and of self, personal with social identity, and the wide spectrum of relational responsibilities with each other, in a thoroughly conscientious and thought-out way. In this thoroughness they were extreme, that is to say far more thorough than we are, but in their blending of the whole wide range of Christian duties set forth in Scripture they were eminently balanced. They lived by 'method' (we would say, by a rule of life), planning and proportioning their time with care, not so much to keep bad things out as to make sure that they got all good and important things in—necessary wisdom, then as now, for busy people! We today, who tend to live unplanned lives at random in a series of non-communicating compartments and who hence feel swamped and distracted most of the time, could learn much from the Puritans at this point.

Second, there are lessons for us in *the quality of their spiritual experience*. In the Puritans' communion with God, as Jesus Christ was central, so Holy Scripture was supreme. By Scripture, as God's word of instruction about divine-human relationships, they sought to live, and here, too, they were conscientiously methodical. Knowing themselves to be creatures of thought, affection, and will, and knowing that God's way to the human heart (the will) is via the human head (the mind), the Puritans practised meditation, discursive and systematic, on the whole range of biblical truth as they saw it applying to themselves. Puritan meditation on Scripture was modelled on the Puritan sermon; in meditation the Puritan would seek to search and challenge his heart, stir his affections to hate sin and love righteousness, and encourage himself with God's promises, just as Puritan preachers would do from the pulpit. This rational, resolute, passionate piety was conscientious without becoming obsessive, law-oriented without lapsing into legalism, and expressive of Christian liberty without any shameful lurches into license. The Puritans knew that Scripture is the unalterable rule of holiness, and never allowed themselves to forget it. Knowing also the dishonesty and deceitfulness of fallen human hearts, they cultivated humility and self-suspicion as abiding attitudes, and examined themselves regularly for spiritual blind spots and lurking inward evils. They may not be called morbid or introspective on this account, however; on the contrary, they found the discipline of self-examination by Scripture (not the same thing as introspection, let us note), followed by the discipline of confessing and forsaking sin and renewing one's gratitude to Christ for his pardoning mercy, to be a source of great inner peace and joy. We today, who know to our cost that we have unclear minds, uncontrolled affections, and unstable wills when it comes to serving God, and who again and again find ourselves being imposed on by irrational, emotional romanticism disguised as super-spirituality, could profit much from the Puritans' example at this point too.

Third, there are lessons for us in *their passion for effective action.* Though the Puritans, like the rest of the human race, had their dreams of what could and should be, they were decidedly not the kind of people that we would call 'dreamy'! They had no time for the idleness of the lazy or passive person who leaves it to others to change the world. They were men of action in the pure Reformed mould—crusading activists without a jot of self-reliance; workers for God who depended utterly on God to work in and through them, and who always gave God the praise for anything they did that in retrospect seemed to them to have been right; gifted men who prayed earnestly that God would enable them to use their powers, not for self-display, but for his praise. None of them wanted to be revolutionaries in church or state, though some of them reluctantly became such; all of them, however, longed to be effective change agents for God wherever shifts from sin to sanctity were called for. So Cromwell and his army made long, strong prayers before each battle, and preachers made long, strong prayers privately before ever venturing into the pulpit, and laymen made long, strong prayers before tackling any matter of importance (marriage, business deals, major purchases, or whatever). Today, however, Christians in the West are found to be on the whole passionless, passive, and, one fears, prayerless; cultivating an ethos which encloses personal piety in a pietistic cocoon, they leave public affairs to go their own way and neither expect nor for the most part seek influence beyond their own Christian circle. Where the Puritans prayed and laboured for a holy England and New England, sensing that where privilege is neglected and unfaithfulness reigns national judgement threatens, modern Christians gladly settle for conventional social respectability and, having done so, look no further. Surely it is obvious that at this point also the Puritans have a great deal to teach us.

Fourth, there are lessons for us in *their program for family stability.* It is hardly too much to say that the Puritans created the Christian family in the English-speaking world. The Puritan ethic of marriage was to look not for a partner whom you *do* love passionately at this moment, but rather for one whom you *can* love steadily as your best friend for life, and then to proceed with God's help to do just that. The Puritan ethic of nurture was to train up children in the way they should go, to care for their bodies and souls together, and to educate them for sober, godly, socially useful adult living. The Puritan ethic of home life was based on maintaining order, courtesy, and family worship. Goodwill, patience, consistency, and an encouraging attitude were seen as the essential domestic virtues. In an age of routine discomforts, rudimentary medicine without pain-killers, frequent bereavements (most families lost at least as many children as they reared), an average life expectancy of just under thirty years, and economic hardship for almost all save merchant princes and landed gentry, family life was a school for character in every sense, and the fortitude with which Puritans resisted the all-too-familiar temptation to relieve pressure from the world by brutality at home, and laboured to honour God in their families despite all, merits supreme praise. At home the Puritans showed themselves (to use my overworked term) mature, accepting hardships and disappointments realistically as from God and refusing to be daunted or soured by any of them. Also, it was at home in the first instance that the Puritan layman practised evangelism and ministry. 'His family he endeavoured to make a Church,' wrote Geree, '. . . labouring that those that were born in it, might be born again to God.'[3] In an era in which family life has become brittle even among Christians, with chicken-hearted spouses taking the easy course of separation rather than working at their relationship, and narcissistic parents spoiling their children materially while neglecting them spiritually, there is once more much to be learned from the Puritans' very different ways.

Fifth, there are lessons to be learned from their *sense of human worth*. Through believing in a great God (the God of Scripture, undiminished and undomesticated), they gained a vivid awareness of the greatness of moral issues, of eternity, and of the human soul. Hamlet's 'What a piece of work is man!' is a very Puritan sentiment; the wonder of human individuality was something that they felt keenly. Though, under the influence of their medieval heritage, which told them that error has no rights, they did not in every case manage to respect those who differed publicly from them, their appreciation of man's dignity as the creature made to be God's friend was strong, and so in particular was their sense of the beauty and nobility of human holiness. In the collectivised urban anthill where most of us live nowadays the sense of each individual's eternal significance is much eroded, and the Puritan spirit is at this point a corrective from which we can profit greatly.

Sixth, there are lessons to be learned from the Puritans' *ideal of church renewal*. To be sure, 'renewal' was not a word that they used; they spoke only of 'reformation' and 'reform', which words suggest to our twentieth-century minds a concern that is limited to the externals of the church's orthodoxy, order, worship forms and disciplinary code. But when the Puritans preached, published, and prayed for 'reformation' they had in mind, not indeed less than this, but far more. On the title page of the original edition of Richard Baxter's *The Reformed Pastor*, the word 'reformed' was printed in much larger type than any other, and one does not have to read far before discovering that for Baxter a 'reformed' pastor was not one who campaigned for Calvinism but one whose ministry to his people as preacher, teacher, catechist and role-model showed him to be, as we would say, 'revived' or 'renewed'. The essence of this kind of 'reformation' was enrichment of understanding of God's truth, arousal of affections God-ward, increase of ardour in one's devotions, and more love, joy, and firmness of Christian purpose in one's calling and personal life. In line with this, the ideal for the church was that through 'reformed' clergy all the members of each congregation should be 'reformed'—brought, that is, by God's grace without disorder into a state of what we would call revival, so as to be truly and thoroughly converted, theologically orthodox and sound, spiritually alert and expectant, in character terms wise and steady, ethically enterprising and obedient, and humbly but joyously sure of their salvation. This was the goal at which Puritan pastoral ministry aimed throughout, both in English parishes and in the 'gathered' churches of con-gregational type that multiplied in the mid-seventeenth century.

The Puritans' concern for spiritual awakening in communities is to some extent hidden from us by their institutionalism; recalling the upheavals of English Methodism and the Great Awakening, we think of revival ardour as always putting a strain on established order, whereas the Puritans envisaged 'reform' at congregational level coming in disciplined style through faithful preaching, catechising, and spiritual service on the pastor's part. Clericalism, with its damming up of lay initiative, was doubtless a Puritan limitation, and one which boomeranged when lay zeal finally boiled over in Cromwell's army, in Quakerism, and in the vast sec-tarian underworld of Commonwealth times; but the other side of that coin was the nobility of the pastor's profile that the Puritans evolved—gospel preacher and Bible teacher, shepherd and physician of souls, catechist and counsellor, trainer and disciplinarian, all in one. From the Puritans' ideals and goals for church life, which were unquestionably and abidingly right, and from their standards for clergy, which were challengingly and search-ingly high, there is yet again a great deal that modern Christians can and should take to heart.

These are just a few of the most obvious areas in which the Puritans can help us in these days.

3

The foregoing celebration of Puritan greatness may leave some readers sceptical. It is, however, as was hinted earlier, wholly in line with the major reassessment of Puritanism that has taken place in historical scholarship. Fifty years ago the academic study of Puritanism went over a watershed with the discovery that there was such a thing as Puritan culture, and a rich culture at that, over and above Puritan reactions against certain facets of medieval and Renaissance culture. The common assumption of earlier days, that Puritans both sides of the Atlantic were characteristically mor-bid, obsessive, uncouth and unintelligent, was left behind. Satirical aloofness towards Puritan thought-life gave way to sympathetic attentiveness, and the exploring of Puritan beliefs and ideals became an academic cottage industry of impressive vigour, as it still is. North America led the way with four books published over two years which between them ensured that Puritan studies could never be the same again. These were: William Haller, *The Rise of Puritanism* (Columbia University Press: New York, 1938); A.S.P. Woodhouse, *Puritanism and Liberty* (Macmillan: London, 1938; Woodhouse taught at Toronto); M.M. Knappen, *Tudor Puritanism* (Chicago University Press: Chicago, 1939); and Perry Miller, *The New England Mind Vol I; The Seventeenth Century* (Harvard University Press: Cambridge, MA, 1939). Many books from the thirties and later have confirmed the view of Puritanism which these four volumes yielded, and the overall picture that has emerged is as follows.

Puritanism was at heart a spiritual movement, passionately concerned with God and godliness. It began in England with William Tyndale the Bible translator, Luther's contemporary, a generation before the word 'Puritan' was coined, and it continued till the latter years of the seventeenth century, some decades after 'Puritan' had fallen out of use. Into its making went Tyndale's reforming biblicism; John Bradford's piety of the heart and conscience; John Knox's zeal for God's honour in national churches; the passion for evangelical pastoral competence that is seen in John Hooper, Edward Dering and Richard Greenham; the view of Holy Scripture as the 'regulative principle' of church worship and order that fired Thomas Cartwright; the anti-Roman, anti-Arminian, anti-Socinian, anti-Antinomian Calvinism that John Owen and the Westminster standards set forth; the comprehensive ethical interest that reached its apogee in Richard Baxter's monumental *Christian Directory*; and the purpose of popularising and making practical the teaching of the Bible that gripped Perkins and Bunyan, with many more. Puritanism was essentially a movement for church reform, pastoral renewal and evangelism, and spiritual revival; and in addition—indeed, as a direct expression of its zeal for God's honour—it was a world-view, a total Christian philosophy, in intellectual terms a Protestantised and updated medievalism, and in terms of spirituality a reformed monasticism outside the cloister and away from monkish vows.

The Puritan goal was to complete what England's Reformation began: to finish reshaping Anglican worship, to introduce effective church discipline into Anglican parishes, to establish righteousness in the political, domestic, and socio-economic fields, and to convert all Englishmen to a vigorous evangelical faith. Through the preaching and teaching of the gospel, and the sanctifying of all arts, sciences, and skills, England was to become a land of saints, a model and paragon of corporate godliness, and as such a means of blessing to the world.

Such was the Puritan dream as it developed under Elizabeth, James, and Charles, and blossomed in the Interregnum, before it withered in the dark tunnel of persecution between 1660 (Restoration) and 1689 (Toleration). This dream bred the giants with whom this book is concerned.

4

The present chapter is, I confess, advocacy, barefaced and unashamed. I am seeking to make good the claim that the Puritans can teach us lessons that we badly need to learn. Let me pursue my line of argument a little further.

It must by now be apparent that the great Puritan pastor-theologians—Owen, Baxter, Goodwin, Howe, Perkins, Sibbes, Brooks, Watson, Gurnall, Flavel, Bunyan, Manton, and others like them—were men of outstanding intellectual power, as well as spiritual insight. In them mental habits fostered by sober scholarship were linked with a flaming zeal for God and a minute acquaintance with the human heart. All their work displays this unique fusion of gifts and graces. In thought and outlook they were radically God-centred. Their appreciation of God's sovereign majesty was profound, and their reverence in handling his written word was deep and constant. They were patient, thorough, and methodical in searching the Scriptures, and their grasp of the various threads and linkages in the web of revealed truth was firm and clear. They understood most richly the ways of God with men, the glory of Christ the Mediator, and the work of the Spirit in the believer and the church.

And their knowledge was no mere theoretical orthodoxy. They sought to 'reduce to practice' (their own phrase) all that God taught them. They yoked their consciences to his word, disciplining themselves to bring all activities under the scrutiny of Scripture, and to demand a theological, as distinct from a merely pragmatic, justification for everything that they did. The applied their understanding of the mind of God to every branch of life, seeing the church, the family, the state, the arts and sciences, the world of commerce and industry, no less than the devotions of the individual, as so many spheres in which God must be served and honoured. They saw life whole, for they saw its Creator as Lord of each department of it, and their purpose was that 'holiness to the Lord' might be written over it in its entirety.

Nor was this all. Knowing God, the Puritans also knew man. They saw him as in origin a noble being, made in God's image to rule God's earth, but now tragically brutified and brutalised by sin. They viewed sin in the triple light of God's law, Lordship, and holiness, and so saw it as transgression and guilt, as rebellion and usurpation, and as uncleanness, corruption, and inability for good. Seeing this, and knowing the ways whereby the Spirit brings sinners to faith and new life in Christ, and leads saints, on the one hand, to grow into their Saviour's image, and, on the other, to learn their total dependence on grace, the great Puritans became superb pastors. The depth and unction of their 'practical and experimental' expositions in the pulpit was no more outstanding than was their skill in the study in applying spiritual physic to sick souls. From Scripture they mapped the often bewildering terrain of the life of faith and fellowship with God with great thoroughness (see *Pilgrim's Progress* for a pictorial gazetteer), and their acuteness and wisdom in diagnosing spiritual malaise and setting out the appropriate biblical remedies was outstanding. They remain the classic pastors of Protestantism, just as men like Whitefield and Spurgeon stand as its classic evangelists.

Now it is here, on the pastoral front, that today's evangelical Christians most need help. Our numbers, it seems, have increased in recent years, and a new interest in the old paths of evangelical theology has grown. For this we should thank God. But not all evangelical zeal is according to knowledge, nor do the virtues and values of the biblical Christian life always come together as they should, and three groups in particular in today's evangelical world seem very obviously to need help of a kind that the Puritans, as we meet them in their writings, are uniquely qualified to give. These I call *restless experientialists*, *entrenched intellectualists*, and *disaffected deviationists*. They are not, of course, organised bodies of opinion, but individual persons with characteristic mentalities that one meets over and over again. Take them, now, in order.

Those whom I call *restless experientialists* are a familiar breed, so much so that observers are sometimes tempted to define evangelicalism in terms of them. Their outlook is one of casual haphazardness and fretful impatience, of grasping after novelties, entertainments, and 'highs', and of valuing strong feelings above deep thoughts. They have little taste for solid study, humble self-examination, disciplined meditation, and unspectacular hard work in their callings and their prayers. They conceive the Christian life as one of exciting extraordinary experiences rather than of resolute rational righteousness. They dwell continually on the themes of joy, peace, happiness, satisfaction and rest of soul with no balancing reference to the divine discontent of Romans 7, the fight of faith of Psalm 73, or the 'lows' of Psalms 42, 88 and 102. Through their influence the spontaneous jollity of the simple extrovert comes to be equated with healthy Christian living, while saints of less sanguine and more complex temperament get driven almost to distraction because they cannot bubble over in the prescribed manner. In their restlessness these exuberant ones become uncritically credulous, reasoning that the more odd and striking an experience the more divine, supernatural, and spiritual it must be, and they scarcely give the scriptural virtue of steadiness a thought.

It is no counter to these defects to appeal to the specialised counselling techniques that extrovert evangelicals have developed for pastoral purposes in recent years; for spiritual life is fostered, and spiritual maturity engendered, not by techniques but by truth, and if our techniques have been formed in terms of a defective notion of the truth to be conveyed and the goal to be aimed at they cannot make us better pastors or better believers than we were before. The reason why the restless experientialists are lop-sided is that they have fallen victim to a form of worldliness, a man-centred, anti-rational individualism, which turns Christian life into a thrill-seeking ego-trip. Such saints need the sort of maturing ministry in which the Puritan tradition has specialised.

What Puritan emphases can establish and settle restless experientialsts? These, to start with. First, the stress on God-centredness as a divine require-ment that is central to the discipline of self-denial. Second, the insistence on the primacy of the mind, and on the impossibility of obeying biblical truth that one has not yet understood. Third, the demand for humility, patience, and steadiness at all times, and for an acknowledgment that the Holy Spirit's main ministry is not to give thrills but to create in us Christlike character. Fourth, the recognition that feelings go up and down, and that God frequently tries us by leading us through wastes of emotional flatness. Fifth, the singling out of worship as life's primary activity. Sixth, the stress on our need of regular self-examination by Scripture, in terms set by Psalm 139:23-24. Seventh, the realisation that sanctified suffering bulks large in God's plan for his children's growth in grace. No Christian tradition of teaching administers this purging and strengthening medicine with more masterful authority than does that of the Puritans, whose own dispensing of it nurtured a marvellously strong and resilient type of Christian for a century and more, as we have seen.

Think now of *entrenched intellectualists* in the evangelical world: a sec-ond familiar breed, though not so common as the previous type. Some of them seem to be victims of an insecure temperament and inferiority feel-ings, others to be reacting out of pride or pain against the zaniness of expe-rientialism as they have perceived it, but whatever the source of their syndrome the behaviour-pattern in which they express it is distinctive and characteristic. Constantly they present themselves as rigid, argumentative, critical Christians, champions of God's truth for whom orthodoxy is all. Upholding and defending their own view of that truth, whether Calvinist or Arminian, dispensational or Pentecostal, national church reformist or Free Church separatist, or whatever it might be, is their leading interest, and they invest themselves unstintingly in this task. There is little warmth about them; relationally they are remote; experiences do not mean much to them; winning the battle for mental correctness is their one great pur-pose. They see, truly enough, that in our anti-rational, feeling-oriented, instant-gratification culture conceptual knowledge of divine things is undervalued, and they seek with passion to right the balance at this point. They understand the priority of the intellect well; the trouble is that intel-lectualism, expressing itself in endless campaigns for their own brand of right thinking, is almost if not quite all that they can offer, for it is almost if not quite all that they have. They too, so I urge, need exposure to the Puritan heritage for their maturing.

That last statement might sound paradoxical, since it will not have escaped the reader that the above profile corresponds to what many still suppose the typical Puritan to have been. But when we ask what emphases Puritan tradition contains to counter arid intellectualism, a whole series of points springs to view. First, true religion claims the affections as well as the intellect; it is essentially, in Richard Baxter's phrase, 'heart-work'. Second, theological truth is for practice. William Perkins defined theology as the science of living blessedly for ever; William Ames called it the science of living to God. Third, conceptual knowledge kills if one does not move on from knowing notions to knowing the realities to which they refer—in this case, from knowing about God to a relational acquaintance with God himself. Fourth, faith and repentance, issuing in a life of love and holiness, that is, of gratitude expressed in goodwill and good works, are explicitly called for in the gospel. Fifth, the Spirit is given to lead us into close companionship with others in Christ. Sixth, the discipline of discursive meditation is meant to keep us ardent and adoring in our love affair with God. Seventh, it is ungodly and scandalous to become a firebrand and cause division in the church, and it is ordinarily nothing more reputable than spiritual pride in its intellectual form that leads men to create parties and splits. The great Puritans were as humble-minded and warm-hearted as they were clear-headed, as fully oriented to people as they were to Scripture, and as passionate for peace as they were for truth. They would certainly have diagnosed today's fixated Christian intellectualists as spiritually stunted, not in their zeal for the form of sound words but in their lack of zeal for anything else; and the thrust of Puritan teaching about God's truth in man's life is still potent to ripen such souls into whole and mature human beings.

I turn finally to those whom I call *disaffected deviationists*, the casualties and dropouts of the modern evangelical movement, many of whom have now turned against it to denounce it as a neurotic perversion of Christianity. Here, too, is a breed that we know all too well. It is distressing to think of these folk, both because their experience to date discredits our evangelicalism so deeply and also because there are so many of them. Who are they? They are people who once saw themselves as evangelicals, either from being evangelically nurtured or from coming to profess conversion within the evangelical sphere of influence, but who have become disillusioned about the evangelical point of view and have turned their back on it, feeling that it let them down. Some leave it for intellectual reasons, judging that what was taught them was so simplistic as to stifle their minds and so unrealistic and out of touch with facts as to be really if unintentionally dishonest. Others leave because they were led to expect that as Christians they would enjoy health, wealth, trouble-free circumstances, immunity from relational hurts, betrayals, and failures, and from making mistakes and bad decisions; in short, a flowery bed of ease on which they would be carried happily to heaven—and these great expectations were in due course refuted by events. Hurt and angry, feeling themselves victims of a confidence trick, they now accuse the evangelicalism they knew of having failed and fooled them, and resentfully give it up; it is a mercy if they do not therewith similarly accuse and abandon God himself. Modern evangelicalism has much to answer for in the number of casualties of this sort that it has caused in recent years by its naivety of mind and unrealism of expectation. But here again the soberer, profounder, wiser evangelicalism of the Puritan giants can fulfil a corrective and therepeutic function in our midst, if only we will listen to its message.

What have the Puritans to say to us that might serve to heal the disaffected casualties of modern evangelical goofiness? Anyone who reads the writings of Puritan authors will find in them much that helps in this way. Puritan authors regularly tell us, first, of the *mystery* of God: that our God is too small, that the real God cannot be put without remainder into a manmade conceptual box so as to be fully understood; and that he was, is, and always will be bewilderingly inscrutable in his dealing with those who trust and love him, so that 'losses and crosses', that is, bafflement and disappointment in relation to particular hopes one has entertained, must be accepted as a recurring element in one's life of fellowship with him. Then they tell us, second, of the *love* of God: that it is a love that redeems, converts, sanctifies, and ultimately glorifies sinners, and that Calvary was the one place in human history where it was fully and unambiguously revealed, and that in relation to our own situation we may know for certain that nothing can separate us from that love (Rom 8:38f), although no situation in this world will ever be free from flies in the ointment and thorns in the bed. Developing the theme of divine love the Puritans tell us, third, of the *salvation* of God: that the Christ who put away our sins and brought us God's pardon is leading us through this world to a glory for which we are even now being prepared by the instilling of desire for it and capacity to enjoy it, and that holiness here, in the form of consecrated service and loving obedience through thick and thin, is the high road to happiness hereafter. Following this they tell us, fourth, about *spiritual conflict*, the many ways in which the world, the flesh and the devil seek to lay us low; fifth, about the *protection* of God, whereby he overrules and sanctifies the conflict, often allowing one evil to touch our lives in order thereby to shield us from greater evils; and, sixth, about the *glory* of God, which it becomes our privilege to further by our celebrating of his grace, by our proving of his power under perplexity and pressure, by totally resigning ourselves to his good pleasure, and by making him our joy and delight at all times.

By ministering to us these precious biblical truths the Puritans give us the resources we need to cope with 'the slings and arrows of outrageous fortune', and offer the casualties an insight into what has happened to them that can raise them above self-pitying resentment and reaction and restore their spiritual health completely. Puritan sermons show that problems about providence are in no way new; the seventeenth century had its own share of spiritual casualties, saints who had thought simplistically and hoped unrealistically and were now disappointed, disaffected, despondent and despairing, and the Puritans' ministry to us at this point is simply the spin-off of what they were constantly saying to raise up and encourage wounded spirits among their own people.

I think the answer to the question, why do we need the Puritans, is now pretty clear, and I conclude my argument at this point. I, who owe more to the Puritans than to any other theologians I have ever read, and who know that I need them still, have been trying to persuade you that perhaps you need them too. To succeed in this would, I confess, make me overjoyed, and that chiefly for your sake, and the Lord's. But there, too, is something that I must leave in God's hands. Meantime, let us continue to explore the Puritan heritage together. There is more gold to be mined here than I have mentioned yet.

CHAPTER THREE

Puritanism as a Movement of Revival

1

I begin by offering definitions, first of Puritanism and then of revival, as a foundation for what I have to say.

Puritanism I define as that movement in sixteenth- and seventeenth-century England which sought further reformation and renewal in the Church of England than the Elizabethan settlement allowed. 'Puritan' itself was an imprecise term of contemptuous abuse which between 1564 and 1642 (these exact dates are given by Thomas Fuller and Richard Baxter[1]) was applied to at least five overlapping groups of people—first, to clergy who scrupled some *Prayer Book* ceremonies and phrasing; second, to advocates of the Presbyterian reform programme broached by Thomas Cartwright and the 1572 *Admonition to the Parliament*; third, to clergy and laity, not necessarily nonconformists, who practised a serious Calvinistic piety; fourth, to 'rigid Calvinists'[2] who applauded the Synod of Dort, and were called doctrinal Puritans by other Anglicans who did not; fifth, to MPs, JPs and other gentry who showed public respect for the things of God, the laws of England and the rights of subjects.[3] Professor and Mrs George have argued that the word 'puritan' 'is the "x" of a cultural and social equation: it has no meaning beyond that given it by the particular manipulator of an algebra of abuse'.[4] In fact, however, there was a specific, though complex and many-sided, reality to which all these uses of the 'odious name' really did pertain. This was a clergy-led movement which for more than a century was held together, and given a sense of identity too deep for differences of judgement on questions

35

of polity and politics to destroy, by three things. The first was a set of shared convictions, biblicist and Calvinist in character, about on the one hand Christian faith and practice and on the other hand congregational life and the pastoral office. The second was a shared sense of being called to work for God's glory in the Church of England by eliminating popery from its worship, prelacy from its government and pagan irreligion from its membership, and so realising in it the New Testament pattern of true and authentic church life.[5] The third was a shared literature, catechetical, evangelistic and devotional, with a homiletical style and experiential emphasis that were all its own. Of the hundred or so authors who wrote it, William Perkins, who died in 1602, was the most formative and Richard Baxter, whose career as a devotional writer began with *The Saints' Everlasting Rest* in 1650, was the most distinguished. Such was the Puritanism that we are to discuss.

Revival I define as a work of God by his Spirit through his word bringing the spiritually dead to living faith in Christ and renewing the inner life of Christians who have grown slack and sleepy. In revival God makes old things new, giving new power to law and gospel and new spiritual awareness to those whose hearts and consciences had been blind, hard and cold. Revival thus animates or reanimates churches and Christian groups to make a spiritual and moral impact on communities. It comprises an initial *reviving*, followed by a maintained state of *revivedness* for as long as the visitation lasts. Taking the early chapters of Acts as a paradigm, and relating them to the rest of the New Testament, which is manifestly a product throughout of revival conditions, we may list as marks of revival an awesome sense of the presence of God and the truth of the gospel; a profound awareness of sin, leading to deep repentance and heartfelt embrace of the glorified, loving, pardoning Christ; an uninhibited witness to the power and glory of Christ, with a mighty freedom of speech expressing a mighty freedom of spirit; joy in the Lord, love for his people, and fear of sinning; and from God's side an intensifying and speeding-up of the work of grace so that men are struck down by the word and transformed by the Spirit in short order, making it appropriate pastorally as well as theologically to baptise adult converts straight after they have professed faith. It is true, of course, that there can be personal revival without any community movement, and that there can be no community movement save as individuals are revived. Nonetheless, if we follow Acts as our paradigm we shall define revival as an essentially corporate phenomenon in which God sovereignly shows his hand, visits his people, extends his kingdom, and glorifies his name.

2

I should observe here that, though these points are drawn directly from the Bible, they are also in a real sense Puritan points, if only because most if not all of them are found in the theology of revival adumbrated by the great Jonathan Edwards, of whom Perry Miller truly said: 'Puritanism is what Edwards was'.[6] I have maintained elsewhere that the understanding of revival embedded in the writings of Edwards' thirties is the most important single contribution that Edwards has to make to evangelical theology today, and remains the classical treatment of its subject;[7] but this is beyond my scope now.

For more than two centuries, since Daniel Neal's *History of the Puritans* first appeared (four volumes, 1732-38), it has been customary to understand the Puritan movement in terms of the power struggle that went on in church and state; and this, of course, is part of the truth, though it leaves the question of Puritan motives somewhat in the air. Here, however, Dr Irvonwy Morgan supplies the vital clue. He writes:

> The essential thing in understanding the Puritans was that they were preachers before they were anything else. . . . Into whatever efforts they were led in their attempts to reform the world through the Church, and however these efforts were frustrated by the leaders of the Church, what bound them together, undergirded their striving, and gave them the dynamic to persist was their consciousness that they were called to preach the Gospel.[8]

And I venture to suggest that for a truly adequate understanding of Puritanism we must await the day when its history will be told as a revival story, in which the church conflict which has hitherto been taken as the key to interpretation is recognised as having all along been subservient to the larger Puritan aim—and, be it said, partial achievement—of a spiritually renewed nation. The day when this story can be told properly is not yet. Analysis of Puritan preaching, teaching, piety, pastoral work, and spiritual experience has begun,[9] but still has far to go, and theological evaluation of this material is in its infancy.[10] Nor have all the source materials yet been assembled. The limited objective of this present paper is simply to make credible the statement that Puritanism was, at its heart, a movement of spiritual revival (like that of the friars, and the Lollards, and the Reformation itself, which the Puritans professedly sought to complete). To establish this point will confirm the need to study Puritanism in the terms stated above and may perhaps become an incentive to doing so. So now in my argument I set out three broad facts, as follows.

The first fact is that *spiritual revival was central to what the Puritans professed to be seeking*. Remarkably, this fact is rarely highlighted and often ignored. Why is that? Three reasons at least may be suggested. First, the Puritans did not seek revival in isolation from their quest for a more scriptural church order, and professional historians and pietistic evangelicals tend to assume (I do not know why) that these are distinct and even contrasting quests on which men do not engage at the same time. Second, the Puritan pursuit of revival was in its own day mocked and not taken seriously (that is what the history of the word 'Puritan' really tells us), and later students have been betrayed hereby into similar failure to take this quest seriously. Third, the Puritans did not use 'revival' as the technical term for what they sought, but expressed their objectives entirely in terms of the vocabulary of 'reform'. When, for instance, in 1656 Richard Baxter published his classic on the ministry, The Reformed Pastor, what he meant by 'reformed' was not Calvinistic in doctrine (he assumed that, at least in a broad sense); what he meant was renewed in vigour, zeal and purpose, in other words revived, as the book itself makes plain. And when he wrote elsewhere, 'If God would but reform the ministry, and set them on their duties zealously and faithfully, the people would certainly be reformed',[11] what he meant by 'reformed' was once again what we would express by saying 'revived'. But historians and evangelicals (again I do not know why) regularly conceive of 'reform' and 'reformation' in the church as a matter of externals only, doctrine publicly professed and order publicly established, without reference to inward renewal of heart and life; so they miss the spiritual dimensions of the goal of 'reform' which the Reformers and Puritans always had at heart.

Yet if we ask why throughout Elizabeth's reign Puritans preached, wrote and petitioned for official action to produce a godly and competent ministry;[12] why Puritans introduced and backed 'prophesyings' (gatherings for biblical exposition), which Elizabeth suppressed;[13] why through lectureships and incumbencies Puritans tried to establish their own network of learned and godly preachers across all England; why they constantly encouraged the wealthy to finance promising young men to the university, to prepare for the ministry; why Puritan feoffees bought patronage rights and endowments (advowsons and impropriations) after 1625, till Laud had them inhibited by law;[14] why the 1642 Parliamentary Committee for Plundered Ministers and the 1654 Cromwellian Committees of Ejectors (to displace incompetent clergy) and Triers (to examine would-be incumbents) were set up—if, in short, we ask why concern for a ministry of evangelical quality was always top of the list of Puritan priorities, as indeed it was—the answer stares us in the face. As Baxter put it: 'All churches either rise or fall as the ministry doth rise or fall (not in riches or worldly grandeur) but in knowledge, zeal and ability for their work.'[15] The Puritans wanted, more than anything else, to see the church in England 'rise' spiritually, and they saw that this could not be without a renewed ministry.

So it was not, as William Haller often implies,[16] that after 1570 the Puritan clergy turned to preaching and pastoral work as a means to the end of building up a lay constituency strong enough to secure the changes in church order which at that time were unattainable by direct action; the truth is rather that, as Edward Dering's John Knox-like sermon before Elizabeth in 1570 and the 1572 Admonition (to look no further) make plain,[17] the end to which all church order, on the Puritan view, was a means, and for which everything superstitious, misleading and Spirit-quenching must be rooted out, was the glory of God in and through the salvation of sinners and the building up of lively congregations in which people met God. And by the salvation of sinners the Puritans meant not just their conversion, but also their growth in fellowship into spiritual health, strength and consecrated obedience—in short, their *holiness* (for the Puritans used that great word in a sense so broad as to include in it every aspect and dimension of the godly life). But without a ministry that was 'powerful', 'painful' (laborious) and 'useful'—the three great Puritan commendations of good clergymen—holiness among the people of England would never become a reality. That was why for more than a century Puritan clergy spent themselves in preaching and pastoral care. The cause they served was not so much that of restructuring as of revival.

This leads to the second fact, which is that *personal revival was the central theme of Puritan devotional literature.* About four-fifths of the way through his 1143-page folio, *A Christian Directory* (sub-titled *A Sum of Practical Theology and Cases of Conscience. Directing Christians, how to use their knowledge and faith; how to improve all helps and means, and to perform all duties; how to overcome temptations, and to escape or mortify every sin*), Richard Baxter reaches 'Ecclesiastical Cases of Conscience', number 174: 'What books, especially of theology, should one choose who for want of money or time can read but few?' In reply, he lists what he calls 'the poorest or smallest library that is tolerable': Bible, concordance, commentary, catechisms, something on the doctrines of the gospel, and 'as many affectionate practical English writers as you can get.' He names some sixty, all but three of them Puritans, and then repeats: 'as many as you can get.'[18] It is this literature, to which Baxter himself contributed so much (his *Directory, Saints Everlasting Rest, Call to the Unconverted, Life of Faith, Dying Thoughts,* and a great deal more), that concerns us now.

What was in these books? Sermons, mostly, expounding Scripture by the characteristic Puritan method of 'doctrine, reason and use'—proposition, confirmation, and application. But the sermons were linked to form treatises, for the Puritans took much latitude in developing the various lines of thought, theological and applicatory, that their passage suggested, and might 'stand on' a text for weeks together while they drew these out. The writers were called 'affectionate' and 'practical' because on paper, just as in the pulpit, they used words in a way calculated not merely to inform, but to make men feel the force of truth and to show them how they should respond to it. The contents of these homiletic treatises may be generally described, in John Downame's words, as 'that part of Divinity . . . which consisteth more in experience and practice, than in theory and application, and more principally tendeth to the sanctification of the heart, than the informing of the judgement and the increasing of knowledge; and to the stirring up of all to the practice of that they know in the duties of a godly life, and in bringing forth the fruits of faith in new obedience. . . .'[19] Specific categories of Puritan books include the following:

1. *Evangelistic books*, dealing with sin and redemption, repentance and faith, conversion and regeneration. 'It hath been one of the glories of the Protestant Religion, that it revived the Doctrine of saving Conversion, and of the new creature brought forth thereby,' wrote Thomas Goodwin and Philip Nye in 1656 in their preface to Thomas Hooker's *The Application of Redemption*; 'but in a more eminent manner, God hath cast the honour hereof upon the Ministers and Preachers of this Nation, who are renowned abroad for their more accurate search into and discoveries hereof.' Puritan theology has indeed been called a theology of regeneration because of its pervasive orientation upon this theme. Many books deal with it directly. To name a few for many: John Rogers' *The Doctrine of Faith* (1627), Ezekiel Culverwell's *Treatise on Faith* (1623), Perkins' *Treatise of the Nature and Practice of Repentance* (1593), Richard Sibbes' *Bruised Reed* (1630), William Whateley's *The New Birth* (1618), and John Flavel's *Method of Grace* (1681), all debouching in exhortation and invitation to seek the Lord while he may be found. In addition, Puritan writers invented the 'wakening persuasive',[20] what we should call the evangelistic tract if 'tract' is an allowable word for books of forty thousand words! Richard Baxter's *Call to the Unconverted to Turn and Live . . . from the Living God* (1658), which sold 20,000 copies in a year and was translated into French, Dutch and Red Indian, was the pioneer work here, followed by Joseph Alleine's *Alarm to the Unconverted* (1672) which borrowed from Baxter and of which, according to Calamy, 70,000 copies were circulated within a generation.[21] Also, as a response to a situation in which nominal Christians and 'gospel hypocrites' abounded, the Puritans wrote much that was designed to crack through their veneer of religiosity and alert them to their need of renewing grace. In this class come books like Daniel Dyke's *Mystery of Selfe-Deceiving* (1614), Thomas Shepard's *Parable of the Ten Virgins*, and Matthew Meade's *The Almost Christian: or the False-Professor Tried and Cast* (1662).

Analysis of this corpus of evangelistic writing is not possible here, but it can safely be said that in declaring the gospel of God's free grace in Christ the Puritans leave nothing to be desired by the standards of any earlier or later age. Their belief, as children of the Reformation, that all the contents of Scripture are either law or gospel led them to an extremely rich exploration of both. The occasionally voiced suggestion that there was something legalistic in their stress on the need for a 'preparatory work' of contrition and humbling for sin before men can close with Christ is quite false: the only point they were making (and, admittedly, sometimes labouring, as the needs of their readers required) was that, because fallen man is naturally in love with sin, it is psychologically impossible for him to embrace Christ whole-heartedly as a Saviour, not just from sin's penalty but from sinning itself, until he has come to hate sin and long for deliverance from it. The 'preparatory work' is simply the creating of this state of mind. On the whole the Puritan account of conversion as a work of man turning to God which is also a work of God turning man to himself seems to mirror exactly what the New Testament says.

2. *Casuistic books*, spelling out the standards of conduct set in God's law so that Christians might be able to live with a good conscience, knowing that they were doing God's will. The century that followed the Reformation was a great age of 'case-divinity' among both Romans and Protestants, but whereas Jesuit casuistry was guidance for the priest in the confessional, that of the Puritans was for the ordinary Christian in everyday life. Perkins was the pioneer here, systematically reforming the medieval heritage on conscience and good works by the Bible; most of the contents of the three folio volumes of his works (1616-1618) prove on inspection to be 'case-divinity'.[22] Baxter's massive *Directory* sums up two generations of work in this field, and between Perkins and Baxter lie abundance of smaller books like the *Plaine and Familiar Exposition of the Ten Commandments* by John Dod and Thomas Cleaver (1603) (nineteen editions in thirty-two years), and many treatments of particular areas where problems of right conduct arose then, as they arise now (marriage and the family; work; the occult; the use of wealth; the stewardship of truth, etc). All this material remains enormously impressive in the depth of its insight into both biblical teaching and the paralogisms of the human heart.

3. *Paraenetic books*, written to 'comfort' (i.e., strengthen and encourage), and to give the Christian both motives and resources for 'cheerful obedience' on a basis of 'triumphing assurance'. Into this category fall countless volumes 'opening' themes of the gospel—the love of God, the work of Christ, the renewing ministry of the Spirit, and the commitment to save made to the believer by all three Persons of the Trinity in the covenant of grace. I venture to affirm that the richness of these treatments is still unparalleled, however antiquated and unwieldy their form. In this category also come books dealing directly with assurance, books designed to help Christians in states of anxiety, morbidity, and dryness ('desertion') to discern the genuineness of their faith in face of feelings of desperation and the reality of their standing in grace in face of temptations to conclude themselves lost. These books were written because throughout the Puritan period there were many troubled souls who needed help of this kind. In many minds the questions 'What must I do to be saved?' 'Am I among the elect?' and 'Am I in a state of grace?' were unhelpfully tangled up with each other, and one of the chief strengths of Puritan pastoral writing, as of Puritan pastoral dealing, was the skill with which these questions were separated and confusions about them sorted out. The pioneer work here was Perkins' *Treatise Tending unto a Declaration whether a man be in the*

estate of Damnation or in the estate of Grace and if he be in the first, how
he may in time come out of it; if in the second, how he may discern it, and
persevere in the same to the end (1586); the classic treatment was perhaps
The Christian's Great Interest by the Scotsman, William Guthrie, which
John Owen much admired.

Such, in brief, was Puritan devotional literature. We could use Bunyan's
Pilgrim's Progress as a pictorial index to its scope and contents. William
Haller, who wrote in 1938 what is still the best introduction to it, speaks
of its 'extraordinary vitality',[23] and there is an abundance of contemporary
testimonies to its usefulness. Baxter himself records how when he was
about fifteen

> a poor pedlar came to the door. . . . And my father bought of him Dr. Sibbes'
> *Bruised Reed*. This . . . opened the *Love of God* to me, and gave me a livelier
> apprehension of the Mystery of Redemption, and how much I was beholden
> to Jesus Christ. . . . After this we had a Servant that had a little Piece of Mr.
> *Perkins's* Works (of *Repentance*, and the right *Art of Living and Dying Well*,
> and *the Government of the Tongue*): And the reading of that did further
> inform me, and confirm me . . . the reading of Mr. *Ezek. Culverwell's* Trea-
> tise of Faith did me much good, and many other excellent Books, were made
> my Teachers and Comforters: And the use that God made of Books, above
> Ministers, to the benefit of my Soul, made me somewhat excessively in love
> with good Books. . . . I remember in the beginning how savoury to my read-
> ing was Mr. *Perkins's* short Treatise of the *Right Knowledge of Christ*
> *crucified*, and his *Exposition of the Creed*; because they taught me how to
> live by Faith on Christ.[24]

This is one sample testimony for many that might be given. The literature as a whole is remarkably homogeneous, and its purpose is
constant—to induce faith, repentance, assurance, and joyful zeal in the life
of pilgrimage, conflict and good works to which the saints are called; in
other words, to create and sustain a spiritual condition for which personal
revival is the truly appropriate name.

The two facts we have so far looked at, namely, the centrality of revival
in Puritan purpose and personal revival as the focus of Puritan literature,
lead on to the third, which is this: *the ministry of Puritan pastors under*
God brought revival. Only in these terms can the remarkable blessing that
increased through the seventeenth century till the Restoration be adequately described.

The pattern for Puritan ministry was set by the Scriptures and the *Prayer*
Book ordinal, which describes clergy as called 'to be messengers, watchmen
and stewards of the Lord; to teach, and to premonish, to feed and provide
for the Lord's family; to seek for Christ's sheep that are dispersed
abroad. . . . ' From the hagiological records of Puritan ministers[25] and from

the ideals set out in Baxter's *Reformed Pastor*[26] (to look no further) we can see clearly enough how this calling was understood and discharged. Many of the pastors were men of great gifts and great unction, whose preaching was 'powerful' in every sense and whose counselling ministry as 'physicians of the soul' transformed many deranged lives. To illustrate this, and the way in which over the years the fruits of faithful ministry increased, here are glimpses of three of these men in action.

Richard Greenham, a pastoral pioneer, was incumbent of Dry Drayton, seven miles from Cambridge, from 1570 to 1590. He worked extremely hard. He rose daily at four and each Monday, Tuesday, Wednesday and Friday preached a sermon at daybreak, to catch his flock before they dispersed into the fields; then on Sunday he preached twice, and in addition catechised the children of the parish each Sunday evening and Thursday morning. Mornings he studied, afternoons he visited the sick or walked out into the fields 'to confer with his Neighbours as they were at Plough'. In his preaching, Henry Holland, his biographer tells us, 'he was so earnest, and took such extraordinary pains, that his shirt would usually be as wet with sweating, as if it had been drenched with water, so that he was forced, as soon as he came out of the Pulpit to shift himself. . . . '[27] He was a pastoral counsellor of uncommon skill. 'Having great Experience and an excellent Faculty to relieve and comfort distressed Consciences,' writes Holland, 'he was sought to, far and near, by such as groaned under spiritual Afflictions and Temptations . . . the fame of this spiritual Physician so spread abroad that he was sent for to very many, and the Lord was pleased so far to bless his labours that by his knowledge and experience many were restored to joy and comfort.' His friends hoped he would write a book on the art of counselling, but he never did; nonetheless, he passed on a great deal of his lore to others by word of mouth. In a letter to his bishop he described his ministry as 'preaching Christ crucified unto my selfe and Country people',[28] and the contents of his posthumously published *Works* (a small folio of over 800 pages) bear this out. Yet, for all his godliness, insight, evangelical message and hard work, his ministry was virtually fruitless. Others outside his parish were blessed through him, but not his own people. 'Greenham had pastures green, but flocks full lean' was a little rhyme that went round among the godly. 'I perceive noe good wrought by my ministry on any but one family'[29] was what, according to Holland, he said to his successor. In rural England in Greenham's day, there was much fallow ground to be broken up; it was a time for sowing, but the reaping time was still in the future.

Now we move on to look at Richard Fairclough, Rector (from 1647 to 1662) of Mells, a village in Somerset, and a friend of the great John Howe, who preached his funeral sermon, as Fairclough had requested in his will. From Howe's *Sermon* come the following sentences.

It was soon observed what a star had risen . . . which made an obscure country village soon become a most noted place; from sundry miles about, thither was the great resort, so that I have wondered to see so thronged an auditory as I have sometimes had the opportunity to observe . . . that did usually attend his most fruitful ministry. And O how hath that congregation been wont to melt under his holy fervours! His prayers, sermons and other ministerial performances had that strange pungency, quickness and authority with them, at some times; that softness, gentleness, sweetness, alluringness at others; that one would think it scarce possible to resist the spirit and power wherewith he spake. And the effect did in a blessed measure correspond; they became a much enlightened, knowing, judicious, reformed . . . religious people. His labours here were almost incredible. Beside his usual exercises on the Lord's day, of praying, reading the Scriptures, preaching, catechising, administering the sacraments . . . he usually five days in the week, betimes in the morning, appeared in public, prayed and preached an expository lecture upon some portion of the Holy Scriptures . . . he always had a considerable congregation. . . . Yet he also found time, not only to visit the sick (which opportunities he caught at with great eagerness) but also, in a continual course, all the families within his charge; and personally and severally to converse with every one that was capable, labouring to understand the present state of their souls, and applying himself to them in instructions, reproofs, admonitions, exhortations and encouragements, suitable thereto; and he went through all with the greatest facility and pleasure imaginable; his whole heart was in his work. Every day, for many years together, he used to be up by three in the mornings, or sooner, and to be with God (which was his dear delight) when others slept. . . .[30]

The lifestyle was essentially the same as with Greenham: but now the harvest was starting to come.

Finally, we glance at Richard Baxter, who ministered at Kidderminster from 1641 to 1660, with a five-year break during the Civil War. Kidderminster was a town of some 2,000 adults, and most of them, it seems, were converted under his ministry. He found them, he tells us, 'an ignorant, rude and revelling people, for the most part . . . they had hardly ever had any lively serious preaching among them.' But his ministry was wonderfully blessed.

When I first entered on my labours I took special notice of everyone that was humbled, reformed or converted; but when I had laboured long, it pleased God that the converts were so many, that I could not afford time for such particular observations . . . families and considerable numbers at once . . . came in and grew up I scarce knew how.

Here is Baxter's retrospect of what went on.

The Congregation was usually full, so that we were fain to build five Galleries after my coming thither. . . . The Church would have held about a thousand without the galleries. Our private Meetings were also full. On the Lord's Days there was no disorder to be seen in the Streets, but you might hear an hundred Families singing Psalms and repeating Sermons, as you passed through the Streets. In a word, when I came thither first, there was about one Family in a Street that worshipped God and called on His Name, and when I came away there were some streets where there was not past one Family in the side of a Street that did not so; and that did not by professing serious Godliness, give us hopes of their sincerity. And those Families that were the worst, being Inns and Alehouses (*sic*) usually *some persons* in each House did seem to be religious. . . . When I set upon Personal Conference and Catechising them, there were very few families in all the Town that refused to come. . . . [Baxter asked them to call on him at his home.] And few families went from me without some tears, or seemingly serious promises of a Godly Life.[31]

What Baxter refers to here is the practice which he describes and commends in *The Reformed Pastor*, and which, as we heard from Howe, Fairclough also followed, of systematically interviewing families for the purpose of personal spiritual dealing. Baxter met families in this way at the rate of seven or eight a day, two days a week, so as to get through all 800 families in the parish every year. 'I first heard them recite the words of the catechism [the *Westminster Shorter Catechism* was the one he used], and then examined them about the sense, and lastly urged them with all possible engaging reason and vehemency to answerable affection and practice. I spent about an hour with a family.' His testimony to the value of this practice is emphatic. 'I find we never took the rightest course to demolish the kingdom of darkness till now. . . . I find more outward signs of success with most . . . than of all my public preaching to them.'[32]
His retrospect continues:

Some of the Poor men did competently understand the Body of Divinity. . . . Some of them were so able in Prayer, that very few Ministers did match them. . . . Abundance of them were able to pray very *laudably* with their Families, or with others. The temper of their Minds, and the innocency of their lives was much more laudable than their Parts [abilities]. The Professors of serious Godliness, were generally of very humble Minds and Carriage. . . .

And, writing in 1665, he was able to say that despite intense anti-Puritan pressure exerted against them during the years since he left them, 'not one, that I hear of . . . are fallen off, or forsake their Uprightness.'[33] His final comment is: 'O, what am I . . . that God should thus abundantly encourage comment is: 'O, what am I . . . that God should thus abundantly encourage me, when the Reverend Instructors of my youth, did labour Fifty years together in one place, and could scarcely say they had Converted one or two of their Parishes!'[34] But by the Interregnum the long-awaited time of harvest had come. My final comment is: was not this revival?

In that connection, Baxter's comment on religion in the Cromwellian period is of deep interest. It was written in 1665.

I must bear this faithful Witness to those times, that as far as I was acquainted, where before there was one godly profitable Preacher, there was then six or ten; and taking One Place with another, I conjecture there was a proportionable increase of truly godly People . . . where the Ministers had excellent parts, and holy lives, and thirsted after the good of Souls, and wholly devoted themselves, their time and strength and estates thereunto, and thought no pains or cost too much, there abundance were converted to serious Godliness. . . . God did so wonderfully bless the Labours of his *unanimous faithful Ministers*, that had it not been for the Faction of the Prelatists . . . and the Factions of the giddy and turbulent Sectaries . . . together with some *laziness* and *selfishness* in many of the Ministry, I say, had it not been for these Impediments, *England* had been like in a quarter of an Age to have become a Land of Saints, and a Pattern of Holiness to all the World, and the unmatchable Paradise of the Earth. Never were such fair opportunities to sanctifie a Nation, lost and trodden underfoot, as have been in this Land of late! Woe be to them that were the causes of it. [He is referring to the wretched events that followed the Restoration.][35]

I defined my task in this study as one of making credible the claim that Puritanism was a movement of revival. I believe that the evidence I have adduced does that. Further study of the Puritan ministry in seventeenth-century England, along the lines of Irvonwy Morgan's book, *The Godly Preachers of the Elizabethan Church*, would, I think, warrant the conclusion that in the middle of that century a work of grace was in progress in England that was every whit as potent and deep as its better-known counterpart a hundred years later. Certainly, the understanding of the gospel and the principles of its ministry in the two periods was identical, apart from the private oddities of John Wesley's theology, which he miscalled Arminianism out of deference to the Wesley family tradition but which is better categorised as inconsistent Calvinism.[36] Recent studies of the evangelical revival have highlighted its debt to Puritanism;[37] and it was Whitefield, the friend of that pure Puritan born out of due time, Jonathan Edwards, who wrote, as we saw, in 1767: 'For these thirty years past I have remarked, that the more true and vital religion hath revived either at home or abroad [he means in Britain or America], the more the good old Puritanical writings . . . have been called for.'[38] Interestingly, it was also Whitefield who wrote in his diary in 1743 of his visit to Kidderminster: 'I was greatly refreshed to find what a sweet savour of good Mr. Baxter's doctrine, works and discipline remained unto this day.'[39] The Puritan and evangelical movements need to be studied together; their links with each other are much stronger and more numerous than is sometimes realised. The great difference, of course, is that whereas after two generations the evangelical revival became socially acceptable, the men of the Restoration systematically scattered and stamped out the fires of Puritan Christianity, as part of their public rejection of the revolutionary order. Further study would, I think, conform Baxter's judgement, based as it was on a far fuller knowledge of the state of religion in England in the 1650s than we yet have, 'Never were such fair opportunities to sanctifie a Nation lost and trodden under foot.'

To be sure, nothing happened in Puritan England quite so spectacular as the Sixmilewater revival in Antrim in the 1620s, that 'bright and hot sun-blink of the gospel' as Robert Fleming called it,[40] when crazy James Glendinning preached the law and struck men down thereby without knowing how to preach the gospel, so that Robert Blair and others had to do it for him; nor anything as overwhelming as that Monday in 1631 at the Kirk o' Shotts when for an hour and a half diffident John Livingstone preached as he never preached again, either before or after, and persons testified afterwards that they had been converted or at least had their Christian lives transformed by the power that attended his words. There was, to be sure, that unforgettable lecture day at Dedham, some time in the 1620s, when the great John Rogers bore down on his 500 hearers for neglecting the Bible:

> He personates God to the people, telling them, 'Well, I have trusted you so long with my Bible . . . it lies in such and such houses all covered with dust and cobwebs; you care not to listen to it. Do you use my Bible so? Well, you shall have my Bible no longer.' And he takes up the Bible from his cushion, and seemed as if he were going away with it and carrying it from them, but immediately turns again and personates the people to God, falls down on his knees, cries and pleads most earnestly. 'Lord, whatever thou dost to us, take not thy Bible from us; kill our children, burn our houses, destroy our goods, only spare us thy Bible, take not away thy Bible'. And then he personates God again to the people: 'Say you so? Well I will try you a while longer; and here is my Bible for you, I will see how you will use it, whether you will love it more . . . observe it more . . . practice it more, and live more according to it.'

And at this point, so Thomas Goodwin, who was there, told John Howe, whose words I have been quoting, the entire churchful of people dissolved in tears, and Goodwin himself 'when he got out . . . was fain to hang a quarter of an hour on the neck of his horse weeping before he had power to mount; so strange an impression was there upon him, and generally upon the people, upon having been expostulated with for the neglect of the Bible.'[41] Generally, however, the Puritan revival seems to have been a comparatively quiet and orderly work, apart from the fanaticism that boiled out of it during the 1640s and 1650s when it was at its height.

3

Further light on the Puritan revival would come from a study of Puritan theology, in particular its unprecedented interest in and concentration on the ministry of the Holy Spirit;[42] and also from a review of Puritan worship, with its stress on 'heart-work', spontaneity, the singing of hymns and psalms, free Spirit-prompted prayer marked by 'familiarity', 'fullness' and 'affection', and the 'plain, pressing, downright' preaching of sin and grace which would 'rip up' the conscience and then pour in gospel balm.[43] Puritan theology and worship, as they developed, showed increasingly their character as both products and adjuncts of revival. Further exploring of the annals of Puritan ministry would also throw fresh light on the movement, as was said above. It would, for instance, be fascinating to learn more about men like Elkanah Wales, of Pudsey, who 'was reckoned the most successful Preacher in Converting Souls, in the whole Country', though, as with Greenham and so many more since, 'more among Strangers and Occasional Hearers, than his own People';[44] or about the itinerant Henry Oasland of Bewdley, 'Who Rode About from Place to Place, Preaching fervently and winning many Souls to God';[45] or Thomas Tregoss of St Mabe in West Cornwall, who 'Dated his Conversion, after he had been some time in the Ministry . . . and a sufferer for *Nonconformity* too';[46] or about Samual Annesley, John Wesley's maternal grandfather, whom Parliament 'intruded' into Cliffe (Kent) in place of a minister who had been scandalous but popular, and whose congregation, resenting the change, attacked him 'with Spits Forks and Stones; threatening him with Death', whereupon he promised to leave them as soon as they were ready to accept another minister of his own type, and who after 'the People were greatly Reform'd, and his Labours had marvellous Success' kept his word and went, 'least any seeming Lightness of his might prove a Scandal to his Young Converts';[47] or about Thomas Lye, the children's evangelist, who was remembered for more than forty years after his ministry ceased for 'his excellent Knack of Catechising Young Ones, whom he by many Artifices entic'd to delight in the getting Knowledge in the best things'.[48] These men (and there were literally hundreds like them) were revival ministers working in revival times, and their stories would take us to the very heart of the Puritan movement. But this book would then be far too long. However, my point has been made, and now I have done.

CHAPTER FOUR

The Practical Writings
of the English Puritans

Richard Baxter's *Christian Directory*, composed in 1664-65 and printed in 1673, contained, in the judgement of Baxter's first editors, 'perhaps the best body of practical divinity that is extant in our own or any other tongue.'[1] In his prefatory 'Advertisement' Baxter says that he wrote it partly so that 'the younger and more unfurnished and unexperienced sorts of ministers, might have a promptuary at hand, for practical resolutions and directions on the subjects that they have need to deal in.'[2] Under the heading 'Ecclesiastical Cases of Conscience' he tackles, as seen in the last chapter, many practical matters on which younger ministers might need guidance, and when in reply to question 174, 'What books, especially of theology, should one choose, who for want of money of time can read but few?'[3] he lists 'the poorest or smallest library that is tolerable', it is of the young minister's bookshelf that he is thinking. His answer, numbered in standard Puritan style, consists of six items, and the sixth, following Bible, concordance, commentary, some English catechisms, and some English books on the doctrine of grace, is: 'As many affectionate practical English writers as you can get.' Having named more than sixty of these (!), he repeats, 'as many as you can get.'[4] His emphatic repetition, and the length of his list,[5] are both remarkable. Clearly he has little hope for young ministers who will not steep themselves in 'affectionate practical English writers'.

Nor is it only to ministers that he recommends them. In the dedicatory letter prefixed to his first written work, *The Saints' Everlasting Rest* (1649; an 844-page bestseller, annually reprinted for the first ten years of its life), he urged his Kidderminster congregation: 'Read much the writings of our old, solid divines.'[6] It was to these same 'affectionate practical' writers that he was referring. The summons to read them, often with particular recommendations, comes many times in Baxter's devotional books, which were themselves put together to augment this corpus. 'I have laboured to fit all, or almost all, for matter and manner, to the capacity of the vulgar,' he wrote in the preface to his sermon on the absolute sovereignty of Christ (1654).

> And though, for the matter, it is as necessary to the greatest, yet it is for the vulgar, principally, that I publish it; and had rather it might be numbered with those books which are carried up and down the country from door to door in pedlars' packs, than with those that lie on booksellers' stalls, or are set up in the libraries of learned divines. And to the same use would I design most of my published labours, should God afford me time and ability. . . .[7]

Baxter himself had learned faith in Christ from Sibbes' *Bruised Reed*, sold to his father over the doorstep by a pedlar a quarter of a century earlier,[8] and he could envisage no higher usefulness for his own books than that they should fulfil just such a ministry. Here, again, is a pointer to the value he found in 'affectionate practical English writers'.

My present task is to introduce or reintroduce these men to a Christian world that habitually neglects them. Popular and prized in their day, and for two centuries after, they are now hardly known. The interest in Puritanism that has stirred in the past half-century is mainly academic, and not many believers seem to read the Puritan reprints that are nowadays happily available.[9] I believe that this neglect impoverishes us grievously, and I would like to see it end.

I shall call these 'affectionate practical English writers' Puritans, as everyone else does. But we should note that this usage dates from the eighteenth century,[10] and is not contemporary with the authors themselves. To make distinction in the field of practical theology, the mark of a Puritan is to use the word in a way that corresponds to none of its applications in the period (1564-1642) when it was current.[11] During that period it was an insult, implying one or both of the two evils of 'pure-church' elitism and priggish censoriousness—two ugly forms of pride. Thus loaded, the word was contemptuously applied to would-be reformers of the national church and to pious people generally, like Richard Baxter's father, who was mocked as a Puritan by his neighbours for staying indoors on Sunday afternoons to read the Bible and pray with his family instead of dancing and playing games on the village green.[12] Apart from the obscure Anabaptists in London of whom John Stowe had heard, who according to his report called themselves 'Puritans, the unspotted lambs of the Lord',[13] no one ever claimed the name, and William Perkins, the father-figure among 'affectionate practical English writers', rejected it as 'vile'.[14] It is certainly slippery, and hard to handle. R.T. Kendall observes with justice that 'if one accepts the term "Puritan" one must, if consistent, either readjust the definition to fit one man at a time, or, if dealing with a tradition, begin with one definition and end up with another'. Kendall opts for calling the 'affectionate practical' school 'experimental predestinarians'—which is apt.[15] For convenience, however, I shall adhere to the conventional description of these writers as Puritans.

The best introduction to the 'affectionate practical' writers is their history, which I shall now quickly review. It is not in fact well known. Much better known is the fact that from 1564 the label 'Puritan' was being fastened on to advocates of more external reform for the Church of England. A host of historians over two centuries have defined Puritanism in terms of this. G.M. Trevelyan, for instance, is typical when he explains Puritanism as 'the religion of all those who wished either to "purify" the usage of the established church from the taint of popery or to worship separately by forms so "purified"'.[16] Rarely, however, has it been recognised that Puritan ecclesiastical agitation was one aspect only of a many-sided religious movement that had evangelism and nurture at its heart. This pastoral movement, in which conformists and nonconformists, Anglicans, Presbyterians, Independents, Baptists, and Erastians were all essentially at one, was unspectacular, as pastoral movements often are. It never won itself a party name and its story has never been adequately written. That story is one of spiritual revival starting small but gaining impetus over most of a century till Restoration policies snuffed it out. In summary form it runs thus.

1

Ten years after the Elizabethan settlement, the Church of England was in a bad way. In the first place, it lacked money. Royal and aristocratic depredations at the time of the Reformation had left many livings so poor as to be unable to support an incumbent. Moreover, it lacked men. Mary's persecutions had taken from it its convinced Protestants; the Oath of Allegiance imposed by Elizabeth had denuded it of its convinced papists; most of the clergy who remained were men of little ability and no clear convictions at all. Many of them were known to be immoral. Livings were held in plurality by nonresidents, and untrained artisans were ordained, for lack of anyone better, to read the services on Sunday while continuing to practise their trade during the week. Many churches had not had a sermon preached in them for years. Nor could the Elizabethan bishops attract young university men into the ministry in sufficient numbers to stop the rot.

The ignorance of mid-sixteenth-century country clergy may be judged from the records of Bishop Hooper's enquiry into conditions in his diocese in 1551. His clergy were asked the following questions:

1. How many commandments are there?
2. Where are they to be found?
3. Repeat them.
4. What are the articles of the Christian faith?
5. Prove them from Scripture.
6. Repeat the Lord's Prayer.
7. How do you know it is the Lord's?
8. Where is it to be found?

Out of 311 examined, only 50 could answer these questions, and 19 of them 'mediocriter'. Ten did not know the Lord's Prayer, and 8 did not answer a single question.[17]

Nothing had happened between 1551 and 1570 to improve this situation; rather the reverse, for as we saw, the ablest men on both the Protestant and the papist side had been lopped off. The only competent protagonists of Reformed religion in England were the returned Marian exiles, and of those who had not become bishops or deans practically all had settled either in the universities (Oxford and Cambridge) or in London. Scarcely one went to the country. For all the difference it had made to religion in England during twenty years, the doctrinal reformation of the English Church might never have happened. In the time of Edward VI, and again after Mary, there had been a superficial move among large sections of the community in the direction of Protestantism; but by 1570 it was clear that this amounted to little more than a violent anti-papalism. The religion of justification by faith was as little known, and superstition was as widespread and deep-rooted, as it has been for the previous century. England might profess a Reformed Protestant religion and come obediently to church on Sundays (it was illegal not to), but England was not yet converted.

In February 1570, Edward Dering, a celebrated young Puritan leader, preaching before Elizabeth, spoke plainly to her concerning this matter.

I would first lead you to your benefices, and behold, some are defiled with impropriations, some with sequestrations, some loaden with pensions, some robbed of their commodities. . . . Look . . . upon your patrons. And lo, some are selling their benefices, some farming them, some keep them for their children, some give them to boys, some to serving men, a very few seek after learned pastors. . . . Look upon your ministry, and there are some of one occupation, some of another, some shake-bucklers, some ruffians, some hawkers and hunters, some dicers and carders, some blind guides and cannot see, some dumb dogs and will not bark. . . .

And yet you, in the meanwhile that all these whoredoms are committed, you at whose hands God will require it, you sit still and are careless. Let men do as they list. It toucheth not, belike, your commonwealth, and therefore you are so well contented to let all alone.[18]

What Dering laments is not the lack of echoes from Geneva in the Church of England but the appallingly barren pastoral situation and Elizabeth's refusal to do anything about it. 'She is in the habit of listening with the greatest patience to bitter and sufficiently cutting discourses'[19] was Cox's testimony to her in 1571; and certainly she refused to let Dering's denunciations shake her out of inactivity. Her only reaction to the sermon was to suspend him from preaching.

It is not easy to see what Elizabeth could have done to improve this situation, even had she wanted to; but in fact she did not want to. For political reasons she wished clergy to be undistinguished men without initiative and to limit themselves to maintaining the status quo. Those, however, who sought the conversion of England and the glory of God in the English Church could not conscientiously sit still as she did. But what did their quest for spiritual quickening require of them? What were they to do? What should their strategy be? To this question different answers were given.

Some, led by veteran Marian exiles, were already campaigning for the removal from the *Prayer Book* of four ceremonies: the clergyman's surplice, the wedding-ring, tracing the cross on the forehead in baptism, and kneeling at Holy Communion. The objection was that, in addition to lacking Scripture sanction, these touches seemed to endorse the medieval superstitions that clergy are mediating priests, marriage is a sacrament, baptism is magic, and transubstantiation is true. Take them away, so it was thought, and God would be honoured and basic Christianity appreciated very much more.

Then, following the deposing of Cambridge's Lady Margaret Professor of Divinity Thomas Cartwright in 1570, for advocating Presbyterianism in his lectures on Acts, agitation began for a radical Presbyterianising of Elizabeth's Church of England by parliamentary enactment. Young men took the lead, and the theoretician's rigidity and over-arguing arrogance that usually appear when youthful revolutionaries get the bit between their teeth were much in evidence. The notorious 'Admonition to the Parliament' by John Field and Thomas Wilcocks, which earned its authors a year in gaol, was the manifesto of this movement. Here, too, the assumption was that God's honour and Englishmen's godliness would be much furthered by the change. Edwin Sandys, Archbishop of York, had been a Marian exile and was always a doughty Protestant, but his view of the Presbyterian agitators was dim. 'New orators are rising up from among us,' he wrote to Bullinger in Zurich in 1573,

> foolish young men who, while they despise authority, and admit of no superiors, are seeking the complete overthrow and rooting up of our whole ecclesiastical polity . . . and are striving to shape out for us, I know not what new platform of a church . . . that you may be better acquainted with the

whole matter, accept this summary of the question at issue reduced under certain heads:

1. The civil magistrate has no authority in ecclesiastical matters. He is only a member of the church, the government of which ought to be committed to the clergy.

2. The church of Christ admits of no other government than that by presbyteries; viz. by the minister, elders and deacons.

3. The names and authority of archbishops, archdeacons, chancellors, commissaries, and other titles and dignities of the like kind, should be altogether removed from the church of Christ.

4. Each parish should have its own presbytery.

5. The choice of ministers of necessity belongs to the people.

6. The goods, possessions, lands, revenues, titles, honours, authorities and all other things relating either to bishops or cathedrals, and which now of right belong to them, should be taken away forthwith and forever.

7. No one should be allowed to preach who is not a pastor of some congregation; and he ought to preach to his own flock exclusively, and no where else. . . .

None of this, Sandys judged, 'will make for the advantage and peace of the church, but for her ruin and confusion. Take away authority, and the people will rush headlong into every thing that is bad. Take away the patrimony of the church, and you will by the same means take away not only sound learning, but religion itself.'[20]

Surely Sandys was right to judge that in the England he knew, where most people were still illiterate and in the grip of ignorance and superstition, the Presbyterian reform programme, whatever its motives and warrants, was doctrinaire, impracticable, and inimical to the cause of godliness. What England needed was not Presbyterianism so much as pastoral care: which meant, precisely, pastors who would care for their flocks. Presbyterianisers spluttered on intermittently for the next twenty years, but created no ground swell of opinion that theirs was the right point of entry into the quest for the sanctifying of England; rather the reverse, and the scurrilous Marprelate tracts of 1588-89 finally destroyed their moral credit. Lampooning dignitaries as the tracts did was no formula for winning souls! It was a further event of 1570 that showed the fruitful way to go.

On 24 November of that year the Abraham of the 'affectionate practical' school of pastors and writers left his Mesopotamia and headed for the promised land. His name was Richard Greenham, and he had resigned his fellowship at Pembroke Hall in Cambridge to become minister of Dry Drayton, some seven miles out of the city. He was the pioneer Reformed Pastor of Baxter's type, the first genuinely able man as far as we can tell to tackle in an authentically apostolic way the task of rooting the gospel in rural England. We have already seen something of his labours.[21] He won himself a great reputation as a pastoral counsellor, or (as he himself conceived it) a spiritual physician, and it was a source of lasting regret to his friends that he did not 'leave to Posterity a Commentary of such particular Maladies as God had made him instrumental in the cure of, together with the means used by him for effecting of the same'. Those are the words of Henry Holland, Greenham's biographer, who expatiates on the theme as follows:

> The diet and cure of souls afflicted is a very great mystery, wherein, but few have travailed to reduce that matter into any good form of art, or to give us any good method of practice . . . wanting art and good experience, we conceive the danger to be greater; for that we rather guess uncertainly to apply good remedies and speeches unto the sick, than know how to proceed by any certain rule of art, and well grounded practice. If the natural Physician might truly say, as touching his faculty, *Vita brevis, etc.* much more assuredly may the spiritual Physician prefix such an aphorism to all this mystery we have in hand. For herein the godly learned know it is a matter far more difficult to judge what secret causes breed the hidden distemper of the soul; and here it is far more dangerous to proceed only by experience, without art and skill. . . .
>
> This reverend man of God M. [=Master] GREENHAM, was a man in his life time of great hope, and could have given best rules for this unknown faculty. . . .[22]

Greenham never wrote the treatise on pastoral direction that his friends desiderated (Holland's own forty-page collection of 'Grave Counsels and Godly Observations', the first item in Greenham's *Works*, shows what its range and thrust might have been); however, he did the next best thing, if not an even better thing: he trained many of the next generation of pastors. Ordinands lived in his home and studied with him as, in effect, apprentices; local ministers and visitors from further afield regularly joined them at the midday meal; and thus in Holland's words Greenham 'was a special Instrument and means under God to encourage and train up many godly and learned young men in the holy service of *Christ*, in the work of the Ministry'.

Though settled at Dry Drayton, Greenham continued to exercise considerable influence in the university, with which he kept in close contact. We find him in the pulpit of Great St Mary's in 1589, inveighing against one of the bishop-baiting Marprelate tracts on the ground that 'the tendency of this Book is to make sin ridiculous, whereas it ought to be made odious'. He consistently opposed Cambridge's Presbyterian agitators. Their course, he told them, was 'tantamount to rearing a roof before laying a foundation'. 'Some, ignorant how to reforme themselves, will be talking of reforming the church.'[23] 'Some busie themselves in Church-discipline, and are slender-sighted in their privie corruptions.'[24]

All his influence in Cambridge was directed to promote personal religion and peace within the church, and against sin and schism. Anything that made against Christian love and peace he regretted and opposed, even when he sympathised with the views expressed. In his personal practice he was a nonconformist as far as the four obnoxious ceremonies were concerned, and sympathised with the vision of Presbyterian reformation; but he never made an issue of it. All he asked was liberty to obey his conscience and to preach the gospel to his people. In 1573 Bishop Cox summonsed him for failing to wear the surplice, and he wrote a full account of his position in reply. He professed himself reluctant to argue about such a matter:

> I perceyve by experience, that dissention of reasons, doeth cause alienation of affections. Agayne, these matters have bin, and are debated betwixt the godly learned, where I a sole poore Countryman, a yong scholler, having occupied my selfe daylie by the space of these three yeares last past, in *preaching Christ crucified unto my selfe and Country people*, am not in these matters anie whit to reason with you. . . .[25]

His own position was not in doubt: 'I neyther can, nor will weare the apparrell, nor subscribe unto it, or the communion booke'; but when faced with the questions, 'What judge you then of so many learned and good men, that thinke that they may beare with the ceremonies?' he would not commit himself:

> I reverence the true disposinges of God his misteries, and their godlines of life; I judge them not in ceremonies, for they may use them to the Lorde, as I desire not to be judged in refusing them, for I doe it to the Lorde.[26]

In conclusion, he gently reminds the bishop that the scriptural criterion of Christ's ministers is not ceremonial conformity. He quotes Matthew 7:15-16 and continues thus:

> Our heauenly maister hath left the true badge, or common liverie, whereby his true servauntes shall bee decerned from others. . . . This kind of traiall, as you onely towardes me have hitherto used, and I have not refused; so I trust so long as I shall abyde it, you will content yourselfe therewith.[27]

In other words, he asks simply to be judged on the quality of his pastoral ministry, and to be left in peace to discharge it. And in this he was typical of the new generation of Puritan pastors whom he led out into the spiritual darkness of rural England. Some of them were nonconformists, but many were satisfied with the existing framework of the established church and deplored only its lack of pastors. Such were Laurence Chaderton, Richard Sibbes, William Perkins, and Robert Bolton. Membership of this brotherhood of 'affectionate practical' teachers and spiritual physicians was not affected by individual views on problems of ecclesiastical polity.

Over the next half-century Cambridge produced many spiritual physicians in Greenham's mould. Christ's College was their nursery at first. Dering was at Christ's, first as an undergraduate, from 1560, then as a fellow. Laurence Chaderton, who became a Protestant during his time as an undergraduate there, was a fellow for the best part of two decades before becoming first Master of Sir Walter Mildmay's new foundation, Emmanuel College, in 1584. Chaderton delivered a weekly 'lecture' (i.e., sermon) in St Clement's Church for fifty years, and when, at eighty-two, he decided to cease preaching he got letters from forty clergy begging him not to and testifying that they owed their conversion to his ministry. It was Chaderton whose apology for preaching all of two hours was once greeted, so Fuller tells us, with the cry from the congregation *For God's Sake Sir Go on, go on*.[28] Richard Rogers, 'another Greenham',[29] minister of Wethersfield from 1574, and Arthur Hildersam, preacher for forty years at Ashby-de-la-Zouch and mentor of William Gouge and John Preston, were both Christ's men; so was William Perkins, Chaderton's pupil, converted as an undergraduate and made a fellow in 1584. Paul Baynes, yet another Christ's man, who succeeded Perkins as weekly lecturer at Great St Andrew's Church when the latter died in 1602, preached to the conversion of Richard Sibbes, who preached to the conversion of John Cotton, who preached to the conversion of John Preston. When Thomas Goodwin went up to Christ's in 1613, aged twelve, the college boasted 'six Fellows that were great Tutors, who professed Religion after the strictest sort, then called Puritans',[30] and a funeral sermon on repentance from Bainbridge, the Master, soon became the human means of Goodwin's own conversion. Chaderton, Rogers, Hildersam, Perkins, Gouge, Baynes, Sibbes, Cotton, Preston, and Goodwin all gained role-model status among 'affectionate practical' pastor-evangelists. So the Cambridge movement progressed, maintaining spiritual depth and gathering numerical strength all the time.

Sadly, though not surprisingly, young men who took their cue from these patriarchal figures had difficulty in finding pastoral charges. We can well imagine that few patrons in those days would want to offer incumbencies to preachers of righteousness and repentance as aggressive and uncompromising as these men sought to be. A plea to Parliment in 1586 from some Cambridge students calls for action in this matter:

> It cannot be denied but this our Universitie doth flourish at this present in all kinds of good literature as much as at any time heretofore, the praise being given to God for the same; yet it cannot be denied likewise but that that part of us which have chosen the studie of the Sacred Scriptures and have prepared ourselves for the holie ministerie do find lesse lawfull entrance into the Church of God and preferment for our labours than in

former times, a lamentable thing to be heard of in this gratious light of the Gospel. There are now in our Universitie of Cambridge . . . able men, furnished with sufficient gifts to teach the ignorant people, a common subject to be wrought upon in most places of this land, as partlie we know by experience, and partlie the generall complaints of the people do show, yet for all that, how fewe of us are called to this business with just and equall conditions, and not rather the unlearned ministers, the verie scumme of the people, preferred to the ruine of thousands of soules, to the shame of the Church of God, and the utter ruine of learning. For if we ourselves use some meanes to have entrance into a charge, the covetousnes of patrons is such, and so insatiable for the most part, that there is no waie by them but by simonie, perjurie, and afterwards almost plaine beggarie. So that, in this great want of labourers we stand idle in the market place all the day, for almost no man regardeth us to use our labours, so lamentable is the state of this our Church at this time.[31]

No official action was taken; but lectureships were endowed in many parishes to provide preaching-posts for these young Puritans, and thus the leaven of the gospel spread through England in the days of Elizabeth, James, and Charles.

2

Every movement of ideas needs its own literature, and pastoral Puritanism was no exception. Perkins, a gifted scholar with a flair for clarity and simplicity, was the pioneer at this point. In 1589 he started a series of popular books written in sermon style to promote Puritan piety: *A treatise tending unto a declaration, whether a man be in a state of damnation, or in the estate of grace* (1589); *A Golden Chain* (1590: a Calvinistic projection of the plan of salvation); *Spiritual Desertions* (1591); *A Case of Conscience . . . how a man may know whether he be the child of God, or no* (1592); *Two treatises; of the nature and practice of repentance; of the conflict of the flesh and spirit* (1593); and many more (in Perkins' collected *Works*, which fill three folios, there are forty-seven separate items).

Others followed where Perkins led. Richard Rogers produced a large work, *Seven Treatises . . . leading and guiding to true happiness, both in this life, and in the life to come . . . the practice of Christianity . . . in the which, more particularly true Christians may learn how to lead a godly and comfortable life every day* (1603; fifth edition, 1630; abridged version, *The Practice of Christianity. Or, an Epitome of Seven Treatises*, 1618). John Downame also wrote a folio, *The Christian Warfare* (1604). Greenham's *Works* appeared in folio in 1599, Perkins' in 1608-9; Dering's were on sale in 1597. The folios were for ministers' bookshelves, but for layfolk there were soon quartos and octavos (i.e., pocket-books) in abundance: Perkins' separate works, already mentioned; the two books that formed Mrs Bunyan's dowry, Arthur Dent's *The Plain Man's Pathway to Heaven* (1601) and Lewis Bayly's *The Practice of Piety* (fortieth edition, 1640); *The Ten Commandments* by John Dod and Robert Cleaver (1603; nineteenth edition, 1635); and a vast number of expository sermons in topical series. England had had no devotional literature worth speaking of until this flow started; hence, writing at layman's level, the same level at which they preached, the pastors were soon able to capture a very large readership, and the influence of their published works in the first half of the seventeenth century was far-reaching and profound.

Some sense of the impact of Puritan books over two generations may be gained by comparing Greenham's ministry at Dry Drayton with Baxter's at Kidderminster. Greenham laboured for twenty years (1570-90) with virtually no fruit; Baxter worked for fourteen (1641-42, 1647-60), in a situation where 'they had hardly ever had any lively serious preaching', and saw the greater part of the town, which was about 800 families and 2,000 adults strong, make a meaningful profession of faith. 'O what am I, a worthless Worm . . . that God should thus abundantly encourage me, when the Reverend Instructors of my Youth, did labour Fifty years together in one place, and could scarcely say they had converted one or two of [i.e., out of] their Parishes!'[32] The means used were essentially the same in both cases; Baxter too could say with truth that he spent his time 'preaching Christ crucified unto my selfe and Country people', both from the pulpit and in personal dealings with individuals; but Baxter's England, leavened by two generations of Puritan preaching and religious writing, was a different place from Greenham's. The fallow ground had been broken up, the seen sown faithfully over many decades, and now harvest time had come. In ministries like Baxter's the vision of converted communities that had led men like Greenham and Rogers into their pastoral charges was finding fulfilment at last.

Though, spiritually speaking, the harvest sun shone brightly in many parts of England during the Commonwealth years, storm clouds soon returned and the story of the 'affectionate practical English writers' ends not happily but in very dark shadows. The Puritans who came to power in the 1640s, for all their oneness of view about personal religion, could not agree politically (which was why Cromwell had to become a reluctant dictator, contrary to what he and most people desired). Again, though they were at one in seeking the glory of God in his church, they could not agree ecclesiastically (which was why Cromwell had to establish a frankly pluralist independency of a non-episcopal, non-Socinian, non-Roman type—an arrangement that satisfied very few).

Moreover, eccentricity and fanaticism came in to upset the Puritan apple-cart. Where the pastors had insisted that conscience must be controlled by the word of God, lay leaders now quoted Scripture to support the promptings of the light within. Where the pastors had taught the art of living on earth in the light of eternity, zealots now dreamed of seeing the kingdom of heaven set up in seventeenth-century England. Where the Puritans had exalted the office of the preacher as he declares God's mind out of his word, people now treated every man bold and uninhibited enough to air his views in public as inspired. Where the preachers had explained that learning without the Holy Spirit will not give understanding of Scripture, education was now thought of as unfitting one to see the Bible's meaning. And when the university-trained, theologically erudite Puritan pastors spoke against these tendencies, Quakers, Ranters, Muggletonians and many more told them they were quenching the Spirit.

Baxter saw something satanic in the field-day the printers were having in all of this. 'I confess,' he wrote in 1653, 'I am . . . apprehensive of the luxurious fertility of licentiousness of the press of late, as being a design of the enemy to bury and overwhelm . . . those judicious, pious, excellent writings, that before were so commonly read by the people.'[33] Confusion and instability, both political and spiritual, were spreading; the Puritan revival was burning itself out; and after Cromwell died, nothing seemed to be under control any more. Restoration of the monarchy and the Church of England was the inevitable reaction, and in 1660 this duly took place.

For the pastors, the result was misery. The vengeful, fear-driven Clarendon Code ejected and repressed them. The ministry which they conscientiously maintained outside the Church of England was made illegal, so that it pitchforked them into prison. They saw the Church of England surrender to latitudinarianism, legalism, and laxity in faith and morals as the country blindly aped its Merry Monarch. The great pastoral theologians—John Owen, Thomas Goodwin, John Howe, Richard Baxter, Stephen Charnock—wrote much of their best material during these years, and Bunyan's wonderful allegories date from this period also. But because the pastors could not totally assent to the Church of England as restored, the universities were barred to them and to young nonconformists with them, and this meant that they could not effectively reproduce their kind. Hence the organised nonconformity that staggered into daylight when toleration came (1689) fell painfully short in stature of the Puritanism that had preceded it. When John Howe, the last of the giants, died in 1705, Puritanism was over.

3

Among Puritan devotional writers Richard Baxter was from the first acknowledged as outstanding for the 'heavenliness' both of his matter and of his manner. Clarity and energy, order and ardour, wisdom and warmth, breadth and depth, ministerial faithfulness and magisterial authority come together in all his 'affectionate practical' productions. With his first book, *The Saints' Everlasting Rest*, which he began to write in order to direct his thoughts upward when he thought he was on his deathbed, he hit the ground running: not only because the book centres, fair and square, on that which was always central to the godliness that he lived and taught, namely the hope of glory strengthening the heart, but because the sublime rush of his rhetoric transcended anything that Puritan stylists had achieved up to that time (1649). Elizabethan Puritan prose, like most of the rest of Elizabethan prose, is pedestrian; early seventeenth-century writers like Richard Sibbes, Robert Bolton, and John Preston had more colour and vividness; but Baxter's high-pressure eloquence on paper put all his peers in the shade. His book 'Of Rest', as he used to call it, became a bestseller, and catapulted him overnight to prominence as a writer on issues of spiritual life.

Old James Usher, Bible chronologist, alp of learning and ex-Archbishop of Armagh, was one in heart with the 'affectionate practical' school, and much appreciated Baxter's quality as an exponent of devotional truth. Meeting Baxter in London in 1654, he put before him a project for the furtherance of religion in England which he judged Baxter supremely fitted to carry out.

> In that short acquaintance I had with that reverend learned servant of Christ, Bishop Usher, he was oft, from first to last, importuning me to write a directory for the several ranks of professed Christians, which might distinctly give each one their portion; beginning with the unconverted, and then proceeding to the babes in Christ, and then to the strong; and mixing some special helps against the several sins that they are addicted to. By the suddenness of motion at our first congress, I perceived that it was in his mind before; and I told him, both that it was abundantly done by many already, and that his unacquaintedness with my weakness, might make him think me fitter for it than I was. But this did not satisfy him, but still he made it his request.[34]

Three years later, after Usher's death, Baxter took the task in hand. In 1657 he wrote:

> ...... I resolved, by God's assistance, to proceed in the order following. First, to speak to the impenitent, unconverted sinners, who are not yet so much as purposing to turn. .... And with these, I thought, a wakening persuasive was a more necessary means. .... My next work must be for those that have some purposes to turn, and are about the work, to direct them for a thorough and a true conversion, that they miscarry not in the birth. The third part must be directions for the younger and weaker sort of Christians, that they may be established, built up, and persevere. The fourth part,

directions for lapsed and backsliding Christians, for their safe recovery. Besides this, there is intended some short persuasions and directions against some special errors of the times, and against some common, killing sins. As for directions to doubting, troubled consciences, that is done already.[35] And then the last part is intended more especially for families, as such, directing the several relations in their duties.[36]

In pursuance of this scheme, Baxter published during the next few years *A Treatise of Conversion* (1657): *A Call to the Unconverted* (1658); *Directions and Persuasions to a Sound Conversion* (1658); *Directions for Weak, Distempered Christians* (1669); *Crucifying the World by the Cross of Christ* (1658); *Catholic Unity* (1659); *Self-Denial* (1660); *The Vain Religion of the Formal Hypocrite Detected* (1660); *The Mischiefs of Self-ignorance* (1662); *The Divine Life* (1664); *The Life of Faith* (1670); while the family vade-mecum swelled into the enormous *Christian Directory* (1673), 'perhaps the best body of practical divinity that is extant in our own or any other tongue', plus the shorter *Poor Man's Family Book* (1674) and *The Catechizing of Families* (1683). This series is a peak point in Puritan devotional writing, and will serve as a convenient orientation point for those seeking to find their way around in the wide world of Puritan spiritual teaching.

4

Our historical survey has indicated the overall aim and character of what the 'affectionate practical English writers' wrote. A reader's introduction to them and their books now follows. Two general points will direct us to approach them rightly.

First, we should appreciate that Puritan practical theology was the envy of continental Protestants. Fighting for their theological life against the Roman Counter-reformation, racked and torn by incessant wars, and with their best minds wholly committed to controversy, Reformed and Lutheran churches had never been free for deep thought about spiritual life. 'It is long ago,' wrote Baxter, in the 'Advertisement' to his *Christian Directory*,

> since many foreign divines subscribed a request, that the English would give them in Latin a sum of our practical theology, which Mr. [John] Dury sent over, and twelve great divines of ours wrote to Bishop Usher . . . to draw them up a form or method. But it was never done among them all. And it is said that Bishop [George] Downame at last undertaking it, died in the attempt. Had this been done, it is like my labour had been spared. But being undone, I have thus made this essay.[37]

How much continental churches valued Puritan practical theology appears from the number of translations they made of it. *The Practice of Piety* went into a string of European languages. Perkins' English works were put into Latin, Dutch, Spanish, Irish (Erse) and Welsh.[38] Baxter was read as far afield as Poland and Hungary,[39] and of translations of his works he wrote in 1691:

> About Twelve of them are Translated into the German tongue; and the Lutherans say they have done good. Some are translated into French; one into the language of the New-England Americans by Mr. John Eliot. Multitudes say, they have been the means of their conversion, and more of their information, confirmation and consolation. And the chief benefit that I expect by them to the world is when I am dead and gone.[40]

The book translated into American was the *Call to the Unconverted*, the 'wakening persuasive' of which Baxter wrote elsewhere:

> In a little more than a year there were about twenty thousand of them printed by my own consent, and about ten thousand since, besides many thousands by stolen impressions. . . . Through God's mercy I have had information of almost whole households converted by this small book, which I set so light by: And as if all this in *England, Scotland and Ireland* were not mercy enough to me, God (since I was silenced) hath sent it on his message to many beyond the seas; for when *Mr. Eliot* had printed the Bible in the *Indians* language, he next translated this. . . . And yet God would make some farther use of it; for *Mr. Stoop* the Pastor of the *French* church was pleased to translate it into elegant *French*, and print it . . . and I hope it will not be unprofitable there; nor in *Germany*, where it is printed in *Dutch*.[41]

Realising that Puritan practical writings were valued all over Europe (not to mention Scotland and New England!) in their own day should prepare us to learn to value them too.

Second, we should appreciate that this devotional literature, though popular in the sense of being expressed simply and not presupposing any technical knowledge, is not popular in the sense of being crude, or frothy, or theologically inept, or ill-informed, or ill-digested, or incompetent in any other way. The modern snobbery of learning whereby professional scholars refuse to popularise and popularisers are expected to apologise for not being professional scholars was not a seventeenth-century syndrome. Puritan authors were learned, strong-minded, well-read, scholarly men in the tradition of Perkins, whom Thomas Fuller rightly hailed as the pioneer who 'first humbled the towering speculations of philosophers into practice and morality',[42] but who in his own day was also known throughout Western

Europe as a top Reformed theologian of the Bezan sort. To bring what they knew about God down to the level of ordinary people in sermons and in print seemed to Puritan clergy a supreme privilege and a prime duty, and they saw their practical writing—sermon material, mostly—as no less important than anything else that they wrote.

As all the world knows, they were great controversialists on questions of doctrine as well as of church order, and saw this as essential to their ministry. Pastors, they said, are responsible for rebuking heresy and defending truth, lest their flocks be misled and thereby enfeebled, if not worse. Biblical truth is nourishing, human error is killing, so spiritual shepherds must guard sound doctrine at all costs. As John Owen put it:

> It is incumbent on them [pastors] to preserve the truth or doctrine of the gospel received and professed in the church, and to defend it against all opposition. This is one principal end of the ministry. . . . And the sinful neglect of this duty is that which was the cause of most of the pernicious heresies and errors that have infested and ruined the church. Those whose duty it was to preserve the doctrine of the gospel entire in the public profession of it have, many of them 'spoken perverse things, to draw away disciples after them'. Bishops, presbyters, public teachers, have been the ringleaders in heresies. Wherefore this duty, especially at this time, when the fundamental truths of the gospel are on all sides impugned, from all sorts of adversaries, is in an especial manner to be attended unto.[43]

But controversy, though a painful necessity when dangerous error was around, had no value save as a prophylactic against evil. Only direct exposition and application of truth would edify in a positive way. It should not, therefore, be thought strange that Puritan intellectuals and academics should put their best efforts into practical writing, view the result as the crown of their achievement, and expect it to prove more useful than anything else they did.

Realising that behind the studied simplicity of Puritan practical books lies the care and competence of brilliant and deeply learned theologians should prepare us to rate this literature at its true worth.

Books are communications from their authors to their readers, and what the authors have to communicate depends on who and what they are themselves. Five positive qualities made the Puritan authors what they were and gave them the message that they still have for those who read them today.

In the first place, they were, as we have seen, *physicians of the soul*. They valued God's revealed truth for its healing power in sinners' lives, and purely theoretical discussions seemed to them false to the true nature of theology. Perkins spoke for them all when he defined theology as 'the science of living blessedly for ever'.[44] 'Blessed life ariseth from the knowledge of God, Ioh. [John] 17:3. . . .' he added. So theology is essentially a practical matter, and is best studied with a practical end directly—existentially, we might say—in view. Baxter's remarks apropos of his bad health in early manhood are significant here:

> Thus was I long kept with the calls of approaching Death at one Ear, and the Questionings of a doubtful conscience at the other! and since then I have found that this method of God's was very wise, and no other was so like to have tended to my good. . . . It set me upon that Method of my Studies, which since then I have found the benefit of, though at the time I was not satisfied with myself. It caused me *first* to seek God's Kingdom and His Righteousness, and most to mind the One thing needful; and to determine first of my Ultimate End; by which I was engaged to choose out and prosecute all other Studies, but as meant to that End: Therefore *Divinity* was not only carried on with the rest of my Studies with an equal hand, but had always the first and chiefest place. And it caused me to study *Practical Divinity* first, in the most *Practical Books*, in a *Practical Order; doing all purposely for the informing and reforming of my own Soul*. So that I had read a multitude of our English Practical Treatises, before I had ever read any other Bodies of Divinity, than *Ursine and Amesius*. . . .[45]

Elsewhere Baxter recommends the same order to others, and in doing so he speaks for the 'affectionate practical' writers as a body. God's revealed truth, they maintained, is for health-giving practice; therefore it is best studied in a practical way; therefore pastors must preach and teach it in that way. Gospel doctrine is to be obeyed; truth is to be, not just acknowledged, but done, in the sense of doing what it requires. So the most biblical theologian will be the most practical theologian, and vice versa; and the preaching style, with practical applications and challenges at every turn, will be the most biblical manner of theologising.

Truth obeyed, said the Puritans, will *heal*. The word fits, because we are all spiritually sick—sick through sin, which is a wasting and killing disease of the heart. The unconverted are sick unto death; those who have come to know Christ and been born again continue sick, but they are gradually getting better as the work of grace goes on in their lives. The church, however, is a hospital in which nobody is completely well, and anyone can relapse at any time. Pastors no less than others are weakened by pressure from the world, the flesh, and the devil, with their lures of profit, pleasure, and pride, and, as we shall see more fully in a moment, pastors must acknowledge that they the healers remain sick and wounded and therefore need to apply the medicines of Scripture to themselves as well as to the sheep whom they tend in Christ's name. All Christians need Scripture truth as medicine for their souls at every stage, and the making and accepting of applications is the administering and swallowing of it. The ability to apply God's truth therapeuticaly implies the prior ability to diagnose spiritual ill-health, and diagnostic ability is learned as much by discovering and keeping track of one's own sins and weaknesses as by any other means. The frequency with which Puritan pastors lament their own sinfulness should not be dismissed as a trivial cultural convention; it is in fact an assurance to us, as it was to their own first hearers and readers, that they know what they are talking about when they 'rip up' our consciences (their phrase), diagnose our spiritual diseases, and prescribe a regimen of biblical directives for our cure. Their own self-examination and self-acquaintance before God is a large part of the secret of the skill with which they probe hearts, nail sins, and show us how Christ's healing power may rescue us from moral and spiritual evil.

In the second place, they were *expositors to the conscience*. Their practical writings are always expositions of Scripture, directed to the ends for which Scripture is profitable: 'doctrine [teaching], reproof, correction, and instruction [nurture, training] in righteousness' (2 Tim 3:16). The Puritan hermeneutic, learned from Scripture itself (more precisely, from the New Testament use of the Old), saw the written word as showing us the nature and mutual relations of God and men, the way in which a covenant-love relation becomes real in Christ, and how to live it out once it has become real. The Puritan expository method was to state the doctrines—that is, the principles concerning the God-and-us relationship—that their texts yielded, and then to apply them. That is why the writers were termed 'practical'. Their applications were directed to the conscience, that is, self-judging practical reason: reason weighing questions of one's duty and one's desert and one's actual relationship to God in each present moment. The Puritans believed that this was the scriptural way to expound Scripture, and they looked to the Holy Spirit to honour it by giving understanding and conviction of the divine truth of what was said, by triggering the process of self-judgement, and by calling forth appropriate responses to the verdict that was reached. These responses would range over the whole area of faith, hope, and love; repentance, humility, and self-distrust; self-denial, self-devotion, and obedience; praise, thanksgiving, adoration and petition; plus the various dispositional 'affections' (not just waves of passing emotion, but set inclinations of heart with a feeling-tone) that contribute to one's actual cleaving to God and communing with God. Their stress on the importance of these dispositions, and their constant efforts to evoke and strengthen them (joy, sorrow, desire, fear, and so on, all directed to their proper objects), explains why the writers were called 'affectionate'.

Built into the Puritan hermeneutic was the belief, argued so successfully by the Reformers that their English successors could in practice take it for granted, that justification by faith through Christ by grace is a God-given grid or prism through which all Scripture should be passed in order fully to see what light and truth it has for us. William Tyndale, who on this as on many other matters may justly be called the grandfather of Puritan practical theology, spelt out this contention as follows:

> Which two points, that is to wit, the law spiritually interpreted, how that all is damnable sin that is not unfeigned love out of the ground and bottom of the heart . . . and that the promises be given unto a repenting soul that thirsteth and cryeth for them out of the fatherly mercy of God, through our faith only, without all deserving of our deeds or merits of our works, but for Christ's sake alone, and for the merits and deserving of his works . . . which two points, I say, if they be written in thine heart, are the keys which open all the scriptures unto thee. . . .[46]

Directions for the study of Scripture follow. Tyndale adduces 2 Timothy 3:16, Romans 15:4 and 1 Corinthians 10:11 and proceeds:

> Seek therefore in the Scripture as thou readest it, first the *law*, what God commandeth us to do; and secondarily the *promises* . . . in Christ Jesus our Lord. Then seek *ensamples*, first of comfort, how God purgeth all them that submit themselves to walk in his ways, in the purgatory of tribulation . . . never suffering any of them to perish that cleave fast to his promises. And finally note the ensamples which are written to fear the flesh, that we sin not; that is, how God suffereth the ungodly and wicked sinners . . . to continue in their wickedness . . . they harden their hearts against the truth, and God destroyeth them utterly.[47]

Again, he instructs

> that thou takest the stories and lives which are contained in the Bible for sure and undoubted ensamples that God will so deal with us unto the world's end.[48]

Once those principles are applied, says Tyndale, Scripture is found to be self-interpreting: 'the Scripture giveth record to itself, and ever expoundeth itself by another open text.'[49] The key is justification by faith, and the door (as we should expect) is the Epistle to the Romans. 'A light and way unto the whole Scripture', Tyndale calls it, and translates Luther's verdict upon it: 'a bright light, and sufficient to give light unto all the Scripture.'[50] These principles of exegesis were handed on to the Puritan brotherhood by Perkins, who laid it down that if one began one's study with Romans, and followed it with John's Gospel, one had the key to the entire Bible;[51] analysis shows that these principles have virtually axiomatic status in all Puritan exegesis.

Puritan accounts of faith—the faith that brings justification, and by which Christians live each day—are not in every respect uniform. All the writers agree that faith is more than bare belief of known facts, but when they seek to show what more it is their definitions diverge somewhat. Perkins, knowing how the Reformers drew on Scripture to correlate faith with the Spirit's witness to God's promise, find faith's essence in applicatory assurance, which he sees as an exercise of the mind; Ames, his disciple, knowing how the Reformers also drew on Scripture to present the living Christ, crucified and risen, as faith's object, and evidently influenced by the voluntarist view of faith held by the Arminians with whom he constantly debated, finds faith's essence in receiving and relying on Christ in personal, covenantal terms, which he sees as an exercise of the will; and most Puritan accounts after Ames, if not before, include both elements.[52] But all the Puritans see faith as involving conscience, the judging of oneself in God's presence by the light of biblical truth, and therefore they structure all their biblical expositions, designed as these are to induce and nurture faith, as sustained addresses and appeals to the conscience. Typical as an indication of their conscious mental discipline in this matter is John Owen's directional guideline at the start of his large and complex treatise on *The Doctrine of Justification by Faith*:

> It is the practical direction of the consciences of men, in their application unto God by Jesus Christ, for deliverance from the curse due unto the apostate state, and peace with him . . . that is alone to be designed in the handling of this doctrine. . . . And whereas we cannot either safely or usefully treat of this doctrine, but *with respect unto the same ends for which it is declared, and whereunto it is applied, in the Scripture*, we should not . . . be turned aside from attending unto this case and its resolution, in all our discourses on this subject. For it is the direction, satisfaction, and peace of the consciences of men, and not the curiosity of notions or subtlety of disputations, which it is our duty to design.[53]

Not only in connection with justification, but at every point, first to last, the Puritan account of faith's focus, exercise, and fruits is structured in terms of conscience receiving God's word and by its light judging how God sees one and how through Christ one may or does stand related to him in covenant mercy. This explains why the writers in their own day were regularly called 'experimental', and what they themselves meant when they spoke of Christian 'experience'. They were not using the word to denote all states of consciousness and emotion as such; they were using it with careful precision to signify all that is involved in living the life of faith through the exercise of conscience on God's word. Nor, when they talked about experience in this sense, was it their own experience that they took as their reference-point; instead, they read the Bible as a book of normative experience, no less than of normative doctrine. And here, in fact, they were pursuing an insight that is a peculiar treasure of Augustinian biblicism, whether in Augustine himself or Bernard or the Reformers or the original Puritans or such latter-day Puritans as C.H. Spurgeon and Martyn Lloyd-Jones. What Augustinians see, as others often do not, is that those biblical documents in which the writers give their teaching by telling of their experience must set standards of spiritual experience, just as they do of divine truth, and must be expounded in a way that brings out and enforces the one as much as the other. If, in particular, apostolic teaching is to be set forth as definitive, so must apostolic experience be, for the apostles regularly recount their doctrine in terms of its effect in their own lives, and the response of their own consciences to it: again and again their message and their experience are stated in terms of each other. (Think of Romans, 2 Corinthians, Galatians, Philippians, and 1 John in particular for illustrations of this.) Here is a further matter about which it is proper to say: What God has joined, let not man put asunder.

In this regard the Puritans were in fact exemplary. Studying the New Testament Epistles, the Psalms, and the 'ensamples' of faith and faithfulness and their opposites in both Testaments, they built up alongside their full formulations of the doctrine of God's grace correspondingly full formulations of the distinctive experience of faith which this doctrine is intended to produce; and just as they learned to refute heresies and correct misstatements that were distorting the apostolic gospel, so they learned to diagnose and prescribe treatment, not like quack doctors, 'blind Empyrikes' as Holland calls them, who are even more of a menace in soul-therapy than they are in bodily medicine, but as true physicians with a proper theoretical basis for their diagnosis and for the remedies they offer. Those who see the Reformers as having given the church classical formulations of the doctrine of God's saving grace should hail the Puritans as classical exponents, through their understanding of faith and conscience, of the application of that doctrine to human spiritual needs. If the Reformers are classic theologians, then the Puritans are classic pastors and spiritual guides, as any who read them will soon find.

In the third place, the Puritans were *educators of the mind*. This point relates to their teaching method. Much thought was given in the sixteenth and seventeenth centuries to educational theory, and the Puritan pastors as a body had a well planned out educational technique, at which we shall now glance.

The starting-point was their certainty that the mind must be instructed and enlightened before faith and obedience become possible. 'Ignorance is almost every error,' wrote Baxter, and one of his favourite maxims about preaching was 'first light—then heat'. Heat without light, pulpit passion without pedagogic precision, would be no use to anyone. Unwillingness on the part of church attenders to learn the faith and accept instruction from sermons was a sure sign of insincerity. 'If ever you would be converted, labour for true knowledge,' Baxter told his working-class congregation, and when they did as a modern congregation would, and objected, 'We are not learned, and, therefore, God will not require much knowledge at our hands,' he replied as follows:

> (1) Every man that has a reasonable soul should know God that made him; and know the end for which he should live; and know the way to his eternal happiness, as well as the learned: have you not souls to save or lose as well as learned have? (2) God hath made plain His will to you in His Word; He hath given you teachers and many other helps; so that you have no excuse if you are ignorant; you must know how to be christians if you are no scholars. You may hit the way to heaven in English, though you have no skill in Hebrew or Greek; but in the darkness of ignorance you can never hit it. (3) . . . If you think, therefore, that you may be excused from knowledge, you may as well think that you may be excused from love and from all obedience; for there can be none of this without knowledge. . . . Were you but as willing to get the knowledge of God and heavenly things as you are to know how to work in your trade, you would have set yourself to it before this day, and you would have spared no cost or pains till you had got it. But you account seven years little enough to learn your trade, and will not bestow one day in seven in diligent learning the matters of your salvation.[54]

And again:

> If heaven be too high for you to think on, and to provide for, it will be too high for you ever to possess.[55]

All the Puritans regarded religious feeling and pious emotion without knowledge as worse than useless. Only when the truth was being felt was emotion in any way desirable. When men felt and obeyed the truth they knew, it was the work of the Spirit of God, but when they were swayed by feeling without knowledge, it was a sure sign that the devil was at work, for feeling divorced from knowledge and urgings to action in darkness of mind were both as ruinous to the soul as was knowledge without obedience. So the teaching of truth was the pastor's first task, as the learning of it was the layman's.

But how was truth to be taught? Principally from the pulpit, by the systematic analysis and application of biblical texts, all of which were approached as utterances of the Holy Spirit. The basic method was set out by Perkins in his *Art of Prophecying*. The preacher must serve his text by becoming the mouthpiece for its message. He should first paraphrase it, give the 'connexion' (context) and point out its structure and component parts, that is, 'divide' it: all to make sure that his readers understood the biblical writer's general meaning and scope. Then he should extract from it one or more doctrinal propositions or theses which the text asserted, implied, presupposed or instanced. Arthur Hildersam, for instance, 'raises' from Psalm 51:1-2 the following three 'doctrines':

> That God's people, when they are in any distress, must fly to God by prayer, and seek comfort that way; That pardon of sin is more to be desired than deliverance from the greatest judgments that can befall us; That the best of God's servants have no other ground of hope to find favour with God, for the pardon of their sins, but only in the mercy of the Lord.[56]

John Owen, on the second half of Romans 8:13, raises these three:

> The choicest believers, who are assuredly free from the condemning power of sin, ought yet to make it their business all their days to mortify the indwelling power of sin; The Holy Ghost . . . only is sufficient for this work . . . ; The vigour and power and comfort of our spiritual life depends on our mortification of the deeds of the flesh.[57]

Baxter's *Call to the Unconverted* is an extended exposition of seven doctrines derived from Ezekiel 33:11:

> It is the unchangeable law of God, that the wicked shall live, if they will but turn; God takes pleasure in men's conversion and salvation, but not in their death or damnation . . . ; This is a most certain truth, which . . . God . . . hath confirmed . . . solemnly by His oath; The Lord doth redouble His commands and persuasions to the wicked to turn; The Lord condescendeth to reason the case with them, and asketh the wicked, why they die? If after all this, the wicked will not return, it is not long of God that they perish, but of themselves . . . they die because they will die.[58]

The doctrines, once stated, are to be 'proved' by further analysis of the text, plus appeal to other passages of Scripture; they must be 'cleared' against possible misunderstandings and difficulties and 'confirmed' against objections that might arise in the listeners' minds. 'Doctrine' must then lead on to application, or 'use'. This was usually subdivided into several particular 'uses', such as the use of information, whereby the truth would be applied to instruct the mind and mould the judgement, so that a man might learn to conform his thoughts and opinions to the revealed mind of God; the use of exhortation or dehortation, whereby the listener was shown in the light of the doctrine what to do and what not to do; the uses of lamentation and persuasion, whereby the preacher sought to impress on his hearers the blind folly of those who fail to respond to God's grace as set forth in the doctrine and to rouse them to lay hold of it for themselves; the use of comfort, whereby the doctrine was shown to be the answer to doubt and uncertainty; the use of trial, or self-examination, whereby the preacher calls the congregation to judge of their own spiritual condition in the light of the doctrine (which may state one of the marks of a regenerate man, or some Christian privilege or duty); and so on. The details of this expository method might be varied, but it was always variation on the theme of doctrine plus use. 'It would be an uncouth sermon,' commented John Owen, 'that should be without doctrine and use.'[59]

Application must always be relevant, otherwise it is hollow histrionics, and since congregations contain people in many different spiritual conditions a wide range of applications must constantly be made. There must be something of application for everyone. Perkins offers preachers a sevenfold pastoral grid for planning application.[60] First, he says, there are 'unbelievers who are both ignorant and unteachable'; the strategy with them must be one of 'reproving in them some notorious sin, that being pricked in heart and terrified, they may become teachable'. Second, 'some are teachable, but yet ignorant': they need to be taught the basic gospel, preferably by use of a question-and-answer catechism (a much favoured Puritan means of instruction) to supplement sermons. Third, 'some have knowledge, but are not as yet humbled': these need to hear how God's law condemns them. Fourth, 'some are humbled': these need to hear 'the doctrine of faith and repentance, and the comforts of the Gospel'. Fifth, 'some do believe': these need grounding in '1. The Gospel touching justification, sanctification and perseverance. 2. The law without the curse, whereby they may be taught to bring forth fruits of new obedience beseeming repentance.' Sixth, 'some are fallen' from true faith or true righteousness: these need 'that doctrine which do cross their error . . . demonstrated and inculcated (or beaten upon them) together with the doctrine of repentance, and that with a brotherly affection'. Seventh, 'there is a mingled people. A mixed people are the assemblies of our Churches.' (This was true. Church attendance was required by law under Elizabeth, on pain of the sizeable fine of one shilling for a first conviction and worse if the offence of non-attendance was repeated. This law, the purpose of which was to winkle out Catholic recusants, gave ministers a captive audience but not always an alert one.) What to do here? Let preachers ring the changes on all these types of application on a regular basis. Each will be right for some hearers, and the well of applicatory material will never run dry. Many forms and levels of 'home-coming' application (the adjective is from Alexander Whyte) can be drawn by inference from just about any text with which the preacher is dealing.

Because this was so, and because so many distinct points of doctrine could be derived from each text as well, and because doctrines, once introduced, were felt to need full and thorough statement lest they be misunderstood, Puritan preachers might 'stand' on the same text for many sermons together, and stay with a single passage for months and years at a time. The result in print looks daunting to the modern eye: the array of numbered headings and sub-headings is forbidding, and one easily loses one's way. One reason why these expositions floor us at first is that they are controlled by a much stronger interest in the Bible as a whole than we are used to. Where we concentrate on focusing the flow of each passage with minimum reference to other Scriptures, Puritan expositors labour throughout to show how each passage reflects and links up with the teaching of the rest of the word of God. Then a second reason why we are floored is that whereas our way of presenting a topic is to assume total ignorance of it and build it up inductively from a chosen starting-point, the Puritan way was to assume some awareness of it and break it down by cross-sectional analysis. The claim of Peter Ramus, a sixteenth-century French Protestant educationist, that dichotomising analysis was the best way to understand any subject, led many Puritans to 'divide' texts and spell out themes that way in the pulpit, in the belief that this would make everything clear and memorable. One hopes that for their own hearers it did, but there is no denying that for us to read the Puritans' preached treatises today is initially hard. Jotting down the headings as one comes to them does, however, help greatly to get the structure of their presentations into one's mind.

Puritan analytical method accounts for the length of Puritan expositions—Joseph Caryl's 6,000 quarto pages on Job; 2,000 plus in folio on Hebrews from John Owen; Hildersam's 152 sermons on Psalm 51:1-7; over 800 pages of small print in all modern editions of William Gurnall's treatment of Ephesians 6:10-20, *The Christian in Complete Armour*; et cetera! What led the Puritans into such long-windedness was their passion for thoroughness in extracting all doctrines and developing all applications. Clearly, once they started drawing out implications and applications they found it hard to stop. Yet their variety of matter is great, repetition is minimal, the sense that they begin in the middle rather than at the beginning is soon overcome, and interest once gained does not fade. You doubt that? Taste and see!

In the fourth place, the Puritans were *enforcers of the truth*. This point relates to their way with words. They turned their back on the airs and graces which won 'witty' preachers reputations at Oxford and Cambridge and court. They chose instead a plain, straightforward style, solemn yet lively and homely, for their messages; and their plainness was with power. Perkins caused comment in Cambridge by resolutely preaching in this simple lucid way; some who heard him wrote him off as 'a barren empty fellow, and a passing mean scholar',[61] but when Thomas Goodwin went up to Cambridge in 1613 he found the memory of Perkins' ministry still vivid, though the man himself had been dead eleven years. At first Goodwin set his heart on becoming a 'witty' preacher like Dr Senhouse of St John's, whose sermons were 'the eminentest farrago of all sorts of flowers of wit that are found in any of the fathers, poets, histories, similitudes, or whatever has the elegancy of wit in it'. After his conversion, however, he renounced such self-display.

> I came to this resolved principle, that I would preach wholly and altogether sound and wholesome words, without affectation of wit and vanity of eloquence. . . . I . . . have continued in that purpose and practice these three-score years [Goodwin was writing at the end of his life]. I have preached what I thought was truly edifying, either for conversion, or bringing them up to eternal life.[62]

This was typical. The Puritans as a body were clear that the preacher's job is to display Christ's grace, not his own learning, and to design his sermons so that they bring benefit to others rather than applause to himself. Therefore Puritan preaching revolved around the three Rs of biblical religion—ruin, redemption, regeneration—and clothed these gospel truths in the vivid dress of studied simplicity.

In the preface to his *Treatise on Conversion*, Richard Baxter seeks to disarm mockers of the 'plain style' by explaining that in the sermons of which the treatise is composed 'I was to preach not only to a popular auditory, but to the most ignorant, sottish part of that auditory'. He continues thus:

> The plainest words are the profitablest oratory in the weightiest matters. Fineness is for ornament, and delicacy for delight; . . . when they are conjunct, it is hard for the . . . hearer or reader to observe the matter of ornament and delicacy, and not to be carried from the matter . . . and to hear or read a neat, concise, sententious discourse, and not to be hurt by it; for it usually hindereth the due operation of the matter, and keeps it from the heart, and stops it in the fancy, and makes it seem as light as the style. We use not to stand upon compliment or precedency, when we run to quench a common fire, nor to call men out to it by an eloquent speech. If we see a man fall into fire or water, we stand not upon mannerliness in plucking him out. . . . I shall never forget the relish of my soul, when God first warmed my heart with these matters, and when I was newly entered into seriousness in religion: when I read such a book as Bishop [Lancelot] Andrewes' Sermons, or heard such kind of preaching, I felt no life in it; methought they did but play with holy things. . . . But it was the *plain and pressing downright preacher*, that only seemed to me to be in good sadness . . . and to speak with life, and light, and weight: and it was such kind of writings that were wonderfully pleasant and savoury to my soul. . . . And yet I must confess, that though I can better digest exactness and brevity, than I could so long ago, yet I as much value seriousness and plainness: and I feel in myself in reading or hearing, a despising of that wittiness as proud foolery, which savoureth of levity, and tendeth to evaporate weighty truths, and turn them

all into very fancies, and keep them from the heart. As a stage-player, or morris-dancer, differs from a soldier or a king, so do these preachers from the true and faithful ministers of Christ: and as they deal liker to players than preachers in the pulpit, so usually their hearers do rather come to play with a sermon, than to attend a message from the God of heaven about the life or death of their souls.[63]

Baxter's 'noble negligence' of style, of which the quotation displays some touches, should not be taken to indicate that Puritan prose was ever slip-shod. Owen's Latinised style is tortuously exact, as was Goodwin's crabbed 'familiar' style; Baxter and Bunyan write with a force and pungency that little if any religious prose since their day has matched, let alone surpassed; while William Perkins, Richard Sibbes, Thomas Watson, Thomas Brooks, Thomas Manton, and William Gurnall (to look no further) are models of tidy lucidity, all of them save Perkins overflowing with vivid analogies and illustrations. By the standards of the day their homespun forthrightness was no eloquence at all, but it was a deliberately chosen idiom, the ratio-nale of which was well if sententiously expressed by John Flavel as follows:

A crucified style best suits the preachers of a crucified Christ. . . . Prudence will choose words that are solid, rather than florid. . . . Words are but ser-vants to matter. An iron key, fitted to the wards of the lock, is more useful than a golden one that will not open the door to the treasures. . . . Prudence will cast away a thousand fine words for one that is apt to penetrate the conscience and reach the heart.[64]

It will be found that Puritan plainness works in this way for the modern reader, just as it did for the preachers' own contemporaries. We, too, expe-rience it as a channel of God's unction and power, and we can forgive occa-sional lapses into diffuseness and redundancy. 'I confess my memory often lets slip the passages that I have before written, and in that forgetfulness I write them again: but I make no great matter of it,' declared Baxter with captivating candour; 'the writing of the same thing is safe to the reader, and why then should it be grievous to me?'[65] There's no answer to that!

In the fifth place, the Puritans were *men of the Spirit*; lovers of the Lord, keepers of his law, and self-squanderers in his service, which are in every age the three main elements of the truly Spirit-filled life. Baxter's *Reformed Pastor* opens by admonishing God's shepherds as follows:

Take heed to yourselves, lest you be void of that saving grace of God which you offer to others . . . be also careful that your graces are kept in vigorous and lively exercise, and that you preach to yourselves the sermons which you study, before you preach them to others . . . watch therefore over your own hearts: keep out lusts and passions, and worldly inclinations; keep up

the life of faith, and love, and zeal; be much at home, and much with God
. . . take heed to yourselves, lest your example contradict your doctrine
. . . lest you unsay with your lives, what you say with your tongues. . . . We
must study as hard how to live well, as how to preach well. We must think
and think again, how to compose our lives, as may most tend to men's salvation, as well as our sermons. . . .[66]

This was what the great Puritans in fact did, and their writings bear witness to the quality of their own Christian living. 'A man preacheth that sermon only well unto others which preacheth itself in his own soul,' wrote
John Owen. 'And he that doth not feed on and thrive in the digestion of
the food which he provides for others will scarce make it savoury unto
them; yea, he knows not but that the food he hath provided may be poison,
unless he have really tasted of it himself. If the word do not dwell with
power *in* us, it will not pass with power *from* us.'[67] Perkins had said: 'Good
words are vain where there is no good life. Let not Ministers think that
their golden words shall do so much good as their leaden lives shall do
hurt. . . . As no man is more honourable than a learned and holy minister,
so none is more contemptible in this world, none more miserable for that
to come than he who by his loose and lewd life doth scandalize his doctrine.'[68] And Calvin had said very bluntly: 'It were better for him [the
preacher] to break his neck going up into the pulpit, if he does not take
pains to be the first to follow God.'[69]

The Puritan teachers saw this to be true, and acted accordingly. Pre-eminently, they were holy men, and the authority that their printed words carry
is the authority not just of Scripture in itself, as the word of God, but of
Scripture in experience—their own experience—as the power of God,
through what they recognised as the illuminating and applying agency of
the Holy Spirit. Of the doctrine of justification Owen wrote:

Unto him that would treat of it in a due manner, it is required that he weigh
every thing he asserts in his own mind and experience, and not dare to propose that unto others which he doth not abide by himself, in the most intimate recesses of his mind, under his nearest approaches unto God, in his
surprisals with dangers, in deep afflictions, in his preparations for death,
and in his most humble contemplations of the infinite distance between God
and him.[70]

The same applied, so the Puritans perceived, to all doctrines. Accordingly it was out of the exercise of their own hearts and consciences at every
point over the truth they had to teach that the preachers addressed the
hearts and consciences of others. Thus they fulfilled Paul's formula that 'as
men of sincerity, as commissioned by God, in the sight of God we speak
in Christ' (2 Cor 2:17).

Spiritual authority is hard to pin down in words, but we recognise it when we meet it. It is a product compounded of conscientious faithfulness to the Bible; vivid perception of God's reality and greatness; inflexible desire to honour and please him; deep self-searching and radical self-denial; adoring intimacy with Christ; generous compassion manward; and forthright simplicity, God-taught and God-wrought, adult in its knowingness while childlike in its directness. The man of God has authority as he bows to divine authority, and the pattern of God's power in him is the baptismal pattern of being supernaturally raised from under burdens that feel like death.

The great Puritans lived out this pattern in their own day as they battled against poor health, circumstantial distractions and distresses, and most of all their own sluggish hearts so as to preach the gospel 'with life, and light, and weight', and we who read three and a half centuries later what they prepared for their own pulpits (for that, as we have seen, is what most of the Puritan material is) will find that their authority still comes through to us. The Reformers left to the church magisterial expositions of what our gracious God does for us; the Puritan legacy is equally authoritative declarations of what that same God does in us. To turn to the works of the 'affectionate practical English writers' is like entering a new world; one's vision is cleared, one's thoughts are purged, one's heart is stirred; one is humbled, instructed, quickened, invigorated, brought low in repentance and raised high in assurance. There is no more salutary experience! Churches and Christians today are sadly Laodicean: complacent, somnolent, shallow, stuffy. We need reviving. What to do? Opening the windows of our souls to let in a breath of fresh air from the seventeenth century would, I suggest, be the wisest possible course.

THE PURITANS AND THE BIBLE

CHAPTER FIVE

John Owen on
Communication from God

1

Who was John Owen? His name has appeared in this book already (and will do so many times more), and he will be properly profiled in Chapter Twelve. Here I need only say that he is by common consent not the most versatile, but the greatest among Puritan theologians. For solidity, profundity, massiveness and majesty in exhibiting from Scripture God's ways with sinful mankind there is no one to touch him. On every topic he handles, apart from the limits he imposes on synods and magistrates, he stands in the centre of the Puritan mainstream, totally in line with the Westminster standards and the developed ideal of godliness. All my chapters on Owen give evidence for this assertion, as will appear. In his own day he was seen as England's foremost bastion and champion of Reformed evangelical orthodoxy, and he did not doubt that God had given him this role; but his interest lay in broadening and deepening insight into the realities that orthodoxy confesses, and a humbled and humbling awareness that his present understanding, though true (so he believed) as far as it went, was deeply inadequate to those realities pervades all that he wrote. In this, as in most things, he was more like John Calvin than was any other of the Puritan leaders.

2

If my present chapter title were construed according to the Owenian idiom, it would license me to range over the whole field of the Holy Spirit's work in applying redemption: for John Owen used the word 'communication' to cover every divine bestowal of benefit upon man. But I am using the word in its modern restricted sense, and what I propose to explore is John Owen's account of *cognitive* communication from God to men—in other words, his doctrine of the Spirit and the word, his answer to the question, how does God bring us to understand him, and to comprehend the world of spiritual reality?

The giving of spiritual understanding is not, of course, an end in itself; as Owen recognises, it is always to be seen and valued as a means to something further—knowing and enjoying God. But it is a subject in itself, which can be clearly delimited in terms of the concept of communication from the mind of God to the minds of men. It was, in fact, in these terms that Owen saw and discussed it, rather than in terms of the formal categories of revelation, inspiration, illumination, and interpretation, which were, and are, the common topical divisions in textbooks of theology. Owen makes use of these categories, of course, but the object of his interest is the communicative action of God as a whole, and what is striking about his presentation of it is the organic way in which, Calvin-like, he holds these themes together in the broad and dynamic context which the thought of God making his mind known to sinners provides.

Owen does not, to my knowledge, anywhere make the point that the image of God in which man was created involves the capacity for receiving, and responding to, communications from the Creator. This, however, is constantly presupposed in his insistence, on the one hand, that the image of God in Adam was a state of actual responsive conformity to God's revealed will, and, on the other hand, that God gives us knowledge of his mind by calling our minds into play. God will instruct us in his mind and will, Owen maintains, in and by the rational faculties of our souls.[1] With all the Reformed theologians of his day, and certainly with the Bible, Owen assumes a direct affinity and correspondence between God's mind and man's, such that God can speak to us in words and we, within the limits of his own self-disclosure, can comprehend him in our thoughts. Not, indeed, that we can in any sense take his measure—God measures man, but not vice versa. We cannot plumb the mystery of his being (he is in that sense wholly incomprehensible to us), and there are many 'secret things' (Deut 29:29) in his plan which he has not told us; moreover, we can be quite sure that, whatever stage in our pilgrimage we may have reached, many of the things that he has told us we have not yet understood. Nevertheless, as far as our thoughts about him correspond to what he says about himself, they are true thoughts about him, and constitute real knowledge about him, knowledge which is fundamental to our actual dealing with him. In this sense Owen, like Calvin, appears as a Christian rationalist, who would have condemned out of hand the irrationalism of the neo-orthodox idea of a 'knowledge' of God derived from non-communicative 'encounters' with him. Basic to our knowledge of God, Owen would have said, is our knowledge about him, and this knowledge he himself gives us by his own verbal self-testimony.

However, Owen, like all mainstream Reformed thinkers, sees a problem here. Sin within us, the anti-God drive in mankind's makeup that is our legacy from Adam, has noetic well as behavioral consequences: it promises a universal unresponsiveness to spiritual truth and reality that the New Testament calls *hardness* and *blindness* of heart. More rational instruction thus proves ineffective; only the illumination of the Holy Spirit, opening our heart to God's word and God's word to our hearts, can bring understanding of, conviction about, and consent to, the things that God declares. No Puritan has a sharper sense than Owen of the tragic darkness and perversity of the fallen human mind, and therefore of the absolute necessity that the Spirit should work in preacher and teacher, hearer and student alike, if effective communication of divine things is ever to take place.

It is convenient to analyse Owen's concept of divine communication under five headings: (1) the giving of revelation; (2) the inspiring of Scripture; (3) the authenticating of Scripture; (4) the establishing of faith in Scripture; (5) the interpreting of Scripture. Each of these headings covers what Owen saw as one distinct element in the complex of activities whereby the Holy Spirit introduces the thoughts that are in God's mind into ours.

The source-documents are chiefly three. The first, published in 1658, is entitled *Of the Divine Originall, Authority, Self-evidencing Light and Power of the Scriptures, with an Answer to that Enquiry, How we know the Scriptures to be the Word of God.* The second and third belong to the series of treatises, of which *Pneumatologia: A Discourse Concerning the Holy Spirit* (1674) was the first, in which Owen works his way systematically through all the biblical material concerning the third Person of the Trinity. The two treatises which concern us, the second and third of Owen's series as well as of our sources, are *The Reason of Faith: or an Answer to the Enquiry, Wherefore we believe the Scripture to be the Word of God; with the causes and nature of that Faith wherewith we do so* (1677), and *Causes, Ways, and Means of Understanding the Mind of God as revealed in His Word, with assurance therein: and a Declaration of the Perspicuity of the Scriptures, with the external means of the Interpretation of them* (1678).[1] All these works hit out on occasion at illuminists and rationalistic theologians, but principally they have an anti-Roman polemical slant; Owen is writing to overthrow the Roman contentions, first, that faith in Scripture as God's word should be based on the church's traditional authentication of it, and, second, that the ordinary Christian should not attempt to interpret the Bible for himself, but should leave that to the institutional church to do for him. Owen's aim is to show that it belongs to the revealed and promised office of the Holy Spirit both to bring God's people to faith in Scripture as divine, and also to lead them into an understanding of Scripture as the law of life and the message of salvation. Since, however, his method of making his points in these treatises, as always, is expository, by means of appeals to texts, and since the treatises themselves are constructive and edificatory in their main purpose, and the polemical note is largely muted (as is common with Owen, though very uncommon in his age), it is easy to read them without thinking of their controversial purpose at all. Note, I did not say that it was easy to read them!—that would not be true; yet I do venture to say that the labour involved in plodding through these ill-arranged and tediously-written treatises will be found abundantly worthwhile.

For there is no question as to the importance for our day of the themes with which Owen deals. The doctrine of revelation is in the melting-pot; the historic evangelical belief in verbal communication from God through the Bible is at a discount; can Owen, the greatest British divine of his day, if not of all time, help us to recover and re-establish the truth? Or is he himself vulnerable to criticism? One feature of the contemporary theological scene is the polemic of Karl Barth and some of his followers against the expositors of Reformed orthodoxy in the seventeenth century for having, as they allege, foreshortened their doctrine of divine communication by 'freezing' the Spirit in the Scriptures. Barth's complaint is that, having started well by asserting the divine origin of Scripture, these theologians allowed rationalism to creep into their biblical exposition and theology, for want of effectively thinking through the doctrine of the Spirit as Lord of, and instructor through, the written word. Since Barth's own doctrine of Scripture makes its divine origin wholly problematical, and his theological interpretations of it seem again and again to be read into the text rather than read out of it, one is tempted simply to retort 'physician, heal thyself', and leave the matter there—but the criticism is a serious one, made in good faith, and if it is valid as a stricture on Owen, who, whatever else he is, is certainly a mainstream Reformed divine, it would certainly limit the extent to which we could look to him for help today. But is it valid? It will be interesting, as we proceed, to see. In fact, we shall find that the criticism, as applied to Owen, is wholly invalid, and that the point at which Barth regards Owen's generation as deficient is actually the point of Owen's greatest mastery.

3

We move, then, to the first of our sub-divisions: *the giving of revelations*. Owen normally used the word 'revelation' to denote any immediate informative communication from God, disclosing things which could not otherwise have been known. Such communications, he tells us, were conveyed to their recipients by means of a voice or inward impression, accompanied on occasion by a dream or a vision. Owen lumps all revelations of this kind under the head of *prophecy*, defining a 'prophet' as 'one who used to receive divine revelations'[2] He affirms that the patriarchs, from Adam onward, who received revelations from God, were 'guided by a prophetical spirit', and may properly be called prophets, as indeed Abraham is in Genesis 20:7.

The giving of these disclosures was the work of the Holy Spirit, who is 'the immediate author of all divine revelations',[3] and it is clear from the narratives that they brought with them assurance of their own divine origin. They evidenced themselves to their recipients as being messages from God, and therefore as requiring absolute adherence and obedience, however inexplicable their content might appear to be—as, for instance, when Abraham was told to sacrifice Isaac. (The nature of this self-evidencing quality will be analysed in a later section.) Adam, Abraham, Moses, and all the others to whom the word of God came did not need to ask what was the source of the message; they knew—that is, they found themselves sure and unable to doubt—that it was from God, and acted accordingly. Thus by faith they obtained their good report.

The revelations given to the prophets were in most cases not primarily for themselves, but for others, to whom they were charged to relay them. Owen knew that the prophets were, in the modern phrase, forthtellers as well as foretellers—as he himself says, 'prophets are the interpreters, the declarers of the word, mind, will, or oracles of God unto others'.[4] In the providence of God, such of these revelations as 'are of general use to the Church'[5] were written down, and thus the Old Testament Scriptures began to grow till they reached their present size. A similar process produced the New Testament: the Spirit enabled the apostles 'infallibly to receive, understand, and declare, the whole counsel of God in Christ',[6] and then to write what they knew for the instruction of later ages. In an anti-Roman passage, Owen sharpens the point that a written record, as distinct from mere oral tradition, is always necessary if God's revelations are to be preserved from corruption and loss:

> Before the committing of the Scriptures to writing, God had given the world an experiment, what keepers men were of this revelation by tradition; within some hundreds of years after the flood, all knowledge of Him, through the craft of Satan, and the vanity of the minds of men, which is unspeakable, was so lost, that nothing, but as it were the creation of a new world, or the erection of a new church-state by new revelations, could relieve it. After that great trial what can be farther pretended on the behalf of tradition I know not.[7]

Once the Scriptures were written, and the prophetic and apostolic witness to Christ was complete, no need remained for private revelations of new truths, and Owen did not believe that any were given. He opposed the 'enthusiasm' of those who, like the Quakers, put their trust in supposed revelations given apart from, and going beyond, the word. In a Latin work Owen calls the Quakers *fanatici*, 'fanatics', for their attitude. He is quick to deploy against them the old dilemma that if their 'private revelations' agree with Scripture, they are needless, and if they disagree, they are false.

In all this, Owen is following the beaten track of Reformed exposition, from Calvin onward, and there is nothing novel in any of the points that he makes.

So we proceed to our second topic: *the inspiring of Scripture*. Here again, the line that Owen follows is the standard Reformed teaching of his day. 'Inspiration' he defines as the inbreathing of the Holy Spirit, whereby revelations are given, received, and transmitted, both orally and in writing. The human subjects of inspiration, says Owen, are passive during the process, in the sense of being non-originative: though their minds are active in a psychological sense, they are being acted upon, or simply, as Owen says, 'acted', by the Spirit, 'moved [borne along] by the Holy Ghost' (2 Pet 1:21). We may quote here some statements from Owen's own exposition of this text. The Spirit, says Owen,

> prepared them [the prophets] for to receive the impressions he made upon them, and confirmed their memories to retain them. He did not indeed so enlighten and raise their minds as to give them a distinct understanding and full comprehension of all the things themselves that were declared unto them. There was more in their inspirations than they could search into the bottom of [Owen is thinking of the statement in 1 Pet 1:10, 11 that the prophets themselves did not know the full meaning of their own words about Christ]. But he so raised and prepared their minds, as that they might be capable to receive and retain those impressions of things which he communicated unto them. As a man tunes the strings of an instrument, that it may in a due manner receive the impressions of his finger, and give out the sounds he intends . . . he himself acted their faculties, making use of them to express his words, not their own conception.[8]

With this may be compared Owen's account of the work of the Holy Spirit in inspiring the writers of Scripture:

> There were, therefore, three things concurring in this work. 1. The inspiration of the minds of these prophets, with the knowledge and apprehension of the things communicated unto them. 2. The suggestion of words unto them, to express what their minds conceived. 3. The guidance of their hands, in setting down the words suggested; or of their tongues, in uttering

them unto those by whom they were committed to writing; as Baruch wrote the prophecy of Jeremiah from his mouth (Jer 36:3, 8). If either of these were wanting, the Scripture could not be absolutely and every way divine and infallible.

This completeness of divine initiative and control did not mean, however, that the human personalities or characteristics of the writers were obliterated.

The Holy Ghost in His work on the minds of men doth not put a force upon them, nor acts them any otherwise than they are in their own natures, and with their present endowments and qualifications meet to be used and acted . . . the words therefore which he suggests unto them are such as they are accustomed unto, and he causeth them to make use of such expressions as were familiar unto themselves. . . . We may also grant and do, that they used their own abilities of mind and understanding in the choice of words and expressions. So the preacher sought to find out acceptable words (Eccles 12:10). But the Holy Spirit who is more intimate unto the minds and skills of men than they are themselves, did so guide, act, and operate in them, as that the words they fixed upon were as directly and certainly from him, as if they had been spoken to them by an audible voice.[9]

The works of the biblical writers, therefore, have God for their ultimate author.

The laws they made known, the doctrines they delivered, the instructions they gave, the stories they recorded, the promises of Christ, the promises of gospel times they gave out and revealed, were not their own, not conceived in their minds, not formed by their reasonings, not retained in their memories from what they heard, not by any means beforehand comprehended by them (1 Pet 1:10, 11), but were all of them immediately from God; there being only a passive concurrence of their rational faculties in their reception.[10]

The inspiration of Scripture is thus both substantial and verbal: not only the matter, but also the words, are directly from God. 'As to the doctrine contained in it [Scripture], and the words wherein that doctrine is delivered, it is wholly his [God's]; what that speaks, he speaks himself. He speaks in it and by it.'[11] It is in this sense, and on this account, that we should receive the Bible as the word of God, 'the supernatural, immediate revelation of his mind unto us'.[12]

As the word of God, Holy Scripture is a direct and primary object of faith, just as the revelations which came to the patriarchs, and the inspired sermons of the prophets and apostles, were direct and primary objects of faith for their original recipients. All faith, says Owen, has the nature of assent on testimony, and Christian faith, which blossoms in consent to God's covenant, trust in his promises, and affiance in his Son, has as its root assent to evangelical truth on the testimony of God. It is thus not 'human', but 'divine'. 'Human' faith in anything is assent on human testimony; 'divine' faith is assent on divine testimony. Human faith in the articles of the Christian creed, and even in the evangelical presentation of Christ—assent, that is, based only on some form of human attestation, that of the church, for instance, or of particular scholars or saints, or on a rational probability-judgement—is not enough. Not only is such 'faith' necessarily unstable, it is not what God wants. The faith which he requires is divine faith springing from a recognition that the basis on which the Christian confession rests—that is, the testimony of Scripture—is God's own infallible testimony to himself. The ground of divine faith in the divine truth of what the Scriptures teach is thus the fact of their 'divine originall', which is the source of their authority (that is, as Owen defines it, their 'power to command and require obedience, in the name of God'[13]). The Scriptures carry God's authority because, quite simply, he wrote them: they are his utterance, his own written word.

When Owen refers to the 'divine originall' of the Scriptures, he means, not only that God *spoke* their contents long ago, when he caused them to be written, but also that he *speaks* the same content now: the Scriptures remain his contemporary utterance to every generation. So faith that is 'divine, supernatural, infallible', to quote a recurring trio of adjectives—true Christian faith, that is, as distinct from attitudes of conventional acquiescence that are less than divine faith—rests on the recognition that what Scripture says, God says, here and now, in direct application to all to whom the Scriptures come. Rational arguments based on facts relating to the Bible—its antiquity, its preservation, its inner unity of message and design, its historic attestation in the church, and its transforming effects wherever it goes—may serve to remove doubts that bother believers, and to bring unbelievers, however reluctantly, to 'a firm opinion, judgment, and persuasion'—a conviction, that is, that it is probable, indeed certain—'that the Scriptures are from God';[14] yet this is at best only human faith, and is not therefore adequate. God requires divine faith in the truth and authority of his written word, and this comes only by recognising that it comes to us as the prophetic oracles came, under the rubric 'thus saith the Lord'.

Owen makes it sound as if ever since the apostolic age saving faith in Christ has in all cases depended necessarily on prior faith in the divinity of Scripture. Did Owen really mean this, we ask. Was it his view that nobody could believe savingly till he knew and accepted the Bible? And what would Owen make of the fact that some today give evidence of 'divine, supernatural, infallible' faith in Christ while professing not fully to share his own faith in the 'divine originall' of Scripture?

To the two former questions, the answer seems to be that Owen's controversial preoccupation explains his form of statement. Against the mistaken Roman thesis that the proper ground of faith in Christ is the church's witness—in other words, human testimony—Owen is insisting that the proper ground of faith is biblical witness—in other words, divine testimony. He is speaking against the background of his own day, in which Bibles were available for all, the plenary inspiration and truthfulness of Scripture were not yet challenged, and the only question at issue was whether faith should rest directly on biblical testimony or not. If asked whether a man could come to true saving faith on the basis of an accurate account of the biblical message which made no reference to the Bible itself (such as missionaries abroad, or apologists at home, might sometimes present), Owen would doubtless have replied that in the beneficent sovereignty of God such a thing might well happen, but that it was not this kind of situation that he was discussing in the writings under review.

On the third question, Owen could in terms of his principles make three sound points, each tending to show that when a person who gives evidence in other ways of saving faith in Christ claims not to accept the 'divine originall' of Scripture, the claim should not be taken as seriously as it is made. (Owen's instincts would probably have led him to start by making the opposite point, that doubt of the divinity of Scripture is so anomalous in a believer as to suggest that such doubters are probably hypocrites!—but his own principles would also lead to the thesis as we are stating.)

First, Owen could observe that the only Christ there is is the Christ of the Bible, and that faith in this Christ necessarily presupposes faith in at least the main substance of what Scripture says about him—which is not very different from saying that real faith in the real Christ rests on faith in the divine truth of a good deal of the Bible.

Second, he could point out that in the New Testament itself faith in Christ is represented as consequent and dependent on receiving the apostolic message as God's own word of truth (see Rom 10:14-17; Col 1:4-7; 1 Thess 1:5-10; 2:13), and that the New Testament is no more, just as it is no less, than the substance of this apostolic message in writing.

Third, he could make the point that the ministry of the Spirit enlightening sinners to receive the man Jesus as the divine Saviour, and the human Scriptures as the divine word, is one ministry, and that everyone in whose heart the Spirit bears witness to the divine saviourhood of Jesus does in fact receive a similar testimony to the 'divine originall' of such of the canonical Scriptures as he knows; though confusion and weakness of mind, springing from the remnants of corruption within him and fomented by anti-Christian thought-currents around him in an age of unbelief, may prevent him from giving adequate intellectual expression to this. Owen would certainly have dwelt on the debilitating effect of this intellectual besetting sin, just as he does elsewhere in connection with errors regarding other doctrines, but there is no reason to ascribe to him the view that a man who was muddle-headed about biblical infallibility could not be a Christian at all.

4

But how does faith in 'God's word written' come about? This brings us to out next two themes, the first of which, and the third in our overall order, is *the authentication of Scripture*.

The Holy Spirit, the Author of Scripture, says Owen, causes his work to be received with divine faith, as God's word, by means of a twofold operation: His *external* witness and His *internal* witness. The latter is 'the internal work of the Holy Spirit on the minds of men, enabling them to believe'; the former is 'the external work of the same Holy Spirit giving evidence in and by the Scripture unto its own divine originall'.[15] The former presupposes, and is correlative to, the latter, and both belong to the statement of the classic Reformed doctrine, first given prominence by Calvin in the *Institutes*, of the witness of the Spirit as the ground of faith in the Scriptures. In stating this against the Church of Rome, which laid emphasis on the external testimony of the church. Calvin had stressed the internal witness of the Spirit and had given no separate attention to the point that there is also an external testimony of the Spirit to which his inward witness in the believer's heart corresponds. What is distinctive about Owen's presentation of this doctrine, as compared with Calvin's, is the stress that he lays on the Spirit's external witness. His doctrine is thus of a double testimony of the Holy Spirit to Scripture; its effect is to draw out and make explicit what is implicit in Calvin's statements on the subject, at points where these statements are not fully developed.[16] It is the external witness of the Spirit that we deal with now.

'Herein consists that testimony which the Spirit gives unto the Word of God that it is so,' writes Owen. 'The Holy Ghost being the immediate author of the whole Scripture, doth therein and thereby give testimony unto the divine truth and original of it, by the characters of divine authority and veracity impressed on it, and evidencing themselves in its power and efficacy'.[17] By this means 'the Scriptures of the Old and New Testament, do abundantly and uncontrollably manifest themselves to be the word of the living God'.[18]

How does the Spirit bring about this effect? By a threefold activity. First, he imparts to the Scriptures the permanent quality of *light*. Owen appeals to biblical references to Scripture as 'light in a dark place' (2 Pet 1:19), a 'light' to men's feet and a lamp to their path (Ps 119:105), a word whose entrance gives 'light' (130), and other similar passages. By light, Owen means that which dispels darkness and illuminates people and situations.

Light, by its very nature, is self-evidencing. 'Let a light be ever so mean and contemptible; yet if it shines, it casts out beams and rays in a dark place, it will evidence itself.'[19] Scripture, through the covenanted action of the Holy Spirit, constantly 'shines', in the sense of giving spiritual illumination and insight as to who and what one is in the sight of God, and who and what Jesus Christ is, both in himself and in relation to one's own self and finally, in the broadest and most inclusive sense, how one ought to live. Thus it makes evident its divine origin.

Second, the Spirit makes the Scriptures *powerful* to produce spiritual effects. They evidence their divine origin by their disruptive and recreative impact on human lives. Owen quotes in this connection the biblical descriptions of the word of God as 'quick and powerful', 'able to build you up', and 'the power of God' (Heb 4:12; Acts 20:31; 1 Cor 1:18).

Third, the Holy Spirit makes Scripture impinge on the individual consciousness as a word *addressed personally* to each man by God himself, evoking awe, and a sense of being in God's presence and under his eye. This is what Owen means when he speaks of the 'majesty' of the Scriptures. So he writes: 'the Holy Ghost speaking in and by the word imparting to it virtue, power, efficacy, majesty, and authority, affords us the witness, that our faith is resolved into'.[20]

Thus, through the action of the Holy Spirit, Scripture evidences and authenticates itself as the word of God. 'Must we not rest at last in that *to theion* [divine quality], which accompanies the true voice of God, evidencing itself and ascertaining the soul beyond all possibility of mistake?'[21]

What Owen is saying here is more straightforward, perhaps, than his language at first reveals. His point is simply that the unique enlightening and convicting power with which the canonical Scriptures come at us is itself 'the public testimony of the Holy Spirit given to all, of the Word, by and in the Word'.[22] Part of the distinctiveness of the canonical books lies in the fact that this testimony constantly accompanies them: 'I fear not to affirm that there are on every individual book of the Scriptures . . . those divine characters and criteria which are sufficient to difference them from all other writings whatever, and to testify their divine authority unto the minds and consciences of believers.'[23] It is in terms of this testimony, this constant outflow of light and power, that the self-evidencing quality of the Bible and its message should, according to Owen, be described and explained. That the Bible, like all messages and revelations from God, has this quality is proved by the fact that it is always the duty of those to whom any part of the written word comes to receive and obey it, and failure to do this is always guilty. (For proof of this, Owen cites, among other passages, Deuteronomy 31:11-13; Luke 16:31; 2 Peter 1:16-21.)

This leads us to our fourth topic: *the establishing of faith in Scripture*. The internal testimony of the Holy Spirit, whereby the external testimony comes to be recognised and received, is not, says Owen, an inward voice, revealing facts otherwise unknown and unknowable (that is, a private revelation), nor is it an unreasoning conviction, objectively groundless, coming to us out of the blue; it is, rather, an activity of inward illumination, whereby a man's natural spiritual blindness is removed, the veil is taken from the eyes of his heart, his pride and his prejudice are alike broken down, and he is given both an understanding and a 'taste' (Heb 5:14) of spiritual realities. This, Owen observes, is what the New Testament is referring to when it uses the verb 'reveal' in texts like Matthew 11:25-27 and Ephesians 1:17-19, and it is also what the apostle John has in mind when he speaks of the Spirit as an 'unction' that 'teaches all things' (1 John 2:27).

The mark of this understanding is that Scripture now appears coherent: to the man enlightened by the Spirit, Scripture is no longer a bewildering jumble of isolated items, as it may well have seemed to him before, but 'under the benefit of this assistance all the parts of the Scripture, in their harmony and correspondency, all the truths of it in their power and necessity, come in together to give evidence one to another, and all of them to the whole.'[24] Part chimes in with part, Scripture meshes with Scripture, and the unified bearing of the whole Bible becomes apparent. The accompanying experience of the 'taste', or 'flavour' of spiritual realities is immediate and ineffable; Owen describes it as follows:

> He [the Spirit] gives unto believers a spiritual sense of the power and reality of the things believed, whereby their faith is greatly established. . . . And on the account of this spiritual experience, is our perception of spiritual things so often expressed by acts of sense, as tasting, seeing, feeling, and the like means of assurance in things natural. And when believers have attained hereunto, they do find the divine wisdom, goodness, and authority of God so present unto them, as that they need neither argument, nor motive, or anything else, to persuade them unto, or confirm them in, believing. And whereas this spiritual experience, which believers obtain through the Holy Ghost, is such as cannot rationally be contended about, seeing those who have received it, cannot fully express it, and those who have not, cannot understand it, nor the efficacy which it has to secure and establish the mind; it is left to be determined on by them alone, who have their 'senses exercised to discern good and evil'. And this belongs unto the internal subjective testimony of the Holy Ghost.[25]

Also, the Spirit upholds those whom he enlightens against temptations to question the divinity of Scripture, from whatever source they spring—lust, unbelief, pressure of opposing argument, waning of the sense of God and his authority, or any other spiritual malaise. All this belongs to the inner witness of the Spirit, as Owen describes it. His is in truth the richest exposition of the subject that I know.

The grounds, then, on which we have faith in Scripture as the word of

God are the Spirit's external witness to its divine origin, which is given in and with it constantly; and the reason why we so believe, is 'because the Holy Ghost hath enlightened our minds, wrought faith in us, and enabled us to believe it'.[26] And the way to bring others to like faith is simply to let the Bible and its message get at them, so that the Spirit may fulfil the same ministry towards them too. As Owen points out, the apostles' way of convincing men that their message was divine was not by 'rational arguments', but 'by preaching the word itself unto them in the evidence and demonstration of the Spirit, by the power whereof manifesting the authority of God in it, they were convinced; and falling down acknowledged God to be in it of a truth' (1 Cor 2:4, 5; 15:25, 26).[27]

5

So we come to our final topic: *the interpreting of the Scriptures.*

Owen's first point under this head is the standard Protestant point that Scripture is perspicuous, in the sense that every Christian who uses the means of grace as he should, can learn from it all that he needs to know for life and godliness. This formula is not, however, a warrant for anyone to go off on his own with a Bible and expect to learn everything by reading it in isolation; Owen makes this plain by listing as the prime means of grace, which personal Bible study presupposes, those afforded by the corporate life of the Christian community, namely the public preaching of the word and informal discussion with Christian people. On the former Owen lays great emphasis, as being the principal means appointed in the church for the instruction of God's people. Of the latter, he writes:

> The mutual instruction of one another in the mind of God out of the Scripture, is also required . . . thus, when our Saviour found His disciples talking of the things of God by the way-side, He bearing unto them the person of a private man, instructed them in the sense of Scripture (Luke 24:26, 27, 32). And the neglect of this duty in the world, which is so great that the very mention of it, or the least attempt to perform it, is a matter of scorn and reproach, is one cause of the great ignorance and darkness that yet abounds among us.[28]

This may be a word in season in our own day. Only in the context of the church's corporate learning from the Scriptures, both formally and informally, does Owen expect the individual to reach a right understanding of biblical teaching.

But even then it is not easy. Inbred spiritual evils—pride, corrupt affection, sloth, a darkened mind, temperamental traditionalism, and sinful rationalisations—hinder our progress, and these evils can only be countered and overcome by spiritual means. So, in a most searching chapter,[29] Owen, having spoken of the need for careful and meditative reading of the biblical text, in large units as well as in small, goes on to list as necessary 'spiritual' means of understanding it, over and above getting acquainted with its linguistic and cultural background and consulting commentaries and the history of exposition, these following: constant prayer for light; a desire to experience the power of whatever truth may be learned; a conscientious practice of obedience to all truth known at present; and a life of worship in the church. Though written in the usual dull style (dull even for him!) which Owen affected when writing about the Scriptures, this chapter is veritable dynamite, and deserves reading and re-reading by all who desire to prove the perspicuity of Scripture for themselves.

Of the contents and layout of the Bible, as Owen saw them, little can be said here. Owen viewed the Bible as a landscape, part of whose charm and impact on the viewer lies in its lack of order in surface arrangement. 'The Holy Spirit hath not in the Scripture reduced and disposed its doctrines or supernatural truths into any system, order, or method', although 'there is indeed in some of the epistles of Paul, especially that unto the Romans, a methodical disposition of the most important doctrines of the gospel.'[30] Generally, Owen saw Scripture as consisting of doctrines (facts about God) and examples of their application—the doctrinal principles interpreting the narratives, and the narratives illustrating the doctrinal principles. Owen insists that the existing arrangement of the biblical books is in fact more practical and useful than any other would be; it summons us to the right kind of meditative study, and shields us against the temptation to intellectual pride in doctrinal knowledge. Moreover, truth as it stands in Scripture is already in a 'posture' to exert 'power and efficacy,' and the demand of adjustment to its style and layout puts students into the right 'posture' to receive and profit from it practically. As we prayerfully wait on God, so the holy message is made known and applied to us in all its converting and transforming power.

Owen makes this point very strikingly in answer to the complaint that the Bible is obscure because 'it is not distributed into *common-places*,' (i.e., distinct topics, each exhaustively expounded in one place), but requires us to gather its truths 'out of a *collection of histories, prophecies, prayers, songs, letters. . . .* ' He writes as follows:

> Such a *systematical proposal of doctrines*, truths, or articles of faith, as some require, would not have answered the great ends of the Scripture itself. All that can be supposed of benefit thereby is only that it would lead us more easily into a *methodical comprehension* of the truths so proposed; but this we may attain, and not be rendered one jot more *like unto God* thereby. The principal end of the Scriptures is of another nature. It is, to beget in the minds of men faith, fear, obedience, and reverence of God—to make

them holy and righteous. . . . Unto this end every truth is disposed of in the Scripture as it ought to be. If any expect that the Scripture should be written with respect unto *opinions, notions,* and *speculations,* to render men *skillful* and cunning in them, able to talk and dispute . . . they are mistaken. It is given to make us *humble, holy, wise* in spiritual things; to direct us in our *duties,* to relieve us in our *temptations,* to comfort us under *troubles,* to make us to love God and to live unto him. . . . Unto this end there is a more glorious power and efficacy in one *epistle,* one *psalm,* one *chapter,* than in all the writings of men. . . . He that hath not experience hereof is a stranger unto the power of God in the Scripture . . . sometimes an *occasional passage in a story,* a word or expressions, shall contribute more to excite faith and love in our souls than a volume of learned disputations. . . .[31]

Thus God communicates with us, to our soul's health.

If we now ask what exactly it is that he communicates, the short answer is, knowledge of ourselves, and of Christ, as set forth in the *Westminster Confession* and in Bunyan's *Pilgrim's Progress*; but we cannot amplify this answer here.[32]

6

Question 4 of the *Westminster Larger Catechism* reads: 'How does it appear that the Scriptures are the word of God?' The answer is:

The Scriptures manifest themselves to be the word of God, by their majesty and purity; by the consent of all the parts, and the scope of the whole, which is to give all glory to God; by their light and power to convince and convert sinners, to comfort and build up believers unto salvation. But the Spirit of God, bearing witness by and with the Scriptures in the heart of man, is alone able fully to persuade it that they are the very word of God.

Owen's doctrine of divine communication, as we have seen, merely spells out this position. That his doctrine is scriptural, suggestive, and spiritual to a high degree will hardly be disputed. That the Barthian criticism does not apply to him (nor, for that matter, to the Westminster divines) is also clear; one could hardly have a more complete or dynamic doctrine of the Spirit bringing home the word to God's people than that which Owen sets forth.

What lessons has this study for us? It reminds us that Scripture is always the best evidence for itself, and that preaching biblical truth in the power of the Holy Ghost will do more than any amount of arguing to bring about faith in biblical inspiration, and in the divine realities which Scripture proclaims. It also challenges us to ask ourselves whether in our own searching and teaching of the Scriptures we are honouring the Holy Ghost as we should. When problems of interpretation arise, how much and how hard do we pray? And are we who preach wholly men of the word? Is it our glory, as Christian instructors, to refuse to do anything save expound and apply the word of God? May our study of Owen's doctrine of communication from God renew our zeal to fulfil such a ministry, and our confidence in the fruitfulness that, under God, such a ministry will have.

CHAPTER SIX

The Puritans as Interpreters of Scripture

We introduce this chapter by repeating John Howe's account of an episode described to him by Dr Thomas Goodwin. During his student days, said Howe, Goodwin,

> having heard much of Mr. Rogers of Dedham [an early Puritan Boanerges] took a journey . . . to hear him preach on his lecture day. . . . Mr. Rogers was . . . on the subject of . . . the Scriptures. And in that sermon he falls into an expostulation with the people about their neglect of the Bible; . . . he personates God to the people, telling them, 'Well, I have trusted you so long with my Bible; you have slighted it, it lies in such and such houses all covered with dust and cobwebs; you care not to listen to it. Do you use my Bible so? Well, you shall have my Bible no longer.' And he takes up the Bible from his cushion, and seemed as if he were going away with it and carrying it from them; but immediately turns again and personates the people to God, falls down on his knees, cries and pleads most earnestly, 'Lord, whatever thou dost to us, take not thy Bible from us; kill our children, burn our houses, destroy our goods; only spare us thy Bible, only take not away thy Bible.' And then he personates God again to the people: 'Say you so? Well, I will try you a while longer; and here is my Bible for you. I will see how you will use it, whether you will love it more . . . observe it more . . . practice it more, and live more according to it.' By these actions (as the doctor told me) he put all the congregation into so strange a posture that . . . the place was a mere Bochim, the people generally . . . deluged with their own tears;

and he told me that he himself, when he got out . . . was fain to hang a quarter of an hour upon the neck of his horse weeping before he had power to mount; so strange an impression was there upon him, and generally upon the people, upon having been expostulated with for the neglect of the Bible.[1]

This anecdote takes us to the very heart of Puritanism. The congregation's reaction shows that Rogers was touching their conscience at its most sensitive point. For Puritanism was, above all else, a Bible movement. To the Puritan the Bible was in truth the most precious possession that this world affords. His deepest conviction was that reverence for God means reverence for Scripture, and serving God means obeying Scripture. To his mind, therefore, no greater insult could be offered to the Creator than to neglect his written word; and, conversely, there could be no truer act of homage to him than to prize it and pore over it, and then to live out and give out its teaching. Intense veneration for Scripture, as the living word of the living God, and a devoted concern to know and do all that it prescribes, was Puritanism's hallmark.

Our present task is to study the principles and methods, and to assess the quality, of Puritan biblical interpretation. Source-material, consisting of both hermeneutical directories and sermons, treatises and commentaries, is abundant. We may draw on these sources indiscriminately, for on all the matters we shall discuss we find the Puritans to be virtually unanimous.

Three general statements about the way the Puritans tackled the interpretative task can be made at once.

First, Puritan exegetes are pre-modern, in the sense that they do not bring to the Bible the pervasive sense of difference and distance between cultures and epochs that is so much part of today's mind-set; nor do they bring with them the imaginative ideas of religious evolution that cripple so many modern biblical scholars and corrupt so much of their expository work. Instead of feeling distant from biblical characters and their experiences because of the number of centuries between them, the Puritans felt kinship with them because they belonged to the same human race, faced, feared, and fellowshipped with the same unchanging God, and struggled with essentially the same spiritual problems. (Was that wisdom? Yes!)

Second, Puritan grammatical-historical exegesis of texts, though often naively expressed, is remarkably competent, as any knowledgeable reader of, for instance, Matthew Henry's great expository commentary on the whole Bible will soon see.

Third, Puritans exegeted Scripture in order to apply it, and as application was the focus of their concern so it was the area of their special strength, as will appear.

Two presuppositions governed their approach to interpretation; six rules sum up their method.

The first presupposition concerns *the nature of Scripture*. To the Puritans, Scripture, as a whole and in all its parts, was the utterance of God: God's word set down in writing, his mind opened and his thoughts declared for man's instruction. The content of Scripture is God's eternal truth, for the historical process which the Bible records and interprets is just the temporal outworking of God's eternal plan, formed before the world was. In this sense, 'what our Scriptures have set down and written, is all but extracts and copies taken out of the Scriptures in God's heart, in which they were written from everlasting.'[2] That which was delivered by such a multiplicity of human authors, of such different background and characters, in such a variety of styles and literary forms, should therefore be received and studied as the unified expression of a single divine mind, a complete and coherent, though complex, revelation of the will and purpose of God. To the Puritan Bible student, it was God who had uttered the prophecies, recorded the histories, expounded the doctrine, declared the praises, written the visions, of which Scripture was made up; and he knew that Scripture must be read, not merely as words which God spoke long ago, in the actual inspiring of the biblical books, but as words which God continues to speak to every reader in every age. 'Think in every line you read that God is speaking to you,' says Thomas Watson[3]—for in truth he is. What Scripture says, God is saying.

Just as God's mind is unfathomable, so there are illimitable depths in Scripture: 'the stores of truth laid up in it are inexhaustible.'[4] It is always the case that, in the famous words ascribed to John Robinson, 'the Lord hath more truth yet to break forth out of his holy word.' As interpreters, we never reach the end of God's thoughts, and must not permit ourselves to imagine otherwise. 'Never think you have knowledge enough; study the word more fully. . . .'[5] God safeguards our humility by keeping us 'in continual dependence on him for teaching and revelations of himself out of the word, never in this world bringing any soul to the utmost of what is from the word to be made out and discovered.'[6] The Puritans often echo Augustine's remark that, just as there are shallows in Scripture where a lamb may wade, so there are depths in Scripture where an elephant may swim—depths which the most learned and godly have yet to plumb. All Christians, therefore, should approach their study of Scripture knowing that they know but little, longing to learn more and looking to God himself to open to them his own word.

This brings us to the second presupposition, which concerns *the subject-matter of Scripture*. 'What do the Scriptures principally teach?' is the third question of the *Shorter Catechism*, and the answer is: '. . . what man is to believe concerning God, and what duty God requires of man.' Consider the implications of this answer. First, Scripture teaches us what to believe about God—that is, it sets before us spiritual truths concerning spiritual realities, truths beyond the grasp of fallen reason which only the Holy Spirit can enable us to discern. Therefore we must distrust ourselves, confess our natural inability and blindness in this realm, and invoke the aid of the Spirit to interpret Scripture to us. 'It was the Spirit that wrote that word,' says Goodwin.

> ... therefore ... no man's or men's private understandings, without the aid of that public secretary of heaven, can understand them ... he only hid the treasures of knowledge in that field, and he only knows where they lie; what an advantage is it then by prayer to unlock God's breast, obtain the key of knowledge that unlocks God's study, and can direct to all his notes and his papers![7]

Less quaintly, but more categorically, Owen makes the same point:

> I suppose ... this may be fixed on as a common principle of Christianity; namely, that constant and fervent prayer for the divine assistance of the Holy Spirit, is such an indispensable means for the attaining the knowledge of the mind of God in the Scripture, as that without it all others will not be available [will not avail].[8]

'Before and after you read the Scripture,' says Baxter, 'pray earnestly that the Spirit which did indite it, may expound it to you, and lead you into the truth.'[9]

Also, Scripture teaches us our duty. Its instruction is for practice. It must be studied, therefore, for the purpose of setting our lives in order. And God will only prosper our study if we continually exercise ourselves to live by what we learn. Then our knowledge will deepen and expand; but otherwise it will run out into sterile verbiage and mental error. Owen says:

> The true notion of holy evangelical truths will not live, at least not flourish, where they are divided from a holy conversation. As we learn all to practise, so we learn much by practice. .... And herein alone can we come unto the assurance, that what we know and learn is indeed the truth. So our Saviour tells us, that 'if any man do the will of God, he shall know of the doctrine whether it be of God' (John 7:17). .... And hereby will they be led continually into farther degrees of knowledge. For the mind of man is capable of receiving continual supplies in the increase of light and knowledge whilst it is in this world, if so be they are improved unto their proper end in obedience unto God. But without this the mind will be quickly stuffed with notions, so that no streams can descend into it from the fountain of truth.[10]

He who would interpret Scripture aright, therefore, must be a man of a reverent, humble, prayerful, teachable and obedient spirit; otherwise, however tightly his mind may be 'stuffed with notions', he will never reach any understanding of spiritual realities.

We turn now to the Puritans' approach to the task of interpretation itself. Their governing principles may be summarised under the following heads:

1. Interpret Scripture *literally and grammatically*. The Reformers had insisted, against the medieval depreciation of the 'literal' sense of Scripture in favour of the various 'spiritual' (allegorical) senses, that the literal—i.e., the grammatical, natural, intended—sense was the only sense that Scripture has, and that it was this sense that must be sought in exposition through careful attention to the context and grammar of each statement. The Puritans fully agreed.

> If you would understand the true sense . . . of a controverted Scripture, then look well into the coherence, the scope and the context thereof.[11]

> There is no other sense in it [Scripture] than what is contained in the words whereof materially it doth consist. . . . In the interpretation of the mind of anyone, it is necessary that the *words* he speaks or writes be rightly understood; and this we cannot do immediately unless we understand the *language* wherein he speaks, as also the idiotism [idiom] of that language, with the common use of and intention of its *phraseology* and expressions. . . . And what perplexities, mistakes and errors, the ignorance of these *original languages* hath cast many expositors into . . . especially among those who pertinaciously adhere unto *one translation* . . . might be manifested by instances . . . without number.[12]

Of course, there might be places in Scripture where the literal sense was itself allegorical. The Puritans all regarded the Song of Solomon as a case in point, and James Durham has some interesting remarks on the subject:

> I grant it hath a literal meaning; but I say, that literal meaning is not . . . that which first looketh out, as in historical Scriptures . . . but that which is spiritually . . . meant by these allegorical and figurative speeches, is the literal meaning of this Song . . . for a literal sense (as it is defined by Rivet out of the school-men) is that which floweth from such a place of Scripture, as intended by the Spirit in the words, whether properly or figuratively used, and is to be gathered from the whole complex of expressions together . . . as in the exposition of parables, allegories and figurative Scriptures is clear.

But, Durham notes, this is quite different from the illegitimate allegorising of which the medievals were guilty; for 'there is a great difference between an allegorical exposition of Scripture and an exposition of allegorical Scripture'.[13] Durham expounds allegorically only when he has reason to think that it is an allegory that he is expounding.

2. Interpret Scripture *consistently and harmonistically*. If Scripture is God's word, the expression of a single divine mind, all that it says must be true, and there can be no real contradiction between part and part. To harp on apparent contradictions, therefore, says Bridge, shows real irreverence. Bridge continues:

> You know how it was with Moses, when he saw two men fighting, one an Egyptian, and another an Israelite, he killed the Egyptian; but when he saw two Hebrews fighting, now, saith he, I will go and reconcile them, for they are brethren; why so, but because he was a good man, and gracious? So also it is with a gracious heart; when he sees the Scripture fighting with an Egyptian, and heathen author, or apocryphal, he comes and kills the heathen ... the Egyptian, or the apocrypha; but when he sees two Scriptures at variance (in view, though in truth not), Oh, saith he, these are brethren, and they may be reconciled, I will labour all I can to reconcile them; but when a man shall take every advantage of seeming difference in Scripture, to say, Do ye see what contradictions there are in this book, and not labour to reconcile them; what doth this argue, but that the corruption of a man's nature, is boiled up to an unknown malice against the word of the Lord; take heed therefore of that.[14]

It is a striking thought, and an acute diagnosis.

Since Scripture is the unified expression of a single divine mind, it follows that 'the infallible rule of interpretation of Scripture is the Scripture itself, and therefore, when there is a question about the true and full sense of any Scripture ... it must be searched and known by other places that speak more clearly.'[15] Two principles derive from this. (1) What is obscure must be interpreted by the light of what is plain. 'The rule in this case,' says Owen, 'is that we affix no sense unto any obscure or difficult passage of Scripture but what is ... consonant unto other expressions and plain testimonies. For men to raise peculiar senses from such places, not confirmed elsewhere, is a dangerous curiosity.'[16] (2) Peripheral ambiguities must be interpreted in harmony with fundamental certainties. No exposition of any text, therefore, is right which does not 'agree with the principles of Religion, the points of Catechism set down in the Creed, the Lord's Prayer, the Ten Commandments, and the doctrine of Sacraments.'[17] These two principles together comprised the rule of interpretation commonly termed 'the analogy of faith,' a phrase borrowed—probably not in the apostle's sense—from Romans 12:6.

Both the foregoing rules concern the form of Scripture; the next four have to do with its matter and content.

3. Interpret Scripture *doctrinally and theocentrically*. Scripture is a doctrinal book: it teaches us about God and created things in their relation to him. Bridge brings this out in a passage where he develops James' image of Scripture as a looking-glass:

> When ye look upon a looking-glass, ye see three things, the glass, yourself, and all the other things, persons, stools or pictures that are in the room. So in looking upon Scripture . . . ye see the truths that are therein contained concerning God and Christ. There is God seen especially, and Christ seen; there also you see yourself, and your own dirty face; there also you see the creatures that are in the room with you, and their emptiness. . . .[18]

Also, Scripture teaches a theocentric standpoint: whereas fallen man sees himself as the centre of the universe, the Bible shows us God as central, and depicts all creatures, man included, in their proper perspective—as existing through God, and for God. One of the points at which the Puritans can help us most is in the recovery of this God-centred standpoint of Scripture, which they themselves grasped so firmly.

4. Interpret Scripture *christologically and evangelically*. Christ is the true subject-matter of Scripture: all was written to bear witness to him. He is 'the sum of the whole Bible, prophesied, typified, prefigured, exhibited, demonstrated, to be found in every leaf, almost in every line, the Scriptures being but as it were the swaddling bands of the child Jesus.'[19] Therefore:

> Keep still Jesus Christ in your eye, in the perusal of the Scriptures, as the end, scope and substance thereof: what are the whole Scriptures, but as it were the spiritual swaddling clothes of the holy child Jesus? 1. Christ is the truth and substance of all the types and shadows. 2. Christ is the substance and matter of the Covenant of Grace, and all administrations thereof; under the Old Testament Christ is veiled, under the New Covenant revealed. 3. Christ is the centre and meeting place of all the promises; for in him the promises of God are yea and Amen. 4. Christ is the thing signified, sealed and exhibited in the Sacraments of the Old and New Testament. 5. Scripture genealogies use to lead us on to the true line of Christ. 6. Scripture chronologies are to discover to us the times and seasons of Christ. 7. Scripture-laws are our schoolmasters to bring us to Christ, the moral by correcting, the ceremonial by directing. 8. Scripture-gospel is Christ's light, whereby we hear and follow him; Christ's cords of love, whereby we are drawn into sweet union and communion with him; yea it is the very power of God unto salvation unto all them that believe in Christ Jesus; and therefore think of Christ as the very substance, marrow, soul and scope of the whole Scriptures.[20]

How richly the Puritans applied this evangelical principle of exegesis can only be appreciated by those who dig into the expository writings of such authors as Owen, Goodwin and Sibbes.

5. Interpret Scripture *experimentally and practically*. The Bible is, from one standpoint, a book of spiritual experience, and the Puritans explored this dimension of it with unrivalled depth and insight. *Pilgrim's Progress*

serves as a kind of pictorial index to the themes which they handled under this head—faith, doubt, temptation, despair, fear, hope, the fight with sin, the attacks of Satan, the peaks of spiritual joy, the dry waste of spiritual desertion. Equally the Bible is a practical book, addressing man in a concrete situation—as he stands before God, guilty, vile, helpless—and telling him in that situation what he must believe and do for his soul's health; and the Puritans recognised that this practical orientation must be retained in exposition. Doctrines must be taught from the standpoint from which, and applied for the purpose for which, Scripture itself presents them. Owen, as we observed earlier, makes this point as he embarks on his analysis of the doctrine of justification:

> It is the practical direction of the consciences of men, in their application unto God by Jesus Christ, for deliverance from the curse due unto the apostate state, and peace with him . . . that is alone to be designed in the handling of this doctrine. . . . And whereas we cannot either safely or usefully treat of this doctrine, but with respect unto the same ends for which it is declared, and whereunto it is applied, in the Scripture, we should not . . . be turned aside from attending unto this case and its resolution, in all our discourses on this subject; For it is the direction, satisfaction, and peace of the consciences of men, and not the curiosity of notions or subtlety of disputations, which it is our duty to design.[21]

Neglect of this rule by many in the Puritan age led to much irresponsible, doctrinaire handling of Holy Scripture, but the great Puritan pastors consistently observe it, and their writings are in consequence 'practical and experimental' (their own regular phrase) in the best and most edifying sense.

6. Interpret Scripture *with a faithful and realistic application*. The application comes out of Scripture; the indicating of the 'uses' of doctrine is therefore part of the work of expounding Scripture. Interpretation means making Scripture meaningful and relevant to those whom one addresses, and the work is not finished till the relevance of doctrine for their 'reproof, correction, instruction in righteousness' (2 Tim 3:16) has been shown. The standard 'uses' (types of application) were the use of information, whereby the point of doctrine under review was applied, and its implications drawn out, to mould men's judgements and outlook according to the mind of God; the use of exhortation, summoning them to action; the use of comfort, whereby the doctrine was shown to be the answer to doubts and uncertainties; and the use of trial, of self-examination, a call to measure and assess one's own spiritual condition in the light of the doctrine set forth (the marks of a regenerate man, perhaps, or the nature of some Christian privilege or duty). The application must be realistic: the expositor must watch that the Bible is made to address men where they are. Yesterday's

application may not speak to their condition today. 'It is but a cheap zeal that declaimeth against antiquated errors, and things now out of use and practice. We are to consider what the present age needeth.'[22] For an expositor to make a truly relevant, searching, edifying application of Scripture (as distinct from a clumsy, inappropriate, confusing one) is, no doubt,

> a work of great difficulty to himself, requiring much prudence, zeal and meditation, and to the natural and corrupt man will be very unpleasant [which consideration will sorely tempt God's messenger to pull his punches, for no normal man likes causing offence]; yet he is to endeavour to perform it in such a manner, that his auditors may feel the word of God to be quick and powerful, and a discerner of the thoughts and intents of the heart; and that, if any unbeliever or ignorant person be present, he may have the secrets of his heart made manifest, and give glory to God.[23]

To apply Scripture realistically, one must know what is in men's heads as well as in their hearts, and the Puritans insisted that the would-be expositor needs to study people as well as the Bible.

Such were Puritan principles in the matter of biblical interpretation. To them, no discipline was so exacting, and no labour so rewarding. The soundness of their method is unquestionable; we shall do well to follow in their footsteps. That will mean asking six questions of each passage or text that we seek to expound:

1. What do these words actually mean?

2. What light do other Scriptures throw on this text? Where and how does it fit into the total biblical revelation?

3. What truths does it teach about God, and about man in relation to God?

4. How are these truths related to the saving work of Christ, and what light does the gospel of Christ throw upon them?

5. What experiences do these truths delineate, or explain, or seek to create or cure? For what practical purpose do they stand in Scripture?

6. How do they apply to myself and others in our own actual situation? To what present human condition do they speak, and what are they telling us to believe and do?

CHAPTER SEVEN

The Puritan Conscience

1

Giving evidence in the famous lawsuit about D.H. Lawrence's novel, *Lady Chatterley's Lover*, Richard Hoggart startled the court by calling Lawrence a Puritan. Asked what he meant (a natural question), he replied that to him a Puritan was a man supremely concerned about conscience. This definition as it stands is either sophistical or stupid, for you could hardly have two more different things than the concern about conscience which Hoggart finds in Lawrence and that which marked the Puritans of history. Nevertheless, Hoggart's formula is a pointer to an important truth. The concern which was really supreme in the minds and hearts of the people called Puritans was a concern about God—a concern to know him truly, and serve him rightly, and so to glorify him and to enjoy him. But just because this was so, they were in fact very deeply concerned about conscience, for they held that conscience was the mental organ in men through which God brought his word to bear on them. Nothing, therefore, in their estimation, was more important for any man than that his conscience should be enlightened, instructed, purged, and kept clean. To them, there could be no real spiritual understanding, nor any genuine godliness, except as men exposed and enslaved their consciences to God's word.

In saying this, the Puritans were doing no more than maintain an emphasis which went back to the first days of the Reformation. One thinks, for example, of Luther's momentous words at Worms: 'My conscience is

107

captive to the Word of God. I cannot and will not recant anything, for to go against conscience is neither right nor safe. Here I stand; there is nothing else I can do. God help me. Amen.' One thinks, too, of the famous sentence about the doctrine of justification in Chapter 20 of the *Augsburg Confession* of 1530: 'This whole doctrine must be related to that conflict of terrified conscience (*illud certamen perterrefactae conscientiae*), and without that conflict it cannot be understood.' Statements like this make plain the centrality of conscience in the Reformers' understanding of what it meant to be a Christian. Conscience, to them, signified a man's knowledge of himself as standing in God's presence (*coram Deo*, in Luther's phrase), subject to God's word and exposed to the judgement of God's law, and yet—if a believer—justified and accepted nonetheless through divine grace. Conscience was the court (*forum*) in which God's justifying sentence was spoken. Conscience was the soil in which alone true faith, hope, peace, and joy could grow. Conscience was a facet of the much-defaced image of God in which man was made; and vital Christianity (the 'Christian religion' of which Calvin wrote the *Institutes*) was rooted directly in the apprehensions and exercises of conscience under the searching address of God's quick and powerful word, and the enlightenment of his Holy Spirit. So the Reformers held; and the Puritans too.

But where do we find such an emphasis today? The frightening fact is that at the present time this note is scarcely ever struck. In Western society as a whole, conscience is in decay; apostasy has set in and hence, as always when faith fails, moral standards are falling. Among intellectuals, conscience is on occasion perverted. One thinks again of D.H. Lawrence and of his camp-followers, and also of Isaiah's curse: 'Woe unto them that call evil good, and good evil!' (Is 5:20). In the Christian church, consciences should be sharp and alert; but are they? It is to be feared that we whom Christ calls to be the salt of the earth have lost much of our proper savour. Are evangelicals noted these days for goodness and integrity? Are we distinguished in society for sensitiveness to moral issues, and compassion towards those in need? Do our preachers, earnest and eloquent as they may be, win for themselves the name that God gave to Noah—'a preacher of *righteousness*' (2 Pet 2:3)? Once, the so-called 'nonconformist conscience' meant something in British national life; but does it mean anything now? Once, Christians were taught to commune with their consciences daily, in the regular discipline of self-examination under the word of God; but how much of this remains today? Do we not constantly give evidence of our neglect of this secret discipline by unprincipled and irresponsible public conduct? We profess our anxiety to keep clear of legalistic bondage, but are we not in much greater danger of Antinomian licence? We rightly repudiate the common view that doctrine does not matter so long as one is upright in life; but if we let our reaction drive us into the opposite extreme of supposing that one's life does not matter so long as one is theologically 'sound' ('a good Calvinist', we say), then the beam in our own eye will be worse than the mote in our brother's. A study of the Puritan conscience, therefore, may well be bracing and salutary for us at the present time.

2

All Puritan theologians from Perkins on are agreed in conceiving of conscience as a rational faculty, a power of moral self-knowledge and judgement, dealing with questions of right and wrong, duty and desert, and dealing with them authoritatively, as God's voice. Often the Puritans appealed to the form of the word (con-science, from the Latin *con-scientia*) as pointing to the fact that the knowledge which conscience possesses is shared knowledge, joint-knowledge, knowledge (*scientia*) held in common with (*con-*) another—namely God. The judgements of conscience thus express the deepest and truest self-knowledge that a man ever has—i.e., knowledge of himself as God knows him. William Ames starts his textbook on conscience and casuistry by reproducing Aquinas' definition of conscience as 'a mans judgement of himselfe, according to the judgement of God of him',[1] and variants of this definition often appear in Puritan writings. Ames appeals to Isaiah 5:3 and 1 Corinthians 11:31 as affording its biblical basis. The Edinburgh professor David Dickson gives a fuller analysis along the same lines, as follows:

> Conscience, as it doth respect ourselves, is . . . the understanding power of our souls examining how matters do stand betwixt God and us, comparing his will revealed, with our state, condition and carriage, in thoughts, words or deeds, done or omitted, and passing judgment thereupon as the case requires.[2]

Conscience, says Thomas Goodwin, is 'one part of practical reason',[3] and the Puritan theologians, still following Aquinas—for they never hesitated to go along with medieval writers when they judged their teaching to be scriptural—all depict the reasonings of conscience as taking the form of a *practical syllogism*: that is, an inference from two premises, major and minor, concerning either our duty (what we should or should not do) or our state before God (obedient or disobedient, approved or under censure, justified or condemned). Dickson gives the following example of a syllogism about duty:

> What God hath appointed to be the only rule of faith and maners, I must take heed to follow it as the rule.
>   But, the holy Scripture, God hath appointed to be the only rule of faith and maners.
>   Therefore, I must take heed to follow the Scripture as the only rule.[4]

Another illustration would be this: *God forbids me to steal* (major premise); *to take this money would be stealing* (minor premise); *therefore I must not take this money* (conclusion).

In a practical syllogism about one's state, the major premise is a revealed truth, functioning as a rule for self-judgement, and the minor is an observed fact about oneself. Ames illustrates with two syllogisms, in the first of which conscience condemns, in the second of which it gives comfort. The first is: '*He that lives in sinne, shall dye: I live in sinne; Therefore, I shall dye.*' The second is: '*Whosoever believes in Christ, shall not dye but live. I believe in Christ; Therefore, I shall not dye but live.*'[5]

Though in experience the reasonings of conscience, like most of our thinking processes, are so compressed that we are consciously aware only of the conclusion, anyone who reflects on the way his conscience functions will soon see that this doctrine of the practical syllogism is in fact a correct analysis.

It is a universal experience that conscience is largely autonomous in its operation; though sometimes we can suppress or stifle it, it normally speaks independently of our will, and sometimes, indeed, contrary to our will. And when it speaks, it is in a strange way distinct from us; it stands over us, addressing us with an absoluteness of authority which we did not give it and which we cannot take from it. To personify conscience and treat it as God's watchman and spokesman in the soul is not, therefore, a mere flight of fancy, it is a necessity of human experience. So that when the Puritans call conscience 'God's deputy and vice-regent within us', 'God's spy in our bosoms', 'God's sergeant he employs to arrest the sinner',[6] we must not dismiss these ideas as just quaint imaginings; they represent a serious attempt to do justice to the biblical conception of conscience, which everyone's experience reflects—namely, the conception of conscience as a witness, declaring facts (Rom 2:15; 9:1; 2 Cor 1:12), a mentor, prohibiting evil (Acts 24:16; Rom 13:5), and a judge, assessing desert (Rom 2:15; cf 1 Jn 3:20f). Such passages amply warrant the Puritan conception of conscience as the faculty which God put in man to be a sounding-board for his word in its application to our lives, or (changing the metaphor) a mirror to catch the light of moral and spiritual truth that shines forth from God and to reflect it in concentrated focus upon our deeds, desires, goals and choices. The Puritans are simply following the Bible when they depict conscience in this fashion, as God's monitor in the soul.

To amplify the last thought, we will now cite three typical and detailed Puritan presentations of conscience and its activity. Here, first, is Richard Sibbes' picture of conscience as *God's court* within us, where the last judgement is anticipated (a very common Puritan thought):

> To clear this further concerning the nature of conscience [Sibbes is expounding 2 Cor 1:12], know that God hath set up in a man a court, and there is in man all that are in a court.

1. There is a *register* to take notice of what we have done. . . . The conscience keeps diaries. It sets down everything. It is not forgotten, though we think it is . . . there is a register that writes it down. Conscience is the register.

2. And then there are *witnesses*. 'The testimony of conscience.' Conscience doth witness, this have I done, this I have not done.

3. There is an *accuser with the witnesses*. The conscience, it accuseth, or excuseth.

4. And then there is the *judge*. Conscience is the judge. There it doth judge, this is well done, this is ill done.

5. Then there is an *executioner*, and conscience is that too. Upon accusation and judgment, there is punishment. The first punishment is within a man alway before he come to hell. The punishment of conscience, it is a prejudice [i.e., a pre-judgement] of future judgment. There is a flash of hell presently [i.e., in the present] after an ill act. . . . If the understanding apprehend dolorous things, then the heart smites, as David's 'heart smote him.' (2 Sam 24:5). . . . The heart smites with grief for the present, and fear for the time to come.

God hath set and planted in man this court of conscience, and it is God's hall, as it were, where he keeps his first judgment . . . his assizes. And conscience doth all the parts. It registereth, it witnesseth, it accuseth, it judgeth, it executes, it doth all.[7]

Here, second, from John Bunyan's *Holy War*, is an account of the career of 'Mr Recorder' of the town of Mansoul, first under sin and then under grace:

Mr. Recorder . . . [was] . . . a man well read in the laws of his king, and also a man of courage and faithfulness, to speak truth at every occasion; and he had a tongue as bravely hung as he had a head filled with judgment. . . . [After Mansoul had fallen under Diabolus] he was much degenerated from his former king . . . but . . . he would now and then think upon Shaddai, and have dread of his law upon him, and then he would speak with a voice as great against Diabolus as when a lion roareth; yea, and would also at certain times when his fits were upon him—for you must know that sometimes he had terrible fits—make the whole town of Mansoul shake with his voice . . . his words . . . were like the rattling thunder, and also like thunder-claps. . . .[8]

In due course Emmanuel, the king's son, broke through Eargate and sent Captains Boanerges, Conviction, and Judgment, to take possession of Mr Recorder's house, an event which shattered the old gentleman and drove him almost to despair; but Emmanuel made him the messenger of 'a large and general pardon' to the townspeople, and put him into office as a preacher, to inculcate the moral law, and with it all that he had learned, or in future might learn, from 'the Lord Secretary' (the Holy Spirit) concerning the will of Emmanuel's father.

Here, finally, is William Fenner, in *A Treatise of Conscience*, elaborating this last thought of conscience as a preacher:

> It is a preacher also to tell us our duty both towards God and towards man; yea, it is a powerful preacher; it exhorteth, urgeth, provoketh; yea, the most powerful preacher that can be; it will cause the stoutest and stubbornest heart under heaven to quake now and then. . . . Conscience is joyned in commission with God's own spirit to be an instructor unto us in the way we should walk; so that the spirit and it are resisted or obeyed together, grieved or delighted together; We cannot sinne against conscience but we sinne also against God's spirit; we cannot check our own conscience but we check and quench the holy spirit of God.[9]

Such, then, was conscience as the Puritans conceived it.

3

To bring out the significance of conscience in the Puritan theological scheme, we shall now set it in relation to some of the other major topics on which the Puritans dwelt, and show how some of their most characteristic emphases were bound up with their view of conscience and reflected in their preaching about it.

First, this teaching reflects the Puritan view of *Holy Scripture*. God, said the Puritans, must control our consciences absolutely. 'The conscience . . . must be subjected to him, and to him alone; for he alone is Lord of the conscience. . . . Conscience is God's deputy, and must in the exercise of this office confine itself to the orders and instructions of the sovereign Lord.'[10] Hence follows an imperative need to get our consciences fully attuned to the mind and will of God. Otherwise, we cannot help going wrong, whatever we do; for flouting conscience, and following an erring conscience, are both sin. 'If you follow it,' Baxter explains, 'you break the law of God in doing that which he forbids you. If you forsake it, and go against it, you reject the authority of God, in doing that which you think he forbids you.'[11] In his twenty-seventh direction 'for faithful serving Christ, and doing good', Baxter warns against the idea that conscience, as such, is an ultimate standard:

> Make not your own judgments or consciences your law, or the maker of your duty; which is but the discerner of the law of God, and of the duty which he maketh you, and of your own obedience or disobedience to him.

There is a dangerous error grown too common in the world [it is commoner still today] that a man is bound to do every thing which his conscience telleth him is the will of God; and that every man must obey his conscience, as if it were the lawgiver of the world; whereas, indeed, it is not ourselves, but God, that is our lawgiver. And conscience is . . . appointed . . . only to discern the law of God, and call upon us to observe it: and an erring conscience is not to be obeyed, but to be better informed. . . .[12]

But how can God's will be known? Can we tell his requirements with certainty and exactness? Is there any way out of the fogs of pious guesswork on this point into the clear light of certainty? Yes, said the Puritans, there is; the way out is to harness our consciences to the Holy Scriptures, in which the mind of God is fully revealed to us. To them, Scripture was more than the fallible and sometimes fallacious human witness to revelation which is all that some moderns allow it to be; it was revelation itself, the living word of the living God, divine testimony to God's own redemptive acts and plans, written by the Holy Ghost through human agents in order to give the church of every age clear direction on all matters of faith and life that could possibly arise.

But, it might be said, such a formula is unrealistic and empty. The Bible is, after all, a very old book, the product of a now long-vanished culture. Most of it was written for people in an utterly different situation from our own. How can it throw clear and direct light on the problems of life today? It can do so, the Puritans would reply, because the God who wrote it remains the same, and his thoughts about man's life do not change. If we can learn to see what principles he was inculcating and applying in his recorded dealings with Israel and the early church, and to reapply them to our own situation, that will constitute the guidance that we need. And it is to help us to do this that the Holy Spirit has been given. Certainly, seeing the relevant principles and applying them correctly in each case is in practice an arduous task; ignorance of Scripture, and misjudgement of situations, constantly lead us astray, and to be patient and humble enough to receive the Spirit's help is not easy either. But it remains true nonetheless that in principle Scripture provides clear and exact guidance for every detail and department of life, and if we come to Scripture teachably and expectantly God himself will seal on our minds and hearts a clear certainty as to how we should behave in each situation that faces us. 'God hath appointed means for the cure of blindness and error,' wrote Baxter, 'Come into the light, with due self-suspicion, and impartiality, and diligently use all God's means, and avoid the causes of deceit and error, and the light of truth will at once show you the truth.'[13]

The Puritans themselves sought clear certainty as to God's truth in its practical bearing, and believed that they had been given it. Their very quest sharpened both their moral sensibilities and their insight into the Bible.

They would not have been interested in vague moral uplift; what they wanted was to grasp God's truth with the same preciseness of application with which they held that he had revealed it. Because of their concern for preciseness in following out God's revealed will in matters moral and ecclesiastical, the first Puritans were dubbed 'precisians'. Though ill-meant and derisive, this was in fact a good name for them. Then as now, people explained their attitude as due to peevish cantankerousness and angularity or morbidity of temperament, but that was not how they themselves saw it. Richard Rogers, the Puritan pastor of Wethersfield, Essex, at the turn of the sixteenth century, was riding one day with the local lord of the manor, who, after twitting him for some time about his 'precisian' ways, asked him what it was that made him so *precise*. 'O sir,' replied Rogers, '*I serve a precise God*.' If there were such a thing as a Puritan crest, this would be its proper motto. A precise God—a God, that is, who has made a precise disclosure of his mind and will in Scripture, and who expects from his servants a corresponding preciseness of belief and behaviour—it was this view of God that created and controlled the historic Puritan outlook. The Bible itself led them to it. And we who share the Puritan estimate of Holy Scripture cannot excuse ourselves if we fail to show a diligence and conscientiousness equal to theirs in ordering our lives according to God's written word.

Second, the Puritans' teaching on conscience reflected their view of *personal religion*. Godliness, to the Puritans, was essentially a matter of conscience, inasmuch as it consisted in a hearty, disciplined, 'considerate' (thoughtful) response to known evangelical truth, and centred upon the getting and keeping of a good conscience. As long as a man is unregenerate, his conscience oscillates between being bad and being asleep. The first work of grace is to quicken his conscience and make it thoroughly bad, by forcing him to face God's demands upon him and so making him aware of his guilt, impotence, rebelliousness, defilement, and alienation, in God's sight. But the knowledge of pardon and peace through Christ makes his bad conscience good. A good conscience is God's gift to those whom, like Bunyan's pilgrim, he enables to look with understanding at the cross. It is maintained through life by seeking to do God's will in all things, and by constantly keeping the cross in view. Let Fenner explain this:

Suppose a man have peace of conscience, what must he do to keep and maintain it? I answer,

First, We must labour to prevent troubles of conscience by taking heed that we do nothing contrarie to conscience. . . . Nothing that we get in any evil way will chear and comfort us in a time of need. . . . Wretched is he that alloweth himself in any course which his conscience findeth fault with. It is a good rule the Apostle giveth. *Blessed is he that condemneth not him-*

self in that which he alloweth (Rom xiv:22): that is, Blessed is he that hath not a condemning conscience. . . .

Secondly, If we will maintain our peace, we must labour to have our hearts grounded in the assurance of the love of God. . . .

Thirdly, We must use the assurance of faith in applying the blood of Christ; we must labour to purge and cleanse our consciences with it. If we find that we have sinned, we must runne presently [at once] to the blood of Christ to wash away our sinne. We must not let the wound fester or exulcerate, but presently get it healed. . . . As we sinne dayly, so he justifieth dayly, and we must dayly go to him for it. . . . We must every day eye the brazen serpent. Justification is an everrunning fountain, and therefore we cannot look to have all the water at once. . . . O let us sue out every day a dayly pardon. . . . Let us not sleep one night without a new pardon. Better sleep in a house full of adders and venomous beasts than sleep in one sinne. O then be sure with the day to clear the sinnes of the day: Then shall our consciences have true peace.[14]

A good conscience, said the Puritans, is the greatest blessing that there is. 'Conscience,' declared Sibbes, 'is either the greatest friend or the greatest enemy in the world.'[15] There is no better friend than a conscience which knows peace with God; for, says Fenner:

First . . . it is the very head of all comforts. A worthy divine calls it *Abrahams bosome to the soule*. . . .

Secondly, A quiet conscience maketh a man to tast the sweetness of things heavenly and spirituall: It maketh the word to be to him, as to David, *Sweeter than hony*. . . . *I have not departed from thy judgment, O Lord,* saith he (thus saith his conscience) now what followeth next? *How sweet are thy words unto my tast! yea, sweeter than hony unto my mouth* (Ps 103). A good conscience maketh a man tast sweetnesse in prayer . . . in a Sabbath . . . in the Sacraments. . . . What is the reason so few of you tast sweetnesse in these things? The reason is this: Because ye have not the peace of a good conscience. . . .

Thirdly, A good quiet conscience maketh a man tast sweetnesse in all outward things, in meat, in drink, in sleep, in the company of friends. . . . The healthy man only can take pleasure in recreations, walks, meats, sports, and the like: they yield no comfort to those that are bedrid, or half-dead. But when the conscience is at peace, the soul is all in good health; and so all things are enjoyed with sweetness and comfort.

Fourthly, It sweetneth evils to a man, as trouble, crosses, sorrows, afflications. If a man have true peace in his conscience, it comforteth him in them all. When things abroad do disquiet us, how comfortable it is to have something at home to chear us? so when troubles and afflictions without turmoil and vex us and adde sorrow to sorrow, then to have peace within, the peace

of conscience, to allay all and quiet all, what happiness is this? When sick-
nesse and death cometh, what will a good conscience be worth then? Sure,
more than all the world besides. . . . The conscience is God's echo of peace
to the soul: in life, in death, in judgement it is unspeakable comfort.[16]

A man with a good conscience can face death with equanimity. In his
famous account of the crossing of Jordan, Bunyan tells us how 'Mr. *Honest*
in his life time had spoken to one *Good-conscience* to meet him there, the
which he also did, and lent him his hand, and so helped him over'.[17] It is
through the gift of a good conscience that God enables one to say, 'Lord,
now lettest thou thy servant depart in peace' (Lk 2:29).

A good conscience is a tender conscience. The consciences of the godless
may be so calloused that they scarcely ever act at all; but the healthy Christian conscience (said the Puritans) is constantly in operation, listening for
God's voice in his word, seeking to discern his will in everything, active in
self-watch and self-judgement. The healthy Christian knows his frailty and
always suspects and distrusts himself, lest sin and Satan should be ensnar-
ing him unawares; therefore he regularly grills himself before God, scru-
tinising his deeds and motives and ruthlessly condemning himself when he
finds within himself moral deficiency and dishonesty. This was the kind of
self-judging that Paul urged upon the Corinthians at Communion time
(1 Cor 11:31). The degree of sharp-sightedness which our consciences
show in detecting our own real sins (as distinct from the imaginary ones
on which Satan encourages us to concentrate) is an index of how well we
really know God and how close to him we really walk—an index, in other
words, of the real quality of our spiritual life. The sluggish conscience of
a 'sleepy', 'drowsy' saint is a sign of spiritual malaise. The healthy Christian
is not necessarily the extrovert, ebullient Christian, but the Christian who
has a sense of God's presence stamped deep on his soul, who trembles at
God's word, who lets it dwell in him richly by constant meditation upon
it, and who tests and reforms his life daily in response to it. We can begin
to assess our real state in God's sight by asking ourselves how much exercise of conscience along these lines goes into our own daily living.

Third, the Puritans' teaching on conscience was reflected in their view
of *preaching*. The most characteristic feature in the Puritan ideal of preaching was the great stress laid on the need for searching applications of truth
to the hearers' consciences. One mark of a 'spiritual', 'powerful' preacher,
in the Puritan estimation, was the closeness and faithfulness of application
whereby he would 'rip up' men's consciences and make them face themselves as God saw them. The Puritans knew that sinful men are slow to
apply truth to themselves, quick though they may be to see how it bears
on others. Hence unapplied general statements of evangelical truth were
unlikely to do much good. Therefore (said the Puritans) the preacher must
see it as an essential part of his job to work out applications in detail, lead-

ing the minds of his hearers step by step down those avenues of practical syllogisms which will bring the word right home to their hearts, to do its judging, wounding, healing, comforting, and guiding work. 'Because of [this] slownesse in men to . . . apply,' declared Ames, 'there is a necessity laid on all Ministers, not only to declare Gods will generally, but likewise so farre as they are able, to helpe, and further both publicly, and in private, the application of it.'[18] Application is the preacher's highway from the head to the heart. This applicatory part of preaching, says the *Westminster Directory*,

> albeit it prove a work of great difficulty . . . requiring much prudence, zeal, and meditation, and to the natural and corrupt man will be very unpleasant; yet he [the preacher] is to endeavour to perform it in such a manner, that his auditors may feel the word of God to be quick and powerful, and a discerner of the thoughts and intents of the heart; and that, if any unbeliever or ignorant person be present, he may have the secrets of his heart made manifest, and give glory to God.

The word must thus cut into the conscience if it is ever to do men good.

Effective application presupposes that the truth applied has first been shown to be a genuine word from God, and not just a bright idea of the preacher's. This means that it must have been drawn out of the preacher's text, in such a way that 'the hearers may discern how God teacheth it from thence' (*Westminster Directory*), and thus be forced to realise that it comes to them with the authority of God himself. Fenner stresses this in connection with his point that 'God's law is the absolute and supreme bond of conscience'.[19]

Whence comes the skill to apply God's truth appropriately in preaching? From the experience of having God apply his truth powerfully to oneself. Ordinarily, said the Puritans, it is those whose own consciences are most deeply exercised by God's truth who have most power to awaken the consciences of others by prudent and piercing applications. This was part of what John Owen meant when he laid it down that 'if the word do not dwell with power *in us*, it will not pass with power *from us*'.[20] And the Puritans would no doubt have said that this was part of the true meaning of Anselm's assertion that it is the heart (*pectus*) that makes the theologian.

It may be asked: does not this stress on the searching of conscience produce a morbid and introspective type of piety? Does not this emphasis on constant self-suspicion and self-examination actually weaken faith, by diverting our gaze from Christ in his fulness to ourselves in our emptiness, so leading us to spiritual despondency and depression? No doubt it would if it were made an end in itself; but, of course, it never was. The Puritans ripped up consciences in the pulpit and urged self-trial in the closet only in order to drive sinners to Christ and to teach them to live by faith in him.

They plied the law only to make way for the gospel, and for the life of dependence on the grace of God. Morbidity and introspectiveness, the gloomy self-absorption of the man who can never look away from himself, is bad Puritanism; the Puritans themselves condemned it repeatedly. A study of Puritan sermons will show that the preachers' constant concern, in all their detailed detecting of sins, was to lead their hearers into the life of faith and a good conscience; which, they said, is the most joyous life that man can know in this world.

4

The Puritan concern for a good conscience lent great ethical strength to their teaching. Of all English evangelicals from the Reformation to the present day, the Puritans were undoubtedly the most conspicuous as preachers of righteousness. They were in truth the salt of society in their time, and on many points they created a national conscience which has only recently begun to be eroded. A demand for the sanctification of the Sabbath; plain speaking against demoralising amusements (bawdy plays, promiscuous dancing, gluttony and drunkenness, salacious fiction); abhorrence of profanity; insistence on a faithful management of one's calling and station in life—these were emphases which are still remembered (sometimes applauded, sometime ridiculed) as 'Puritan'. Just as Laud had a policy of 'thorough' in ecclesiastical affairs, so the Puritans had a policy of 'thorough' in ethical realm; and they went to great pains to give detailed guidance on the duties involved in the various relationships to God and man in which the Christian stood. Among the memorials of their work in this field are the many printed expositions of the Ten Commandments; major works like Richard Rogers' *Seven Treatises . . . the Practice of Christianity* (1603), Perkins' and Ames' volumes on conscience and casuistry, and Baxter's *Christian Directory* (1670); plus countless small vade-mecums on the Christian life, from Arthur Dent's *Plain Man's Pathway to Heaven* (1601) down to Thomas Gouge's *Christian Directions Shewing how to Walk with God All the day Long* (1688).

Was all this detailed teaching on Christian conduct a lapse into a new legalism and a curtailing of Christian liberty? Does it mark a decline into pharisaic ways?

No; for first, all this ethical teaching was evangelically based, as that of the New Testament is. The supreme ethical motives in Puritanism were gratitude for grace received, and a sense of responsibility to walk worthy of one's calling, and there was not the least room in Puritan teaching for self-righteousness; for not only was it constantly stressed that the Christian works *from* life, rather than *for* life, but it was also repeatedly emphasised that our best works are shot through with sin, and contain something that needs to be forgiven.

Then, secondly, this ethical teaching was all given (again, just as in the New Testament) not as a code of routine motions to go through with mechanical exactness, but in the form of attitudes to be maintained and principles to be applied, so that however much teaching and advice a man received, he was always left to make the final decisions and determinations (whether to follow his pastor's advice; how to apply the given principles in this or that case; etc) on his own initiative, as spontaneous, responsible acts of his own conscience in the sight of God.

Thirdly, Puritan ethical teaching was not authoritarian; it was offered as exposition and application of Scripture, and was to be checked against Scripture by those who received it, according to the Protestant principle of the duty of private judgement. The Puritans did not wish men's consciences to be bound to their own teaching, as such, but to the word of God only, and to Puritan teaching only so far as it was demonstrably in accord with that word.

Fourthly, Puritan ethical teaching took the form of a positive ideal of zealous and wise godliness, at which Christians must always be aiming even though they never fully reach it in this world; and unattained positive ideals are the death of the legalistic spirit, which can only flourish in an atmosphere of negative restriction where abstinence is regarded as the essence of virtue. In reality nothing less legalistic in spirit and content than the ethical teaching of the Puritans can well be imagined.

But, it may be said, did not their habitual attention to the minutiae of righteousness, however evangelically motivated, impair their sense of proportion, and make them scrupulous about small matters in which no issues of principle were involved, and which therefore they should have taken in their stride? This was a constant accusation in the Puritans' own day, especially with regard to their insistence that the worship of the Church of England needed to be purified further than had been done in the Elizabethan settlement. The Puritan objections to the surplice, the wedding ring, the cross in baptism, and kneeling at Communion were put down to a 'peevish humour' rationalising itself in an adverse judgement. Again, in 1662, it appeared to many that Richard Baxter and those clergy who shared his views (the majority, it seems, of the ejected) had really no sufficient reason for taking exception to the terms of the Act of Uniformity. What happened on August 24, 1662 is usually called the Great Ejection, and certainly a wish to eject any Puritans who would not become Vicars of Bray was present, but historically it is more accurate to call this event the Great Withdrawal of those who would not take the oath that the Act of Uniformity prescribed. Did the Puritans in their brave and costly refusal actually make mountains out of molehills? Was their heroism really necessary? Let us try to see.

Of the poignancy of the choice which Baxter and his friends made there can be no question. They believed in the idea of a national Protestant

Church of England; they regarded themselves as already ministers of that church, and only wanted to continue as such. They were not divine-right Presbyterians; they had no objection to a fixed liturgy (provided it was scriptural), nor to episcopacy (provided it was not prelatical); they accepted the ideal of a national uniformity of religion. Yet they felt bound to refuse the Caroline settlement, and to withdraw, either into silence, or into surreptitious, sectarian forms of church life—two alternatives both of which were to them intensely undesirable, quite apart from the persecution to which the second would expose them. It was a terribly painful decision. Why did they feel obliged to make it? They had five main reasons.

First, they could not conscientiously declare 'unfeigned assent and consent' to the 1662 Prayer Book, as the Act of Uniformity required them to do. Not only did that book still retain the ceremonies to which Puritans had been objecting for a century, on the grounds that (1) being tainted with superstitious associations, they were undesirable, and (2) not being scriptural, they should not be made obligatory; it also retained phraseology to which the Puritan spokesmen at the Savoy Conference had definitely objected, such as the declaratory assertion of regeneration in the baptism service, the strong absolution in the visitation of the sick, and the reference to the dead man as a brother in the Lord in the funeral service. Even so, had they merely been asked by the Act to assent to the book in the sense of accepting it for regular use, they might have felt free to do so (after all, it was virtually the same book that earlier Puritans had used, many of them without any deviations, up to 1640). But what the Act required was a public declaration of 'unfeigned assent and consent'; and this seemed to them to imply a degree of approval which they dare not undertake to give, lest they involve themselves in the guilt of perjury.

Second, the Act required them to abjure the Solemn League and Covenant of 1645 (an undertaking to further the work of reforming the English Church so as to bring it closer into line with other Reformed churches, especially the Church of Scotland, and to extirpate the traditional Anglican ecclesiastical hierarchy). But many of the Puritans, even those who did not believe that the New Testament prescribes a thoroughgoing Presbyterianism, felt unable to renounce the Covenant as an 'unlawful oath': neither constitutionally nor theologically could they see anything that was demonstrably unlawful about it. Again, therefore, rather than risk perjury, they declined the abjuration.

Third, the Act required them to declare it unlawful under any circumstances to take up arms against the king, and to bind themselves never to do it. The requirement was understandable, but the many who thought Parliament had been right to fight naturally found it unacceptable, as involving a recantation that they could not honestly make and an advance acceptance of any form of royal absolutism that might develop. Here, too, conscience compelled them to take the stand they took.

Fourth, they objected to the demand that English clergy who had not hitherto received episcopal orders should be episcopally ordained forthwith. To accept this demand, they held, would be not merely to condemn as invalid their own previous ministrations, but also to condemn by implication all the non-episcopal ministries of Protestant Christendom throughout the world; and this they could not do.

Finally, these Puritan clergy were prevented from trying to stretch their consciences by the sense that the eyes of their own flocks—indeed, of all Englishmen—were upon them, and that they could not even appear to compromise principles for which they had stood in the past without discrediting both themselves, their calling, and their previous teaching. Calamy records a contemporary comment which focuses their fear: 'had the ministers conformed, people would have thought there was nothing in religion.' It had become a question of credibility. The Puritan clergy held that they should be ready to confirm what they had publicly maintained as truth by suffering, if need be, rather than risk undermining their whole previous ministry by what would look like time-serving abandonment of principle. Therefore, once they had become clear that the terms of the Act of Uniformity were *prima facie* intolerable, they did not expend any energy on trying to find ways and means of wriggling round them. Rather than appear to be trifling with truth, they withdrew into the wilderness.

Was this scrupulosity? Was their attitude a case of a mere rationalised peevishness? Surely not. It is, rather, the supreme illustration of the Puritan conscience in action. Two ruling axioms of Puritan casuistry were (1) that no known truth must be compromised or denied in practice and (2) that no avoidable sin must be committed, however great the good to which such compromise and sin might lead. Expediency is no warrant for unprincipled action; the end does not justify the means. Whether Baxter and his friends were right in their verdict on the Restoration settlement we need not now discuss, any more than we need pass judgement on the action of men like Gurnall and Trapp, who conformed, Reynolds who became Bishop of Norwich, and Leighton, who received both episcopal ordination and consecration to become a bishop in Scotland. All I wish to do here is to display the action of Baxter and his friends as an instance of costly conscientiousness. The suggestion that—to put it bluntly—the root of their nonconformity was cussedness, wounded pride, and an obstinate refusal to climb down is simply ridiculous. Perjury, and reformation, and the sufficiency of Scripture, and the dispensability of bishops were matters of theological principle as far as they were concerned; and they kept a good conscience in the only way open to them, or to any Christian—by following truth as it appears from Scripture, and refusing to sell it, or betray it, for any consideration in the world.

So the conclusion I would draw is simply this: that such conscientiousness as marked all Puritan religion, and was supremely manifested in the ejections of 1662, is a necessary Christian virtue at all times. It is man's proper response to God's immutable revealed truth. It may be costly, as it was in 1662; but without it, churchmanship becomes irreligion, and one's Christian profession becomes an insult to God. These are compromising days in the church's life; that, perhaps, is only to be expected when the very existence of revealed truth is so widely doubted or denied. But if we believe that God has spoken in his Son, and that the Bible is his own word of testimony to that revelation—if, in other words, we hold the Puritan view of Scripture—then, as we said earlier, the uncompromising fidelity to Bible truth which marked the Puritans should mark us also. May God give us light to see his truth, consciences to apply it and live by it, and conscientiousness to hold it fast, whatever the cost, in these Laodicean days.

The Puritans and the Gospel

CHAPTER EIGHT

'Saved by His Precious Blood': An Introduction to John Owen's The Death of Death in the Death of Christ

1

The Death of Death in the Death of Christ (Owen, *Works*, X:139-148) is a polemical piece, designed to show, among other things, that the doctrine of universal redemption is unscriptural and destructive of the gospel. There are many, therefore, to whom it is not likely to be of interest. Those who see no need for doctrinal exactness and have no time for theological debates which show up divisions between so-called evangelicals may well regret its reappearance. Some may find the very sound of Owen's thesis so shocking that they will refuse to read his book at all, so passionate a thing is prejudice, and so proud are we of our theological shibboleths. But it is hoped that this classic may find itself readers of a different spirit. There are signs today of a new upsurge of interest in the theology of the Bible: a new readiness to test traditions, to search the Scriptures and to think through the faith. It is to those who share this readiness that Owen's treatise is now offered, in the belief that it will help us in one of the most urgent tasks facing evangelical Christendom today—the recovery of the gospel.

This last remark may cause some raising of eyebrows, but it seems to be warranted by the facts.

There is no doubt that evangelicalism today is in a state of perplexity and unsettlement. In such matters as the practice of evangelism, the teaching of holiness, the building up of local church life, the pastor's dealing with

125

souls and the exercise of discipline, there is evidence of widespread dissatisfaction with things as they are and of equally widespread uncertainty as to the road ahead. This is a complex phenomenon, to which many factors have contributed; but, if we go to the root of the matter, we shall find that these perplexities are all ultimately due to our having lost our grip on the biblical gospel. Without realising it, we have during the past century bartered that gospel for a substitute product which, though it looks similar enough in points of detail, is as a whole a decidedly different thing. Hence our troubles; for the substitute product does not answer the ends for which the authentic gospel has in past days proved itself so mighty. Why?

We would suggest that the reason lies in its own character and content. It fails to make men God-centred in their thoughts and God-fearing in their hearts because this is not primarily what it is trying to do. One way of stating the difference between it and the old gospel is to say that it is too exclusively concerned to be 'helpful' to man—to bring peace, comfort, happiness, satisfaction—and too little concerned to glorify God. The old gospel was 'helpful', too—more so, indeed, than is the new—but (so to speak) incidentally, for its first concern was always to give glory to God. It was always and essentially a proclamation of divine sovereignty in mercy and judgement, a summons to bow down and worship the mighty Lord on whom man depends for all good, both in nature and in grace. Its centre of reference was unambiguously God. But in the new gospel the centre of reference is man. This is just to say that the old gospel was *religious* in a way that the new gospel is not. Whereas the chief aim of the old was to teach people to worship God, the concern of the new seems limited to making them feel better. The subject of the old gospel was God and his ways with men; the subject of the new is man and the help God gives him. There is a world of difference. The whole perspective and emphasis of gospel preaching has changed.

From this change of interest has sprung a change of content, for the new gospel has in effect reformulated the biblical message in the supposed interests of 'helpfulness'. Accordingly, the themes of man's natural inability to believe, of God's free election being the ultimate cause of salvation, and of Christ dying specifically for his sheep are not preached. These doctrines, it would be said, are not 'helpful'; they would drive sinners to despair, by suggesting to them that it is not in their own power to be saved through Christ. (The possibility that such despair might be salutary is not considered: it is taken for granted that it cannot be, because it is so shattering to our self-esteem.) However this may be (and we shall say more about it later), the result of these omissions is that part of the biblical gospel is now preached as if it were the whole of that gospel; and a half-truth masquerading as the whole truth becomes a complete untruth. Thus, we appeal to men as if they all had the ability to receive Christ at any time; we speak of his redeeming work as if he had done no more by dying than make it possible for us to save ourselves by believing; we speak of God's love as if it were no more than a general willingness to receive any who will turn and trust; and we depict the Father and the Son, not as sovereignly active in drawing sinners to themselves, but as waiting in quiet impotence 'at the door of our hearts' for us to let them in.

It is undeniable that this is how we preach; perhaps this is what we really believe. But it needs to be said with emphasis that this set of twisted half-truths is something other than the biblical gospel. The Bible is against us when we preach in this way; and the fact that such preaching has become almost standard practice among us only shows how urgent it is that we should review this matter. To recover the old, authentic, biblical gospel, and to bring our preaching and practice back into line with it, is perhaps our most pressing present need. And it is at this point that Owen's treatise on redemption can give us help.

2

'But wait a minute,' says someone, 'it's all very well to talk like this about the gospel; but surely what Owen is doing is defending limited atonement—one of the five points of Calvinism? When you speak of recovering the gospel, don't you mean that you just want us all to become Calvinists?'

These questions are worth considering, for they will no doubt occur to many. At the same time, however, they are questions that reflect a great deal of prejudice and ignorance. 'Defending limited atonement'—as if this was all that a Reformed theologian expounding the heart of the gospel could ever really want to do! 'You just want us all to become Calvinists'—as if Reformed theologians had no interest beyond recruiting for their party, and as if becoming a Calvinist was the last stage of theological depravity, and had nothing to do with the gospel at all! Before we answer these questions directly, we must try to remove the prejudices which underlie them by making clear what Calvinism really is; and therefore we would ask the reader to take note of the following facts, historical and theological, about Calvinism in general and the 'five points' in particular.

First, is should be observed that the 'five points of Calvinism,' so-called, are simply the Calvinistic answer to a five-point manifesto (the Remonstrance) put out by certain 'Belgic semi-Pelagians'[1] in the early seventeenth century. The theology which it contained (known to history as Arminianism) stemmed from two philosophical principles: first, that divine sovereignty is not compatible with human freedom, nor therefore with human responsibility; second, that ability limits obligation. (The charge of semi-Pelagianism was thus fully justified.) From these principles, the Arminians drew two deductions: first, that since the Bible regards faith as a free and responsible human act, it cannot be caused by God, but is exercised independently of him; second, that since the Bible regards faith as obligatory on the part of all who hear the gospel, ability to believe must be universal. Hence, they maintained, Scripture must be interpreted as teaching the following positions: (1) Man is never so completely corrupted by sin that he cannot savingly believe the gospel when it is put before him, nor (2) is he ever so completely controlled by God that he cannot reject it. (3) God's election of those who shall be saved is prompted by his foreseeing that they will of their own accord believe. (4) Christ's death did not ensure the salvation of anyone, for it did not secure the gift of faith to anyone (there is no such gift); what it did was rather to create a possibility of salvation for everyone if they believe. (5) It rests with believers to keep themselves in a state of grace by keeping up their faith; those who fail here fall away and are lost. Thus, Arminianism made man's salvation depend ultimately on man himself, saving faith being viewed throughout as man's own work and, because his own, not God's in him.

The Synod of Dort was convened in 1618 to pronounce on this theology, and the 'five points of Calvinism' represent its counter-affirmations. They stem from a very different principle—the biblical principle that 'salvation is of the Lord';[2] and they may be summarised thus: (1) Fallen man in his natural state lacks all power to believe the gospel, just as he lacks all power to believe the law, despite all external inducements that may be extended to him. (2) God's election is a free, sovereign, unconditional choice of sinners, as sinners, to be redeemed by Christ, given faith, and brought to glory. (3) The redeeming work of Christ had as its end and goal the salvation of the elect. (4) The work of the Holy Spirit in bringing men to faith never fails to achieve its object. (5) Believers are kept in faith and grace by the unconquerable power of God till they come to glory. These five points are conveniently denoted by the mnemonic TULIP: Total depravity, Unconditional election, Limited atonement, Irresistible grace, Preservation of the saints.

Now, here are two coherent interpretations of the biblical gospel, which stand in evident opposition to each other. The difference between them is not primarily one of emphasis, but of content. One proclaims a God who saves; the other speaks of a God who enables man to save himself. One view presents the three great acts of the Holy Trinity for the recovering of lost mankind—election by the Father, redemption by the Son, calling by the Spirit—as directed towards the same persons, and as securing their salvation infallibly. The other view gives each act a different reference (the objects of redemption being all mankind, of calling, all who hear the gospel, and of election, those hearers who respond), and denies that any man's salvation is secured by any of them. The two theologies thus conceive the plan of salvation in quite different terms. One makes salvation depend on the work of God, the other on a work of man; one regards faith as part of God's gift of salvation, the other as man's own contribution to salvation;

one gives all the glory of saving believers to God, the other divides the praise between God, who, so to speak, built the machinery of salvation, and man, who by believing operated it. Plainly, these differences are important, and the permanent value of the 'five points', as a summary of Calvinism, is that they make clear the areas in which, and the extent to which, these two conceptions are at variance.

However, it would not be correct simply to equate Calvinism with the 'five points'. Five points of our own will make this clear.

In the first place, Calvinism is something much broader than the 'five points' indicate. Calvinism is a whole world-view, stemming from a clear vision of God as the whole world's Maker and King. Calvinism is the consistent endeavour to acknowledge the Creator as the Lord, working all things after the counsel of his will. Calvinism is a theocentric way of thinking about all life under the direction and control of God's own word. Calvinism, in other words, is the theology of the Bible viewed from the perspective of the Bible—the God-centred outlook which sees the Creator as the source, and means, and end, of everything that is, both in nature and in grace. Calvinism is thus theism (belief in God as the ground of all things), religion (dependence on God as the giver of all things), and evangelicalism (trust in God through Christ for all things), all in their purest and most highly developed form. And Calvinism is a unified philosophy of history which sees the whole diversity of processes and events that take place in God's world as no more, and no less, than the outworking of his great preordained plan for his creatures and his church. The five points assert no more than that God is sovereign in saving the individual, but Calvinism, as such, is concerned with the much broader assertion that he is sovereign everywhere.

Then, in the second place, the 'five points' present Calvinistic soteriology in a negative and polemical form, whereas Calvinism in itself is essentially expository, pastoral and constructive. It can define its position in terms of Scripture without any reference to Arminianism, and it does not need to be forever fighting real or imaginary Arminians in order to keep itself alive. Calvinism has no interest in negatives, as such; when Calvinists fight, they fight for positive evangelical values. The negative cast of the 'five points' is misleading chiefly with regard to the third (limited atonement, or particular redemption), which is often read with stress on the adjective and taken as indicating that Calvinists have a special interest in confining the limits of divine mercy. But in fact the purpose of this phraseology, as we shall see, is to safeguard the central affirmation of the gospel—that Christ is a redeemer who really does redeem. Similarly, the denials of an election that is conditional and of grace that is resistible are intended to safeguard the positive truth that it is God who saves. The real negations are those of Arminianism, which denies that election, redemption and calling are saving acts of God. Calvinism negates these negations in order to assert the positive content of the gospel, for the positive purpose of strengthening faith and building up the church.

Thirdly, the very act of setting out Calvinistic soteriology in the form of five distinct points (a number due, as we saw, merely to the fact that there were five Arminian points for the Synod of Dort to answer) tends to obscure the organic character of Calvinistic thought on this subject. For the five points, though separately stated, are really inseparable. They hang together; you cannot reject one without rejecting them all, at least in the sense in which the Synod meant them. For of Calvinism there is really only *one* point to be made in the field of soteriology: the point that *God saves sinners*. *God*—the Triune Jehovah, Father, Son and Spirit; three Persons working together in sovereign wisdom, power and love to achieve the salvation of a chosen people, the Father electing, the Son fulfilling the Father's will by redeeming, the Spirit executing the purpose of Father and Son by renewing. *Saves*—does everything, first to last, that is involved in bringing man from death in sin to life in glory: plans, achieves and communicates redemption, calls and keeps, justifies, sanctifies, glorifies. *Sinners*—men as God finds them, guilty, vile, helpless, powerless, blind, unable to lift a finger to do God's will or better their spiritual lot. *God saves sinners*—and the force of this confession may not be weakened by disrupting the unity of the work of the Trinity, or by dividing the achievement of salvation between God and man and making the decisive part man's own, or by soft-pedalling the sinner's inability so as to allow him to share the praise of his salvation with his Saviour. This is the one point of Calvinistic soteriology which the 'five points' are concerned to establish and Arminianism in all its forms to deny: namely, that sinners do not save themselves in any sense at all, but that salvation, first and last, whole and entire, past, present and future, is of the Lord, to whom be glory for ever; amen!

This leads to our fourth remark, which is this: the five-point formula obscures the depth of the difference between Calvinistic and Arminian soteriology. There seems no doubt that it seriously misleads many here. In the formula, the stress falls on the adjectives, and this naturally gives the impression that in regard to the three great saving acts of God the debate concerns the adjectives merely—that both sides agree as to what election, redemption, and the gift of internal grace are, and differ only as to the position of man in relation to them: whether the first is conditional upon faith being foreseen or not; whether the second intends the salvation of every man or not; whether the third always proves invincible or not. But this is a complete misconception. The change of adjective in each case involves changing the meaning of the noun. An election that is conditional, a redemption that is universal, an internal grace that is resistible is not the same kind of election, redemption, internal grace that Calvinism asserts. The real issue concerns, not the appropriateness of adjectives, but the definition of nouns. Both sides saw this clearly when the controversy first began, and it is important that we should see it too, for otherwise we cannot discuss the Calvinist-Arminian debate to any purpose at all. It is worth setting out the different definitions side by side.

1. God's act of election was defined by the Arminians as a resolve to receive to sonship and glory a duly qualified class of people—believers in Christ.[3] This becomes a resolve to receive individual persons only in virtue of God's foreseeing the contingent fact that they will of their own accord believe. There is nothing in the decree of election to ensure that the class of believers will ever have any members; God does not determine to make any man believe. But Calvinists define election as a choice of particular undeserving persons to be saved from sin and brought to glory, and to that end to be redeemed by the death of Christ and given faith by the Spirit's effectual calling. Where the Arminian says, 'I owe my election to my faith', the Calvinist says, 'I owe my faith to my election.' Clearly, these two concepts of election are very far apart.

2. Christ's work of redemption was defined by the Arminians as the removing of an obstacle (the unsatisfied claims of justice) which stood in the way of God's offering pardon to sinners, as he desired to do, on condition that they believe. Redemption, according to Arminianism, secured for God a right to make this offer, but did not of itself ensure that anyone would ever accept it; for faith, being a work of man's own, is not a gift that comes to him from Calvary. Christ's death created an opportunity for the exercise of saving faith, but that is all it did. Calvinists, however, define redemption as Christ's substitutionary endurance of the penalty of sin in the place of certain specified sinners, through which God was reconciled to them, their liability to punishment was for ever destroyed, and a title to eternal life was secured for them. In consequence of this, they now have in God's sight a right to the gift of faith, as the means of entry into the enjoyment of their inheritance. Calvary, in other words, not merely made possible the salvation of those for whom Christ died; it ensured that they would be brought to faith and their salvation made actual. The cross *saves*. Where the Arminian will only say; 'I could not have gained my salvation without Calvary', the Calvinist will say, 'Christ gained my salvation for me at Calvary.' The former makes the cross the *sine qua non* of salvation, the latter sees it as the actual procuring cause of salvation, and traces the source of every spiritual blessing, faith included, back to the great transaction between God and his Son carried through on Calvary's hill. Clearly, these two concepts of redemption are quite at variance.

3. The Spirit's gift of internal grace was defined by the Arminians as 'moral suasion', the bare bestowal of an understanding of God's truth. This, they granted—indeed, insisted—does not of itself ensure that anyone will ever make the response of faith. But Calvinists define this gift as not merely an enlightening, but also a regenerating work of God in men, 'taking away their heart of stone, and giving unto them a heart of flesh; renew-

ing their wills, and by his almighty power determining them to that which is good; and effectually drawing them to Jesus Christ; yet so as they come most freely, being made willing by his grace.'[4] Grace proves irresistible just because it destroys the disposition to resist. Where the Arminian, therefore, will be content to say, 'I decided for Christ', 'I made up my mind to be a Christian,' the Calvinist will wish to speak of his conversion in more theological fashion, to make plain whose work it really was:

> Long my imprisoned spirit lay
>   Fast bound in sin and nature's night:
> Thine eye diffused a quickening ray;
>   I woke; the dungeon flamed with light;
> *My chains fell off: my heart was free:*
> I rose, went forth, and followed thee.[5]

Clearly, these two notions of internal grace are sharply opposed to each other.

Now, the Calvinist contends that the Arminian idea of election, redemption and calling as acts of God which do not save cuts at the very heart of their biblical meaning; that to say in the Arminian sense that God elects believers, and Christ died for all men, and the Spirit quickens those who receive the word, is really to say that in the biblical sense God elects nobody, and Christ died for nobody, and the Spirit quickens nobody. The matter at issue in this controversy, therefore, is the meaning to be given to these biblical terms, and to some others which are also soteriologically significant, such as the love of God, the covenant of grace, and the verb 'save' itself, with its synonyms. Arminians gloss them all in terms of the principle that salvation does not directly depend on any decree or act of God, but on man's independent activity in believing. Calvinists maintain that this principle is itself unscriptural and irreligious, and that such glossing demonstrably perverts the sense of Scripture and undermines the gospel at every point where it is practised. This, and nothing less than this, is what the Arminian controversy is about.

There is a fifth way in which the five-point formula is deficient. Its very form (a series of denials of Arminian assertions) lends colour to the impression that Calvinism is a modification of Arminianism; that Arminianism has a certain primacy in order of nature, and developed Calvinism is an offshoot from it. Even when one shows this to be false as a matter of history, the suspicion remains in many minds that it is a true account of the relation of the two views themselves. For it is widely supposed that Arminianism (which, as we now see, corresponds pretty closely to the new gospel of our own day) is the result of reading the Scriptures in a 'natural', unbiased, unsophisticated way, and that Calvinism is an unnatural growth, the product less of the texts themselves than of unhallowed logic working on the texts, wresting their plain sense and upsetting their balance by forcing them into a systematic framework which they do not themselves provide.

Whatever may have been true of individual Calvinists, as a generalisation about Calvinism nothing could be further from the truth than this. Certainly, Arminianism is 'natural' in one sense, in that it represents a characteristic perversion of biblical teaching by the fallen mind of man, who even in salvation cannot bear to renounce the delusion of being master of his fate and captain of his soul. This perversion appeared before in the Pelagianism and semi-Pelagianism of the patristic period and the later scholasticism, and has recurred since the seventeenth century both in Roman theology and, among Protestants, in various types of rationalistic liberalism and modern evangelical teaching; and no doubt it will always be with us. As long as the fallen human mind is what it is, the Arminian way of thinking will continue to be a natural type of mistake. But is is not natural in any other sense. In fact, it is Calvinism that understands the Scriptures in their natural, one would have thought inescapable, meaning; Calvinism that keeps to what they actually say; Calvinism that insists on taking seriously the biblical assertions that God saves, and that he saves those whom he has chosen to save, and that he saves them by grace without works, so that no man may boast, and that Christ is given to them as a perfect Saviour, and that their whole salvation flows to them from the cross, and that the work of redeeming them was finished on the cross. It is Calvinism that gives due honour to the cross. When the Calvinist sings,

> There is a green hill far away,
>   Without a city wall,
> Where the dear Lord was crucified,
>   *Who died to save us all;*
> *He died that we might be forgiven,*
>   He died to make us good;
> *That we might go at last to Heaven,*
>   Saved by His precious blood . . .

he means it. He will not gloss the italicised statements by saying that God's saving purpose in the death of his Son was a mere ineffectual wish, depending for its fulfilment on man's willingness to believe, so that for all God could do Christ might have died and none been saved at all. He insists that the Bible sees the cross as revealing God's power to save, not his impotence. Christ did not win a hypothetical salvation for hypothetical believers, a mere possibility of salvation for any who might possibly believe, but a real salvation for his own chosen people. His precious blood really does 'save us all'; the intended effects of his self-offering do in fact follow, just because the cross was what it was. Its saving power does not depend on faith being added to it; its saving power is such that faith flows from it. The cross secured the full salvation of all for whom Christ died. 'God forbid,' therefore, 'that I should glory, save in the cross of our Lord Jesus Christ.'[6]

Now the real nature of Calvinistic soteriology becomes plain. It is no artificial oddity, nor a product of over-bold logic. Its central confession, that *God saves sinners*, that *Christ redeemed us by his blood*, is the witness both of the Bible and of the believing heart. The Calvinist is the Christian who confesses before men in his theology just what he believes in his heart before God when he prays. He thinks and speaks at all times of the sovereign grace of God in the way that every Christian does when he pleads for the souls of others, or when he obeys the impulse of worship which rises unbidden within him, prompting him to deny himself all praise and to give all the glory of his salvation to his Saviour. Calvinism is the natural theology written on the heart of the new man in Christ, whereas Arminianism is an intellectual sin of infirmity, natural only in the sense in which all such sins are natural, even to the regenerate. Calvinistic thinking is the Christian being himself on the intellectual level; Arminian thinking is the Christian failing to be himself through the weakness of the flesh. Calvinism is what the Christian church has always held and taught when its mind has not been distracted by controversy and false traditions from attending to what Scripture actually says; that is the significance of the patristic testimonies to the teaching of the 'five points', which can be quoted in abundance. (Owen appends a few on redemption; a much larger collection may be seen in John Gill's *The Cause of God and Truth*.) So that really it is most misleading to call this soteriology 'Calvinism' at all, for it is not a peculiarity of John Calvin and the divines of Dort, but a part of the revealed truth of God and the catholic Christian faith. 'Calvinism' is one of the 'odious names' by which down the centuries prejudice has been raised against it. But the thing itself is the just the biblical gospel.[7]

3

In the light of these facts, we can now give a direct answer to the questions with which we began.

'Surely all that Owen is doing is defending limited atonement?' Not really. He is doing much more than that. Strictly speaking, the aim of Owen's book is not defensive at all, but constructive. It is a biblical and theological enquiry; its purpose is simply to make clear what Scripture actually teaches about the central subject of the gospel—the achievement of the Saviour. As its title proclaims, it is 'a treatise of the redemption and reconciliation that is in the blood of Christ: with the merit thereof, and the satisfaction wrought thereby.' The question which Owen, like the Dort divines before him, is really concerned to answer is just this: what is the gospel? All agree that it is a proclamation of Christ as Redeemer, but there is a dispute as to the nature and extent of his redeeming work. Well, what saith the Scripture? What aim and accomplishment does the Bible assign to the work of Christ? This is what Owen is concerned to elucidate. It is true that he tackles the subject in a directly controversial way, and shapes his book as a polemic against the 'spreading persuasion . . . of a *general ransom*, to be paid by Christ for all; that he dies to redeem *all and every one*'.[8] But his work is a systematic expository treatise, not a mere episodic wrangle. Owen treats the controversy as providing the occasion for a full display of the relevant biblical teaching in its own proper order and connection. As in Hooker's *Laws of Ecclesiastical Polity*, the polemics themselves are incidental and of secondary interest; their chief value lies in the way that the author uses them to further his own design and carry forward his own argument.

That argument is essentially very simple. Owen sees that the question which has occasioned his writing—the extent of the atonement—involves the further question of its nature, since if it was offered to save some who will finally perish, then it cannot have been a transaction securing the actual salvation for all for whom it was designed. But, says Owen, this is precisely the kind of transaction that the Bible says it was. The first two books of his treatise are a massive demonstration of the fact that according to Scripture the Redeemer's death actually saves his people, as it was meant to do. The third book consists of a series of sixteen arguments against the hypothesis of universal redemption, all aimed to show, on the one hand, that Scripture speaks of Christ's redeeming work as effective, which precludes its having been intended for any who perish, and, on the other, that if its intended extent had been universal, then *either* all will be saved (which Scripture denies, and the advocates of the 'general ransom' do not affirm), or *else* the Father and the Son have failed to do what they set out to do—'which to assert,' says Owen, 'seems to us blasphemously injurious to the wisdom, power and perfection of God, as likewise derogatory to the worth and value of the death of Christ.' Owen's arguments ring a series of changes on this dilemma.[9]

Finally, in the fourth book, Owen shows with great cogency that the three classes of texts alleged to prove that Christ died for persons who will not be saved (those saying that he died for 'the world', for 'all', and those thought to envisage the perishing of those for whom he died), cannot on sound principles of exegesis be held to teach any such thing; and, further, that the theological inferences by which universal redemption is supposed to be established are really quite fallacious. The true evangelical evaluation of the claim that Christ died for every man, even those who perish, comes through at point after point in Owen's book. So far from magnifying the love and grace of God, this claim dishonours both it and him, for it reduces God's love to an impotent wish and turns the whole economy of 'saving' grace, so-called ('saving' is really a misnomer on this view), into a monumental divine failure. Also, so far from magnifying the merit and worth of Christ's death, it cheapens it, for it makes Christ die in vain. Lastly, so far from affording faith additional encouragement, it destroys the scriptural ground of assurance altogether, for it denies that the knowledge that Christ died for me (or did or does anything else for me) is a sufficient ground for inferring my eternal salvation; my salvation, on this view, depends not on what Christ did for me, but on what I subsequently do for myself.

Thus, this view takes from God's love and Christ's redemption the glory that Scripture gives them, and introduces the anti-scriptural principle of self-salvation at the point where the Bible explicitly says 'not of works, lest any man should boast'.[10] You cannot have it both ways: an atonement of universal extent is a depreciated atonement. It has lost its saving power; it leaves us to save ourselves. The doctrine of the general ransom must accordingly be rejected, as Owen rejects it, as a grievous mistake. By contrast, however, the doctrine which Owen sets out, as he himself shows, is both biblical and God-honouring. It exalts Christ, for it teaches Christians to glory in his cross alone, and to draw their hope and assurance only from the death and intercession of their Saviour. It is, in other words, genuinely evangelical. It is, indeed, the gospel of God and the catholic faith.

It is safe to say that no comparable exposition of the work of redemption as planned and executed by the Triune Jehovah has ever been done since Owen published his. None has been needed. Discussing this work, Andrew Thomson notes how Owen 'makes you feel when he has reached the end of his subject, that he has also exhausted it'.[11] That is demonstrably the case here. His interpretation of the texts on the points of issue is sure; his power of theological construction is superb; nothing that needs discussing is omitted, and (so far as this writer can discover) no arguments for or against his position have been used since his day which he has not himself noted and dealt with. One searches his book in vain for the leaps and flights of logic by which Reformed theologians are supposed to establish their positions; all that one finds is solid, painstaking exegesis and a careful following through of biblical ways of thinking. Owen's work is a constructive, broad-based biblical analysis of the heart of the gospel, and must be taken seriously as such. It may not be written off as a piece of special pleading for a traditional shibboleth, for nobody has a right to dismiss the doctrine of the limitedness, or particularity, of atonement as a monstrosity of Calvinistic logic until he has refuted Owen's proof that it is part of the uniform biblical presentation of redemption, clearly taught in plain text after plain text. And nobody has done that yet.

4

'You talked about recovering the gospel,' said our questioner; 'don't you mean that you just want us all to become Calvinists?'

This question presumably concerns, not the word, but the thing. Whether we call ourselves Calvinists hardly matters; what matters is that we should understand the gospel biblically. But that, we think, does in fact mean understanding it as historic Calvinism does. The alternative is to mis-understand and distort it. We said earlier that modern evangelicalism, by and large, has ceased to preach the gospel in the old way, and we frankly admit that the new gospel, insofar as it deviates from the old, seems to us a distortion of the biblical message. And we can now see what has gone wrong. Out theological currency has been debased. Our minds have been conditioned to think of the cross as a redemption which does less than redeem, and of Christ as a Saviour who does less than save, and of God's love as a weak affection which cannot keep anyone from hell without help, and of faith as the human help which God needs for this purpose. As a result, we are no longer free either to believe the biblical gospel or to preach it. We cannot believe it, because our thoughts are caught in the toils of syn-ergism. We are haunted by the Arminian idea that if faith and unbelief are to be responsible acts, they must be independent acts; hence we are not free to believe that we are saved entirely by divine grace through a faith which is itself God's gift and flows to us from Calvary. Instead, we involve our-selves in a bewildering kind of double-think about salvation, telling our-selves one moment that it all depends on God and next moment that it all depends on us. The resultant mental muddle deprives God of much of the glory that we should give him as author and finisher of salvation, and our-selves of much of the comfort we might draw from knowing that God is for us.

And when we come to preach the gospel, our false preconceptions make us say just the opposite of what we intend. We want (rightly) to proclaim Christ as Saviour; yet we end up saying that Christ, having made salvation possible, has left us to become our own saviours. It comes about in this way. We want to magnify the saving grace of God and the saving power of Christ. So we declare that God's redeeming love extends to everyone, and that Christ has died to save everyone, and we proclaim that the glory of divine mercy is to be measured by these facts. And then, in order to avoid universalism, we have to depreciate all that we were previously extolling, and to explain that, after all, nothing that God and Christ have done can save us unless we add something to it; the decisive factor which actually saves us is our own believing. What we say comes to this—that Christ saves us with our help; and what that means, when one thinks it out, is this—that we save ourselves with Christ's help. This is a hollow anticlimax. But if we start by affirming that God has a saving love for all, and Christ died a saving death for all, and yet balk at becoming universalists, there is nothing else that we can say. And let us be clear on what we have done when we have put the matter in this fashion. We have not exalted grace and the cross; we have cheapened them. We have limited the atonement far more drastically than Calvinism does, for whereas Calvinism asserts that Christ's death, as such, saves all whom it was meant to save, we have denied that Christ's death, as such, is sufficient to save any of them.[12] We have flattered impenitent sinners by assuring them that it is in their power to repent and believe, though God cannot make them do it. Perhaps we have also trivialised faith and repentance in order to make this assurance plausible ('it's very simple—just open your heart to the Lord . . .'). Certainly, we have effectively denied God's sovereignty, and undermined the basic conviction of true religion—that man is always in God's hands. In truth, we have lost a great deal. And it is, perhaps, no wonder that our preaching begets so little reverence and humility, and that our professed converts are so self-confident and so deficient in self-knowledge and in the good works which Scripture regards as the fruit of true repentance.

It is from degenerate faith and preaching of this kind that Owen's book could set us free. It we listen to him, he will teach us both how to believe the Scripture gospel and how to preach it. For the first: he will lead us to bow down before a sovereign Saviour who really saves, and to praise him for a redeeming death which made it certain that all for whom he died will come to glory. It cannot be overemphasised that we have not seen the full meaning of the cross till we have seen it as the divines of Dort display it—as the centre of the gospel, flanked on the one hand by total inability and unconditional election, and on the other by irresistible grace and final preservation. For the full meaning of the cross only appears when the atonement is defined in terms of these four truths. Christ died to save a certain company of helpless sinners upon whom God had set his free saving love. Christ's death ensured the calling and keeping—the present and final salvation—of all whose sins he bore. That is what Calvary meant, and means. The cross *saved*; the cross *saves*. This is the heart of true evangelical faith; as Cowper sang:

> Dear dying Lamb, *Thy precious blood*
> *Shall never lose its power,*
> *Till all the ransomed church of God*
> *Be saved to sin no more.*

This is the triumphant conviction which underlay the old gospel, as it does the whole New Testament. And this is what Owen will teach us unequivocally to believe.

Then, second, Owen could set us free, if we would hear him, to preach the biblical gospel. This assertion may sound paradoxical, for it is often imagined that those who will not preach that Christ died to save every man are left with no gospel at all. On the contrary, however, what they are left with is just the gospel of the New Testament. What does it mean to preach 'the gospel of the grace of God'? Owen only touches on this briefly and incidentally,[13] but his comments are full of light. Preaching the gospel, he tells us, is not a matter of telling the congregation that God has set his love on each of them and Christ has died to save each of them, for these assertions, biblically understood, would imply that they will all infallibly be saved, and this cannot be known to be true. The knowledge of being the object of God's eternal love and Christ's redeeming death belongs to the individual's assurance,[14] which in the nature of the case cannot precede faith's saving exercise; it is to be inferred from the fact that one has believed, not proposed as a reason why one should believe. According to Scripture, preaching the gospel is entirely a matter of proclaiming to men, as truth from God which all are bound to believe and act on, the following four facts:

1. that all men are sinners, and cannot do anything to save themselves;

2. that Jesus Christ, God's Son, is a perfect Saviour for sinners, even the worst;

3. that the Father and the Son have promised that all who know themselves to be sinners and put faith in Christ as Saviour shall be received into favour, and none cast out—which promise is 'a certain infallible truth, grounded upon the superabundant sufficiency of the oblation of Christ in itself, for whomsoever (fewer or more) it be intended';[15]

4. that God has made repentance and faith a duty, requiring of every man who hears the gospel 'a serious full recumbency and rolling of the soul upon Christ in the promise of the gospel, as an all-sufficient Saviour, able to deliver and save to the utmost them that come to God by him; ready, able and willing, through the preciousness of his blood and sufficiency of his ransom, to save every soul that shall freely give up themselves unto him for that end.'[16]

The preacher's task, in other words, is to *display Christ*, to explain man's need of him, his sufficiency to save, and his offer of himself in the promises as Saviour to all who truly turn to him; and to show as fully and plainly as he can how these truths apply to the congregation before him. It is not for him to say, nor for his hearers to ask, for whom Christ died in particular. 'There is none called on by the gospel once to enquire after the purpose and intention of God concerning the particular object of the death of Christ, every one being fully assured that his death shall be profitable to them that believe in him and obey him.' After saving faith has been exercised, 'it lies on a believer to assure his soul, according as he find the fruit of the death of Christ in him and towards him, of the good-will and eternal love of God to him in sending his Son to die for him in particular';[17] but not before. The task to which the gospel calls him is simply to exercise faith, which he is both warranted and obliged to do by God's command and promise.

Some comments on this conception of what preaching the gospel means are in order.

First, we should observe that the old gospel of Owen contains no less full and free an offer of salvation than its modern counterpart. It presents ample grounds for faith (the sufficiency of Christ, and the promise of God), and cogent motives to faith (the sinner's need, and the Creator's command, which is also the Redeemer's invitation). The new gospel gains nothing here by asserting universal redemption. The old gospel, certainly, has no room for the cheap sentimentalising which turns God's free mercy to sinners into a constitutional softheartedness on his part which we can take for granted; nor will it countenance the degrading presentation of Christ as the baffled Saviour, balked in what he hoped to do by human unbelief; nor will it indulge in maudlin appeals to the unconverted to let Christ save them out of pity for his disappointment. The pitiable Saviour and the pathetic God of modern pulpits are unknown to the old gospel. The old gospel tells men that they need God, but not that God needs them (a modern falsehood); it does not exhort them to pity Christ, but announces that Christ has pitied them, though pity was the last thing they deserved. It never loses sight of the divine majesty and sovereign power of the Christ whom it proclaims, but rejects flatly all representations of him which would obscure his free omnipotence.

Does this mean, however, that the preacher of the old gospel is inhibited or confined in offering Christ to men and inviting them to receive him? Not at all. In actual fact, just because he recognises that divine mercy is sovereign and free, he is in a position to make far more of the offer of Christ in his preaching than is the expositor of the new gospel; for this offer is itself a far more wonderful thing on his principles than it can ever be in the eyes of those who regard love to all sinners as a necessity of God's nature, and therefore a matter of course. To think that the holy Creator, who never needed man for his happiness and might justly have banished our fallen race for ever without mercy, should actually have chosen to redeem some of them! And that his own Son was willing to undergo death and descend into hell to save them! And that now from his throne he should speak to ungodly men as he does in the words of the gospel, urging upon them the command to repent and believe in the form of a compassionate invitation to pity themselves and choose life! These thoughts are the focal points round which the preaching of the old gospel revolves. It is all wonderful, just because none of it can be taken for granted.

But perhaps that most wonderful thing of all—the holiest spot in all the holy ground of gospel truth—is the free invitation which 'the Lord Christ' (as Owen loves to call him) issues repeatedly to guilty sinners to come to him and find rest for their souls. It is the glory of these invitations that it is an omnipotent King who gives them, just as it is a chief part of the glory of the enthroned Christ that he condescends still to utter them. And it is the glory of the gospel ministry that the preacher goes to men as Christ's ambassador, charged to deliver the King's invitation personally to every sinner present and to summon them all to turn and live. Owen himself enlarges on this in a passage addressed to the unconverted.

> Consider the infinite condescension and love of Christ, in his invitations and calls of you to come unto him for life, deliverance, mercy, grace, peace and eternal salvation. Multitudes of these invitations and calls are recorded in the Scripture, and they are all of them filled up with those blessed encouragements which divine wisdom knows to be suited unto lost, convinced sinners. . . . In the declaration and preaching of them, Jesus Christ yet stands before sinners, calling, inviting, encouraging them to come unto him.
>
> This is somewhat of the word which he now speaks unto you: Why will ye die? why will ye perish? why will ye not have compassion on your own souls? Can your hearts endure, or can your hands be strong, in the day of wrath that is approaching. . . . Look unto me, and be saved; come unto me, and I will ease you of all sins, sorrows, fears, burdens, and give rest unto your souls. Come, I entreat you; lay aside all procrastinations, all delays, put me off no more; eternity lies at the door . . . do not so hate me as that you will rather perish than accept of deliverance by me.
>
> These and the like things doth the Lord Christ continually declare, proclaim, plead and urge upon the souls of sinners. . . . He doth it in the preaching of the word, as if he were present with you, stood amongst you, and spake personally to every one of you. . . . He hath appointed the ministers of the gospel to appear before you, and to deal with you in his stead, avowing as his own the invitations which are given you in his name (2 Cor 1:19, 20).[18]

These invitations are *universal*; Christ addresses them to sinners, as such, and every man, as he believes God to be true, is bound to treat them as God's words to him personally and to accept the universal assurance which accompanies them, that all who come to Christ will be received. Again, these invitations are *real*; Christ genuinely offers himself to all who hear the gospel, and is in truth a perfect Saviour to all who trust him. The question of the extent of the atonement does not arise in evangelistic preaching; the message to be delivered is simply this—that Christ Jesus, the sovereign Lord, who died for sinners, now invites sinners freely to himself. God commands all to repent and believe; Christ promises life and peace to all who do so. Futhermore, these invitations are *marvellously gracious*; men despise and reject them, and are never in any case worthy of them, and yet Christ still issues them. He need not, but he does. 'Come unto me

... and I will give you rest' remains his word to the world, never cancelled, always to be preached. He whose death has ensured the salvation of all his people is to be proclaimed everywhere as a perfect Saviour, and all men invited and urged to believe on him, whoever they are, whatever they have been. Upon these three insights the evangelism of the old gospel is based.

It is a very ill-informed supposition that evangelistic preaching which proceeds on these principles must be anaemic and half-hearted by comparison with what Arminians can do. Those who study the printed sermons of worthy expositors of the old gospel, such as Bunyan (whose preaching Owen himself much admired), or Whitefield, or Spurgeon, will find that in fact they hold forth the Saviour and summon sinners to him with a fullness, warmth, intensity and moving force unmatched in Protestant pulpit literature. And it will be found on analysis that the very thing which gave their preaching its unique power to overwhelm their audiences with broken-hearted joy at the riches of God's grace—and still gives it that power, let it be said, even with hard-boiled modern readers—was their insistence on the fact that grace is *free*. They knew that the dimensions of divine love are not half understood till one realises that God need not have chosen to save nor given his Son to die; nor need Christ have taken upon him vicarious damnation to redeem men, nor need he invite sinners indiscriminately to himself as he does; but that all God's gracious dealings spring entirely from his own free purpose. Knowing this, they stressed it, and it is this stress that sets their evangelistic preaching in a class by itself.

Other evangelicals, possessed of a more superficial and less adequate theology of grace, have laid the main emphasis in their gospel preaching on the sinner's need of forgiveness, or peace, or power, and on the way to get them by 'deciding for Christ'. It is not to be denied that their preaching has done good (for God will use his truth, even when imperfectly held and mixed with error), although this type of evangelism is always open to the criticism of being too man-centred and pietistic; but it has been left (necessarily) to Calvinists and those who, like the Wesleys, fall into Calvinistic ways of thought as soon as they begin a sermon to the unconverted, to preach the gospel in a way which highlights above everything else the free love, willing condescension, patient long-suffering and infinite kindness of the Lord Jesus Christ. And, without doubt, this is the most Scriptural and edifying way to preach it; for gospel invitations to sinners never honour God and exalt Christ more, nor are more powerful to awaken and confirm faith, than when full weight is laid on the free omnipotence of the mercy from which they flow. It looks, indeed, as if the preachers of the old gospel are the only people whose position allows them to do justice to the revelation of divine goodness in the free offer of Christ to sinners.

Then, in the second place, the old gospel safeguards values which the new gospel loses. We saw before that the new gospel, by asserting universal redemption and a universal divine saving purpose, compels itself to cheapen grace and the cross by denying that the Father and the Son are sovereign in salvation; for it assures us that, after God and Christ have done all that they can, or will, it depends finally on each man's own choice whether God's purpose to save him is realised or not.

This position has two unhappy results. The first is that it compels us to misunderstand the significance of the gracious invitations of Christ in the gospel of which we have been speaking; for we now have to read them, not as expressions of the tender patience of a mighty Sovereign, but as the pathetic pleadings of impotent desire; and so the enthroned Lord is suddenly metamorphosed into a weak, futile figure tapping forlornly at the door of the human heart, which he is powerless to open. This is a shameful dishonour to the Christ of the New Testament. The second implication is equally serious: for this view in effect denies our dependence on God when it comes to vital decisions, takes us out of his hand, tells us that we are, after all, what sin taught us to think we were—masters of our fate, captain of our souls—and so undermines the very foundation of man's religious relationship with his Maker. It can hardly be wondered at that the converts of the new gospel are so often both irreverent and irreligious, for such is the natural tendency of this teaching.

The old gospel, however, speaks very differently and has a very different tendency. On the one hand, in expounding man's need of Christ, it stresses something which the new gospel effectively ignores—that sinners cannot obey the gospel, any more than the law, without renewal of heart. On the other hand, in declaring Christ's power to save, it proclaims him as the Author and Chief Agent of conversion, coming by his Spirit as the gospel goes forth to renew men's hearts and draw them to himself. Accordingly, in applying the message, the old gospel, while stressing that faith is man's duty, stresses also that faith is not in man's power, but that God must give what he commands. It announces, not merely that men *must* come to Christ for salvation, but also that they *cannot* come unless Christ himself draws them. Thus it labours to overthrow self-confidence, to convince sinners that their salvation is altogether out of their hands, and to shut them up to a self-despairing dependence on the glorious grace of a sovereign Saviour, not only for their righteousness but for their faith too.

It is not likely, therefore, that a preacher of the old gospel will be happy to express the application of it in the form of a demand to 'decide for Christ', as the current phrase is. For, on the one hand, this phrase carries the wrong associations. It suggests voting a person into office—an act in which the candidate plays no part beyond offering himself for election, everything then being settled by the voter's independent choice. But we do not vote God's Son into office as our Saviour, nor does he remain passive while preachers campaign on his behalf, whipping up support for his cause. We ought not to think of evangelism as a kind of electioneering. And then, on the other hand, this phrase obscures the very thing that is essential in repentance and faith—the denying of self in a personal approach to Christ. It is not at all obvious that deciding *for* Christ is the same as coming *to* him and resting *on* him and turning *from* sin and self-effort; it sounds like something much less, and is accordingly likely to instill defective notions of what the gospel really requires of sinners. It is not a very apt phrase from any point of view.

To the question; 'What must I do to be saved?', the old gospel replies: believe on the Lord Jesus Christ. To the further question; 'What does it mean to believe on the Lord Jesus Christ?', its reply is: it means knowing oneself to be a sinner, and Christ to have died for sinners; abandoning all self-righteousness and self-confidence, and casting oneself wholly upon him for pardon and peace; and exchanging one's natural enmity and rebellion against God for a spirit of grateful submission to the will of Christ through the renewing of one's heart by the Holy Ghost. And to the further question still, 'How am I to go about believing on Christ and repenting, if I have no natural ability to do these things?', it answers: look to Christ, speak to Christ, cry to Christ, just as you are; confess your sin, your impenitence, your unbelief, and cast yourself on his mercy; ask him to give you a new heart, working in you true repentance and firm faith; ask him to take away your evil heart of unbelief and to write his law within you, that you may never henceforth stray from him. Turn to him and trust him as best you can, and pray for grace to turn and trust more thoroughly; use the means of grace expectantly, looking to Christ to draw near to you as you seek to draw near to him; watch, pray, and read and hear God's word, worship and commune with God's people, and so continue till you know in yourself beyond doubt that you are indeed a changed being, a penitent believer, and the new heart which you desired has been put within you. The emphasis in this advice is on the need to call upon Christ directly, as the very first step.

> Let not conscience make you linger,
>   Nor of fitness fondly dream;
> All the fitness He requireth
>   Is to feel your need of Him—

So do not postpone action till you think you are better, but honestly confess your badness and give yourself up here and now to the Christ who alone can make you better; and wait on him till his light rises in your soul, as Scripture promises that it shall do. Anything less than this direct dealing with Christ is disobeying the gospel. Such is the exercise of spirit to which the old evangel summons its hearers. 'I believe—help thou mine unbelief': this must become their cry.

And the old gospel is proclaimed in the sure confidence that the Christ of whom it testified, the Christ who is the real speaker when the Scriptural invitations to trust him are expounded and applied, is not passively waiting for man's decision as the word goes forth, but is omnipotently active, working with and through the word to bring his people to faith in himself. The preaching of the new gospel is often described as the task of 'bringing men to Christ'—as if only men move, while Christ stands still. But the task of preaching the old gospel could more properly be described as bringing Christ to men, for those who preach it know that as they do their work of setting Christ before men's eyes, the mighty Saviour whom they proclaim is busy doing his work through their words, visiting sinners with salvation, awakening them to faith, drawing them in mercy to himself.

It is the older gospel which Owen will teach us to preach: the gospel of the sovereign grace of God in Christ as the Author and Finisher of faith and salvation. It is the only gospel which can be preached on Owen's principles, but those who have tasted its sweetness will not in any case be found looking for another. In the matter of believing and preaching the gospel, as in other things, Jeremiah's words still have their application: 'Thus saith the Lord, Stand ye in the ways, and see, and ask for the old paths, where is the good way, and walk therein, and ye shall find rest for your souls.'[19] To find ourselves debarred, as Owen would debar us, from taking up with the fashionable modern substitute gospel may not, after all, be a bad thing, either for us or for the church.

More might be said, but to go further would be to exceed the limits of an introduction. The foregoing remarks are made simply to show how important it is at the present time that we should attend most carefully to Owen's analysis of what the Bible says about the saving work of Christ.

5

It only remains to add a few remarks about this treatise itself. It was Owen's second major work, and his first masterpiece. (Its predecessor, *A Display of Arminianism*, published in 1642, when Owen was twenty-six, was a competent piece of prentice-work, rather of the nature of a research thesis.)

The Death of Death is a solid book, made up of detailed exposition and close argument, and requires hard study, as Owen fully realised; a cursory glance will not yield much. ('Reader . . . If thou are, as many in this pretending age, a *sign or title gazer*, and comest into books as Cato into the theatre, to go out again—thou has had thy entertainment; farewell!'[20]) Owen felt, however, that he had a right to ask for hard study, for his book was a product of hard work ('a more than seven-years' serious inquiry . . . into the mind of God about these things, with a serious perusal of all which I could attain that the wit of man, in former or latter days, hath published in opposition to the truth'[21]), and he was sure in his own mind that a certain finality attached to what he had written. ('Altogether hopeless of success I am not; but fully resolved that I shall not live to see a solid answer given unto it.'[22]) Time has justified his optimism.[23]

Something should be said about his opponents. He is writing against three variations on the theme of universal redemption: that of classical Arminianism, noted earlier; that of the theological faculty at Saumur (the position known as Amyraldism, after its leader exponent); and that of Thomas More, a lay theologian of East Anglia. The second of these views originated with a Scots professor at Saumur, John Cameron; it was taken up and developed by two of his pupils, Amyraut (Amyraldus) and Testard, and became the occasion of a prolonged controversy in which Amyraut, Daillé and Blondel were opposed by Rivet, Spanheim and Des Marets (Maresius). The Saumur position won some support among Reformed divines in Britain, being held in modified form by (among others) Bishops Usher and Davenant, and Richard Baxter. None of these, however, had advocated it in print at the time when Owen wrote.[24]

Goold's summary of the Saumur position may be quoted.

> Admitting that, by the purpose of God, and through the death of Christ, the elect are infallibly secured in the enjoyment of salvation, they contended for an antecedent decree, by which God is free to give salvation to all men through Christ, on the *condition* that they believe on him. Hence their system was termed *hypothetic(al) universalism*. The vital difference between it and the strict Arminian theory lies in the absolute security asserted in the former for the spiritual recovery of the elect. They agree, however, in attributing some kind of universality to the atonement, and in maintaining that, on certain *condition*, within the reach of fulfilment by all men . . . all men have access to the benefits of Christ's death.

From this, Goold continues:

> the readers of Owen will understand . . . why he dwells with peculiar keenness and reiteration of statement upon a refutation of the conditional system. . . . It was plausible; it had many learned men for its advocates; it had obtained currency in the foreign churches; and it seems to have been embraced by More.[25]

More is described by Thomas Edwards as 'a great Sectary, that did much hurt in Lincolnshire, Norfolk, and Cambridgeshire; who was famous also in Boston, [King's] Lynn, and even in Holland, and was followed from place to place by many.'[26] Baxter's description is kinder: 'a Weaver of *Wisbitch* and *Lyn*, of excellent Parts.'[27] (More's doctrine of redemption, of course, was substantially Baxter's own.) Owen, however, has a poor view of his abilities, and makes no secret of the fact.

More's book, *The Universality of God's Free Grace in Christ to Mankind*, appeared in 1646 (not, as Goold says, 1643), and must have exercised a considerable influence, for within three years it had evoked four weighty works which were in whole or part polemics against it: *A Refutation . . . of Thomas More*, by Thomas Whitfield, 1646; *Vindiciae Redemptionis*, by John Stalham, 1647; *The Universalist Examined and Convicted*, by Obadiah Howe, 1648; and Owen's own book, published in the same year.

More's exposition seems to be of little intrinsic importance; Owen, however, selects it as the fullest statement of the case for universal redemption that had yet appeared in English and uses it unmercifully as a chopping-block. The modern reader, however, will probably find it convenient to skip the sections devoted to refuting More (I:viii, the closing pages of I:iii and IV:vi) on his first passage through Owen's treatise.

Finally, a word about the style of this work. There is no denying that Owen is heavy and hard to read. This is not so much due to obscure arrangement as to two other factors. The first is his lumbering literary gait. 'Owen travels through it [his subject] with the elephant's grace and solid step, if sometimes also with his ungainly motion,' says Thomson.[28] That puts it kindly. Much of Owen's prose reads like a roughly-dashed-off translation of a piece of thinking done in Ciceronian Latin. It has, no doubt, a certain clumsy dignity; so has Stonehenge; but it is trying to the reader to have to go over sentences two or three times to see their meaning, and this necessity makes it much harder to follow an argument. The present writer, however, has found that the hard places in Owen usually come out as soon as one reads them aloud. The second obscuring factor is Owen's austerity as an expositor. He has a lordly disdain for broad introductions which ease the mind gently into a subject, and for comprehensive summaries which gather up scattered points into a small space. He obviously carries the whole of his design in his head, and expects his readers to do the same. Nor are his chapter divisions reliable pointers to the structure of his discourse, for though a change of subject is usually marked by a chapter division, Owen often starts a new chapter where there is no break in the thought at all. Nor is he concerned about literary proportions; the space given to a topic is determined by it intrinsic complexity rather than its relative importance, and the reader is left to work out what is basic and what is secondary by noting how things link together. Anyone who seriously tackles *The Death of Death* will probably find it helpful to use a pencil and paper in his study of the book and jot down the progress of the exposition.

We would conclude by repeating that the reward to be reaped from studying Owen is worth all the labour involved, and by making the following observations for the student's guidance. (1) It is important to start with the epistle 'To the Reader', for there Owen indicates in short compass what he is trying to do, and why. (2) It is important to read the treatise as a whole, in the order in which it stands, and not to jump into Parts III and IV before mastering the contents of Parts I and II, where the biblical foundations of Owen's whole position are laid. (3) It is hardly possible to grasp the strength and cogency of this massive statement on a first reading. The work must be read and reread to be appreciated.

CHAPTER NINE

The Doctrine of Justification in Development and Decline Among the Puritans

1

'The *confession* of divine justification touches man's life at its heart, at the point of its relationship to God; it defines the preaching of the Church, the existence and progress of the life of faith, the root of human security, and man's perspective for the future.'

So Professor G.C. Berkouwer[1] evaluates justification as set forth by Paul and reapprehended at the Reformation: a truth which all the reforming leaders in Germany, Switzerland, France, and Britain, and all the confessions which they sponsored, were at one in highlighting, and which they all saw as *articulus stantis vel cadentis ecclesiae*—the point on which depends the standing or falling of the church.

Luther, the pioneer, predicted, as a sure inference from what he knew of satanic strategy, that after his death this truth of present justification by faith only which he had been so instrumental in making known would come under stronger attack, and theology would develop in a way tending to submerge it once more in error and incomprehension. We find Puritan writers voicing a similar sense that the doctrine was very vulnerable, and only grace could keep it from being lost. It is worth setting out their reasons for thinking this.

First, they said, justification is a *gospel mystery*—a matter, that is, of divine revelation by grace. As such, it is doubly humbling. It humbles pride of intellect, because it could never have been guessed or worked out by unaided religious reason, and it humbles moral pride by assuming that all men are hopeless and helpless in sin. Naturally, people resent this, and, as Robert Traill said with abiding truth in his masterly *Vindication of the Protestant Doctrine concerning Justification* (1692), 'this enmity in men to the wisdom of God, is . . . a temptation to many ministers to patch up and frame a gospel that is more suited to, and taking with, and more easily understood by such men, than the true gospel of Christ is.'[2] The mystery of justification is thus threatened constantly by *human pride*.

Second, justification is a *climactic mystery*, like the top rung of a ladder which you reach via the other rungs, or the keystone of an arch supporting, and supported by, the bricks that flank it. Wrote Traill:

> All the great fundamentals of Christian truth, centre in this of justification. The trinity of persons in the God-head; the incarnation of the only begotten of the Father; the satisfaction paid to the law and justice of God, for the sins of the world, by His obedience, and sacrifice of Himself in that flesh He assumed; and the divine authority of the scriptures, which reveal all this, are all straight lines of truth, that centre in this doctrine of the justification of a sinner by the imputation and application of that satisfaction.[3]

Traill's point, in context, is that to deny justification is to deny these other realities too;[4] but the contrary point, that to query them is to lose justification also, is no less true. This has happened in our own day: misbelief about biblical authority, God's wrath, and the atonement has removed for many all basis for asserting justification in the biblical sense. Thus *heretical theology* becomes a second threat to the mystery of justification.

Third, justification is a *spiritual mystery*, which only the enlightened conscience of the man convicted of sin can appreciate. 'The theme of justification hath suffered greatly by this,' complains Traill, 'that many have employed their hands and pens, who never had their hearts and consciences exercised about it.'[5] In the preface to his classic work, *The Doctrine of Justification by Faith* (1677), John Owen, as indeed we have already seen, lays down the positive point thus:

> It is the practical direction of the consciences of men, in their application unto God by Jesus Christ, for deliverance from the curse due unto the apostate state, and peace with Him, with the influence of the way thereof unto universal gospel obedience, that is alone to be designed in the handling of this doctrine. And therefore, unto him that would treat of it in a due manner, it is required that he weigh every thing he asserts in his own mind and experience, and not dare to propose that unto others which he doth not abide by himself, in the most intimate recesses of his mind, under his nearest

approaches unto God, in his surprisals with dangers, in deep afflictions, in his preparations for death, and most humble contemplations of the infinite distance between God and him. Other notions . . . not seasoned with these ingredients . . . are insipid and useless. . . .[6]

The 'light, frothy, trifling temper' of the 1690s seemed to Traill a major hindrance to right thinking about justification. (What would he have said had he lived in our day?) *Spiritual frivolity*, lacking seriousness and experience in approaching God, thus threatens the mystery of justification from a third angle.

Fourth, justification is a *life-giving mystery*, the source of all true peace of conscience, hope, love, joy, holiness, and assurance. Therefore the Puritans, like Luther, saw *satanic hostility* as a fourth threat to the mystery of justification; for they knew that the adversary of God and God's people must wish to suppress a truth so productive of glory to God and good to men.

Fifth, justification is a *contradicted mystery*. Justification by works is the natural religion of mankind, and has been since the Fall, so that, as Traill says, 'all the ignorant people that know nothing of either law or gospel', 'all proud secure sinners', 'all formalists' and 'all the zealous devout people in a natural religion' line up together as 'utter enemies to the gospel'.[7] The Puritans saw that trio of theological relatives, Pelagianism, Arminianism, and Counter-reformation Romanism, as the bastard offspring of natural religion fertilised by the gospel. So (to take one for many) Traill writes: 'The principles of Arminianism are the natural dictates of a carnal mind, which is enmity both to the law of God, and to the gospel of Christ; and, next to the dead sea of Popery (into which also this stream runs), have, since Pelagius to this day, been the greatest plague of the Church of Christ. . . .' Again, 'There is not a minister that dealeth seriously with the souls of men, but he finds an Arminian scheme of justification in every unrenewed heart.'[8] *Natural religion* is thus a fifth threat to the mystery of justification.

My personal agreement with the Puritans in all this will be clear from the way I have put their position. Many moderns discuss Paul's emphatic assertion in Romans, Galatians, and elsewhere of justification through faith in Christ apart from works of law as merely an anti-Jewish controversial ploy, quite distant from the heart of his own positive theology and spirituality. I reject this view as a grievous and killing error, and explain its prevalence today in terms of the the five threats just listed. I believe that in equating the Reformation doctrine of justification with that of the New Testament, and in their analysis of the dangers and conflicts to which it stood exposed, the Puritans were profoundly right, and it is from this standpoint that I shall now attempt to trace out ways in which the Reformation doctrine both developed and declined in the Puritan period—that is, for our purposes, from the last quarter of the sixteenth century (the age of Perkins) to the end of the seventeenth (the last publications of Owen, Baxter, Goodwin, and others of their generation). The developments, as we should expect, come from circles where the fires of spiritual vitality burned bright; the decline took place under influences which were rationalistic, naturalistic, and in the long run hostile to evangelical piety, though claiming to operate in its interest. We take the developments first.

2

Luther's account of justification was never coolly analytical; in the lecture-room he was no less proclamatory and passionate on this theme than he was in the pulpit and in his publications, as his commentaries (actually, class lectures) on Roman, Galatians, Hebrews and the Psalms abundantly show. His concern was always to set forth the fact that the living God justifies sinners through the cross as the heart of the gospel, and he expounded justification as God's merciful answer to man's desperate question, 'How may I find a gracious God? What must I do to be saved?' Puritans, standing in the mainstream of second- and third-generation Reformed theology, took over Luther's emphasis and added to it a further interest, namely a concern to grasp accurately the place and work and glory of the Lord Jesus Christ in our salvation. If Luther's concern was *evangelical* and a function of preaching, this further concern was *doxological* and a function of worship. (Both concerns, of course, derive directly from the New Testament, and they are complementary, not contradictory.)

The Reformers' exposition of justification boiled down to the following seven points.

1. Every man faces the judgement seat of God, and must answer to God for himself. The church cannot shield him from this.

2. Every man is a sinner by nature and practice, a nonconformist so far as God's law is concerned, and therefore can only expect God's wrath and rejection.

3. Justification is God's judicial act of pardoning the guilty sinner, accepting him as righteous, and receiving him as a son.

4. The source of justification is grace, not human effort or initiative.

5. The ground of justification is Christ's vicarious righteousness and blood-shedding, not our own merit.

6. The means of justification, here and now, is faith in Jesus Christ.

7. The fruit of faith, the evidence of its reality, is a manifested repentance and a life of good works.

The occasion of the later Reformed development was controversy with Romanism and Arminianism. This prompted closer reflection on the nature of the saving union between Christ and Christians, and led to development of thought on three matters, thus:

First, *the ground of justification*. The Council of Trent had defined justification as inner renewal plus pardon and acceptance, the renewal being the basis of the pardon, and had gone on to affirm that the 'sole formal cause' (*unica formalis causa*) of justification, in both its aspects, was God's righteousness (*iustitia*) imparted through baptism as the instrumental cause.[9] 'Formal cause', in the language of the schools, denoted that which gave a thing its quality (thus, heat was the formal cause of a thing being hot, or having the quality of hotness). The thesis therefore was that the ground of our being pardoned was the quality of actual divine righteousness infused into us: God declares us righteous, and not liable to punishment for our sins, because we have been made genuinely righteous in ourselves. In the more biblical terminology of Protestantism, this was to make regeneration, or the commencement of sanctification, the ground of justification. In reply, a host of Reformed divines, continental and British, episcopal and nonconformist,[10] drew out at length the position already made explicit by Calvin,[11] that the 'sole formal cause' of justification is not *God's* righteousness *imparted*, but *Christ's* righteousness *imputed*; and to make their meaning more clear they drew a distinction between Christ's *active* obedience to God's law, in keeping its precepts, and his *passive* obedience to it, in undergoing its penalty, and insisted that our acceptance as righteous depends on the imputing to us of Christ's obedience in both its aspects. The same point was pressed against the Arminians, who held that faith is 'counted for righteousness' because it is in itself actual personal righteousness, being obedience to the gospel viewed as God's new law. The argument against both Romans and Arminians was that by finding the ground of justification in the believer himself they ministered to human pride on the one hand, and on the other hand robbed the Son of God of the glory which was his due. It is not enough, the Reformed writers held, to say that without Christ our justification would be impossible; one must go on to say that it is on the ground of his obedience, as our representative and substitutionary sin-bearer, and that alone, that righteousness is reckoned to us, and sin cancelled.

Though the phrase 'formal cause', and the distinction between active and passive obedience, do not appear in the statement on justification in the *Westminster Confession*, nonetheless this statement is a classic expression of the precision and balance of thought, as well as the polemical thrusts, that were learned in these exchanges. Says the *Confession*:

Those whom God effectually calleth He also freely justifieth; not by infusing righteousness into them, but by pardoning their sins, and by accounting and accepting their persons as righteous; not for anything wrought in them, or done by them, but for Christ's sake alone; not by imputing faith itself, the act of believing, or any other evangelical obedience, to them as their righteousness; but by imputing the obedience and satisfaction of Christ unto them, they receiving and resting on Him and His righteousness by faith; which faith they have not of themselves; it is the gift of God (XI:i).

Second, *regeneration and justification*. Roman theologians attacked the Reformers from the first on the grounds that in denying inner renewal and subjective righteousness to be any part of justification they were affirming that justification can exist without regeneration and faith without good works. Roman thinking on the latter point was evidently ruled by the typical legalist assumption that if good works do not bring salvation, but salvation is given freely without them, then no reason for doing them remains. The Reformers' reply, that it is the nature of biblical faith, which is a gift of the Holy Spirit, to be active in good works all the time, made little impact: theological understanding, and spiritual perception of the Holy Spirit's work in the believer, were alike lacking on the Roman side. The Puritans found themselves facing this same Roman polemic, and with it the Arminian thesis that justifying faith is, in the last analysis, not only man's act but also his work, an independent achievement of which prevenient grace, though the necessary precondition, is not the effective source. On this basis, of course, no divine guarantee that faith will work by love can exist. Thus the Arminians appeared to Reformed thinkers to be playing into Rome's hands at this point: Rome complained that justification according to Protestants was divorced from subjective renewal, and Arminianism admitted that faith might fail to produce good works every time.

The Puritans' response to this situation was twofold. First, they reaffirmed the Reformers' point, that 'faith . . . the alone instrument of justification . . . is . . . not alone in the person justified, but is ever accompanied with all other saving graces, and is no dead faith, but worketh by love' (*Westminster Confession*, XI:ii). Second they emphasised that justifying faith is given by God through *effectual calling*, which includes *regeneration*—that is, vitalising union with the risen Christ through the sovereign work of the Spirit, from which, as a work of new creation, flows the sinner's response to the gospel. (Rightly did George Smeaton describe Puritan divinity as 'a theology of regeneration cultivated and expanded as a topic in itself', a theology of which 'it was the prominent peculiarity to bring out the distinction between nature and grace'.[12]) This emphasis both answered the Romans, by showing that though justification and regeneration are distinct the former cannot take place without the latter, and dealt with the Arminians, by showing how completely man's faith is God's gift.[13]

Third, *the covenant context of justification*. The Puritans developed what has been called 'covenant theology'; they saw this as the scriptural setting in which the jewel of justification by faith should be exhibited. They defined the gospel as declaring:

the Covenant of grace: whereby [God] freely offereth unto sinners life and salvation by Jesus Christ, requiring of them faith in him, that they may be saved; and promising to give unto all those that are ordained unto life his Holy Spirit, to make them willing and able to believe (*Westminster Confession*, VII:iii).

They valued this covenant concept, first, because it links God's promise to save believers with his purpose to bring his elect to faith; second, because it gives justification its place in the 'golden chain' of stages in God's saving purpose (election, redemption, and effectual calling going before; sanctification and glorification coming after); third, because it brings into sharp focus the saving ministry of Christ, as Mediator and Federal Head of his people. The *Westminster Confession* embodies Puritan covenant theology in its classical form. Its biblical correctness is something which the student of the Scripture proofs adduced by the *Confession* may safely be left to estimate for himself.

The final element in the Puritan development of the doctrine of justification was to safeguard it against mis-statement within the Puritan camp. Chapter XI of the *Westminster Confession* wards off two such aberrations. The first is that justification is from eternity, i.e., *before* faith. William Twisse, first prolocutor of the Assembly, had maintained this as part of his case against Arminianism, but in addition to being unscriptural the idea is pastorally disastrous, for it reduced justifying faith to discovering that one is justified already, and so sets seekers waiting on God for assurance instead of exerting active trust in Christ. The trouble here was the assimilating of justification to election, and the *Confession* deals with it by drawing the correct distinction; 'God did, from all eternity, decree to justify all the elect . . . nevertheless they are not justified until the Holy Spirit doth in due time actually apply Christ unto them' (XI:iv).

The second misconception was that God takes no notice of the sins of the justified. This was the position called 'Antinomian' by the orthodox, which created a major stir in the 1640s.[14] In their zeal to magnify the liberty, peace, and joy of the man in Christ, the Antinomians (none of whom were front-rank theologians) had largely lost sight of two distinctions: that between God's law as a covenant of works and as a rule of life, and that between justification and adoption, or God's relationship to believers as Judge and as Father. Hence their failure to see, and say, with adequate clarity that the moral law still binds believers, as expressing God's will for his adopted children, and that the Father-son relationship between him and them will be spoiled if his will is ignored or defied. The *Confession* says what is necessary:

God doth continue to forgive the sins of those that are justified: and although they can never fall from the state of justification, yet they may by their sins fall under God's fatherly displeasure, and not have the light of His countenance restored unto them, until they humble themselves, confess their sins, beg pardon, and renew their faith and repentance (XI:v).

3

Now we turn to the sadder side of the picture, and trace out those influences which distorted the doctrine of justification in England, and progressively robbed it of its proper influence, even among the Puritans themselves. This part of our story deals with two movements: Arminianism, and the Neonomianism (so called) of Richard Baxter.

Arminianism, as broached by Jacob Hermandzoon (Arminius) at the turn of the sixteenth century, formulated in the Remonstrance of 1610, and taught by Episcopius, Curcellaeus, and Limborch at the Remonstrant Seminary in Amsterdam, was essentially a denial of some basic Reformed assertions.

The first denial relevant to our theme was that already noticed, namely that man's act of faith is wholly God's gift.

The second relevant denial was that there is a direct correlation in God's plan between the obtaining of redemption by Christ's obedience, active and passive, and the saving application of redemption by the Holy Spirit—direct, that is, in the sense that the former secures and guarantees the latter. The Arminian alternative was that the atonement made salvation possible for all but not necessarily actual for any. This involved abandoning the concept of the atonement as *substitutionary*, for substitution is, by its very nature, an effective relationship, securing actual immunity from obligation for the person in whose place the substitute acts.

> Payment God cannot twice demand—
> First at my bleeding Surety's hand,
> And then again at mine.[15]

Grotius' famous, or infamous, theory of the atonement as an *example* of punishment was one of several ways in which the Arminian conception was spelled out.

The third relevant denial was that the covenant of grace is a relationship which God imposes unilaterally and unconditionally, by effectual calling, saying to his elect, 'I will . . . and you shall . . .' The Arminian alternative was that the covenant of grace is a new law, offering present pardon on condition of present faith and final salvation on condition of sustained faith.

The fourth relevant denial was that faith is essentially *fiducial* (a matter of trusting another, and what he has done). The Arminian alternative was that faith is essentially *volitional* (a matter of committing oneself to do something, i.e., live by the new law which Christ procured).

The fifth relevant denial was that the ground of justification is Christ's righteousness imputed. The Arminian alternative was that faith itself is the ground of justification, being itself righteousness (obedience to the new law) and accepted by God as such. Appeal was made to the references in Roman 4:3, 5, 9 (cf 11, 13) to faith being 'reckoned for righteousness,' but the absence from Romans of the 'new law' idea, the insistence that the Christian's righteousness is God's gift (5:15-17), and the repeated emphasis that sinners, though ungodly (4:5; 5:6-8), are justified through Christ's blood irrespective of their own works makes the Arminian understanding of Paul's thought really impossible.

Arminianism made small inroads into the Puritan ranks: the only Arminian Puritan of ability was John Goodwin, author of *Imputatio Fidei* (on Romans 4), *An Exposition of Romans 9*, *Redemption Redeemed*, and *The Banner of Justification Displayed*. But Caroline Anglicans, Cambridge Platonists and later Latitudinarians took up with Arminianism, linked to a strong anti-Calvinist polemic, and after the Restoration the mainstream of English Christianity flowed in this channel. Typical of the later outlook was the (unhappily) influential Bishop Bull, who interpreted Paul by James and understood both as teaching justification by works (faith being, on Bull's view, 'virtually the whole of evangelical obedience', and thus a work in the fullest sense).[16] Arminian doctrine of this kind led inevitably to a new legalism of which the key thought was that the exerting of steady moral effort now is the way to salvation hereafter. The meaning of faith as trust in Christ's Person and work was forgotten; the experiences of conversion and assurance were dismissed as 'enthusiasm', dangerous to the soul, and present justification ceased to be an issue of importance or interest.

One effect of the Arminian controversy on the continent was to spark off the mediating theology of the 'new methodists' of Saumur seminary. This teaching, pioneered by the Scot John Cameron, who taught at Saumur from 1618 to 1621, was developed by Moise Amyraut and has gone down in history under the name of Amyraldism. A.W. Harrison calls it a 'half-way house between Calvinism and Arminianism';[17] it adopts the Arminian view of the covenant of grace and indefinite (universal) redemption, but retains the Calvinistic belief in particular election, effectual calling, and final preservation. Its importance for our story is that Richard Baxter, perhaps the greatest of Puritan writers on Christian practice, advocated a version of it, which as a result of more than forty years' campaigning by him in its interest became both popular and notorious in England and Scotland at the turn of the seventeenth century. In the 1690s it was referred to as 'Baxterianism' and (because of the prominence it gave to the 'new law' idea) 'Neonomianism'.[18]

Baxter's view sprang from natural theology; he thought Bible teaching about God's kingdom and rule should be assimilated to contemporary political ideas, or, as he put, it, that theology should follow a 'political method'. God should be thought of as governor, and the gospel as part of his legal code. Our salvation requires a double righteousness: Christ's which led to the enacting of God's new law, and our own, in obeying that new law by genuine faith and repentance. Faith is imputed for righteousness because it is real obedience to the gospel, which is God's new law. Faith, however, involves a commitment to keep the moral law, which was God's original code, and every believer, though righteous in terms of the new law, needs pardon every moment for his shortcomings in relation to the old law. Jesus Christ, who procured the new law for mankind by satisfying the prescriptive and penal requirements of the old one, should be thought of as Head of God's government, enthroned to pardon true believers. Into this 'political' frame of concepts, learned mainly from the Arminian Hugo de Groot (Grotius), Baxter fitted the Amyraldean soteriology.

Baxter was convinced that those who held the ground and formal cause of our justification to be the imputing to us of Christ's own righteousness (i.e., his fulfilment of the precept and penalty of the moral law) were logically committed to Antinomianism, on the 'payment-God-cannot-twice-demand' principle. At this point in his thinking (though not elsewhere) Baxter assumed, with his Roman and Socinian contemporaries, that law-keeping has no relevance for God or man save as work done to earn acceptance and salvation, so that if the law has been kept once in our name no basis remains for requiring us to keep it a second time in our own persons. It is an odd mistake to find him making; but he never got this streak of legalism out of his theological system. Naturally, his conviction on this point (of which he made no secret) led to vigorous debate at several periods in his life, including, sadly, his last months on earth, when by assaulting as Antinomian the reprinted sermons of Tobias Crisp (first in a Pinner's Hall lecture, and then in *The Scripture Gospel Defended*, 1691) he effectively wrecked the ' Happy Union' between Presbyterians and Independents almost before it had been contracted.[19]

The Crispian controversy produced much heated writing, but the best contribution was the coolest—Robert Traill's *Vindication of the Protestant Doctrine concerning Justification, and of its Preachers and Professors, from the unjust charge of Antinomianism. In a Letter from the Author, to a Minister in the Country* (1692). Quietly but effectively Traill made the two points which really scupper Baxter's scheme. First, the scheme demonstrably fails to come to terms with the representative headship of Christ, the Second Adam, as this is set forth in Romans 5:12ff. It is, of course, on this unique federal relationship between Christ and his people that the imputing to them of his righteousness is based. Then, second, the scheme is so artificial as to be spiritually unreal; for a sinner pressed in conscience by the burden of uncleanness and guilt finds relief, not by reminding himself that his faith is evangelical righteousness according to the new law, but by looking to the cross of Christ. 'My Saviour's obedience and blood /Hides all my transgressions from view.' Talk of one's faith as one's righteousness at such a time is at best a frivolity and at worst a snare.

Nor is this all that needs to be said. Baxter was a great and saintly man; as pastor, evangelist, and devotional writer, no praise for him can be too high; but as a theologian he was, though brilliant, something of a disaster. On his 'political' theology, viewed as an attempt to explicate Bible teaching, the following points have to be made:

1. The 'political' method is itself rationalistic. To make concepts of monarchy, legislation, and ideal government, borrowed from the world of seventeenth-century political theory, into a strait-jacket for the scriptural proclamation of God the King and Christ the Lord, is not merely quaint; it is theologically vicious, and has bad effects all along the line.

2. The 'political' idea of *sin* represents it as primarily transgression and guilt, analogous to crime. This externalises sin, so that its essential nature as spiritual sickness, blindness, and perversity, its indwelling power in the individual, and its demonic corporate influence are under-stressed.

3. The 'political' idea of *Christ* as Head of God's government rather than of his people, and of his death as one presupposition of our sins being remitted rather than the procuring cause of it, and of the remission of sins itself as public pardon rather than personal forgiveness, makes the Lord Jesus seem remote to a degree, and more like a Judge than a Saviour. Its natural, indeed inevitable tendency is to obscure his substitution for us on the cross, and to play down his sympathy for us from the throne.

4. The 'political' idea of *faith* as allegiance and commitment loses sight of the dimension of self-despairing trust: faith appears less as the outstretched empty hand of a spiritual bankrupt than as the signing-on of a resolute volunteer, a work of some strength and merit.

5. The 'political' idea of *God* in a real sense loses God. It is important to see this. Baxter follows Grotius in maintaining that when God purposed to glorify himself by restoring fallen man, he carried out his plan not by satisfying the law, but by changing it. A new law was brought in, which waived the penal requirement of the original law. This assumes that the demand for retribution in the original law was not grounded in the nature of God, but only in the exigencies of government. What is at issue here is the divine holiness. Reformed theology sees both the precept and the penalty of the law of God as a permanent expression of God's eternal and unchangeable holiness and justice, and argues that God does not save sinners at his law's expense; rather, he saves them by satisfying his law on their behalf, so that he continues to be just when he becomes their justifier. Baxter's scheme makes the wrath of God against sin something less than a rev-

elation of his abiding character, and so opens the door to the idea that benevolence is really the whole essence of his moral being: an idea made explicit by the liberalism of a later age.

Thus Baxter, by the initial rationalism of his 'political method', which forced Scripture into an *a priori* mould, actually sowed the seeds of *moralism* with regard to sin, *Arianism* with regard to Christ, *legalism* with regard to faith and salvation, and *liberalism* with regard to God. In his own teaching, steeped as it was in the older affectionate 'practical' Puritan tradition, these seeds lay largely dormant, but later Presbyterianism in both England and Scotland reaped the bitter crop. It is sadly fitting that the Richard Baxter Church in Kidderminster today should be Unitarian. What we see in Baxter is an early stage in the decline, not simply of the doctrine of justification among the Puritans, but of the Puritan insight into the nature of Christianity as a whole.

4

So, after more than a century of clear gospel light, Arminianism brought darkness back to the minds of conformists, and Baxterianism did the same for nonconformists. Natural theology and religious moralism triumphed in England, and, just as Luther had foreseen and Traill feared, the Scripture doctrine of justification was for a time lost to view—until the day when a tremendous voice rang across the country elaborating sermon scripts such as this:

> Are any of you depending upon a righteousness of your own? Do any of you here think to save yourselves by your own doings? I say to you . . . your righteousness shall perish with you. Poor miserable creatures! What is there in your tears? What in your prayers? What in your performances, to appease the wrath of an angry God? Away from the trees of the garden; come, ye guilty wretches, come as poor, lost, undone, and wretched creatures, and accept of a better righteousness than your own. As I said before, so I tell you again, the righteousness of Jesus Christ is an everlasting righteousness; it is wrought out for the very chief of sinners. Ho, every one that thirsteth, let him come and drink of this water of life freely. Are any of you wounded by sin? Do any of you feel you have no righteousness of your own? Are any of you perishing for hunger? Are any of you afraid ye will perish for ever? Come, dear souls, in all your rags; come, thou poor man; come, thou poor distressed woman; you, who think God will never forgive you, and that your sins are too great to be forgiven: come, thou doubting creature, who art afraid thou wilt never get comfort; arise, take comfort, the Lord Jesus Christ, the Lord of life, the Lord of glory, calls for thee. . . . O let not one poor soul stand at a distance from the Saviour. . . . O

come, come! Now, since it is brought into the world by Christ, so, in the name, in the strength, and by the assistance of the great God, I bring it now to the pulpit; I now offer this righteousness, this free, this imputed, this everlasting righteousness, to all poor sinners who will accept of it. . . . Think, I pray you, therefore, on these things; go home, go home, go home, pray over the text, and say, 'Lord God, Thou hast brought an everlasting righteousness into the world by the Lord Jesus Christ; by the blessed Spirit bring it into my heart!' then, die when ye will, ye are safe; if it be tomorrow, ye shall be immediately translated into the presence of the everlasting God; that will be sweet! Happy they who have got this robe on; happy they that can say, 'My God hath loved me, and I shall be loved by Him with an everlasting love!' That every one of you may be able to say so, may God grant, for the sake of Jesus Christ, the dear Redeemer; to whom be glory for ever. Amen.[20]

Whose voice? Why, George Whitefield's: a man who knew, and could express, what the Scripture gospel of justification by faith is all about. With him a new era opened in British Christianity—but that is another story, beyond the scope of this chapter.

The Puritan View of Preaching the Gospel

1

In 1955, at the Puritan and Reformed Studies Conference, I gave a paper entitled 'Puritan Evangelism' which appears in this book as Chapter Eighteen. It was meant as a contribution to the ongoing debate on evangelistic methods. In it, I showed how the Puritan approach to the task of winning souls was controlled by the knowledge that fallen men cannot turn to God by their own strength, nor is it in the power of evangelists to make them do so. The Puritan position was that only God, by his Spirit, through his word, can bring sinners to faith, and that he does this, not to our order, but according to his own free purpose. Our evangelistic practice, the Puritans would say, must be in accord with this truth. Modes of action which imply another doctrine cannot be approved.

The Puritan position seems indubitably biblical, and, as I partly showed in the paper, its implications are of great importance for the reforming of inherited evangelistic traditions today. It implies, to start with, that all devices for exerting psychological pressure in order to precipitate 'decisions' must be eschewed, as being in truth presumptuous attempts to intrude into the province of the Holy Ghost. It means, further, that to abjure such devices is no loss, since their use can contribute nothing whatever to the effectiveness of evangelistic preaching. Indeed, it will in the long run detract from it; for while psychological pressures, skillfully handled, may produce the outward form of 'decision', they cannot bring about regeneration and a change of heart, and when the 'decisions' wear off those who registered them will be found 'gospel-hardened' and antagonistic. Such forcing tactics can only do damage, perhaps incalculable damage, to men's souls. It follows, therefore, that high-speed evangelism is not a valid option. Evangelism must rather be conceived as a long-term enterprise of patient teaching and instruction, in which God's servants seek simply to be faithful in delivering the gospel message and applying it to human lives, and leave it to God's Spirit to draw men to faith through this message in his own way and at his own speed.

But this raises a further question: What is the message? How much is involved in declaring the gospel?

This question is rarely raised in evangelical circles; we assume—too readily—that we all know the answer. But it needs raising; two factors in our situation compel us to face it.

The first is a *minimising approach to the task of teaching Christians truth*. This has infected Protestant clergy very widely. The modern minister does not usually ask, how much ought I to teach but rather, how little need I teach? What is the minimum of doctrine that will do? One reason for this, no doubt, is the reluctance of those in the pews to learn. But this is no new thing. Baxter met it three centuries ago in his working-class congregation at Kidderminster, and gave it short shrift.

> Were you but as willing to get the knowledge of God and heavenly things as you are to know how to work in your trade, you would have set yourself to it before this day, and you would have spared no cost or pains till you had got it. But you account seven years little enough to learn your trade, and will not bestow one day in seven in diligent learning the matters of your salvation.[1]

Baxter did not humour this ungodly unwillingness; but the modern minister often does, and when he finds that some aspect of biblical truth arouses no immediate interest or approval in his congregation his instinct is to jettison it. And the tendency today is to encourage him to do so. Thus, for instance, some will assure us that it is a waste of time preaching to modern hearers about the law and sin, for (it is said) such things mean nothing to them. Instead (it is suggested) we should just appeal to the needs which they feel already, and present Christ to them simply as One who gives peace, power and purpose to the neurotic and frustrated—a super-psychiatrist, in fact.

Now, this suggestion excellently illustrates the danger of the minimising approach. If we do not preach about sin and God's judgement on it, we cannot present Christ as Saviour from sin and the wrath of God. And if we are silent about these things, and preach a Christ who saves only from self and the sorrows of this world, we are not preaching the Christ of the

Bible. We are, in effect bearing false witness and preaching a false Christ. Our message is 'another gospel, which is not another'. Such preaching may soothe some, but it will help nobody; for a Christ who is not seen and sought as a Saviour from sin will not be found to save from self or from anything else. An imaginary Christ will not bring a real salvation; and a half-truth presented as the whole truth is a complete untruth. Thus the minimising approach threatens to falsify the gospel by emptying it of doctrinal elements that are essential to it. In face of this prevalent habit of mind, it is vital that we raise the question: *how much* does preaching the gospel involve?

The second factor in our situation is a *widespread uncertainty about the evangelistic implications of the Reformed faith*. Many today see the scripturalness of the doctrine of grace set out in the so-called 'five points of Calvinism', but do not see how on this basis one can preach evangelistically. If the doctrines of total inability, unconditional election and effectual calling are true—if, that is, sinners cannot of themselves turn to God, and faith and repentance are graces given only to the elect—what sense does it make to command all men indiscriminately to repent and believe? If the doctrine of particular redemption is true—if, that is, Christ died to win salvation, not for all men inclusively (and for many ineffectively), but for the elect only—we can never tell an unconverted man that Christ died for him; on what grounds, therefore, can we exhort him to trust the Saviour? Are we indeed entitled to make a 'free offer' of Christ to sinners at all? Some, perplexed by these questions, feel themselves shut up to a choice between either preaching the gospel like Arminians—addressing the unconverted, that is, as if it were in their own power to receive Christ, and God were simply waiting for them to do so—or else not preaching evangelistically at all. It would be tragic if the current return to Reformed theology, instead of invigorating evangelism, as it should, had the effect of strangling it; but it seems clear that many today have ceased to preach evangelistically because they do not see how an evangelistic application of this theology can be made. Thus, as the minimising approach leads some to empty the gospel of its doctrinal content, so this perplexity causes others to empty it of its practical application. And either mode of evisceration nullifies the gospel as effectively as the other.

In this situation, we return to the Puritans in search of further guidance. How much, we ask them, needs saying, by way of both information and application, if the gospel is to be truly proclaimed? What are the essential ingredients in evangelistic preaching?

Only one aspect of this subject—the need to preach the law when proclaiming Christ—received formal discussion in the Puritan period; but there is ample evidence to show how they would answer our question.

A word about this evidence. It consists of printed sermons. The Puritans did not regard evangelistic sermons as a special class of sermons, having their own peculiar style and conventions; the Puritan position was, rather, that, since all Scripture bears witness to Christ, and all sermons should aim to expound and apply what is in the Bible, all proper sermons would of necessity declare Christ and so be to some extent evangelistic. The Lord Jesus Christ, said Robert Bolton, is 'offered most freely, and without exception of any person, every Sabbath, every Sermon, either in plaine, and direct termes, or implyedly, at the least'.[2] The only difference was that some sermons aimed more narrowly and exclusively at converting sinners than did others. Such were those published in Richard Baxter's *A Call to the Unconverted, A Treatise of Conversion*, and *Directions and Persuasions to a Sound Conversion*, and in Joseph Alleine's *An Alarme to the Unconverted*. But there are five further classes of Puritan sermons and expositions which are equally relevant, being just as directly, if less exclusively, evangelistic in intent:

1. *Treatises on sin*: e.g., Edward Reynolds, *The Sinfulnesse of Sin*; Thomas Goodwin, *Aggravation of Sin* and *An Unregenerate Man's Guiltiness before God*; Jeremiah Burroughs, *The Evil of Evils, or the Exceeding sinfulness of Sin*: ('Wherein is shewed,' continued the title page, '(1) There is more Evil in the least Sin than there is in the greatest Affliction. (2) Sin is most opposite to God. (3) Sin is most opposite to Man's Good. (4) Sin is opposite to all Good in general. (5) Sin is the Poyson, or Evil of all other Evils. (6) Sin hath a kind of Infiniteness in it. (7) Sin makes a man conformable to the Devil. All these several Heads are branched out into very many Particulars.' The work is 527 pages long.)

2. *Treatises on the office and work of Christ*: e.g., Thomas Goodwin, *Christ set Forth*; *Of Christ the Mediator*; *The Heart of Christ in Heaven towards Sinners on Earth*; *The Knowledge of God the Father and His Son Jesus Christ*; Bunyan, *The Work of Christ as an Advocate*; *Christ a Complete Saviour*; Philip Henry, *Christ Is All*; John Owen, *The Glory of Christ*.

3. *Treatises on faith and conversion*: e.g., Ezekiel Culverwell and John Ball each wrote *A Treatise of Faith*; John Rogers, *The Doctrine of Faith*; William Whately, *The New Birth*; Thomas Hooker, *The Application of Redemption* (and many more works on the same subject); Thomas Shepard, *The Sound Believer*; Giles Firmin, *The Real Christian*; John Flavel, *The Method of Grace*.

4. *Treatises on the covenant of grace*, exploring the riches of the relationship with God into which Christ brings believers: e.g., John Preston, *The New Covenant*; Richard Alleine, *Heaven Opened*; E. Fisher, *The Marrow of Modern Divinity*.

5. *Treatises on hypocrisy and nominal Christianity*: e.g., Daniel Dyke, *The Mystery of Selfe-Deceiving*; Shepard, *The Parable of the Ten Virgins*; Matthew Meade, *The Almost Christian; or, the False-Professor Tried and Cast*.

Nearly all these works began life as courses of sermons. They bear the marks that distinguish Puritan sermons; they are textual and expository, practical and applicatory, analytical and thorough. They are uniformly doctrinal—that is to say, their real subject is always God and his ways, even when the formal object of consideration is man. And together they show clearly what the Puritans took to be involved in preaching the gospel.

2

Note, first, *the comprehensiveness of the gospel* as the Puritans understood it. Observe how much they took the word 'gospel' to cover. It denoted to them the whole doctrine of the covenant of grace. Sometimes they included as part of it the preparatory message of sin and judgement as well. Thus, to preach the gospel meant to them nothing less than declaring the entire economy of redemption, the saving work of all three Persons of the Trinity. This appears from the following words of Thomas Manton:

> The sum of the gospel is this, that all who, by true repentance and faith, do forsake the flesh, the world, and the devil, and give themselves up to God the Father, Son, and Holy Spirit, as their creator, redeemer, and sanctifier, shall find God as a father, taking them for his reconciled children, and for Christ's sake pardoning their sin, and by his Spirit giving them his grace; and, if they persevere in this course, will finally glorify them, and bestow upon them everlasting happiness; but will condemn the unbelievers, impenitent, and ungodly to everlasting punishment. That this is the sum of the gospel appeareth by Mk. xvi. 15, 16: 'Go, preach the gospel to every creature. He that believeth, and is baptized, shall be saved; but he that believeth not shall be damned;'—where you have all the Christian religion laid before you in one short view and prospect.[3]

'The sum of the gospel'—'all the Christian religion . . . in one short view and prospect.' We are doing something less than preaching the gospel, the Puritans would tell us, if our preaching contains less than this.

Their view of the comprehensiveness of the gospel comes out in many different connections. We give three further examples. Here, first, is Goodwin, telling us how much is involved in relating the gospel story:

> As there are three persons . . . who have a joint hand in that work of salvation, the subject of the gospel, so the whole story of the gospel hath three parts also, in every of which some one of them bears an especial part.
> The *first* part God the Father had the chiefest hand in, who drew the platform of this great work, contrived it, made the motion first to his Son. . . .
> The *second*, God the Son, when he came down and took flesh and . . . transacted the redemption of the world according to that draft.

As after him, when he was off the stage, came the Spirit, to apply what he had done, and all the benefits of it, whose work makes up the *third* part.[4]

And all three parts must receive mention if the gospel story is to be told properly.

Here, again, is John Owen, showing us how much is involved in declaring the promises of the gospel:

Gospel promises then are: (1) The free and gracious dispensations; and, (2) discoveries of God's good-will and love; to, (3) sinners; (4) through Christ; (5) in a covenant of grace; (6) wherein, upon his truth and faithfulness, he engageth himself to be their God, to give his Son unto them, and for them, and his Holy Spirit to abide with them, with all things that are either required in them, or are necessary for them, to make them accepted before him, and to bring them to an enjoyment of him.[5]

And proclaiming the gospel in its character as God's word of promise involves elucidating all this.

Here, finally, is Richard Baxter, giving his first three 'directions . . . to a sound conversion'—directions designed to lay the foundation for an intelligent and responsible commitment to Christ.

First: 'labour after a right understanding of the true nature of Christianity, and the meaning of the gospel;' begin by clarifying your mind about the Christian message as a whole. Second: study the Scriptures for this purpose. Third: 'Be much in the serious consideration of the truths which you understand'—that you were made to serve God; that you have fallen short of this end; that you are now in a wretched state, for 'you have made God your enemy'; how happy the converted are; how adequate Christ's redemption is; how disastrous it will be to reject redemption; and—before any of the rest—'the nature of that God with whom ye have to do'.

If he be good, and infinitely good, there is all the reason in the world that you should love him; and there is no show of reason that you should love the world or sin before him. If he be faithful and true, his threatenings must be feared, and his promises must not be distrusted; and there is no reason that you should make any question of his word. If he be holy . . . then he must be an enemy to sin, and to all that are unholy, because they are contrary to his nature. Consider that he is almighty, and there is no resisting him . . . in the twink of an eye can he snatch thy guilty soul from thy body, and cast it where sin is better known. A word of his mouth can set all the world against thee, and set thine own conscience against thee too . . . and if he be thine enemy, it is no matter who is thy friend; for all the world cannot save thee, if he do but condemn thee. . . . He was from eternity, and thou art but as it were of yesterday; thy being is from him; thy life is always in his hands, thou canst not live an hour without him, thou canst not fetch a breath without him, nor think a thought, nor speak a word, nor stir a foot or a hand without him . . . no love can be great enough, and no praises can be high enough, and no service can be holy and good enough for such a God . . . this is not a God to be neglected, or dallied with; nor a God to be resisted, nor provoked by the wilful breaking of his laws. . . . O therefore dwell on the meditations of the almighty![6]

This knowledge of God, Baxter insists, is fundamental to a sound conversion. Evidently, therefore, it too must find its place in the preaching of the gospel.

The importance of all this is that it challenges our modern idea that preaching 'gospel sermons' means just harping on a few great truths—guilt, and atonement, and forgiveness—set virtually in a theological vacuum. The Puritan view was that preaching 'gospel sermons' means teaching the whole Christian system—the character of God, the Trinity, the plan of salvation, the entire work of grace. To preach Christ, they held, involved preaching all this. Preach less, they would tell us, and what you do preach will not be properly grasped. What the good news of a restored relationship with God through Christ means for religion cannot be understood further than it is seen in this comprehensive context. Gospel preaching centres always upon the theme of man's relationship to God, but around that centre it must range throughout the whole sphere of revealed truth, viewing the centre from every angle of vision that the Bible provides. In this way, they would say, preaching the gospel involves preaching the whole counsel of God. Nor should the preaching of the gospel be thought of as something confined to set evangelistic occasions, as if at other times we should preach something else. If one preaches the Bible biblically, one cannot help preaching the gospel all the time, and every sermon will be, as Bolton said, at least by implication evangelistic.

And we must not be afraid to start with the basic facts about God the Creator. Revealed truth has a structure, and this is its foundation. When Paul preached to the pagan Athenians, he laid this foundation before going further. He had to, or else the point of his witness to our Lord would not have been grasped. For knowledge of sin and salvation presupposes some knowledge of the Creator; nobody can see what sin is till he has learned what God is. That is why Baxter directed the seeking soul to fix his mind first and foremost on the nature and majesty of God. In the pagan West today, we need to lay the same foundation as Paul laid at Athens. We complain that our 'gospel preaching' (in the modern sense) does not register with those who hear it. May not this be in the first instance because they know nothing about the God with whom they have to do? Have we taken pains to teach them who God is? The irony of our situation is that if we spend time preaching to modern pagans about the character of God we shall be told that we are not preaching the gospel. But the Puritans would not tell us that; nor would Paul.

3

Note, second, *the emphases of the gospel* as the Puritans preached it. We note a few of the major points.

1. They diagnosed *the plight of man* as one, not merely of guilt for sins, but also of pollution in sin and bondage to sin. And by bondage to sin they meant, not bondage to *sins*—particular weaknesses of character and bad habits—but the state of being wholly dominated by an inbred attitude of enmity to God. They sought to expose the sinfulness that underlies sins, and convince men of their own utter corruption and inability to improve themselves in God's sight. This, they held, was a vital part of the work of a gospel preacher; for the index of the soundness of a man's faith in Christ is the genuineness of the self-despair from which it springs.

2. They analysed *the issue of sin* in terms of God's hostility in the present, as well as his condemnation in the future. Their constant aim was to make men feel that to be in a wrong relationship with God was intolerable here and now; hence, contrary to common belief, they made even more of the first thought than they did of the second.

3. They stressed that *the goal of grace* is the glory and praise of God, and our salvation is a means to this end. God, they said, has chosen to redeem us, not for our sakes, but for his own name's sake.

4. They stressed *the sufficiency of Christ*. They did not teach men to trust a theory of the atonement, but a living Redeemer, the perfect adequacy of whose saving work they never tired of extolling.

5. They stressed *the condescension of Christ*. He was never to them less than the divine Son, and they measured his mercy by his majesty. They magnified the love of the cross by dwelling on the greatness of the glory which he left for it. They dwelt on the patience and forbearance expressed in his invitations to sinners as further revealing his kindness. And when they applied Revelation 3:20 evangelistically (as on occasion they did), they took the words 'Behold, I stand at the door and knock' as disclosing, not the impotence of his grace apart from man's cooperation (the too-prevalent modern interpretation), but rather the grace of his omnipotence in freely offering himself to needy souls.

These were the emphases which characterised the Puritan preaching of the gospel, and indeed all preaching of it by evangelicals from Puritan times onward till about a century ago.

4

Note, third, *the demands of the gospel* as the Puritans presented them. The gospel, they said, summons sinners to faith in Christ. Faith means assent to the good news as divine truth and consent to receive Jesus Christ as the divine Saviour. Faith is not a meritorious work, but the stretching out of an empty hand to lay hold of a Saviour and with him salvation. 'What doth the Lord offer in the gospel?' asks Thomas Shepard. 'Is it not first Christ, and then all the benefits of Christ?'[7] The Lord Jesus Christ must be received in his whole mediatorial office, as Saviour and Lord, as Prophet, Priest and King; for 'never did any man take Jesus Christ savingly, who took him not for a Husband and a Lord, to serve, love and obey him for ever after, as well as a Saviour to disburden him of his sinnes; as a King to govern him by his Word and Spirit, as well as a Priest to wash him in his Blood.'[8] To accept Jesus Christ as Saviour and Priest is evangelical faith; to enthrone him as Lord and King is evangelical repentance.

The persons invited and commanded to believe are sinners, as such. The Saviour is freely offered in the gospel to all who need him. The question of the extent of the atonement does not therefore arise in evangelism, for what the gospel commands the unconverted man to believe is not that Christ died with the specific intention of securing his individual salvation, but that here and now the Christ who died for sinners offers himself to this individual sinner, saying to him personally, 'Come unto me . . . and I will give you rest' (Mt 11:28). The whole warrant of faith—the ground, that is, on which believing becomes permissible and obligatory—is found in this invitation and command of the Father and the Son.

The above assertion, however, has been disputed. C.H. Spurgeon, in a sermon on 1 John 3:23, entitled 'The Warrant of Faith', which he preached in 1863, affirmed that some of the Puritans, like the opponents of the Marrowmen in eighteenth-century Scotland and the hypercalvinistic Baptists of Spurgeon's own day, taught that the ground on which believing became permissible was a preliminary work of grace, convicting of sin.

Spurgeon declared:

Some preachers in the Puritanic times erred much in this matter. . . . Alleine and Baxter . . . Rogers of Dedham, Shepherd [Shepard], the author of *The Sound Believer*, and especially the American, Thomas Hooker, who has written a book upon qualifications for coming to Christ. These excellent men had a fear of preaching the gospel to any except those whom they styled as 'sensible sinners'. . . . They preached repentance and hatred of sin as the warrant of a sinner's trusting to Christ. According to them, a sinner might reason thus—'I possess such-and-such a degree of sensibility on account of sin, therefore I have a right to trust in Christ.' Now, I venture to affirm that such reasoning is seasoned with fatal error. . . .[9]

Spurgeon's theological judgement is surely sound; but equally surely he has put the wrong people in the dock. One wonders whether he had read the authors to whom he refers (after all, he was only twenty-nine at the time); certainly, he misrepresents their teaching. To state the facts correctly, we must distinguish two questions: that of the *warrant of faith*, and that of the *way to faith*.

All the Puritans agreed that the way by which God brings sinners to faith is through a 'preparatory work', longer or shorter, of contrition and humbling for sin. This is not repentance (actual turning from sin, which follows faith), but the soil out of which, upon their believing, repentance will spring. The reason why they held this preparatory work to be necessary has nothing to do with the question of the warrant of faith; it is simply because fallen man is naturally in love with sin, and it is a psychological impossibility for him to close whole-heartedly with Christ as a Saviour from sin until he has come to hate sin and long to be delivered from it.

Now, three of the authors whom Spurgeon names—John Rogers (in *The Doctrine of Faith*, 1627), Thomas Hooker (in *The Soul's Preparation for Christ*, 1632, and other books), and Thomas Shepard (in *The Sound Believer*, 1645)—delineated the stages of this preparatory work in great detail; and their writings on the subject may justly be criticised on three counts:

First, they gave the impression (despite parenthetical disclaimers) that God's work of humbling men for sin invariably followed the same course, in every detail of the process, and if you had not experienced it all you must be a stranger to true grace. In his teens, Richard Baxter went through much fear and distress, because, examine himself as he might, 'I could not distinctly trace the Workings of the Spirit upon my heart in that method which . . . *Mr. Hooker, Mr Rogers*, and other Divines describe.' Later, however, he realized 'that God breaketh not all Men's hearts alike', and escaped from the pietistic strait-jacket which these giants of experimental religion had forged.[10]

Second, Hooker and Shepard went beyond Scripture in teaching that the sign of true humiliation for sin was that the sinner, acknowledging his guilt, should be content to be damned for the glory of God. Baxter and, later, Giles Firmin (in *The Real Christian*, 1670) took them to task for this, arguing that it was not required by God nor psychologically possible for any man ever to be content to be damned.

Third, by concentrating attention on this preliminary work of grace, and harping on the need for it to be done thoroughly, these writers effectively discouraged seeking souls from going straight to Christ in their despair. 'If you that are now converted had lived in our younger days,' wrote Goodwin in later life, 'you would have seen that we were held long under John Baptist's water, of being humbled for sin.'[11] This naturally led to much morbidity.

But on the question of the warrant of faith, these authors are not open to criticism; when they speak of it, their doctrine is exactly Spurgeon's, that the warrant of faith is the command and promise of God to sinners, and that faith is required of everyone who hears the gospel. Firmin spoke for the entire Puritan school when he laid it down that 'it is the duty of all the sons and daughters of Adam, who hear the gospel preached, and Christ offered to them, to believe in, or receive, Christ, whether they be prepared or not prepared', and quoted 1 John 3:23 and John 6:29 as proof.[12] John Rogers, discussing the warrant of faith, quotes the same two texts in support of the statement that 'faith is one of the commandments of the gospel'.[13] Shepard speaks of the 'commandment to receive Christ' in 1 John 3:23 which 'binds conscience to believe, as you will answer for the contempt of this rich grace at the great day of account'.[14] If any hearer of the gospel does not believe, it is not for want of being divinely directed and laid under obligation to do so. The truth is that to all the Puritans it was one of the wonders of free grace that the Lord Jesus Christ invites sinners, just as they are, in all their filthy rags, to receive him and find life, and they never waxed more impassioned and powerful than when dilating on what John Owen, in his stately way, calls 'the infinite condescension, grace and love of Christ, in His invitations of sinners to come unto him that they may be saved'.[15]

So much for faith; what, now, of repentance? The New Testament links repentance with faith as a second aspect of the response for which the gospel calls, and the Puritans did the same. In the *Westminster Confession*, Chapter XIV, 'Of Saving Faith', is followed by Chapter XV, 'Of Repentance unto Life'. The chapter starts by defining repentance as 'an evangelical grace' whereby

a sinner, out of the sight and sense not only of the danger, but also of the filthiness and odiousness of his sins, as contrary to the holy nature, and righteous law of God; and upon the apprehension of his mercy in Christ to such as are penitent, so grieves for, and hates his sins, as to turn from them all unto God, purposing and endeavouring to walk with him in all the ways of his commandments.

Repentance, the *Confession* continues, 'is of such necessity to all sinners, that none may expect pardon without it', and 'it is every man's duty to endeavour to repent of his particular sins, particularly.'[16]

Repentance is a fruit of faith. 'Repentance, the soul's pump, is dry . . . until faith pour in the blood of Christ, and water of gospel-promises. So that faith must precede repentance, as the cause to the effect, the mother before the daughter.'[17] When faith has primed the pump of the human heart, repentance is the way of living that results.

Repentance is thus a character quality of the regenerate, a supernaturally inwrought dispositional attitude that finds expression in a constant flow of heartfelt penitent acts—'fruit in keeping with repentance', as John the Baptist put it (Mt 3:8, NIV). As a dispositional dynamic, repentance involved *humiliation* (conviction of guilt plus contrition of heart for offending God) and *conversion* (recession from sin and reversion to God), and finds expression in *confession* of sin and *petition* for pardon at the throne of grace.[18] The gospel of Christ, as the Puritans understood it, specifies that faith must express itself in a life of continual contrition, confession, and conversion. Without these habits of the heart there is no genuine repentance, and where there is no genuine repentance there is no genuine faith either.

Repentance, explains Zachary Crofton,

> is a habit, power, principle, spring, root, and disposition; not a bare, single, and transient action. . . . Repentance is different and distinct from all penitential acts. . . . Repentance is not the work of an hour, or a day: but a constant frame, course, and bent of the soul . . . birth, breeding, education, instruction, art, knowledge, moral suasion, friendly advice, and gospel-ministry itself, cannot work it, without the immediate operation of an Omnipotent Spirit . . . it is the sole and singular prerogative of Jesus Christ exalted 'to give repentance' . . . Repentance is not . . . the effect of the law; but a pure gospel-grace; preached by the gospel, promised in the covenant, sealed in baptism, produced by the Spirit, properly flowing from the blood of Christ; and so is every way supernatural; so that every returning sinner must pray to God: 'Turn thou me, and I shall be turned'. . . .[19]

Crofton offers a checklist of

> false notions about repentance: as that, 1. Repentance is the result of nature, and at man's command; we may repent when we will, as the Arminians teach: but you must remember, it is 'supernatural'. 2. That penance is a transient act of confession and self-castigation, as the Papists teach; you must know that it is a grace or habit. 3. That repentance is before faith, and not the result of the gospel, an effect of the blood of Christ. . . . 4. That conviction, contrition, and confession, are not necessary to repentance, as the antinomians teach. . . .[20]

All Crofton's points belong to the mainstream of Puritan teaching; his statement is entirely representative.

How then did the Puritans direct the unconverted to comply with the summons to repent that the gospel delivers to them? Crofton's answer, which is once again typical, is as follows:

> First. *Sit with care, constancy, and conscience under the word of truth, and gospel of grace.* . . . Secondly, *Study the nature of God* . . . acquaint yourself with his attributes,—his holiness, power, justice, mercy, and the like. Your souls will never be drawn from sin, or driven into a course of true repen-

tance, until God becomes your dread. . . . Thirdly, *Sit close to the work of self-scrutiny.* . . . The worst of men, by a short conference with their own soul, would soon see a necessity of repentance. . . . Be serious in self-examination. Fourthly, *Sit loose to the world* . . . true penitentiaries [penitents] must be pilgrims in the earth. Fifthly, *See the shortness of life.* . . . Hopes of long life, and thoughts of repentance at pleasure, help many a soul to hell. . . . Sixthly, *Seriously expect approaching judgment.* . . . Seventhly, *Seriously apprehend the possibility* . . . of pardon . . . .it is thing with certainty, if received with a prostrate soul, and sued out by serious repentance. . . . Eighthly, *Soak the heart in the blood of Jesus*—Take every day a turn of meditation in Mount Calvary. . . . Be persuaded daily to contemplate the cross of Christ. Ninthly, *Speed will much facilitate repentance.* . . . Linger not in what you will be rid of; for the longer you linger, you will be more loath to part. . . . Tenthly, *Sue for it* [repentance] *at the hands of God.*

Ask God to bless to you the means of grace specified in the first nine directives as you seek to put them into practice; 'so shall your stony heart be taken from you, and you shall possess this necessary grace of repentance in the truth of it.'[21]

And that new penitent habit of heart will be proof positive that in and through Christ you have passed from death to life.

The underlying theology is clear. We sinners cannot change our own hearts, but we can employ means of grace (in this case, lines of disciplined prayerful thought) via which God changes hearts. God ordinarily gives faith, the mother, and repentance, the daughter, to those who are resolutely, self-distrustfully, imploringly reaching after both. The Puritan evangelist's message was: start reaching now!

5

Thus the Puritans preached the gospel of free and sovereign grace. Like Baxter, they were motivated by 'a thirsty desire of Men's Conversion and Salvation'. But two other motives weighed with them also, both greater even than this: the double desire to glorify God, and to magnify Christ. The latter point is, perhaps, the one that at present we most need to apply to ourselves. All of us who preach the gospel, I suppose, desire men's conversion. Many, no doubt, are concerned also to glorify God by a faithful declaration of his truth. But how many, when preaching the gospel, are consumed by the longing to magnify Christ—to extol the richness, and freedom, and glory of his grace, and the perfection of his saving work? The cheap and perfunctory way in which the Person of the Saviour is sometimes

dealt with in modern evangelistic preaching forces this question upon us.
Puritan gospel preaching was concerned above all things to *honour Christ*:
to show his glory to needy men and women. It is much to be wished that
we who preach the gospel in these days might recover the same overmas-
tering concern to exalt this mighty Saviour.

THE PURITANS AND THE HOLY SPIRIT

CHAPTER ELEVEN

The Witness of the Spirit in Puritan Thought

'The Spirit itself beareth witness with our spirit, that we are the children of God,' wrote Paul (Rom 8:16, KJV). Our aim in this chapter is to discover what the Puritans taught about the Spirit's work in assuring believers of their salvation. The work of the Holy Spirit is the field in which the Puritans' most valuable contributions to the church's theological heritage were made, and the subject of assurance in particular is treated with great fullness and profundity by some of the finest Puritan minds—notably Richard Sibbes, the 'sweet dropper', in his exposition of 2 Corinthians 1 (on v 22; *Works*, III), in 'a Fountain sealed' on Ephesians 4:30 (*Works*, V) and elsewhere; Thomas Brooks, one of the greatest of the later Puritans, in *Heaven on Earth. Or, a Serious Discourse touching a well-grounded Assurance* (1654; *Works*, II); and Thomas Goodwin, in his three sermons on Ephesians 1:13 and in the second book of the second part of his great treatise *Of the Object and the Acts of Justifying Faith* (*Works*, I, VIII). Alexander Whyte called Goodwin 'the greatest pulpit exegete of Paul that has ever lived', and perhaps justly; Goodwin's biblical expositions are quite unique, even among the Puritans, in the degree to which they combine theological breadth with experimental depth. John Owen saw into the mind of Paul as clearly as Goodwin—sometimes, on points of detail, more clearly—but not even Owen saw so deep into Paul's heart. Goodwin, Sibbes and Brooks will be our leaders in this study. We shall find them in substantial agreement (especially Sibbes and Goodwin, between whose thoughts on this subject there is an evident genealogical connection); and they represent the main current of Puritan thinking. At the close, we shall introduce John Owen, who makes some necessary exegetical adjustments to his predecessors' position without disputing its theological and experiential substance. Let us see now what these teachers have to say.

1

The Puritans speak of assurance sometimes as a fruit of faith, sometimes as a quality of faith; they talk both of assurance growing out of faith and of faith growing into assurance. Assurance is to them faith full grown and come of age; there can be faith without assurance, but where assurance is present it is present as an aspect of faith, organically related to it, not as something distinct and separable from it. This being so, we must start our study by reviewing what the Puritans taught about the nature of faith in general.

Faith, said the Puritans, begins in the mind, with belief of the truth of the gospel message. It results from spiritual illumination. In illumination, the Spirit both enlightens the mind, making it capable of receiving spiritual things, and impresses on the mind the objective reality of those things of which the word of God bears witness. The knowledge of spiritual realities thus given is as immediate and direct in its way as is the knowledge of material things which we gain by sense, and it brings with it a quality of immediate conviction analogous to that which sense-perception brings. Scripture refers to the process in terms borrowed from the senses—seeing, hearing, tasting (Jn 6:40; Eph 4:21; Heb 6:5)—and tells us that it yields *full assurance of understanding* (Col 2:2). This spiritual appreciation of spiritual things is mediated to man, as a thinking being, by reasoned exposition of Scripture and rational reflection upon it. Man cannot come to know any spiritual object except through the use of his mind; but spiritual knowledge goes beyond reason. It is not a mere logical or imaginative construction, nor is its certainty the derived certainty of an inference drawn from more certain premises; its certainty springs from an immediate awareness of and contact with the thing known. It is not a 'notional, swimming knowledge', second-hand and unstable; it is 'real' and 'solid' knowledge, the product of a direct cognisance by spiritual sense of the things known. The divine operation whereby it is given is what Calvin and his successors called the *testimonium internum Spiritus Sancti*—the inner witness of the Holy Ghost. Paul refers to it in 1 Corinthians 2:4 as the 'demonstration of the Spirit'.

Goodwin puts it thus: 'The Holy Ghost, when he doth work faith in us . . . doth two things: *First*, He doth . . . give us a new understanding . . . 1 Jn 5:20 . . . a new eye to see Christ with. . . . *Secondly*, himself cometh with a light upon this new understanding, thus bestowing a spiritual sight' of spiritual realities.[1] This spiritual knowledge is in fact more certain than anything else. It may be obscured by temptations; one who has it may for a long period be so out of touch with himself, or so inwardly confused and depressed, as to doubt and deny it; but it will prove dominant in the end, and in the long run the effect of his lapses from it will be to make him realise how utterly and unshakeably he is in his heart convinced of it. Such is the knowledge of divine things given to all true believers, and it is the quality of certainty attaching to it which guarantees them against finally falling away. This witness of the Spirit to the objective truth of the gospel is the fundamental factor in personal faith, and this 'full assurance of understanding' of the gospel that the Spirit gives is prerequisite for personal assurance of salvation.

Faith is, of course, more than mental enlightenment. It extends from the head to the heart, and expresses itself in what Baxter calls a 'practical trust' in God through Christ. Man turns from self-reliance and sin to rest his soul on Christ and the promises. Hereby he both expresses and establishes the habit of faith in his soul; and faith, once established, asserts itself as the dynamic of a new life. It begets hope; it works by love; it steels itself to patience; it lays itself out in well-doing; it causes joy and peace to arise naturally and spontaneously in the heart. 'Faith is the master-wheel; it sets all the other graces running.'[2] 'Faith is the spring in the watch that sets all the golden wheels of love, joy, comfort and peace a-going.'[3] Faith is thus regarded as containing a measure of assurance within itself from the outset; the believer hopes, loves, serves and rejoices because he believes that God has had mercy on him.

But this is not the 'settled, well-grounded' assurance which the Puritans regarded as alone worthy of the name. The young convert may in exceptional cases enjoy continual strong consolation, but usually such assurance is not given till faith has been tried and seasoned, ripened and strengthened, by conflict with doubt and fluctuations of feeling. The Puritans were somewhat suspicious when transports of rapture accompanied the first profession of faith; they never forgot that in Jesus' parable it was the stony-ground hearers who received the word with such notable joy. True, sound, thorough converts, they held, do not usually start like that. 'Full assurance' is a rare blessing, even among adults; it is a great and precious privilege, not indiscriminately bestowed. 'Assurance is a mercy too good for most men's hearts. . . . God will only give it to his best and dearest friends.' 'Assurance is the beauty and top of a Christian's glory in this life. It is usually attended with the strongest joy, with the sweetest comforts, and with the greatest peace. It is a . . . crown that few wear. . . .' 'Assurance is meat for strong men; few babes, if any, are able to bear it, and digest it.'[4]

Assurance is not normally enjoyed except by those who have first laboured for it and sought it, and served God faithfully and patiently for some time without it.

Assurance comes in as a reward of faith. . . . A man's faith must fight first, and have a conquest, and then assurance is the crown, the triumph of faith . . . and what tries faith more than temptation, and fears, and doubts, and reasonings against a man's own estate? That triumphing assurance, Rom. 8:37, 39 . . . comes after a trial, as none are crowned till they have striven.[5]

Assurance of this kind is not essential to faith; as Brooks puts it, it is of faith's *bene esse*, not of its *esse*.[6] It is, in fact, an aspect of faith which normally appears only when faith has reached a high degree of development, far beyond its minimal saving exercise. Goodwin speaks of assurance as both 'a branch and appendix of faith, an addition or complement to faith' and 'faith elevated and raised up above its ordinary rate; the Scripture speaks of it,' he says, 'as a thing distinct from faith (though it doth coalesce with it, and they both make one).'[7] This was the general Puritan conception of assurance.

It is evident that 'assurance' to the Puritans was something quite other than the 'assurance' commonly given to the convert of five minutes' standing in the enquiry room ('You believe that John 1:12 is true and you have "received him"? Then you are a son of God'). The Puritans would not have called mere formal assent to such an inference *assurance* at all. Professions of faith, they said, must be tested before they may be trusted, even by those who make them; and assurance, to the Puritan, was in any case more than a bare human inference; it was a God-given conviction of one's standing in grace, stamped on the mind and heart by the Spirit in just the same way as the truth of the gospel facts was stamped on the mind when faith was born, and carrying with it the same immediate certainty. 'Assurance,' says Brooks, 'is the reflex act of a gracious soul, whereby he clearly and evidently sees himself in a gracious, blessed and happy state; it is a sensible feeling and an experimental discerning of a man's being in a state of grace.'[8] The operative words here are *sensible* and *experimental*. Assurance is the conscious fruit of supernatural enlightenment, and cannot exist till it pleases God to give it. The young convert's position is really this: as he believes and obeys, he will know a measure of peace and joy, for real believing at once brings real comfort ('no man looks upon Christ but cometh off more cheerly';[9] 'there is a voice of God's Spirit speaking peace to his people upon their believing'[10]). He may *think* and *hope*, and with reason, that he is a child of God. But he cannot say, in the unqualified sense of John's first Epistle, that he *knows* his sonship until the Spirit sets this certainty home on his heart. Till the Spirit does so, in the Puritan sense, at any rate, he lacks assurance; which, said the Puritans, seems to be the case with most Christian people.

When this supernatural assurance dawns, it transforms a man's entire Christian life. 'It is a new conversion,' says Goodwin; 'it will make a man differ from himself in what he was before in that manner almost as conversion doth before he was converted. There is a new edition of all a man's graces.'[11] This sounds startling, but Goodwin means what he says, and works the idea out. Assurance, he tells us, increases faith (faith 'receives a new degree'[12]); and this invigoration of faith results in a new release of energy at every point in one's Christian life.

In the first place, it deepens one's communion with the Triune God in meditating on the 'plot' of redeeming love.

> In assurance . . . a man's communion and converse is . . . sometimes with the Father, then with the Son, and then with the Holy Ghost; sometimes his heart is drawn out to consider the Father's love in choosing, and then the love of Christ in redeeming, and so the love of the Holy Ghost, that searcheth the deep things of God, and revealeth them to us, and taketh all the pains with us. . . .[13]

Nor is this all. The coming of assurance quickens the spiritual understanding: by it 'the eye of the soul is strengthened to see further into truths; all truths are more clearly known by this'.[14] It makes a man bold and powerful in prayer. It makes him holier, though he was holy before: 'all assurance that is true assurance . . . maketh a man holy';[15] 'nothing makes the heart more in the love, study, practice, and growth of holiness, than the glorious testimony of the Holy Spirit.'[16] Assurance makes a man tireless in Christian service: 'when once . . . the love of God is shed abroad in a man's heart, it makes a man work for God ten times more than before';[17] 'assurance will strongly put men upon the winning of others. . . . A soul under assurance is unwilling to go to heaven without company.'[18] Finally, assurance brings with it the 'joy unspeakable and full of glory' of 1 Peter 1:8, which is one of Goodwin's favourite texts in this connection. Such assurance as this, so far from encouraging presumption and laziness, is in fact the strongest possible incentive against sin, for its possessor knows that by sinning he will jeopardise his assurance, prompting God to withdraw it, and there is nothing that he is more anxious to avoid than that. These, then, are the chief fruits of assurance.

2

How does the Spirit assure? One's answer to this question turns on the sense given to Romans 8:16, which speaks of two witnesses giving evidence together, the Holy Spirit corroborating the testimony of our spirit. The Puritans identified 'our spirit' with the Christian's conscience, which, with the Spirit's aid, is able to discern in his heart the marks which Scripture specifies as tokens of the new birth and to conclude from them that he is a child of God. The Spirit 'writes first all graces in us, and then teaches our consciences to read his handwriting'.[19] Without the Spirit's aid, man can never recognise the Spirit's handiwork in himself; 'if he do not give in his testimony with them, your graces will give no witness at all.'[20] Sometimes the Spirit's help here is given in full measure; sometimes, however, to chasten us for sin, or to try our faith for a time, this help is partly or wholly withdrawn; and because the Spirit is not always active to enable us to know ourselves to the same degree, the witness of our spirit inevitably fluctuates: 'a man shall find the same signs sometimes witness to him, and sometimes not, as the Spirit irradiates them.'[21] We must recognise that God is sovereign here, to give more or less assurance in this way as he pleases. Thus far, all Puritans are agreed.

But what is meant by 'the Spirit beareth witness'? Here, there is a difference. Some of the Puritans equate the witness of the Spirit to which Paul refers with the work of the Spirit in enabling our spirits to bear witness, as described above. Thus, John Goodwin, the Arminian Puritan, writes:

The expression of witnessing with our spirits plainly implies that it is but one and the same act of witnessing . . . jointly in common ascribed unto the Spirit of God and the spirit of man, and that the Spirit of God doth not bear any such witness . . . apart from the spirit of man . . . from whence it appears, that the witness, or joint-witnessing, of the Spirit here spoken of, is only a fortifying, strengthening, raising and enriching of the witness of testimony of a man's own spirit.[22]

On this view, the Spirit bears witness when the believer finds himself able to infer with confidence from the evidence of his heart and life that he is a child of God. But Sibbes, Brooks and Goodwin, among others, hold a different view. They take the text as referring to two distinct modes of witness, the first being inferential, as described above, and the second being that of the Spirit testifying, no longer indirectly, but immediately and intuitively; not merely by prompting us to infer our adoption, but by what Goodwin calls an 'overpowering light' whereby he bears direct witness to the Christian of God's everlasting love to him, of his election, and his sonship, and his inheritance.

Sibbes says:

The Spirit . . . witnesses . . . by . . . whatsoever of Christ's is applied to us by the Spirit. But, besides witnessing with these witnesses, the Spirit hath a distinct witness by way of enlarging the soul; which is joy in the apprehension of God's fatherly love. . . . The Spirit doth not always witness . . . by force of argument from sanctification, but sometimes immediately by way of presence; as the sight of a friend comforts without help of discourse.[23]

There is a twofold assurance of salvation, says Goodwin:

the one way is *discoursive*; a man gathereth that God loves him from the effects [i.e., marks of regeneration], as we gather that there is fire because there is smoke. But the other is *intuitive* . . . it is such a knowledge as whereby we know that the whole is greater than the part. . . . There is light that cometh and overpowereth a man's soul, and assureth him that God is his, and he is God's, and that God loveth him from everlasting.[24]

Goodwin analyses this direct witness in much detail. It is, he tells us, self-evidencing and self-authenticating; and it is analogous in character to the Spirit's witness to the objective truth of the gospel. In each case, the Spirit witnesses to the truth of the word of God and its application to the individual. In creating faith, he convinces the sinner that the conditional promises of the gospel are held out by God to him (e.g., 'come unto me, all ye that labour . . . and I will give you rest'), and prompts him to make the appropriate response, i.e., to trust. In giving assurance, he convinces the Christian that the absolute promises of Scripture include him in their scope (e.g., 'my sheep . . . shall never perish'), and moves him to make the appropriate response, i.e., to rejoice. Goodwin explains:

When we say that [assurance] is an immediate testimony, the meaning is not that it is without the Word; no, it is by a promise; but the meaning is, it is immediate in respect of using your own graces as an evidence or witness: but he bringeth home a promise to the heart, some absolute promise. . . . We do not speak for enthusiasms; it is the Spirit applying the Word to the heart that we speak of.[25]

What happens is that

God says unto a man's soul (as David desires) 'I am thy salvation,' and as Christ said on earth to some few, 'Thy sins are forgiven thee,' so from Heaven is it spoken by his Spirit . . . that a man's sins are forgiven him, and he is owned by the whole trinity to be God's child.[26]

The Spirit applies words and thoughts of Scripture to the heart so powerfully and authoritatively that the believer is left in no doubt that they are being spoken by God to him.

This direct testimony does not normally begin to be given until a man has first gained assurance by the lower road of Spirit-guided inference; our spirit is the first to witness, and God's Spirit joins his witness with it later; but when the direct testimony is experienced, it creates a degree of joy to which the other could never give rise. 'It works that joy in the heart which the saints shall have in heaven. . . . It is not a bare conviction that a man shall go to heaven; but God telleth him in part what heaven is, and lets him feel it.'[27] It is pre-eminently as thus witnessing to our adoption that the

Spirit is the 'earnest of our inheritance' (Eph 1:14), Goodwin thinks. The Spirit's immediate testimony takes a man's mind off himself, and centres him wholly upon God, and through it he foretastes heaven on earth. Goodwin insists that Christians do not enjoy the full riches of assurance till they know, not merely the Spirit's indirect witness through conscience, but his direct witness also; those who lack it, therefore, should stir themselves up to seek it from God.

Goodwin expounds the phrase in Ephesians 1:13, 'sealed with the Holy Spirit of promise', as a reference to this direct testimony. In so doing he identifies with a line of thought that goes back through Sibbes and John Preston to the architect of so much Puritan practical theology, William Perkins;[28] but he makes more of it than any of his predecessors had done. He suggests that 'sealing' is a part of the ministry of the Spirit promised by Christ in John 14, and calls attention to the words 'in that day ye shall *know* that I am in my Father, and *ye in me, and I in you*', and to the promise that Christ himself would manifest himself to the disciples (vv 20-21). These promises, he holds, are fulfilled in the Spirit's direct witnessing; and whenever the New Testament mentions the receiving of the Spirit at some point subsequent to believing, the reference is to a conscious experiencing of the Spirit's direct witness. This, he suggests, is the inner, experiential aspect of the charismatic outpourings of the Spirit recorded in Acts and in such passages as Galatians 3:2.

In his capacity as a 'sealer', the Spirit was not given before Jesus was glorified (Jn 7:38f); full assurance is a specifically New Testament blessing. Clearly, Christ had to be glorified before the Spirit could witness to believers of their union with him in glory.

Then Goodwin proceeds to a remarkable piece of sacramental theology. This 'sealing', he says, 'is the great fruit of your baptism.' Here he develops a line of thought peculiar to himself. Its basis is the scriptural and Reformed conception of baptism as a sign and a seal. As a sign, it signifies God's reception and appropriation of a person into saving union with himself: one is 'baptized into the name of the Father, Son and Holy Ghost' (Mt. 28:19). As a seal, it assures that person, as did circumcision in Old Testament times, that God has entered into covenant with him, pardoning his sins and making him an heir of the promised inheritance. Says Goodwin:

> The seal of the Spirit is the proper work that answereth to baptism. Therefore . . . it is called 'baptizing with the Holy Ghost' (Acts 1:5, 11:16), because it is that which is the fruit of baptism, it answereth that outward seal. . . . Peter biddeth them be baptized, and they should receive the promise, Acts 2:38.[29]

The gift of the Spirit thus witnessing brings home to the believer what his baptism symbolically proclaimed to him: an assurance that he is now

God's, and God is henceforth his. In the early church, says Goodwin, 'baptism was the ordinance to the newly converted, which conveyed the Spirit as sealing';[30] the outward and inward seals were commonly received together, as Acts shows, and the Epistles suggest that 'almost all the saints in the primitive times [were] sealed.'[31] The position for later ages, however, is that the two are normally not conjoined, most of God's people being baptised in infancy; but believers who have received the outward seal of baptism are thereby authorised and encouraged to seek from God in faith the complementary inward seal of the Spirit. When, or whether, God will give it to them they cannot know in advance; they must bow to his sovereignty here; but they can be sure that they will not find it unless they seek it, and that it is supremely worth seeking.

To confirm his view of the connection between baptism and the 'seal' as he conceived it, Goodwin makes a striking appeal to the baptism of Christ, the representative Head of God's elect. He lays down the principle that, since it is of Christ's fullness that we receive, 'whatsoever work God doth upon us, he doth upon Christ first.' Now, Christ was *sealed* (Jn 6:27) at his baptism, when the Spirit descended on him and he heard his Father say: 'This is my beloved Son.' This, says Goodwin, was a giving of direct assurance analogous to that which the 'seal' brings to believers.

> Though [Christ] had the assurance of faith that he was the Son of God
> . . . out of the Scriptures, by reading all the prophets . . . yet to have it sealed
> to him with joy unspeakable . . . this was deferred to the time of his baptism.
> He was then anointed with the Holy Ghost [Acts 10:38]. . . . Answerably
> [cf 2 Cor 1:22] [God] hath sealed and anointed us, just as he sealed and
> anointed Christ in his baptism.[32]

And the mode of the sealing of Christ conformed precisely to the mode of the sealing of Christians.

> It is always, I say, by a promise. . . . Jesus Christ was sealed . . . by a
> promise. . . . What was it? 'This is my beloved Son, in whom I am well
> pleased.' This is a Scripture promise . . . Is. 42:1. . . . That which had been
> spoken before of the Messiah was brought home to his heart.[33]

3

How much of this line of exposition is acceptable? Certain facts are clear. The reception of the Spirit after believing certainly had experimental repercussions for New Testament Christians, as Acts and Galatians 3:2, etc, make plain; it produced, not merely charismatic action (prophecy, tongues,

miracles) but also great joy, boldness and vigour in Christian life and service. John 14—16, as Goodwin points out, certainly links the coming of
the Comforter with a new depth of assurance and a new intimacy of communion with God. Romans 8:16 certainly admits, grammatically, of either
of the exegeses reviewed above, and certainly refers on any view to a strong
God-created and God-sustained conviction of one's standing in grace,
which Paul and his readers shared. It seems certain that the Puritans are
in fact directing our attention to one of the experiential dimensions of New
Testament faith of which we know too little today, whichever mode of conceiving the twofold witness we adopt.

But it seems incorrect to equate the dawning of assurance, direct or indirect, with the 'seal of the Spirit' referred to in Ephesians 1:13, 4:30 and
2 Corinthians 1:21. Goodwin's interpretation, that the Spirit is the sealer,
the 'efficient cause' of the sealing operation, and that the sense of assurance
is the seal, is not what the Greek means. John Owen, discussing these texts,
rightly dissents from this exposition. 'It is not said that the *Holy Spirit seals
us*, but that *we are sealed with him*. He is God's seal unto us.'[34] Nor is he
called a 'seal' because he makes us sure that God's promises are true and
apply to us: 'This were to seal the promises of God, and not believers. But
it is persons, and not promises, that are said to be sealed.'[35] Owen's own
alternative is as follows: 'This is to seal a thing,—to stamp the character
of the seal on it. . . . The Spirit in believers, really communicating the image
of God, in righteousness and true holiness, unto the soul, sealeth us.'[36] If
safe-keeping is part of the thought that the metaphor of God 'sealing' us
is meant to convey, then 'it denotes not an act of sense in the heart', but a
guaranteeing of security to the person.[37] Assurance, as a conscious condition of mind and heart induced by the Spirit's witnessing activity, comes
as a spinoff from the sealing rather than being integral to the act of sealing
as such.

Christ's baptism, which Owen discusses in detail,[38] was certainly the
prototype of our sealing; but the seal given to him was the gift of the Holy
Spirit in all fullness, anointing him for his messianic public ministry, and
the word of assurance given with it was something distinct from it. Correspondingly, 'God's sealing of believers . . . is his gracious communication
of the Holy Ghost unto them . . . to enable them unto all the duties of their
holy calling, evidencing them to be accepted with him . . . and asserting
their preservation unto eternal salvation.'[39] Assurance may come with the
gift, but it is not to be equated with it. The seal is not any particular operation of the Spirit, but the gift of the Spirit himself.

From the vantage-point of his insight that, since we are sealed with the
Spirit 'in Christ' (Eph 1:13), we must understand our sealing in the light
and by the pattern and paradigm of his, Owen writes: 'It hath been generally conceived that the sealing with the Spirit . . . gives assurance . . . and
so indeed it doth, although the way whereby it doth it, hath not been

rightly apprehended.'[40] The truth is that it is the presence of the Spirit, as manifested by his total action in the life, and not any single element in that action, which is the ground of the believer's assurance that he is God's (1 Jn 3:24; 4:13; Rom 8:9). Consequently the assertion that Spirit-sealing is chronologically a post-conversion event must be given up and the aorist participle of Ephesians 1:13 must be taken, in a way that is perfectly natural in Greek, to mean: '*upon believing* you were sealed. . . .' For Scripture forbids us to postulate an interval of time between believing and being sealed. All who believe have the Spirit; all who have the Spirit have been sealed with the Spirit; and those who have not been thus sealed are not Christians at all.

However, the doctrine of the Spirit's witness through the awakening of joy in the light of the knowledge of God's love has a much broader scriptural basis than a particular exegesis of the 'seal' texts. Owen affirmed the reality of this witness by God's sovereign gift of supernatural joy, though he would not identify it with the 'seal'. He wrote:

> Of this joy there is no account to be given, but that the Spirit worketh it when and how he will; he secretly infuseth and distils it into the soul, prevailing against all fears and sorrows, filling it with gladness, exultations; and sometimes with unspeakable raptures of mind.[41]

Owen's statement would, I think, have been subscribed by all the Puritans. Whether or not they regarded such experiences as experiences of assurance in the strict sense, whether or not they believed that Romans 8:16, or the 'seal' texts, referred to them, none of them doubted that such things happened, and that it was supremely desirable for every Christian that such things should happen to him. This is the central fact to fasten on in our assessment of the Puritan teaching on this whole subject, and our reflections on its relevance to ourselves today.

CHAPTER TWELVE

The Spirituality of John Owen

1

The Puritan John Owen, who comes closer than anyone else to being the hero of this book, was one of the greatest of English theologians. In an age of giants, he overtopped them all. C.H. Spurgeon called him the prince of divines. He is hardly known today, and we are the poorer for our ignorance.

Owen was born in 1616, in the Oxfordshire village of Stadham, where his father was the hardworking, uncompromising Puritan vicar. Welsh blood ran in his veins, which may partly account for one of the qualities that make his writings distinctive, namely the grand scale on which he portrays, on the one hand, the greatness of God and the need for the deepest humility before him and, on the other hand, the poignant inward drama of the individual facing the issues of eternity—for Celtic evangelicals regularly outstrip their more matter-of-fact Anglo-Saxon peers in their grasp of these things. He entered Queen's College, Oxford, at the age of twelve, and took his MA in 1635. He studied ferociously hard, driven forward by his ambitions after political or ecclesiastical eminence; but, though a churchman, he was not yet a Christian in the true sense. In his early twenties, however, God showed him his sins, and the torment of conviction threw him into such a turmoil that for three months he avoided the company of others and, when addressed, could scarcely utter a coherent sentence. Slowly he learned to trust Christ, and so found peace.

In 1637, by reason of conscientious objections to Chancellor Laud's statutes, he left the university, and with it, as far as he could foresee, all hope of advancement. But after Laud's fall, under the Long Parliament, he rose rapidly and in 1651 was made Dean of Christ Church, becoming Vice-Chancellor of the university the following year. Oxford had been the Royalist headquarters during the Civil War, and Owen found the university bankrupt and in chaos. He reorganised it, however, with conspicuous success. After 1660, he led the Independents through the bitter years of persecution. He was offered the presidency of Harvard, but declined. He died in 1683, after years of martyrdom to asthma and gallstones.[1]

The epitaph engraved on the monument that adorns Owen's tomb in Bunhill Fields reflects the respect in which he was held by his contemporaries, and indicates something of his quality as a man of God and a teacher of godliness. Here is a translation:[2]

John Owen, born in Oxfordshire, son of a distinguished theologian, was himself a more distinguished one, who must be counted among the most distinguished of this age. Furnished with the recognised resources of humane learning in uncommon measure, he put them all, as a well-ordered array of handmaids, at the service of theology, which he served himself. His theology was polemical, practical, and what is called casuistical, and it cannot be said that any one of these was peculiarly his rather than another.

In polemical theology, with more than herculean strength, he strangled three poisonous serpents, the Arminian, the Socinian, and the Roman.

In practical theology, he laid out before others the whole of the activity of the Holy Spirit, which he had first experienced in his own heart, according to the rule of the Word. And, leaving other things aside, he cultivated, and realised in practice, the blissful communion with God of which he wrote; a traveller on earth who grasped God like one in heaven.

In casuistry, he was valued as an oracle to be consulted on every complex matter.

A scribe instructed in every way for the kingdom of God, this pure lamp of gospel truth shone forth on many in private, on more from the pulpit, and on all in his printed works, pointing everyone to the same goal. And in this shining forth he gradually, as he and others recognized, squandered his strength till it was gone. His holy soul, longing to enjoy God more, left the shattered ruins of his once-handsome body, full of permanent weaknesses, attacked by frequent diseases, worn out most of all by hard work, and no longer a fit instrument for serving God, on a day rendered dreadful for many by earthly powers but now made happy for him through the power of God, August 25, 1683. He was 67.

This encomium brings before us all the themes and motifs that will occupy us in the present study.

Owen was a theologian of enormous intellectual energy. His knowledge and memory were vast, and he had an unusual power of organising his material. His thought was not subtle nor complicated, as, for instance, was Baxter's. His ideas, like Norman pillars, leave in the mind an impression of massive grandeur precisely by reason of the solid simplicity of their structure. Of their content, it is enough to say that for method and substance Owen reminds one frequently of Calvin, frequently too of the *Westminster* and *Savoy Confessions* (the *Savoy* is in fact the *Westminster*, lightly revised, mainly by Owen himself), and time and again of all three together; he is constantly and consciously near the centre of seventeenth-century Reformed thought throughout. His studied unconcern about style in presenting his views, a conscientious protest against the self-conscious literary posturing of the age, conceals their uncommon clarity and straightforwardness from superficial readers; but then, Owen did not write for superficial readers. He wrote, rather, for those who, once they take up a subject, cannot rest till they see to the bottom of it, and who find exhaustiveness not exhausting, but satisfying and refreshing. His works have been truly described as a series of theological systems, each organised around a different centre. He would never view parts in isolation from the whole.

His spiritual stature matched his intellectual gifts. 'Holiness', said David Clarkson in his funeral sermon, 'gave a divine lustre to his other accomplishments, it stirred in his whole course, and was diffused throughout his conversation.'[3] Owen's holiness—that is, the habitual Christlikeness that people saw in him—had a twofold source. First, as noted above, he was a *humble* man. 'There are two things that are suited to humble the souls of men,' he wrote; '. . . a due consideration of God, and then of ourselves. Of God, in his greatness, glory, holiness, power, majesty and authority; of ourselves, in our mean, abject and sinful condition.'[4] God taught Owen to consider both: to let God, the Sovereign Creator, be God in his thought and life, and to recognise his own guilt and uncleanness. The latter, he held, was especially important; 'the man that understands the evil of his own heart, how vile it is, is the only useful, fruitful and solidly believing and obedient person. . . .'[5] A man must abhor himself before he can serve God aright. Owen, proud by nature, had been brought low in and by his conversion, and thereafter he kept himself low by recurring contemplation of his inbred sinfulness.

Again, Owen *knew the power of his gospel*. Preachers, he held, must have 'experience of the power of the truth which they preach in and upon their own souls. . . . A man preacheth that sermon only well unto others which preacheth itself in his own soul.'[6] Therefore he made this rule:

> I hold myself bound in conscience and in honour, not even to imagine that I have attained a proper knowledge of any one article of truth, much less to publish it, unless through the Holy Spirit I have had such a taste of it, in

its spiritual sense, that I may be able, from the heart, to say with the psalmist, 'I have believed, and therefore have I spoken.'[7]

Hence the authority and skill with which he probes the dark depth of the human heart. 'Whole passages flash upon the mind of the reader', wrote A. Thomson of his *Temptation*, 'with an influence that makes him feel as if they had been written for himself alone.'[8] When Rabbi Duncan told his students to read Owen's *Indwelling Sin* he added: 'But prepare for the knife.'

Owen's style is often stigmatised as cumbersome and tortuous. Actually it is a Latinised spoken style, fluent but stately and expansive, in the elaborate Ciceronian manner. When Owen's prose is read aloud, as didactic rhetoric (which is, after all, what it is), the verbal inversions, displacements, archaisms and new coinages that bother modern readers cease to obscure and offend. Those who think as they read find Owen's expansiveness suggestive and his fulsomeness fertilising. 'Owen is said to be prolix,' wrote Spurgeon, 'but it would be truer to say that he is condensed. His style is heavy because he gives notes of what he might have said, and passes on without fully developing the great thoughts of his capacious mind. He requires hard study, and none of us ought to grudge it.'[9] I shall not dispute Spurgeon's verdict; I hope that my readers will not dispute it, either.

2

We now focus attention on John Owen's central teaching about the Christian life. For this I draw material mainly from his sermonic treatises on *Indwelling Sin*, *Mortification of Sin*, and *Temptation*, and his more highly wrought *Discourse concerning the Holy Spirit*.

The Puritan teachers as a body constantly insisted that realistic self-knowledge is a *sine qua non* for living the Christian life, and Owen is no exception. There are four items of self-knowledge of which he never tires of reminding the believer:

First, the Christian is a *man*, created for rational action and equipped to that end with a trinity of faculties: understanding, will and affection. (1) 'The mind or understanding is the leading faculty of the soul . . . its office is to guide, direct, choose and lead'; 'it is the eye of the soul.'[10] (2) As the mind is a power of apprehension, so the will is a power of action: 'a rational appetite: rational as guided by the mind, and an appetite as excited by the affections . . . it chooseth nothing but *sub ratione boni*, as it hath an appearance of good. . . . God is its natural and necessary object.'[11] (Owen here builds on the traditional scholastic doctrine that what is *good* is also desirable, and that objects are actually desired in virtue of the goodness, real or illusory, which is attributed to them. One who truly appreciates God's goodness, therefore, cannot but desire him; and desire, Owen holds, is the root and heart of love.) (3) The affections are the various dispositional 'drives', positive and negative, with their emotional overtones—love, hope, hate, fear and so on—which elicit choices by drawing man to or repelling him from particular objects. No choice is ever made without some degree of affection. Therefore 'affections are in the soul, as the helm is in the ship; if it be laid hold on by a skilful hand, it turneth the whole vessel which way he pleaseth.'[12] What enlists affection wins the man; 'it is in vain to contend with anything that hath the power of our affections in its disposal; it will prevail at the last.'[13]

Man was made to know good with his mind, to desire it, once he has come to know it, with his affections, and to cleave to it, once he has felt its attraction, with his will; the good in this case being God, his truth and his law. God accordingly moves us, not by direct action on the affections or will, but by addressing our mind with his word, and so bringing to bear on us the force of truth. Our first task, therefore, if we would serve God, is to learn the contents of 'God's Word written'.[14] Affection may be the helm of the ship, but the mind must steer; and the chart to steer by is God's revealed truth.

Consequently, it is the preacher's first task to teach his flock the doctrines of the Bible, eschewing emotionalism (the attempt to play directly on the affections) and addressing himself constantly to the mind. Owen habitually spoke of himself as a *teacher*, and conducted his own ministry on these principles, as his published sermons and practical treaties show.

Second, the Christian is a *fallen* man. Sin not only alienated him from God, but also from himself. The fruit of sin is disorder in the soul and disintegration of the character: 'the faculties move cross and contrary one to another; the will chooseth not the good which the mind discovers . . . commonly the affections . . . get the sovereignty, and draw the whole soul captive after them.'[15] Fallen man is no longer rational, but unstable, inconstant, distracted by conflicting passions and blind impulses, and 'without strength' to obey God (Rom 5:6). For the root of sin is an ingrained disaffection and antipathy towards the Creator (Rom 8:7), an irrational ingrained lust to dodge, defy, and disobey him. Of indwelling sin, Owen wrote: 'its nature and formal design is to oppose God; God as a lawgiver, God as holy, God as the author of the gospel, a way of salvation by grace and not by works, are the direct object of the law of sin.'[16] Ungodliness, unrighteousness, unbelief and heresy are its natural forms of self-expression. It pervades and pollutes the whole man: 'it adheres as a depraved principle unto our minds, in darkness and vanity; unto our affections in sensuality; unto our wills, in a loathing of, and aversion from, that which is good; and . . . is continually putting itself upon us, in inclinations, motions, or suggestions, to evil.'[17] And, as we shall see, it resists the whole work of grace, from first to last: 'when Christ comes with his spiritual power upon the soul to conquer it to himself, he hath no quiet landing place. He can set foot on no ground but what he must fight for.'[18]

Christian living, therefore, must be founded upon self-abhorrence and self-distrust because of indwelling sin's presence and power. Self-confidence and self-satisfaction argue self-ignorance. The only healthy Christian is the humble, broken-hearted Christian:

> *Constant self-abasement*, condemnation, and abhorrency, is another duty that is directly opposed unto the . . . rule of sin in the soul. No frame of mind is a better antidote against the poison of sin. . . . It is the soil wherein all grace will thrive and flourish. A constant due sense of sin as sin, of our interest therein by nature, and in the course of our lives, with a continual afflictive remembrance of . . . instances of it . . . is the soul's best posture. . . . To keep our souls in a constant state of mourning and self-abasement is the most necessary part of our wisdom . . . and it is so far from having any inconsistency with those consolations and joys, which the gospel tenders unto us in believing, as that it is the only way to let them into the soul in a due manner.[19]

Third, the Christian is a *redeemed* man. He was one of those for whom Christ became surety in the eternal 'covenant of redemption', to pay his debts, to earn him life, and to free him from sin's guilt, and who now lives to deliver him from sin's power. Redemption by Christ is the heart of Christian doctrine, and faith and love to Christ must be the heart of Christian devotion. With Thomas Goodwin and Samuel Rutherford, Owen saw this as clearly as any man has ever seen it.

> They know nothing of the life and power of the gospel, nothing of the reality of the grace of God, nor do they believe aright one article of the Christian faith, whose hearts are not sensible of the love of Christ herein. Nor is he sensible of the love of Christ, whose affections are not therein drawn out unto him. I say, they make a pageant of religion . . . whose hearts are not really affected with the love of Christ, in the susception and discharge of the work of mediation, so as to have real and spiritually sensible affections for him. Men . . . have no real acquaintance with Christianity, who imagine that the placing of the most intense affections of our souls on the person of Christ, the loving him with all our hearts because of his love, our being overcome thereby, until we are sick of love, the constant motions of our souls towards him with delight and adherence, are but fancies and imaginations.[20]

Fourth, the Christian is a *regenerate* man, a new creature in Christ. A new principle of life, and habit of obedience, has been implanted in him. This is the prophesied 'circumcision of the heart'. 'Whereas the blindness,

obstinacy, and stubbornness in sin, that is in us by nature, with the prejudices which possess our minds and affections, hinder us from conversion
unto God, by this circumcision they are taken away',[21] and man's first act
of true, saving faith in Jesus Christ, his conscious 'conversion', is its immediate result. This act, though directly caused by the Spirit's regenerative
operation in the depths of his being, is perfectly free (i.e., deliberate): 'in
order of nature, the acting of grace in the will in our conversion is
antecedent unto its own acting; though in the same instant of time wherein
the will is moved, it moves; and when it is acted, it acts itself, and preserves
its own liberty in its exercise.'[22]

Regeneration makes man's heart a battlefield, where 'the flesh' (the old
man) tirelessly disputes the supremacy of 'the spirit' (the new man). The
Christian cannot gratify the one without interference from the other (Gal
5:17; Rom 7:23). Sin, from which by repentance he has formally dissoci-
ated himself, seems to take on a life of its own; Paul likens it 'to a person,
a living person, called "the old man," with his faculties and properties, his
wisdom, craft, subtlety, strength.'[23] It is always at work in the heart; a temporary lull in its assaults means, not that it is dead, but that it is very much
alive. 'Sin is never less quiet, than when it seems to be most quiet, and its
waters are for the most part deep, when they are still.'[24] Its strategy is to
induce a false sense of security as a prelude to a surprise attack.

> By sin we are oftentimes, ere we are aware, carried into distempered affec-
> tions, foolish imaginations, and pleasing delightfulness in things that are
> not good nor profitable. When the soul is doing . . . quite another thing
> . . . sin starts that in the heart . . . that carries it away into that which is evil
> and sinful. Yea, to manifest its power, sometimes when the soul is seriously
> engaged in the mortification of any sin, it will, by one means or other, lead
> it away into a dalliance with that very sin whose ruin it is seeking. . . . I
> know no greater burden in the life of a believer than these involuntary sur-
> prisals. . . . And it is in respect unto them, that the apostle makes his com-
> plaint, Rom. 7:24. . . .[25]

The fight with sin is lifelong.

> Sometimes a soul thinks or hopes that it may through grace be utterly free
> from this troublesome inmate. Upon some secret enjoyment of God, some
> full supply of grace, some return from wandering, some deep affliction,
> some thorough humiliation, the poor soul begins to hope that it shall now
> be freed from the law of sin. But after a while . . . sin acts again, makes good
> its old station.[26]

And the man who claims perfection is self-deceived, and riding for a fall.
'You'll never get out of the seventh of Romans while I'm your minister,'

Alexander Whyte once told his Edinburgh congregation; and Owen, could he have stepped forward two and a half centuries to stand in Whyte's shoes, would have told them the same.

3

God's purpose for the Christian during his life on earth is *sanctification*. So said Calvin; so says Owen; and so says Holy Scripture (1 Thess 4:3; 1 Peter 1:15f). In stressing, as he constantly does, the necessity and cruciality of sanctification, Owen is only echoing the New Testament.

> Sanctification is an immediate work of the Spirit of God on the souls of believers, purifying and cleansing of their natures from the pollution and uncleanness of sin, renewing in them the image of God, and thereby enabling them from a spiritual and habitual principle of grace, to yield obedience unto God. . . . Or more briefly; it is the universal renovation of our natures by the Holy Spirit into the image of God, through Jesus Christ. Hence it follows, that our *holiness*, which is the fruit and effect of this work . . . as it compriseth the renewed . . . image of God wrought in us, so it consists in a holy obedience unto God, by Jesus Christ, according to the terms of the covenant of grace.[27]

Thus, 'holiness is nothing but the implanting, writing and realising of the gospel in our souls,'[28] 'the word changed into grace in our hearts . . . the Spirit worketh nothing in us, but what the word first requireth of us . . . growth is nothing but . . . increase in conformity to that word.'[29] This increase is progressive (or should be) throughout a Christian's life.

Holiness is both God's promised gift and man's prescribed duty: 'neither can we perform our duty herein without the grace of God; nor doth God give us this grace unto any other end but that we may rightly perform our duty.' He who would be holy must have a due regard both to God's law, which is itself holy, just, good and binding, and peremptorily requires of him all those good works of which holiness consists, and to God's promise of strength through Christ to keep this law.

> And we have a due regard unto the promise . . . when (1) we walk in a constant sense of our inability to comply with the command . . . from any power in ourselves. . . . (2) When we adore that grace which hath provided help and relief for us. . . . (3) When we act faith in prayer and expectation on the promise for supplies of grace enabling us to holy obedience.[30]

We must pray for help, and fight the good fight of faith in God's strength, and give thanks to him for the victories we win.

Sanctification has a double aspect. Its positive side is *vivification*, the growing and maturing of the new man; its negative side is *mortification*, the weakening and killing of the old man.

We grow in grace by the deliberate stirring up and exercise of the new powers and inclinations which regeneration implanted within us.

> Frequency of acts doth naturally increase and strengthen the habits whence they proceed. And in spiritual habits [e.g., faith, hope, love] it is so, more-over, by God's appointment. . . . They grow and thrive in and by their exercise . . . the want thereof is the principal means of their decay.[31]

The Christian, therefore, must use the means of grace assiduously, hearing, reading, meditating, watching, praying, worshipping; he must animate himself to 'universal obedience', an all-round, all-day conformity to God's revealed will; and he must persevere in it with resolution and resilience. Yet he must remember that the power is from God, not himself, and do it all in the spirit of prayerful dependence, or else he will fail. For

> the actual aid, assistance and internal operation of the Spirit of God is nec-essary . . . unto the producing of every holy act of our minds, wills and affec-tion, in every duty whatsoever. . . . Notwithstanding the power or ability which believers have received by habitual grace, they still stand in need of actual grace in . . . every single . . . act or duty towards God.[32]

This continual assistance will be withheld from those who forget their need of it and omit to ask for it.

Seeking thus to grow in grace means battling directly against the world, just as mortifying sin means battling directly against the flesh (see the next section). Owen points this up in the preface to *The Grace and Duty of Being Spiritually Minded*, in words which, though spoken of the late seventeenth century (the book was published in 1681), seem uncannily applicable to today. Owen wrote:

> The world is at present in a mighty hurry, and being in many places cut off from all foundations of steadfastness, it makes the minds of men giddy with its revolutions, or disorderly in the expectations of them . . . hence men walk and talk as if the world were all, when comparatively it is nothing. And when men come with their warmed affections, reeking with thoughts of these things, unto the performance of or attendance unto any spiritual duty, it is very difficult for them, if not impossible, to stir up any grace unto a due and vigorous exercise.[33]

Thoughts must therefore be guarded, the heart must be watched, and habits of disciplined meditation formed, or one will never be able to sustain the spiritual-mindedness that is the seed-bed of true growth in the life of grace and holiness.

Mortification is more than the mere suppression, or counteraction, of sinful impulse. It is nothing less than a gradual eradication of it. 'Mortify' means 'kill', and 'the end aimed at in this duty is destruction, as it is in all killing: the utter ruin, destruction and gradual annihilation of all the remainders of this cursed life of sin . . . to leave sin with neither being, nor life, nor operation. . . .'[34] The sin that indwells the believer was killed in principle on the cross; Christ's death will in time be its death. It was dethroned in fact by regeneration, and now, with the Spirit's aid, the Christian is to spend his lifetime draining its lifeblood (Rom 8:13). 'The whole work is by degrees to be carried on towards perfection all our days.'[35] We may never relax, for sin 'will no otherwise die, but by being gradually and constantly weakened; spare it, and it heals its wounds, and recovers strength.'[36] 'The work . . . consists in a constant taking part with grace . . . against the principle, acts and fruits of sin.'[37] It is often painful and ungrateful; Christ compared it to plucking out an eye, or cutting off a limb; but it is the way of life, and it is disastrous to neglect it.

The condition of successful assault on particular sins is, first, maintained humility ('no frame of mind is a better antidote against the poison of sin') and, second, sustained growth in grace.

> Growing, thriving and improving in universal holiness is the great way of the mortification of sin. The more vigorous the principle of holiness is in us, the more weak, infirm and dying will be that of sin. . . . This is that which will ruin sin, and without it nothing else will contribute anything thereunto.[38]

Especially, 'live and abound in the actual exercise of all those graces, which are most directly opposed to those . . . corruptions that we are most exercised withal.'[39]

The activity by which the Christian directly secures the mortification of his sins is prayer. This includes *complaint*, in which he spreads before God his sin and extremity and afflicts his soul by humbly acknowledging how justly his wrongdoing has provoked God's wrath against him, and *petition*, whereby he earnestly and importunately pleads God's promises of deliverance and sustains his faith in their accomplishment by recalling those events in which already God has evidenced his love for him. (The Psalms are full of examples of this.) The effect of prayer, subjectively, is twofold. First, grace is strengthened. 'The soul of a believer is never raised to a higher intension of spirit in the pursuit of, love unto, and delight in, holiness, nor is more confirmed unto it or cast into the mould of it, than it is in prayer.'[40] Second, sin is weakened and withers as the believer looks in faith and love to Christ. 'Let faith look on Christ in the gospel as he is set forth dying and crucified for us. Look on him under the weight of our sins, praying, bleeding, dying: bring him in that condition into the heart by faith; apply his blood so shed to thy corruptions; do this daily. . . .'[41] Sin nowhere appears so hateful as at Calvary, and lust shrivels up in the Christian's heart while he keeps Calvary in view. Again:

> Christ as crucified is the great object of our love, or should be . . . in the death of Christ do his love, his grace, his condescension, most gloriously shine forth . . . the effects of love, as of all true love, are first, *Adherence*; secondly, *Assimilation*:—[First] *Adherence*: Love in the Scriptures is frequently expressed by this effect; the soul of one did *cleave*, or was *knit*, unto another. . . . So it produceth a firm adherence unto Christ crucified, that makes a soul to be in some sense always present with Christ on the cross. And hence ensues, [Secondly], *Assimilation*, or conformity. . . . Love . . . begets a likeness between the mind loving and the object beloved. . . . A mind filled with the love of Christ as crucified . . . will be changed into its image and likeness, by the effectual mortification of sin. . . .[42]

The cross and the Spirit are thus the two focal realities in Owen's teaching about the Christian life. Christ merited the gift of the Spirit to the elect sinner by dying for him; the Spirit comes to him to show him what the cross reveals of Christ's love for him, to bring home to him the pardon Christ won for him, to change his heart, and to make him love his Saviour. The Spirit leads us to Christ's cross, God's guarantee to us that our sins, so far from bringing about our death eternally, shall themselves die, and brings the cross of Christ into our hearts, with its sin-killing power,[43] so ensuring that our sins do die.

It ought to be said before we go further, that this dichotomised scheme of sanctification as a matter of vivifying our graces and mortifying our sins, which Owen sets forth with such masterful and searching brilliance, is not in any way peculiar to him. It is conventional Puritan teaching, going back through Calvin to Romans 6 and Colossians 2:20—3:17. Here, as elsewhere, Owen stands in the main Puritan stream.

4

To stop short here, however, would be an injustice to Owen. For him, as for all the Puritans, sanctification was just one facet and cross-section of the more comprehensive reality that is central to Christian existence—namely, *communion with God*.

The thought of communion with God takes us to the very heart of Puritan theology and religion. This becomes clear as soon as we see how this subject stands related to other themes which stood in the forefront of Puritan interest.

We all know, for instance, that the Puritans were deeply concerned with the many-sided problem of man—man's nature and place in the world, man's powers and possibilities for good and evil, man's sufferings, hopes, fears, and frustrations, man's destiny, man in the 'fourfold state' of innocence, of sin, of grace, and of glory. And to their minds the whole end and purpose of man's existence was that he should have communion with God. 'Man's chief end is to glorify God, and to enjoy him for ever.'[44]

Again: we all know that the Puritans were deeply and constantly concerned with the doctrine of the covenant of grace—its nature, its terms, its promises, its blessings, the modes of its dispensation, its seals and ordinances. The covenant of grace has been called the characteristic Puritan doctrine, as justification by faith was the characteristic doctrine of Luther. And to the minds of the Puritans the direct end and purpose of the covenant of grace was to bring men into union and communion with God.

Or again: the Puritans never tired of dwelling on the mediation of Christ in the covenant of grace—his humiliation and exaltation, his satisfaction and intercession, and all his gracious relations as Shepherd, Husband, Friend, and the rest, to his own covenant people. And the Puritan view of the immediate end and purpose of the mediation of Christ is made plain to us by John Owen when he speaks of Christ's 'great undertaking, in his *life, death, resurrection, ascension*, being a mediator between God and us . . . to bring us to an enjoyment of God'.[45] This is the reality of communion.

Once more: Puritanism first emerged as a quest for the reform of England's public worship, and the substance, mode, and practice of corporate as well as individual worship remained a central Puritan concern throughout the movement's history. Of no one was this more true than of Owen himself, as his works bear witness: over and above his frequent treatments of worship in its various aspects as a distinct topic, he relates just about every theological theme to the worship of God somewhere in his writings. Why this sustained focus on worship? Not only because worship's primary aim is to give God the glory and praise that is his due, but also because worship's secondary end and purpose, inseparably bound up with the first, is to lead worshippers into the sunshine of communion with God—a true foretaste of heaven, in which all spiritual souls find their highest delight.

Thus, to the Puritans, communion between God and man is the end to which both creation and redemption are the means; it is the goal to which both theology and preaching must ever point; it is the essence of true religion; it is, indeed, the definition of Christianity.

To this subject Owen devoted his treatise, *Of Communion with God the Father, Son and Holy Ghost, each person distinctly, in love, grace and consolation; or, the Saint's Fellowship with the Father, Son, and Holy Ghost, unfolded*. This work, first published in 1657, was reprinted in 1674 with a prefatory epistle by Daniel Burgess, who called it 'the only [treatise] extant, upon its great and necessary subject'. This was true, however, only from a formal standpoint; the substance of what Owen says is found in less systematic form in very many Puritan expositions. One of the richest of these is Thomas Goodwin's *The Object and Acts of Justifying Faith*. (Goodwin, a fellow-Independent in church principles, was Owen's close colleague in the 1650s when Owen was Oxford's Vice-Chancellor and Goodwin was President of Magdalen College.) Other relevant sources for comparison would be Puritan expositions of the Song of Solomon (Sibbes, Collinges, Durham, and others), and of the favourite Puritan theme of 'walking with God' (for instance, Robert Bolton, *Some General Directions for a Comfortable Walking with God*, Richard Baxter's *The Divine Life*, and Thomas Gouge's *Christian Directions Shewing how to Walk with God All the Day Long*).

5

Owen's analysis of communion with God can be set out in five propositions.

1. *Communion with God is a relationship of mutual interchange between God and man.* Such is the idea which the New Testament word *koinonia* (translated in the English Bible as both 'fellowship' and 'communion') expresses. In general, *koinonia* denotes a joint participation in something by two or more parties, an active sharing in which the parties give to and receive from each other. 'Communion consists in *giving* and *receiving*.'[46] Such a relationship naturally implies the existence of some prior bond between the parties concerned. Accordingly, Owen defines *koinonia* between God and men as follows:

Our communion . . . with God consisteth in his *communication of himself unto us, with our returnal unto him* of that which he requireth and accepteth, flowing from that *union* which in Jesus Christ we have with him . . . [a] mutual communication in giving and receiving, after a most holy and spiritual manner, which is between God and the saints, while they walk together in a covenant of peace, ratified by the blood of Jesus.[47]

2. *Communion with God is a relationship in which the initiative and power are with God.* Note how Owen identifies the starting-point of communion with God as 'his communication of himself to us', with 'our returnal unto him of that which he requireth' coming in only on the basis of this. Communion with God is a relationship which God himself creates by giving himself to us; only so can we know him, and respond to him. In the narrow sense of our communing with God, communion is a Christian duty; in the broader and more fundamental sense of God's communicating himself to us, whether to prompt our communing or to reward it, communion

is a divine gift. Thus conceived, the idea of communion with God is broader than in our common present-day usage. We tend always to think of communion with God subjectively and anthropocentrically; we limit it to our conscious experience of God, our deliberate approach to him and his felt dealings with us. But the Puritans thought of communion with God objectively and theocentrically, taking the idea to cover, first, God's approach to us in grace, pardoning, regenerating, and making us alive to himself; next, all his subsequent self-giving to us; and only then extending it to our own conscious seeking after, and tasting of, his gracious presence. They were not less concerned about experiential acquaintance with God than we are—rather, indeed, the reverse—but they did not isolate this concern in their minds from their broader theological concern about the doctrine of divine grace. Thus they were saved from the peril of false mysticism, which has polluted much would-be Christian devotion in recent times. The context and cause of our experienced communion with God, said the Puritans, is God's effective life-giving communion with us; the former is always to be thought of as a consequence and, indeed, an aspect of the latter. The idea of communion with God thus covers the whole of the grace-and-faith relationship with God in which we stand, a relationship which God himself initiates and in which at each stage the initiative remains in his hands. The Barthians of our day proclaim that God is the active subject in all human relationships with him as if this were a new discovery, but Puritans like Owen knew this long ago.

3. *Communion with God is a relationship in which Christians receive love from, and respond in love to, all three Persons of the Trinity.* Owen constantly insisted that the doctrine of the Trinity is the foundation of Christian faith, and that if it falls, everything falls. The reason for this insistence was that the Christian salvation is a trinitarian salvation, in which the economic relations of the three divine Persons as they work out salvation together mirror their essential and eternal relations in the glorious life of the Godhead. The first Person, the Father, is revealed as the One who initiates, who chooses a people to save and his Son to save them, and who plans a way of salvation that is consistent with his holy character. The second Person is revealed as Son and Word in relation to the Father, imaging and embodying in himself the Father's nature and mind and coming forth from the Father to do his will by dying to redeem sinners. The third Person proceeds from the first two as their executive, conveying to God's chosen the salvation which the Son secured for them. All three are active in fulfilling a common purpose of love to unlovely men; all three give distinct gifts of their bounty to the chosen people, and all three, therefore, should be distinctly acknowledged in faith, with an appropriate response, by Christian believers. This is Owen's theme in his treatise *Of Communion.*

Consider first the Father, says Owen. His special gift to us may be described as an attitude and exercise of fatherly love: 'free, undeserved, and eternal . . . This the Father peculiarly fixes upon the saints: this they are immediately to eye in him, to receive of him, and to make such returns thereof, as he is delighted withal.'[48] Owen points out that in the New Testament love is singled out as the special characteristic of the Father in his relation to us (1 Jn 4:8; 1 Cor 13:14; Jn 3:16; 14:27; Rom 5:5; Tit 2:4).

The way to receive the Father's love is by faith; that is, in this case, by believing and acknowledging that Christ comes to us, not of his own initiative, but as the gift to us of a loving heavenly Father.

> It is true, there is not an *immediate* acting of faith upon the Father, but by the Son. He is 'the way, the truth, and the life: no man cometh unto the Father, but by' him (Jn 14:6). . . . But this is that I say: When by and through Christ, we have an access unto the Father, we then . . . see his love that he peculiarly bears unto us, and act faith thereon. We are then, I say, to eye it, to believe it, to receive it, as in him; the issues and fruits thereof being made out unto us through Christ alone. Though there be no light for us but in the beams, yet we may by the beams see the sun, which is the fountain of it. Though all our refreshments actually lie in the streams, yet by them we are led up to the *fountain*. Jesus Christ, in respect of the love of the Father, is but the beam, the stream, wherein though actually all our light, our refreshment lies, yet by him we are led to the fountain, the sun of eternal love itself. Would believers exercise themselves herein, they would find it a matter of no small spiritual improvement in their walking with God. . . . The soul being thus by faith through Christ . . . brought unto the bosom of God, into a comfortable persuasion, and spiritual perception and sense of his love, there reposes and rests itself. . . .[49]

How should we respond to the Father's love? By love in return: that is, says Owen, 'by a peculiar delight and acquiescing in the Father, revealed effectually as love unto the soul.'[50] He goes on to analyse this love which we owe him as consisting of four elements—rest, delight, reverence, and obedience, in combination together.

Next, Owen says, consider the Son. His special gift to us is grace—communicated free favour, and all the spiritual benefits which flow from it. All grace is found in him, and is received by receiving him.

> There is no man whatever that hath any want in reference unto the things of God, but Christ will be unto him that which he wants. . . . Is he *dead*? Christ is *life*. Is he *weak*? Christ is the *power* of God, and the *wisdom* of God. Hath he the *sense of guilt* upon him? Christ is complete *righteousness*. . . . Many poor creatures are sensible of their wants, but know not where their remedy lies. Indeed, whether it be life or light, power or joy, all is wrapped up in him.[51]

All this, says Owen, is in the mind of Paul when he speaks of 'the grace of our Lord Jesus Christ' (2 Cor 13:14), and of John when he says, 'of his fullness have we all received, and grace for grace' (Jn 1:16). In expounding the meaning of Christ's grace, Owen makes much of the 'conjugal relationship' between Christ and his people, and offers a detailed christological exegesis of the Song of Songs, 2:1-7 and 5, at which we shall be looking shortly.

The way we receive Christ's love is by faith; that is, in this case,

> free, willing consent to receive, embrace and submit unto the Lord Jesus, as their husband, Lord and Saviour,—to abide with him, subject their souls unto him, and to be ruled by him for ever. . . . When the soul consents to take Christ on his own terms, to save him in his own way, and says, 'Lord . . . I am now willing to receive thee and to be saved in thy way,—merely by grace; and though I would have walked according to my own mind, yet now I wholly give myself to be ruled by the Spirit, for in thee have I righteousness and strength, in thee am I justified and do glory;'—then doth it carry on communion with Christ. . . . Let believers exercise their hearts abundantly unto this thing. This is choice communion with the Son Jesus Christ. Let us receive him in all his excellencies as he bestows himself upon us;—be frequent in thoughts of faith, comparing him with other beloveds, sin, world, legal righteousness; and preferring him before them, counting them all loss and dung in comparison of him . . . and we shall not fail in the issue of sweet refreshment with him.[52]

How should we respond to the conjugal affection and loyalty of Christ towards us? By maintaining marital chastity towards him, says Owen: that is, by refusing to trust or hanker after any but him for our acceptance with God; by cherishing his Holy Spirit, sent to us for our eternal benefit; and by maintaining his worship undefiled, according to the Scripture pattern. This necessitates a daily deliberate submission to him as our gracious Lord. Daily we should rejoice before him in the knowledge of his perfection as a Saviour from sin; daily we should take the sins and infirmities of that day to his cross to receive forgiveness ('this is every day's work; I know not how any peace can be maintained with God without it'[53]); daily we should look to Christ, and wait on him, for the supply of his Spirit to purify our hearts and work holiness in us. Holiness, according to the Puritans, cannot be attained without the exercise of faith, any more than it can be perfected without the effort of fighting sin. The saints, says Owen:

> look upon him [Christ] as . . . the only dispenser of the Spirit and of all grace of sanctification and holiness . . . he is to sprinkle that blood upon their souls; he is to create the holiness in them that they long after. . . . In this state they look to Jesus; here faith fixes itself, in expectation of his giving

out the Spirit for all these ends and purposes; mixing the promises with faith and so becoming actual partakers of all this grace. This is . . . their communion with Christ; this is the life of faith as to grace and holiness. Blessed is the soul that is exercised therein.[54]

Finally, says Owen, consider the Spirit. He is called the Comforter, and comfort—strength and encouragement of heart, with assurance and joy—is his special gift to us. This comfort is conveyed in and through the understanding which he gives us of the love of God in Christ, and of our share in God's salvation (Jn 14:26f; 16:14; Rom 5:15; 8:16). The Spirit's ministry as our Comforter consists in

> his bringing the promises of Christ to remembrance, glorifying him in our hearts, shedding abroad the love of God in us, witnessing with us, as to our spiritual state and condition, sealing us to the day of redemption; being the earnest of our inheritance, anointing us with . . . consolation, confirming our adoption, and being present with us in our supplications. Here is the wisdom of faith,—to find out, and meet with the Comforter in all these things; not to lose their sweetness, by lying in the dark [as] to their author, nor coming short of the returns which are required of us.[55]

How are we to respond to the comforting work of the Spirit? By taking care not to grieve him by negligence or sin (Eph 4:30), nor to quench him by opposing or hindering his work (1 Thess 5:19), nor to resist him by refusing the word (Acts 7:51), but to give him constant thanks, and to pray to him for a continuance of his peace and goodness. (Owen finds in Revelation 1:4 a precedent for such prayer to the Spirit.)

This then, according to Owen, should be the pattern of our regular communion with the three Persons of the Godhead, in meditation, prayer, and a duly ordered life. We should dwell on the special mercy and ministry of each Person towards us, and make our proper response of love and submission distinctly to each. Thus we are to maintain a full-orbed communion with God.

Thomas Goodwin propounds a similar conception, with less concern for verbal precision but greater exuberance and warmth than we find in what James Moffatt once called 'the dark grey pool of Owen's ratiocination'. Owen has shown us intercourse with the Triune God as a part of Christian duty; in the following passage, Goodwin sets it before us as a part of God's gift of assurance. Apropos of 1 John 1:3 and John 14:17-23, Goodwin writes:

> There is communion and fellowship with all the persons, Father, Son, and Holy Ghost, and their love, severally and distinctly. . . . Christ putteth you upon labouring after a distinct knowing of, and communion with all three

persons . . . rest not until all three persons manifest their love to thee . . . in
assurance, sometimes a man's communion and converse is with the one,
sometimes with the other; sometimes with the Father, then with the Son,
and then with the help of the Holy Ghost; sometimes his heart is drawn out
to consider the Father's love in choosing, and then the love of Christ in
redeeming, and so the love of the Holy Ghost, that searcheth the deep things
of God, and revealeth them to us, and taketh all the pains with us; and so
a man goes from one witness to another distinctly, which I say, is the communion that John would have us to have. . . . And this assurance it is not
a knowledge by way of argumentation or deduction, whereby we infer that
if one loveth me then the other loveth me, but it is intuitive, as I may so
express it, and we should never be satisfied till we have attained it, and till
all three persons lie level in us, and all make their abode with us, and we
sit as it were in the midst of them, while they all manifest their love to us
. . . this is the highest that ever Christ promised in this life (in his last sermon,
John 14).[56]

Owen did not express himself this way; but would he have assented to
Goodwin's statements? I think he would.

4. *Communion with God is a relation of active, forward-looking friendship between God and man.* This thought brings into perspective at once
the whole of John Owen's complex analysis. Communion with God means
simply behaving as a friend of the God who has called you his friend.
Thomas Goodwin dwells on the love of Christ, who, when we had fallen
into sin and enmity against God, died to make us his friends again—though
'he could have created new ones cheaper'[57]—and develops powerfully the
thought that friendship is not a means to an end, but an end in itself, and
that true friendship is expressed in the cultivation of our friend's company
for its own sake:

Mutual communion is the soul of all true friendship and a familiar converse
with a friend hath the greatest sweetness in it . . . [so] besides the common
tribute of daily worship you owe to [God], take occasion to come into his
presence on purpose to have communion with him. This is truly friendly,
for friendship is most maintained and kept up by visits; and these, the more
free and less occasioned by urgent business . . . they are, the more friendly
they are. . . . We use to check our friends with this upbraiding, You still
[always] come when you have some business, but when will you come to
see me? . . . When thou comest into his presence, be telling him still how
well thou lovest him; labour to abound in expressions of that kind, than
which . . . there is nothing more taking with the heart of any friend. . . .[58]

Once more, Owen's style appears cooler and less intimate; yet he makes
identical points, in his own way. He dwells on Christ's delight in his saints,

assuring us that 'his heart is glad in us, without sorrow. And every day whilst we live is his *wedding-day*'; also, that 'the thoughts of communion with the saints were the joy of his heart from eternity'.[59] 'He useth them as friends, as bosom friends in whom he is delighted,'[60] telling them all that in his heart that concerns them. Then, on the other side, 'the saints delight in Christ: he is their joy, their crown, their rejoicing, their life, food, health, strength, desire, righteousness, salvation, blessedness'—and 'in that pattern of communion with Jesus Christ which we have in the Canticles, this is abundantly insisted on.'[61] Owen here aligns himself with those many Puritans who follow in the footsteps of Bernard and other medievals in expounding the Song of Solomon as a parable (they themselves were perhaps unwisely willing to say, allegory) of the mutual love of Christ and his spiritual bride, sometimes the church and sometimes the Christian. In the course of his analysis of communion with Christ Owen gives some of his own thumbnail exposition of parts of the Song, and I cannot do better than cite here some paragraphs from Sinclair Ferguson's excellent summary of it.[62]

The theme of Canticles is this, essentially:

The Christian's sense of the love of Christ, and the effect of it in communion with him, by prayer and praises, is divinely set forth in the book of Canticles. The church therein is represented as the spouse of Christ; and, as a faithful spouse she is always either solicitous about his love, or rejoicing in it (II:46). . . .

The theme is worked out in this way:

Christ and the Christian are the two main characters. The *daughters of Jerusalem* represent 'all sorts of professors' (II:55). The *watchmen* represent office-bearers in the church, and the city represents the visible church itself. And while, occasionally, the corporate aspect of the Christian life appears in his exposition, the major concentration is on the individual's experience and the communion he enjoys with his Lord Jesus.

Owen develops this theme in several central passages:

2:1-7: here Christ is seen, describing his own character and significance to the Christian. He is the Rose of Sharon, the Lily of the Valley. That is, he is pre-eminent in all his personal graces, just as the Rose abounds in perfume, and the Lily in beauty. Indeed, the Rose is from the fertile plain of Sharon, in which the choicest herds are reared.

What does all this mean? Christ 'allures' (II:42) the Christian, says Owen—there is an irresistible attraction to him; the believer enjoys the scent of him as the Rose . . . he is compared to the apple tree (2:3)—it provides fruit for food, and shade for protection. . . . Christ . . . provides shelter, 'from wrath without, and . . . because of weariness within. . . . From the power of *corruptions*, trouble of temptations, distress of persecutions, there is in him quiet, rest, and repose' (II:43-44).

And so in the verses that follow, our communion with the Lord Jesus is delineated for us. It is marked by four things:

(i) *Sweetness of fellowship.* 'He brought me to the banqueting-house', v. 4, where he reveals all the treasures of his grace in the Gospel. Indeed, says Owen, we find in this book (1:2) that his love is better than wine, since it is righteousness, peace, joy in the Holy Spirit. . . .

(ii) *Delight in fellowship.* The maiden is overcome with all this, and she wants to know more of the love of her beloved. She is 'sick of love'—v. 5, 'not (as some suppose) fainting for want of a sense of love,' but, 'made sick and faint, even overcome, with the mighty actings of that divine affection, after she had once tasted of the sweetness of Christ in the banqueting-house' (II:44).

(iii) *Safety* v. 4—his banner over her was love—a symbol of protection, and a token of success and victory. . . . Christ's banner stands over the believer. . . . Only what Christ gives to us in his love for us will ever come to us. It is the great argument of Romans 8:32—he that spared not his own Son, how shall he not with him also freely give us all things? This is our resting place and safety!

(iv) *Support and Consolation* v. 6. His left hand is under her head, and his right hand embraces her. What is this? asks Owen. It is the picture of Christ supporting the church, and at the same time cherishing it and nourishing it! And so, v. 7—their fellowship together is continued and sustained.

In Canticles 2:9 Christ reappears. In the Song, the lover shows himself through the lattice, and this is interpreted as follows: 'Our sight of him here is as it were by glances,—liable to be clouded by many interpositions.' There is 'instability and imperfection in our apprehension of him', that is our present mortal state; 'In the meantime he looketh through the *windows* of the ordinances of the Gospel' (II:126). When the Christian has turned away in heart, Christ comes, searching and longing for the loving service of the church. If he does not receive it, he will withdraw. It would be impossible within the general framework of Owen's theology to suppose that this involves severed relationships; but it does imply disjointed experience and broken fellowship. Christ is still the Christian's possession and vice-versa, but the *sense* [awareness] of this has gone.

In chapter 3 the spouse discovers that her lover has withdrawn. She is perplexed. Owen is not clear whether this is the cause or the effect of the 'night' in which she discovers herself, but points to the application: 'in the greatest peace and opportunity of ease and rest, a believer finds none in the absence of Christ: though he be on his bed, having nothing to disquiet him, he rests not, if Christ, his rest, be not there' (II:128). So the soul searches for Christ, first of all in the ordinary duties of faith (II:613), but 'This is not a way to recover a sense of lost love' (II:353), rather there must be 'Resolutions for new, extraordinary, vigorous, constant applications unto God,'—'the first general step and degree of a sin-entangled soul acting towards a recovery' (*ibid*). It is evident that here the soul has lost its sense of forgiveness, and that the search for its restoration involves two things: first, a search of one's own *soul* to discover the cause of Christ's absence, and, second, a search of the *promises* of God to discover the means of his return. Self-examination must be followed by a reapplication to the Covenant of Grace. If this yields no success, the solution is to be found in extraordinary duties, as Owen has already hinted. So the spouse goes about the city (the visible church) looking for her lover. If Christ is not found in private, it is the Christian's duty to make a special search for him in public, through worship, the preaching of the word, and the sacraments. In her search the maiden is found by the watchmen (office-bearers in the church visible) . . . who take notice of the plight of the spouse. This is the duty of faithful office-bearers. Exactly how Christ is discovered is not indicated in the passage, but Owen detects some significance in this too. When Christ comes, it is in his own mysterious way by the Spirit.

By chapter 5 the spouse has sunk again into sloth and indolence. The shepherd-lover comes to meet with her, but she excuses herself by the unsuitableness of the time and her lack of preparation for her duties (II:520). Christ, thus rebuffed, leaves the believer and 'long it is before she obtains any recovery' (II:346). He returns later in the chapter and the description given in 5:10-16 provides Owen with a further opportunity to celebrate what the Christian finds in his Saviour who is described as being 'white and ruddy'. 'He is *white* in the glory of his *deity*, and *ruddy* in the preciousness of his *humanity*' (II:49). . . . It is this excellence, through the union of the 'white and ruddy' that fits him to be the Saviour, and brings salvation through union and communion with him. . . .

In the following verses the maiden goes on to describe Christ more fully. His *head* is as fine gold—conveying the splendour and durability of Christ as the head of the government of the kingdom of God (II:71). His *locks* are said to be 'bushy' or curled, 'black as a raven'. To first appearance the hair is tangled, but in fact it is well and precisely ordered, thus representing the wisdom of Christ in his mediatorial administration. The hair is black to indicate that he ways are past finding out (II:72), and, in a natural sense, emphasising his comeliness and vigour (II:73). His *eyes* are like those of the dove—not a bird of prey—indicating the wealth of his knowledge and discernment. They are tender and pure as he discerns the thoughts and intentions of men (*ibid*). His *cheeks* are like beds of spices, sweet of savour, beautiful in their orderliness (II:75); so the graces of Christ, in his human nature, are gathered by Christians in prayer, from the Covenant promises of God which are well ordered (2 Samuel 23:5). These graces are eminent indeed, like 'towers of perfumes' (marginal reading adopted by Owen, II:76). His *lips* are like lilies, dropping myrrh—a description of the riches of Christ's word (*ibid*).

His *hands* (v. 14), refers to the work he has accomplished, as the fruit of his love. His *belly* (in the sense of bowels) reminds us of his tender mercy and loving affection. His *legs, countenance* and *mouth* (v. 15) remind us of the stability of his kingdom, the grace and faithfulness of his promises. He is completely worthy of the desires and affections of his followers (v. 16) in his birth, life, and death, in the glory of his ascension and coronation, in the supply of the Spirit of God, in the ordinances of worship, in the tenderness of his care, in the justice of his vengeance on his enemies, as well as in the pardon he dispenses to all his own people. And this Christ, says Owen, often comes by surprise to the Christian: when he is engaged in ordinary occupations, he finds his mind drawn out in love for Jesus. Weigh these experiences against those when Satan invades the mind with worldly thoughts, says Owen, lest you be led to despair.

Owen adds much more of the same kind, but we cannot follow him further in it now.

It is, as Ferguson says, of secondary importance how far we go along with Owen's allegorising here. What matters is the clear evidence which it affords that at the heart both of his understanding of true Christian piety and of his own personal commitment lay loving fellowship with the living Lord Jesus: fellowship which gave shape, substance and strength both to Owen's laborious discipleship through troubled times and to his personal hope.

In the love affair that is Christianity, the links between faith, love and hope are strong and obvious. On the one hand, God's promises in the covenant of grace guarantee us not only immunity from past sins and protection under present pressures, but also the felicity of closer and richer fellowship in the future, when faith is superseded by sight. On the other hand, as earthly lovers long to be together, with all five senses (sight, hearing, touch, taste, smell) actively involved with the active mind in joyfully apprehending each other, so it is, naturally and spontaneously, with the saints in relation to their Saviour. Writes Owen:

> To have the eternal glory of God in Christ, with all the fruits of his wisdom and love while we ourselves are under the full participation of the effects of them, immediately, directly revealed, proposed, made known unto us, in a divine and glorious light, our souls being furnished with a capacity to behold and perfectly comprehend them,—this is the heaven which, according to God's promise, we look for.[63]

Sustained by such a hope, the believer can and should face the last enemy squarely and get ready to take death in stride when it comes; and such preparation of heart and mind for passage out of this world into the immediate presence of God was, in fact, a major theme of all Puritan spirituality.

How Owen had prepared himself appears from his deathbed reply on the morning of 24 August 1683 to the news which a fellow minister, William Payne, had brought him that his last work, entitled appropriately enough *Meditations and Discourses of the Glory of Christ*, was now in the press. 'I am glad to hear it,' said Owen, 'but O brother Payne! The long wished for day is come at last, in which I shall see that glory in another manner than I have ever done, or was capable of doing, in this world.'[64] He knew that he was dying, and before the day ended he was gone. Right to the end Owen's lumbering Latinised linguistic precision stayed with him, so that what was almost his last utterance was phrased like a public address, and that was, to say the least, quaint—but I ask you, leaving the stylistic question aside, was there ever a lovelier or sweeter or indeed nobler exit line?

5. *Communion with God in Christ is enjoyed in a special way at the Lord's Table.* The typical Puritan view of the Lord's Supper was not a bare memorialism, as if eucharistic worship was a matter merely of recalling Christ's death without fellowshipping with him in the process. It was, to be sure, no part of the Puritan belief that the communicant receives in the Supper a unique grace which he could not otherwise have; the Puritans would all agree with the Scot, Robert Bruce, that 'we get no other thing in the Sacrament, than we get in the Word'.[65] But there is a special exercise of faith proper to the Lord's Table, where Christ's supreme act of love is set before us with unique vividness in the sacramental sign; and from this should spring a specially close communion with the Father and the Son. Let Richard Baxter introduce this teaching:

> Also in the sacrament of the body and blood of Christ, we are called to a familiar converse with God. He there appeareth to us by a wonderful condescension in the representing, communicating signs of the flesh and blood of his Son, in which he hath most conspicuously revealed his love and goodness to believers: there Christ himself with his covenant gifts are all delivered to us by these investing signs of his own institution. . . . No where is God so near to man as in Jesus Christ; and no where is Christ so familiarly represented to us, as in his holy sacrament. Here we are called to sit with him at his table, as his invited, welcome guests; to commemorate his sacrifice, to feed upon his very flesh and blood; that is, with our mouths upon his representative flesh and blood, by such a feeding as belongs to faith. The marriage covenant betwixt God incarnate and his espoused ones, is there publicly sealed, celebrated and solemnized. There we are entertained by God as friends . . . and that at the most precious costly feast. If ever a believer may on earth expect his kindest entertainment, and near access, and a humble intimacy with his Lord, it is in the participation of this sacrifice feast, which is called The Communion, because it is appointed as well for our special communion with Christ as with one another. It is here that we

fullest intimation, expression, and communication of the wondrous love of God; and therefore it is here that we have the loudest call, and best assistance, to make a large return of love; and where there is most of this love between God and man, there is most communion, and most of heaven, that can be had on earth.[66]

Owen and Baxter did not see eye to eye on everything—on the nature of the atonement, the ground of justification, and a number of church questions, they were in fact a fair distance apart—but in regarding the Lord's Supper as an occasion and means of communion with Christ they were truly at one. Owen never wrote about the Lord's Supper, but from a series of informal sacramental sermons that were taken down in shorthand as he preached[67] his view of the matter becomes plain. The last sentence of the last sermon expresses his basic position: 'We say, we have in these things *experience of a peculiar communion* with Christ, in a way made proper to this ordinance, which is not to be found in any other ordinance.'[68] Once again, Sinclair Ferguson offers an admirable summary of Owen's development of his theme, which we may quote:[69]

The communion of the Supper is *commemorative* since it involves a profession and proclamation of Christ's death. It is *eucharistical*, and *federal* (IX:527) in that God *confirms* his covenant . . . and believers renew themselves in covenant obligations.

But how is Christ present in the Supper? Owen believers he is present 'in an special manner' (IX:572) . . . his presence is not corporeal. . . . Christ is present by representation, exhibition and obsignation.

Representation is a favourite expression (IX:563, 593, 595, 605, 606). Christ is shown as the one who suffered for men's sins and as 'newly sacrificed' (IX:564, cf III:440) is food for their souls. This representation is seen with respect to God's setting him forth; his passion; his exhibition in the promise; his incorporation with the believer in union; and his [the believer's] participation with Christ by faith (IX:540-41).

Christ is also *exhibited* in the Supper. Here the important thing for Owen is that *it is Christ who exhibits himself*. He is not proposed as the object of faith by the Father or the Spirit, but by himself (IX:589). This makes the Supper a 'peculiar' ordinance as Christ sets himself forth as Prophet, Priest and King (IX:621-22). 'It is himself, as accompanied with all the benefits of that great part of his mediation, in dying for us' (IX:590).

Christ is also present by *obsignation*: the covenant has been made and confirmed by the blood of Christ; 'he comes and seals the covenant with his own blood in the administration of this ordinance' (IX:574).

Communion with Christ then becomes a matter of acknowledging his presence in the power of his reconciling sacrifice and of observing the ordinance with reverent confidence that in it Christ comes to pledge his saving love to each one personally, so that 'we sit down at God's table as those that are the Lord's friends . . . there being now no difference [contention] between him and us'.[70] We should prepare ourselves for the occasion by '*Meditation* on the guilt of sin, the holiness of God, and salvation in Christ (IX:559); *Self-examination* in a spirit of repentance . . . and faith . . . ; *Supplication*, in which prayer is added "which may inlay and digest all the rest in the soul" (IX:562); and *expectation* that God will keep his promise, and "meet us according to the desire of our hearts" (*ibid*).'[71] Then we may confidently expect an enlivening encounter with our beloved Lord, resulting in more joy, peace, grateful love, and humble devotion, than was ours before; for it is not Christ's way to disappoint those who seek him by a proper use of the means of grace.

6

This completes our mapping of the structure of spirituality, theological and experiential, that was taught by the magisterial instructor who has always been regarded as the prince of the Puritans. At every point he speaks for the entire school of Puritan pastoral theologians, differing from others only in the weight and wisdom with which he formulates their common certainties. So the general reflections that are now in order will have in view, not just Owen, as if he stood alone, but the whole heritage of which he was so distinguished a mouthpiece.

Anyone who knows anything at all about Puritan Christianity knows that at its best it had a vigour, a manliness, and a depth which modern evangelical piety largely lacks. This is because Puritanism was essentially an experimental faith, a religion of 'heart-work', a sustained practice of seeking the face of God, in a way that our own Christianity too often is not. The Puritans were manlier Christians just because they were godlier Christians. It is worth noting three particular points of contrast between them and ourselves.

First, we cannot but conclude that whereas to the Puritans communion with God was a *great* thing, to evangelicals today it is a comparatively *small* thing. The Puritans were concerned about communion with God in a way that we are not. The measure of our unconcern is the little that we say about it. When Christians meet, they talk to each other about their Christian work and Christian interests, their Christian acquaintances, the state of the churches, and the problems of theology—but rarely of their daily experience of God. Modern Christian books and magazines contain much about Christian doctrine, Christian standards, problems of Christian conduct, techniques of Christian service—but little about the inner realities of fellowship with God. Our sermons contain much sound doctrine—but little relating to the converse between the soul and the Saviour. We do not spend much time, alone or together, in dwelling on the wonder of the fact that God and sinners have communion at all; no, we just take that for granted, and give our minds to other matters. Thus we make it plain that communion with God is a small thing to us. But how different were the Puritans! The whole aim of their 'practical and experimental' preaching and writing was to explore the reaches of the doctrine and practice of man's communion with God. In private they talked freely of their experiences of God, for they had deep experiences to talk about, like the 'three or four poor women sitting at a door in the sun' whom Bunyan met at Bedford:

> Their talk was about a new birth, the work of God on their hearts, also how they were convinced of their miserable state by nature; they talked how God had visited their souls with his love in the Lord Jesus, and with what words and promises they had been refreshed, comforted, and supported against the temptations of the devil. Moreover, they reasoned of the suggestions and temptations of Satan in particular; and told each other by which they had been afflicted, and how they were borne up under his assaults. . . . And methought they spake as if joy did make them speak. . . .[72]

And the Puritans never ceased to feel a sense of awe and wonder that access to God in peace and friendship was possible for them at all. 'Truly for sinners to have fellowship with God, the infinitely holy God, is an astonishing dispensation,' wrote Owen,[73] and Puritan hearts thrilled again and again at the wonder of God's 'astonishing' grace. To them it was the most marvellous thing in the world. Yet we in our day, much as we love to sing 'Amazing Grace' (I suppose, because we like the tune), are not inwardly amazed by grace as the Puritans were; it does not startle us that the holy Creator should receive sinners into his company; rather, we take it for granted! 'God will forgive; that's his *job*' was the final scoff with which the French cynic went to meet his Maker. 'God will receive; that his *job*' seems to be our bland assumption today. Surely something is wrong here.

Then, second, we observe that whereas the experimental piety of the Puritans was *natural and unselfconscious*, because it was so utterly God-centred, our own (such as it is) is too often *artificial and boastful*, because it is so largely concerned with ourselves. Our interest focuses on religious experience, as such, and on man's quest for God, whereas the Puritans were concerned with the God of whom men have experience, and in the manner of his dealings with those whom he draws to himself. The difference of interest comes out clearly when we compare Puritan spiritual autobiography—*Grace Abounding*, say, or Baxter's autobiography, or the memoirs of Fraser of Brea—with similar works our own day.[74] In modern spiritual autobiography, the hero and chief actor is usually the writer himself; he is the centre of interest, and God comes in only as a part of his story. His theme is in effect 'I—and God'. But in Puritan autobiography, God is at the centre throughout. He, not the writer, is the focus of interest; the subject of the book is in effect 'God—and me'. The pervasive God-centredness of Puritan accounts of spiritual experience is a proof of their authenticity, and a source of their power to present God to the modern reader. But when experience of God is told in a dramatised and self-glorifying way, it is a sure sign that the experience itself, however poignant, lacked depth, if, indeed, it was genuine at all.

Third, it seems undeniable that the Puritans' passion for spiritual integrity and moral honesty before God, their fear of hypocrisy in themselves as well as in others, and the humble self-distrust that led them constantly to check whether they had not lapsed into religious play-acting before men with hearts that had gone cold towards God, *has no counterpart in the modern-day evangelical ethos*. They were characteristically cautious, serious, realistic, steady, patient, persistent in well-doing and avid for holiness of heart; we, by contrast, too often show ourselves to be characteristically brash, euphoric, frivolous, superficial, naive, hollow and shallow. Owen's advice to 'my fellow-labourers and students in divinity' about the way to approach the task of upholding the faith against falsehood and folly climaxes with a call to 'diligent endeavour to have the power of the truths professed and contended for abiding upon our hearts';[75] surely in saying this Owen plots the path from where we are to where the Puritans were, and where we should be, and need to be, in the quality of our own walk with God. The whole passage calls for quotation.

> When the heart is cast indeed into the mould of the doctrine that the mind embraceth; . . . when not the sense of the words only is in our heads, but the sense of the things abides in our hearts; when we have communion with God in the doctrine we contend for,—then shall we be garrisoned, by the grace of God, against all the assaults of men. And without this all our contending is, as to ourselves, of no value. What am I the better if I can dispute that Christ is God, but have no sense of sweetness in my heart from hence that he is a God in covenant with my soul? What will it avail me to evince, by testimonies and arguments, that he hath made satisfaction for sin, if, through my unbelief, the wrath of God abideth on me, and I have no experience of my own being made the righteousness of God in him? . . . Will it be any advantage to me, in the issue, to profess and dispute that God worketh the conversion of a sinner by the irresistible grace of his Spirit, if I was never acquainted experimentally with the deadness and utter impotency to good, that opposition to the law of God, which is in my own soul by nature, [and] with the efficacy of the exceeding greatness of the power of God in quickening, enlightening, and bringing forth the fruits of obedience in me? . . . Let us, then, not think that we are any thing the better for our conviction

power of God in quickening, enlightening, and bringing forth the fruits of obedience in me? . . . Let us, then, not think that we are any thing the better for our conviction of the truths of the great doctrines of the gospel . . . unless we find the power of the truths abiding in our own hearts and have a continual experience of their necessity and excellency in our standing before God and our communion with him.[76]

A word to the wise? There was once a day when God sent Jeremiah to say to Israel, 'Ask for the ancient paths, ask where the good way is, and walk in it, and you will find rest for your souls' (Jer 6:16). As we study Owen on the spiritual life, may it be that God is speaking in similar terms to us? Owen's instructions and directions are indeed 'old paths', as old as the Bible, but they are paths which the Puritans as a body found to be in truth 'the good way'. We shall do well to seek for grace to start walking in them ourselves. 'And you will find rest for your souls.'

CHAPTER THIRTEEN

John Owen on Spiritual Gifts

1

The subject of spiritual gifts was not much debated in Puritan theology, and the only full-scale treatment of it by a major writer, so far as I know, is John Owen's *Discourse of Spiritual Gifts*. This, the last instalment of Owen's great analysis of biblical teaching on the Holy Spirit, seems to have been written in 1679 or 1680,[1] though it was not printed till 1693, ten years after his death. Owen's *Discourse* is fully characteristic both of himself and of the general Puritan view of its theme.

It is desirable to delimit explicitly the area within which our study of Owen will move, for there could be false expectations here. To many Christians today, the phrase 'spiritual gifts' suggests a wider range of questions and concerns than it did to the Puritans. Throughout the century that separated William Perkins' pioneer ventures in pastoral theology (*The Arte of Prophecying*, Latin 1592, English 1600; *The Calling of the Ministerie*, 1605) from Owen's *Discourse*, Puritan attention when discussing gifts was dominated by their interest in the ordained ministry, and hence in those particular gifts which qualify a man for ministerial office, and questions about other gifts to other persons were rarely raised. Preoccupied as they were—and as their times required them to be—with securing high standards in the ministry, and educating layfolk out of superstition and fanaticism, the Puritans had both their minds and their hands full, and modern questions about laymen's gifts and service were given less of an airing than we might have expected or hoped for. Two such questions in particular may be noted here, since they bulk so large in present-day debate.

First, *how should we evaluate 'Pentecostalism' (the so-called 'charismatic movement') in modern evangelical life?*

The Pentecostal movement, in both its denominational and its interdenominational forms, claims to be in essence a renewal of neglected but authentic elements in Christianity—namely, the gifts of tongues, prophecy, and healing. (The details of the claim vary from group to group.) Can the Puritans help us to assess these claims? Only indirectly, for there was no such movement in Puritan times. Seventeenth-century England did not, to my knowledge, produce anyone who claimed the gift of tongues,[2] and though claimants to prophetic and healing powers were not unknown, particularly in the wild days of the forties and fifties, the signs of enthusiasm (fanatical delusion) and mental unbalance were all too evident.[3]

It was partly, no doubt, Owen's experience with such people that prompted him to write, of the class of 'gifts which in their own nature exceed the whole power of all our faculties' (in which class he puts tongues, prophetic disclosure, and power to heal), that 'that dispensation of the Spirit is long since ceased, and where it is now pretended unto by any, it may justly be suspected as an enthusiastical delusion'.[4] But does this mean that, like B.B. Warfield,[5] Owen would rule out *a priori* all possibility of renewal, for any purpose, of the *charismata* which were given in the apostolic age to authenticate the apostles' personal ministry and message? Owen nowhere says so much, and it would be rash to ascribe to him this dogmatic *a priori* negation, which, as has often been pointed out, is not inevitably implied by any biblical passage. Rather, it may be supposed (though this, in the nature of the case, can only be a guess) that were Owen confronted with modern Pentecostal phenomena he would judge each case *a posteriori*, on its own merit, according to these four principles:

1. Since the presumption against any such renewal is strong, and liability to 'enthusiasm' is part of the infirmity of every regenerate man, any extra-rational manifestation like glossolalia needs to be watched and tested most narrowly, over a considerable period of time, before one can, even provisionally, venture to ascribe it to God.

2. Since the use of a person's gifts is intended by God to further the work of grace in his own soul (we shall see Owen arguing this later), the possibility that (for instance) a man's glossolalia is from God can only be entertained at all as long as it is accompanied by a discernible ripening of the fruit of the Spirit in his life.

3. To be more interested in extraordinary gifts of lesser worth[6] than in ordinary ones of greater value; to be more absorbed in seeking one's own spiritual enrichment than in seeking the edifying of the church; and to have one's attention centred on the Holy Spirit, whereas the Spirit himself is concerned to centre our attention on Jesus Christ—these traits are sure signs

of 'enthusiasm' wherever they are found, even in those whom seem most saintly.

4. Since one can never conclusively prove that any charismatic manifestation is identical with what is claimed as its New Testament counterpart, one can never in any particular case have more than a tentative and provisional opinion, open to constant reconsideration as time and life go on.

Owen was deeply concerned to bring out the supernaturalness of the Christian life, and to do justice to the Spirit's work in it, but whether he could have felt close sympathy with any form of modern Pentecostalism is a question about which opinions might differ.

The second modern issue that calls for mention is, *how should we develop congregational life in our churches so as to secure an 'every-member ministry'?*

The New Testament pictures the local church as a body in which every member—that is, literally 'limb'—has its own part to play in advancing the welfare and growth of the whole. But the churches we know today have inherited over-centralised patterns of life, so that most congregations contain passengers, and our institutional rigidity inhibits our impact on local communities. We are coming increasingly to see that small-group patterns of fellowship, prayer, study, and Christian action—meetings, 'cells' and the like—need to be developed within our congregations on a much larger scale than we have done hitherto. Again we ask, can the Puritans help us here? Again the reply is, only indirectly; for over-centralisation was not a Puritan problem, and the strength and influence of the family as a religious unit in Puritan times made the quest for other small-group structures less pressing.

However, though the Puritans give us no blue-print for modern group meetings, we find them vindicating with emphasis the fact that such meetings are right, desirable, and beneficial. Thus Owen, for one, included in his first book, *The Duties of Pastors and People Distinguished* (1643),[7] a chapter entitled 'Of the liberty and duty of gifted uncalled Christians in the exercise of divers acts of divine worship', in which he argued that

> for the improving of knowledge, the increasing of Christian charity, for the furtherance of a strict and holy communion of that spiritual love and amity which ought to be among the brethren, they may of their own accord assemble together, to consider one another, to provoke unto love and good works, to stir up the gifts that are in them, yielding and receiving mutual consolation by the fruits of their most holy faith.[8]

Christians may rightly meet to pray together (cf Acts 12:12), and to minister to each other encouragement (cf Mal 3:16) and spiritual help (cf Is 50:5; Ja 5:16). The only provisos are that they should not become a splinter group, withdrawing from the church's public worship, or despising and dis-

regarding their pastors, or taking up with doctrinal and expository novelties. Owen ridicules the idea that such gatherings had the nature of 'schis-
matic conventicles', affirming them rather to be lawful and proper means
whereby Christians 'may help each other forward in the knowledge of godliness and the way towards heaven'.[9]

> It is the loss of those spiritual gifts which hath introduced among many an
> utter neglect of these duties, so as that they are scarce heard of among the
> generality of them that are called Christians. But, blessed be God, we have
> large and full experience of the continuance of this dispensation of the
> Spirit, in the eminent abilities of a multitude of private Christians . . . by
> some, I confess, they [gifts] have been abused: some have presumed on them
> beyond the line and measure which they have received; some have been
> puffed up with them; some have used them disorderly in churches and to
> their hurt; some have boasted of what they have not received;—all which
> miscarriages also befell the primitive churches. And I had rather have the
> order, rule, spirit, and practice of those churches that were planted by the
> apostles, with all their troubles and disadvantages, than the carnal peace
> of others in their open degeneracy from all those things.[10]

It is clear that, were Owen with us today, he would be urging us by all
means to seek a recovery of 'every-member ministry', through a renewed
quest for the 'best gifts' of the Holy Spirit.

2

What we have cited from Owen has already made plain the nature of his
concern about spiritual gifts. It is an aspect of the consuming, comprehensive concern that marked him all his days—his concern, that is, for *authenticity of church life*. In pursuing this concern, he appears as at once a
reforming theologian, opposing false structures, dead formalism, and
unspiritual disorder; a pastoral theologian, challenging distortions of the
gospel, mechanical religious routines, and barren professions of faith; and
a Christ-centred theologian, insisting throughout that the honour of the
Saviour was directly bound up with the state of the visible church. (All of
which is only to say that Owen appears as a true Reformed theologian, a
kindred spirit to Calvin himself.) The relevance of spiritual gifts to this concern, in Owen's view, was simply that *there can be no authentic church life
without their exercise*. On this he is explicit and emphatic.

Gifts of the Spirit, says Owen at the outset of his *Discourse*, are 'that
without which the Church cannot subsist in the world, nor can believers
be useful unto one another and the rest of mankind, unto the glory of
Christ, as they ought to be'.[11] Gifts are 'the powers of the world to come'

referred to in Hebrews 6:5, and 'the ministration of the Spirit' mentioned in 2 Corinthians 3:8—for 'the promises of the plentiful effusion of the Spirit under the New Testament . . . are frequently applied to him as he works evangelical gifts extraordinary and ordinary in men',[12] and the use of his gifts is 'the great means whereby all grace is ingenerated and exercised'.[13] Thus gifts are truly 'the great privilege of the New Testament.'[14]

Gifts of the Spirit give the church its inward organic life and its outward visible form. 'This various distribution of gifts [i.e., that referred to in 1 Corinthians 12:16-25] . . . makes the Church an organical body; and in this composure, with the peculiar uses of the members of the body, consists the harmony, beauty, and safety of the whole.'[15] 'That profession which renders a Church visible according to the mind of Christ, is the orderly exercise of the spiritual gifts bestowed on it, in a conversation evidencing the invisible principle of saving grace.'[16]

Gifts of the Spirit were, and are, Christ's sole weapons for setting up, extending, and maintaining his kingdom.

It is inquired what power the Lord Christ did employ . . . for . . . the erecting of that kingdom or church-state, which being promised of old, was called the *world to come, or the new world* . . . and I say, it was these gifts of the Holy Ghost. . . . By them it was, or in their exercise, that the Lord Christ erected His empire over the souls and consciences of men, destroying both the work and kingdom of the devil. It is true, it is the word of the gospel itself that is the rod of his strength which is sent out of Sion to erect and dispense his rule: but that hidden power which made the word effectual in the dispensation of it, consisted in these gifts of the Holy Ghost.[17] By these gifts doth the Lord Christ demonstrate His power, and exercise His rule.[18]

One secret of the abundance of life enjoyed by the early church was that 'all gospel administrations were in those days avowedly executed by virtue of spiritual gifts'.[19]

Without gifts, the church is a mere shadow of itself. The round of worship becomes sterile, for 'gospel ordinances are found to be fruitless and unsatisfactory, without the attaining and exercising of gospel gifts'.[20] The church falls into the ditch of formalism and the mire of superstition. Unconcern about gifts, writes Owen,

was that whereby in all ages countenance was given unto apostasy and defection from the power and truth of the gospel. The names of spiritual things were still retained, but applied to outward forms and ceremonies, which thereby were substituted insensibly into their room, to the ruin of the gospel in the minds of men.[21] As the neglect of internal saving grace, wherein the power of godliness doth consist, hath been the bane of Christian profession as to obedience . . . so the neglect of these gifts hath been the ruin of the same profession as to worship and order, which hath thereon issued in fond superstitions.[22]

Owen judged the Church of Rome to be a case in point:

We have an instance in the Church of Rome, what various, extravagant, and endless inventions the minds of men will put them upon to keep up a show of worship, when by the loss of spiritual gifts spiritual administrations are lost also. This is that which their innumerable forms, modes, sets of rites and ceremonies, seasons of worship are invented to supply, but to no purpose at all; but only the aggravation of their sin and folly.[23]

Owen's further generalisation, 'a ministry devoid of spiritual gifts is sufficient evidence of a Church under a degenerating apostasy',[24] suggests thoughts that might well disturb Protestants, too, at the present time.

3

The overall thrust of Owen's thinking, and the theological and practical importance for him of the question of gifts, is now clear. In the light of this, we may profitably go on to focus attention on four specific subjects: the nature of spiritual gifts; their place in church life; the different kinds of gifts, ordinary and extraordinary; and the place of gifts in the economy of grace. These themes will occupy the rest of our study.

1. *The nature of spiritual gifts.* Spiritual gifts are abilities bestowed and exercised by the power of God; not natural, therefore, but supernatural; not human but divine. Owen starts the argument of his *Discourse* by reviewing the New Testament phraseology for spiritual gifts, observing that this of itself tells us a good deal about their nature. The words may be arranged in four groups (Owen arranges them in three, lumping together the last two). Group one points to the thought that the gifts are free and undeserved bestowals. The words here are *dorea* and *domata*, 'present' and 'presents', and *charismata*, from *charis* (grace), on which Owen comments: 'It is absolute freedom in the bestower of them that is principally intended in this name.'[25] Group two highlights the thought that the author of these abilities is the Holy Spirit. Key words here are *pneumatika*, literally 'spirituals', in 1 Corinthians 12:1, and the phrases 'manifestation of the Spirit' in verse 7 and 'distributions of the Holy Ghost' in Hebrews 2:4 (KJV and RV margin). Group three expresses the idea that a gift is actually God's work in a man, not the actualising of a human capacity but a dynamic divine operation. This thought is focused in the word *energemata*, 'operations', literally 'effectual workings' (1 Cor 12:6). Group four pinpoints the function which gifts fulfil: they are 'ministrations', 'activities of service'

(1 Cor 12:5), 'powers and abilities whereby some are enabled to administer spiritual things unto the benefit, advantage, and edification of others'.[26]

A one-sentence definition of a gift, in line with Owen's analysis, would be this: a spiritual gift is an ability, divinely bestowed and sustained, to grasp and express the realities of the spiritual world, and the knowledge of God in Christ, for the edifying both of others and of oneself. This definition appears to be entirely scriptural. However, it must be noted that whereas Paul, in directing Christians to use their gifts, speaks of expressing one's knowledge of God's mercy in Christ by the way one gives, rules, loves one's brethren, and shows hospitality, as well as by prophesying, teaching, and exhorting (Rom 12:4-13), Owen conceives of ordinary gifts (as distinct from those, like miracles and tongues, which 'consisted only in a transient operation of an extraordinary power') solely in terms of having thoughts of divine things, with power to voice them in words. He does not treat any other capacity for service as a 'gift' at all. This intellectualism comes out in his assertion that 'spiritual gifts are placed and seated in the mind or understanding only . . . and they are in the mind as it is notional and theoretical, rather than as it is practical. They are intellectual abilities and no more.'[27] This appears to have been the general Puritan view; it rested on the assumption that 1 Corinthians 12:7-11 is a complete enumeration of all the gifts there are, or ever were—an assumption which Chapter IV of the *Discourse* shows that Owen shared. But the assumption is unprovable, and Owen's view is surely at this point incomplete. Has Paul only intellectual abilities in view when he says that God has set in the church 'helps' and 'governments' (1 Cor 12:28)? Significantly, perhaps, Owen makes no reference to these either in the *Discourse* or, so far as I can find, in any of his writings on the local church; probably, like other Puritan expositors, he did not suppose that the functions to which these names referred were manifestations of a distinct spiritual gift at all.[28] But it seems clear that the category of spiritual gifts, as Paul views it, includes graces of character and practical wisdom, as well as powers of theoretical reasoning and discourse about divine truths.

Gifts are bestowed by the Lord Jesus Christ (Eph 4:8) through shedding forth on men the Holy Spirit (Acts 2:23). Owen equates the 'power' of the Spirit in Acts 1:4, 1 Corinthians 2:4 with the bestowal and exercise of gifts. Though gifts are often given through sanctification of natural abilities, they are not natural abilities, and sometimes this is marked by non-development in Christians of the gifts that their natural abilities would lead one to expect, and the manifesting in them of gifts for which their natural powers gave no foundation at all. But all gifts alike are increased by use of the means of grace—prayer, meditation, constant self-abasement, and active service in God's cause.

2. *Spiritual gifts and ecclesiastical office.* Though, as we saw, Owen recognises that Christ gives gifts to all, and that the local church should

accordingly display a pattern of 'every-member ministry' in its regular life, the official ministry is central in Owen's interest, and it is in terms of the relation and distinction between gifts and ecclesiastical office that he expounds (in Chapters III to VIII of the *Discourse*) the place of the gifts in the church.

He begins by analysing the notion of 'office' in terms of *power* plus *duty* (in the sense of defined responsibility). He declares that 'ecclesiastical office is an especial power given by Christ unto any person or persons for the performance of especial duties belonging unto the edification of the Church in an especial manner'.[29] He affirms the standard Reformed view of ordination as an act of Christ conferring office through the action of the church, rather than as an act of the church delegating to the ordinand its own inherent powers. He also sets forth exactly the standard Reformed distinction between the offices of apostle, evangelist, and prophet, which were temporary and extraordinary, ceasing with the apostolic age, and the office of presbyter, which is permanent and ordinary, and is to last till the Lord returns. Laying down the principle that 'all office-power depends on the communication of gifts, whether extraordinary or ordinary',[30] he argues that extraordinary gifts presupposed both an extraordinary call and extraordinary gifts, and that in the absence of the latter, no less than of the former, it is impossible that the apostles, the evangelists (whom he understands to have been the apostles' personally appointed assistants), and the prophets could have successors today.[31] All this is familiar ground to those who have read Calvin's *Institutes* IV:iii, and therefore we need not stay on it. Owen's adoption of Independent principles of polity did not affect in the least his adherence to Presbyterian principles regarding ministerial order, character, and authority.

Nor is he anything other than typical of the whole Reformed tradition when he declares that 'spiritual gifts of themselves make no man actually a minister, yet no man can be made a minister according to the mind of Christ, who is not partaker of them'.[32] His point is that a minister is Christ's gift to the church (Eph 4:8) only because, and in so far as, he is gifted by Christ for ministry in his Master's name, and the church has no right to call and send into the Lord's vineyard men whose gifts do not warrant the confidence that the Lord himself has called them to this service.

> The Church hath no power to call any unto the office of the ministry, where the Lord Christ hath not gone before it in the designation of him by an endowment of spiritual gifts; for if the whole authority of the ministry be from Christ, and if he never give it but where he bestows these gifts with it for its discharge, as in Ephesians 4:7, 8, etc., then to call any to the ministry whom he hath not so previously gifted is to set him aside, and act in our own name and authority.[33]

The main application of our Lord's parable of the talents, in Owen's view, is to the ordained ministry, and its main lesson is that 'wherever there is a ministry in the Church that Christ owneth or regardeth as used and employed by him, there persons are furnished with spiritual gifts from Christ by the Spirit, enabling them unto the discharge of that ministry; and where there are no such spiritual gifts dispensed by him, there is no ministry that he either accepteth or approveth'.[34]

3. *Ordinary and extraordinary gifts.* The last point leads on to the question, what gifts are required for the ordinary presbyteral ministry? Owen's answer is, not the extraordinary gifts mentioned in 1 Corinthians 12:5-11 (faith that works miracles, healing powers, immediate discernment of spirits, tongues, and interpretation of tongues), but the ordinary ones, wisdom and knowledge at an extraordinary pitch. Ministers must be able 'in an eminent degree' (Owen's constant phrase) to preach the word with application, to pray with unction, and to rule with wisdom. To speak to men for, and from, God, and to speak to God for, and as the mouthpiece of, God's flock, is no small undertaking. For it, says Owen, men need three gifts in particular.

The first gift is 'wisdom, or knowledge, or understanding':

> such a comprehension of the scope of the Scripture and of the revelation of God therein; such an acquaintance with the systems of particular doctrinal truths, in their rise, tendency, and use; such a habit of mind in judging of spiritual things, and comparing them one with another; such a distinct insight into the springs and course of the mystery of the love, grace, and will of God in Christ, as enables them in whom it is to declare the counsel of God, to make known the way of life, of faith and obedience, unto others, and to instruct them in their whole duty to God and man therein.[35]

Then, secondly, 'with respect unto the doctrine of the gospel . . . there is required . . . skill to divide the word aright, which is also a peculiar gift of the Holy Ghost, (2 Tim 2:15).'[36] This gift of 'right dividing' Owen understands, not in the exotic latter-day sense of distinguishing dispensations, but in the standard Puritan sense of making appropriate application of God's truth to the condition of individuals. Whether, as Owen, with Calvin, believed, the picture here is of discriminating distribution of food to the family, rather than, as most modern expositors hold, cutting a straight furrow, is not the main issue; the central question is rather, will a minister be approved by God as a good workman, handling the word of truth in a manner appropriate to its nature and purpose, and winning the praise of the God whose word it is, if he misapplies it, or fails to apply it at all? One of the most valuable elements in Puritan teaching on the ministry is the constant stress laid on the need for discerning and discriminating application. Owen lays out in detail what this requires of a man:

(1) A sound judgment in general concerning the state and condition of those unto whom any one is so dispensing the word. It is the duty of a shepherd to know the state of his flock; and unless he do so, he will never feed them profitably. He must know whether they are babes, or young men, or old; whether they need milk or strong meat . . . whether in the judgment of charity they are converted unto God, or are yet in an unregenerate condition; what probably are their principal temptations, their hindrances and furtherances; what is their growth or decay. . . .

(2) An acquaintance with the ways and methods of the work of God's grace on the minds and hearts of men, that he may pursue and comply with its design in the ministry of the word. . . . He . . . who is unacquainted with the ordinary methods of the operation of grace fights uncertainly in his preaching of the word like a man beating of the air. It is true, God can, and often doth, direct a word of truth, spoken as it were at random, unto a proper effect of grace, on some or other, as it was when the man drew a bow at a venture, and smote the king of Israel between the joints of the harness. But ordinarily a man is not likely to hit a joint, who knows not how to take his aim.

(3) An acquaintance with the nature of temptation. . . . Many things might be added on this head. . . .

(4) A right understanding of the nature of spiritual diseases, distempers, and sicknesses, with their proper cures and remedies, belongeth hereunto. For the want hereof the hearts of the wicked are oftentimes made glad in the preaching of the word, and those of the righteous filled with sorrow; the hands of sinners are strengthened, and those who are looking towards God are discouraged or turned out of the way. [37]

The question of the best syllabus of study for ministerial candidates is often discussed today. Would it not be in our interest to reconsider this syllabus of Owen's? How dare we, in this or any age, contemplate ordaining men who have not first mastered it?

Thirdly, with knowledge of God's truth and skill to apply it must go the gift of utterance, which, says Owen, 'is particularly reckoned by the apostle among the gifts of the Spirit' (1 Cor 1:5; 2 Cor 8:4; cf Eph 6:19; Col 4:3).[38] This is not the same as rehetorical skill, or a pretty wit, or 'a natural volubility of speech, which . . . is so far from being a gift of the Spirit . . . that it is usually a snare to them that have it, and a trouble to them that hear them'; it consists of naturalness appropriate to the subject-matter, plus 'boldness and holy confidence', plus gravity and 'that authority which accompanieth the delivery of the word when preached in demonstration of these spiritual abilities.'[39] 'All these things are necessary,' Owen concludes, 'that the hearers may receive the word, not as the word of man, but as it is indeed the word of God.'

This rather shattering list of qualifications needed for acceptable ministry prompts the cry, 'who is sufficient for these things?' This leads us straight to our final topic:

4. *Gifts and grace*. Owen's concern for authenticity and reality in the life of the church and of Christians prompts him, when discussing the relation of gifts and grace in Chapter II of the *Discourse*, to lay stress on the negative point that a man can have gifts without grace—that is, one can be skilled in Christian comprehension and communication without having been born again. Owen insists that here are two distinct types of operation by the Spirit of God, and that only the work of grace, producing 'the fruit of the Spirit' in a renewed heart and a transformed character, is saving. Gifts belong to the outward administration of the covenant of grace only; it does not follow that a man with spiritual abilities is therefore in the inward saving relationship with God at which the covenant aims. The thrust of this is that none may presume on his gifts, and conclude from his having theological interests and abilities that therefore he has eternal life; it does not follow. Only the man who has come to know his sin and has been led in repentance and faith to the cross of Christ is in grace; a merely gifted man, however theologically articulate, may be under wrath still. The need to make this point, in our day as in Owen's, is too obvious to require emphasis from me. We should thank Owen for reminding us of it—and examine ourselves.

But there is another side to the picture, a word of encouragement and incentive to balance the word of warning. Where 'saving graces and spiritual gifts . . . are bestowed on the same persons,' writes Owen,

> they are exceedingly helpful unto each other. A soul sanctified by saving grace, is the only proper soil for gifts to flourish in. Grace influenceth gifts unto a due exercise, prevents their abuse, stirs them up unto proper occasions, keeps them from being a matter of pride or contention, and subordinates them in all things unto the glory of God. When the actings of grace and gifts are inseparable, as when in prayer the Spirit is a spirit of grace and supplication, the grace and gift of it working together, when utterance in other duties is always accompanied with faith and love, then is God glorified, and our own salvation promoted. Then have edifying gifts a beauty and lustre upon them, and generally are most successful, when they are clothed and adorned with humility, meekness, a reverence of God, and compassion for the souls of men. . . . Gifts on the other side excite and stir up grace into its proper exercise and operations. How often is faith, love and delight in God excited and drawn forth unto especial exercise in believers by the use of their own gifts.[40]

Do we deplore that so little of the life of God appears in our souls? Is it our complaint that our gifts are so small? Use your gifts and graces, such as they are, to stir each other up to exercise, Owen is saying, and you will have more of both. Do we seek to grow in grace through the exercise of our gifts? When we speak to others of the things of God, do we seek to feed our own souls on the same truths? Equally, do we seek to increase our gifts through stirring up our hearts to seek God? When we speak of divine things to others, and lead them in prayer, do we seek to feel the reality of the things we speak of? Small gifts may have great usefulness when backed by honest, sincere feeling and unaffected holiness. Are we depressed about our Christian service, finding it largely barren and ourselves largely impotent? Let us go back to our God for wisdom to learn how his grace and gifts in us may help each other. Covet earnestly the best gifts—and with them a humble, loving heart. This is the way of growth and fruitfulness.

THE PURITAN CHRISTIAN LIFE

CHAPTER FOURTEEN

The Puritans and the Lord's Day

1

If we are to profit from studying Puritan teaching on this or any subject, our approach to it must be right. For it is all too easy for admirers of the Puritans to study their work in a way which the Puritans themselves would be the first to condemn. Thus, we can have a wrong attitude to the men; we can revere them as infallible authorities. But they would scarify us for such a gross lapse into what they would regard as papalism and idolatry. They would remind us that they were no more than servants and expositors of God's written word, and they would charge us never to regard their writings as more than helps and guides to understanding that word. They would further assure us that, since all men, even Puritans, can err, we must always test their teaching with the utmost rigour by that very word which they sought to expound. Or, again, we can make a wrong application of their teaching. We can parrot their language and ape their manners, and imagine that thereby we place ourselves in the true Puritan tradition. But the Puritans would impress on us that that is precisely what we fail to do if we act so. They sought to apply the eternal truths of Scripture to the particular circumstances of their own day—moral, social, political, ecclesiastical, and so forth.

If we would stand in the true Puritan tradition, we must seek to apply those same truths to the altered circumstances of our own day. Human nature does not change, but times do; therefore, though the application of divine truth to human life will always be the same in principle, the details of it must vary from one age to another. To content ourselves with aping the Puritans would amount to beating a mental retreat out of the twentieth century, where God has set us to live, into the seventeenth, where he has not. This is as unspiritual as it is unrealistic. The Holy Spirit is pre-eminently a realist, and he has been given to teach Christians how to live to God in the situation in which they are, not that in which some other saints once were. We quench the Spirit by allowing ourselves to live in the past. And such an attitude of mind is theologically culpable. It shows that we have shirked an essential stage in our thinking about God's truth—that of working out its application to ourselves. Application may never be taken over second-hand and ready-made; each man in each generation must exercise his conscience to discern for himself how truth applies, and what it demands, in the particular situation in which he finds himself. The application *may* be similar in detail from one generation to another, but we must not assume in advance that it will be so. And therefore our aim in studying the Puritans must be to learn, by watching them apply the word to themselves in their day, how we must apply it to ourselves in ours.

This point is crucial for us who believe that modern evangelicalism stands in need of correction and enrichment of a kind which the older evangelical tradition can supply. It seems that modern evangelicalism is guilty of just this error of living in the past—in this case, in the recent, late nineteenth-century past. We are too often content today to try and get along by rehashing the thin doctrinal gruel and the sometimes questionable ideas about its ethical, ecclesiastical and evangelistic application which were characteristic of that decadent period in evangelical history. But the answer to this situation is emphatically not that we should retreat still further, and start living, not now in the nineteenth, but in the seventeenth century. Such a cure would in many ways be worse than the disease. We certainly need to go back behind the nineteenth century and reopen the richer mines of older evangelical teaching; but then we must endeavour to advance beyond the nineteenth-century mentality into a genuine appreciation of our twentieth-century situation, so that we may make a genuinely contemporary application of the everlasting gospel.

And this principle is as relevant when we study the subject of the Lord's Day as it is anywhere. For here, surely, is a subject on which fresh thinking about the contemporary application of biblical principles is long overdue. Our thoughts and speech about it often betray a degree of negative legalism as it is. If we rigidly imposed on ourselves the application of the Fourth Commandment which the Puritans worked out in terms of their own age, we would merely increase and perpetuate that legalism. Yet, if we resist the temptation to take over this application ready-made, and set ourselves to reapply God's law realistically to our own present-day situation, we shall find in the Puritan expositions an incomparably rich and suggestive presentation of the positive principles that must guide our judgement in this matter.

2

First, however, we must fill in the historical background of our study.[1]

The Puritans created the English Christian Sunday—that is, the conception and observance of the first day of the week as one on which both business and organised recreations should be in abeyance, and the whole time left free for worship, fellowship and 'good works'. This ideal was never generally accepted by continental Protestants; as Baxter observed: 'England hath been the happiest in this piece of reformation.'[2] The history of the Puritan achievement spans a century. At the end of the sixteenth century, it was the Englishman's custom after church was over to pass the rest of Sunday in 'frequenting of bawdy stage plays . . . may-games, church-ales, feasts and wakes; in piping, dancing, dicing, carding, bowling, tennis-playing, in bear-baiting, cock-fighting, hawking, hunting and such like; in keeping of fairs and markets on the Sabbath . . .;' in 'football-playing, and such other devilish pastimes.'[3] Serious Christians ('Puritans' in the popular sense) grew increasingly concerned about this. The 'Puritan' point of view on the subject, which Dennison shows to have been already affirmed in essence by Bishops Hooper[4] and Latimer,[5] Dean Edmund Bunny[6] and Gervase Babington,[7] received its first full statement in print in Dr Nicholas Bound's *True Doctrine of the Sabbath* (1595)—though the first exposition of it to be written seems to have been Richard Greenham's *Treatise of the Sabbath*,[8] which was privately circulated for some years prior to this.

James I's Declaration of Sports (1618) laid it down that, apart from bull- and bear-baiting and bowls, all the popular games of the day might be played on Sundays after church. In fact, James hereby 'simple reiterated what had been the law of the State and of the Church since the early days of the Reformation'; but his Declaration brought consternation to the rapidly growing body of Puritan clergy and laity. In 1633 Charles I republished it, and ordered the bishops to see that all clergy read it from their pulpits; some refused to do so, and lost their livings as a result. What things in the country were like at this time appears from these words of Baxter:

> In my youth . . . one of my father's own tenants was the town piper, and the place of the dancing assemble was not a hundred yards from our door, and we could not on the Lord's day either read a chapter, or pray, or sing a Psalm, or catechize or instruct a servant, but with the noise of the pipe and tabor and the shoutings in the street continually in our ears; and . . . we were the common scorn of all the rabble in the streets and called Puritans, Precisians, Hypocrites, because we rather chose to read the Scriptures than

do as they did. . . . And when the people by the book [i.e., the Declaration, 1633] were allowed to play and dance out of public service time, they could so hardly break off their sports that many a time the reader was fain to stay till the pipe and players would give over; and sometimes the morris dancers would come into the church in all their linen and scarves and antic dresses, with morris bells jingling at their legs, and as soon as common prayer was read did haste out presently to their play again. Was this a heavenly conversation?[9]

But Puritan teaching had its effect. As a result of Baxter's work at Kidderminster, what had previously been a brawling, drunken, irreligious community was so changed that 'on the Lord's Day; there was no disorder to be seen in our Streets; but you might hear a hundred Families singing Psalms and repeating Sermons as you passed through the Streets.'[10]

A similar reformation took place in many other places where Puritans ministered. The Long Parliament and its successors, prompted by Puritan convictions, passed a series of ordinances forbidding games, trading and travel on Sunday. Finally, in 1677, when the Puritans were out of power and in disgrace, a violently anti-Puritan Parliament passed the Sunday Observance Act, which repeated, and confirmed, Commonwealth legislation on this subject. It prescribed that all should spend Sunday, not in trading, travelling, 'worldly labour, business, or work of their ordinary callings', but in 'exercising themselves . . . in the duties of piety and true religion, publicly and privately'. The significance of this piece of legislation is clear. England had come generally to accept the Puritan ideal for Sunday. Royalist and republican, conformist and nonconformist alike were agreed on it. The Puritan teaching had created a national conscience on the subject; and this despite the fact that the Caroline divines had consistently opposed the Puritans' view as being theologically incorrect.

3

Against this background of history we now turn to the Puritan teaching itself.

1. *The meaning of the Fourth Commandment* (Ex 20:8-11). Here the Puritans advanced on the Reformers. These latter had followed Augustine and medieval teaching generally in denying that the Lord's Day was in any sense a Sabbath. They held that the Sabbath, which the Fourth Commandment prescribes, was a Jewish typical ceremony, foreshadowing the 'rest' of a grace-faith relationship with Christ. So Calvin explains it:

The analogy between the external sign and the thing signified is most apt, inasmuch as our sanctification consists in the mortification of our own will. . . . We must desist from all the acts of our own mind that, God working in us, we may rest in him, as the apostle teaches (Heb 3:13; 4:3, 9).[11]

But now that Christ has come the type is cancelled, and it would be as wrong to perpetuate it as to continue offering Levitical sacrifices. Calvin appeals here to Colossians 2:16, which he interprets as referring to the weekly day of rest. He allows that, over and above its typical significance, the Fourth Commandment also teaches the principle that there must be public and private worship, and a day of rest for servants and employees, so that its full Christian interpretation is threefold:

First, that throughout our whole lives we may aim at a constant rest from our own works, in order that the Lord may work in us by His Spirit; second, that each man should diligently exercise himself in devout meditation on the works of God, and . . . that all should observe the lawful order appointed by the Church for hearing the word, administering the sacraments, and public prayer; thirdly, that we should avoid oppressing those subject to us.[12]

But he speaks as if he regards this as being all that the commandment now prescribes, and finds nothing in it, in its Christian sense, to prohibit work or play on the Lord's Day out of church time. Most of the Reformers spoke in the same way. Yet the extraordinary thing is that their statements in other contexts show that 'the Reformers, as a body, *did* hold the divine authority and binding obligation of the fourth command, as requiring one day in seven to be employed in the worship and service of God, admitting only of works of necessity and mercy to the poor and afflicted'.[13] Why they never saw the inconsistency between asserting this in general terms and yet offering an Augustinian exegesis of the Christian Sunday is a standing puzzle. One can only suppose that unwillingness to entertain the thought that Augustine might be wrong blinded them to the fact that they were riding two horses.

The Puritans, however, corrected the inconsistency. They insisted, with virtual unanimity, that, although the Reformers were right to see a merely typical and temporary significance in certain of the detailed prescriptions of the Jewish Sabbath, yet the principle of one day's rest for public and private worship of God at the end of each six days' work was a law of creation, made for man as such, and therefore binding upon man as long as he lives in this world. They pointed out that, standing as it does with nine undoubtedly moral and permanently binding laws in the Decalogue, it could hardly be of a merely typical and temporary nature itself.

In fact, they saw it as integral to the first table of the law, which deals systematically with worship: 'the first command fixes the object, the second the means, the third the manner, and the fourth the time.'[14]

They noted that the Fourth Commandment begins 'Remember . . .' thus looking back to a pre-Mosaic institution. They observed that Genesis 2:1ff represents the seventh-day rest as God's own rest after creation, and that the sanction attached to the Fourth Commandment in Exodus 20:8ff looks back to this, depicting the day as a weekly memorial of creation 'to be observed to the glory of the Creator, as an engagement upon ourselves to serve him, and an encouragement to us to trust in Him who made heaven and earth. By the sanctification of the Sabbath, the Jews declared that they worshipped the God who made the earth. . . .' So speaks that entirely representative latter-day Puritan Matthew Henry, commenting on Exodus 25:11. Henry further pointed out that the commandment declares God to have sanctified the seventh day (i.e., appropriated it to himself) and blessed it (i.e., 'put blessings into it, which He has encouraged us to expect from Him in the religious observance of that day'); and that Christ, though he reinterpreted the Sabbath law, did not cancel it, but rather established it by keeping it himself and showing that he expected his disciples to continue keeping it (cf Mt 24:20).

All this, the Puritans argued, showed that the seventh-day rest was more than a Jewish type; it was a memorial of creation, and a part of the moral law (first table, prescribing proper worship of the Creator), and as such it was perpetually obligatory for all men. So that when we find the New Testament telling us that Christians met for worship on the first day of the week (Acts 23:7; 41; 1 Cor 16:1), and kept that day as 'the Lord's day' (Rev 1:10), this can only mean one thing: that by apostolic precept, and probably in fact by dominical injunction during the forty days before the Ascension, this had been made the day on which men were henceforth to keep the Sabbath of rest which the Fourth Commandment prescribes. The Puritans observed that this change from the seventh day of the week, the day which marked the end of the old creation, to the first, the day of Christ's resurrection, which marked the start of the new, was not precluded by the words of the Fourth Commandment, which 'merely determined, that we should rest and keep as a Sabbath every seventh day . . . but . . . in no way determine where those six days shall begin. . . . There is no direction in the fourth commandment how to reckon the time.'[15] Therefore nothing hinders the supposition, which the New Testament seems to require, that the apostles actually made this change. In that case, it becomes clear that the condemnation (in Col 2:16) of Jewish sabbatarianism has nothing to do with the keeping of the Lord's Day at all. Such, in outline, were the considerations on which the Puritans based their doctrine of the Lord's Day; which is well summed up in the *Westminster Confession*, XXI:vii-viii.

2. *The character of the Fourth Commandment.* 'The sabbath,' writes Matthew Henry, commenting on Mark 2:27,

is a sacred and divine institution; but we must receive and embrace it as a privilege and a benefit, not as a task and a drudgery. First, God never designed it to be an imposition upon us, and therefore we must not make it so to ourselves. . . . Secondly, God did design it to be an advantage to us, and so we must make and improve it. . . . He had much more regard for our souls. The sabbath was made a day of rest, only in order to its being a day of holy work, a day of communion with God, a day of praise and thanksgiving; and the rest from worldly business is therefore necessary, that we may closely apply ourselves to this work, and spend the whole time in it, in public and private. . . . See here what a good master we serve, all whose institutions are for our own benefit. . . .

This quotation fairly sums up the Puritans' approach to the Lord's Day. Here we would merely underline three of Henry's points, and add a fourth by way of corollary.

(a) Sabbath-keeping means action, not inaction. The Lord's Day is not a day for idleness. 'Idleness is a sinne every day: but much more on the Lord's Day.'[16] We do not keep the Sabbath holy by lounging around doing nothing. We are to rest from the business of our earthly calling in order to prosecute the business of our heavenly calling. If we do not spend the day doing the latter, we fail to keep it holy.

(b) Sabbath-keeping is not a tedious burden, but a joyful privilege. The Sabbath is not a fast, but a feast, a day for rejoicing in the works of a gracious God, and joy must be its temper throughout (cf Is 58:3). 'Joy suits no person so much as a saint, and it become no season as well as a sabbath.'[17]

It is the duty and glory of a Christian to rejoice in the Lord every day, but especially on the Lord's Day. . . . To fast on the Lord's Day, saith Ignatius, is to kill Christ; but to rejoice in the Lord this day, and to rejoice in all the duties of the day . . . this is to crown Christ, this is to lift up Christ.[18]

Joy must be the keynote of public worship. Baxter in particular deplores drab, mournful services. There must be no gloom on the Lord's Day. And those who say that they cannot find joy in the spiritual exercises of a Christian Sunday thereby show that there is something very wrong with them.

(c) Sabbath-keeping is not a useless labour, but a means of grace.

God hath made it our duty, by his institution, to set apart this day for a special seeking of his grace and blessing. From which we may argue, that he will be especially ready to confer his grace on those who thus seek it. . . . The sabbath day is an accepted time, a day of salvation, a time wherein God especially loves to be sought, and loves to be found. . . .[19]

So speaks Edwards, and every Puritan would have agreed. George Swinnock waxes lyrical on the grace of the Christian Sabbath:

Hail thou that art highly favoured of God, thou golden spot of the week, thou marker-day of souls, thou daybreak of eternal brightness, thou queen of days, the Lord is with thee, blessed art thou among days. . . . Oh how do men and woman flutter up and down on the weekdays, as the dove on the waters, and can find no rest for their souls, till they come to thee their ark, til thou put forth thy hand and take them in! Oh how they sit under thy shadow with great delight, and find thy faith sweet to their taste! Oh the mountings of mind, the ravishing happiness of heart, the solace of soul, which on thee they enjoy in the blessed Saviour![20]

(d) Sabbath-breaking brings chastisement, as does the abuse of any God-given privilege and means of grace. Spiritual decline and material loss accrue to both individuals and communities for this sin. The good gifts of God may not be despised with impunity. Thomas Fuller thought that the Civil War, Brooks that the fire of London, came as judgements on the nation for Sabbath-breaking.

The admirable positive and evangelical character of this approach to the Lord's Day could scarcely be bettered.

3. *Practical principles for keeping the Lord's Day holy.* The Puritans were methodical men, and nothing if not thorough; and we find them giving detailed attention to this aspect of our subject. Four principles in particular fall to be considered here.

(a) Preparation must be made for the Lord's Day. First, the Puritans tell us, we must realise the importance of the Lord's Day, and learn to value it rightly. It is a great day for the church and for the individual; a 'market-day for the soul', a day for entering the very 'suburbs of heaven' in corporate praises and prayers. We must never, therefore, let our Sundays become mere routine engagements; in that attitude of mind, we shall trifle them away by a humdrum formality. Every Sunday is meant to be a great day, and we should approach it expectantly, in full awareness of this. Therefore we must plan our week, so that we may make the most of our Sabbaths. Haphazard improvidence will preclude our profiting here, just as it will in any other enterprise.

That policie and discretion which we see in naturall men about the market of their bodies, we must learne about the market of our souls: they will be providing, and thinking before what they must buy . . . and sell there . . . so, if ever we will make good markets for our souls, we must [all the week before] be preparing our hearts . . . that we may then be burdened with no sinne nor worldly care. . . . We *must* . . . stop out all distractions and encumbrances, and raise up our hearts against deadness and dulness . . . if ever we will comfortably and profitably spend the Lord's day in the Lord's work.[21]

Preparing the heart is the most important matter of all, for the Lord's Day is pre-eminently 'a day for heart-work.'[22] From this point of view, the battle for our Sundays is usually won or lost on the foregoing Saturday night, when time should be set aside for self-examination, confession and prayer for the coming day. Richard Baxter's young people's fellowship used to spend three hours each Saturday evening preparing together for the Sabbath in this way. 'If thou wouldst thus leave thy heart with God on the Saturday night,' Swinnock assures us, 'thou shouldest find it with him in the Lord's-day morning.'[23] The last rule for preparation comes from the supremely practical mind of Richard Baxter: 'Go seasonably to bed, that you may not be sleepy on the Lord's Day.'[24]

(b) Public worship must be central on the Lord's Day. The day must be built round public worship, morning and afternoon or evening ('the publike exercises are twice at the least to be used every Sabbath'[25]). Private devotions must take second place to this, if one or the other for any reason has to go. But we must get up on Sunday mornings in time to prepare our hearts afresh to praise and pray and hear God's word preached, for 'if we come rudely into the Lord's House from brawling or chiding at home or so soone as he is out of his bed . . . the Word shall be but a tediousness and serve to the further hardening of his heart.'[26]

Puritan services might last anything up to three hours; but the Puritans had little sympathy with those who complained at their length. Baxter's comment is simply that those who found a church service tedious, and yet could spend a far longer time in a public house, or at a public entertainment, without boredom, must have very bad hearts; though he then takes occasion to speak a word in season to preachers and suggest to them

an honester way to cure people's weariness. Preach with such life and awakening seriousness . . . and with such easy method and with such variety of wholesome matter that the people may never be weary of you. Pour out the rehearsal of the love and benefits of God; open so to them the privileges of faith, the joys of hope, that they may never be angry. How oft have I heard the people say of such as these, I could hear him all day and never be weary! They are troubled with the shortness of such sermons, and wish they had been longer. . . .[27]

(c) The family must function as a religious unit on the Lord's Day. The *Westminster Larger Catechism*, question 118, is emphatic on this: 'The charge of keeping the Sabbath is more specially directed to government of families, and other superiors, because they are bound not only to keep it themselves, but to see that it be observed by all that are under their charge.' The head of the house must conduct family prayers twice, take the family to church, and examine and catechise the children and servants afterwards to make sure that they had thoroughly absorbed the sermon. The principle here is that the man of the house has an inalienable responsibility to care for the souls of the household, and that it is on the Lord's Day supremely that he must exercise it. The Puritan pastor, unlike his modern counterpart, did not scheme to reach the men through the women and children, but vice versa. Was he not perhaps wiser, and more scriptural too?

(d) The pitfalls of legalism and pharisaism must be avoided in regard to the Lord's Day. These wrong attitudes threaten here, as in all other spiritual concerns. There was no dispute among the Puritans that, as the answer to question 60 of the *Westminster Shorter Catechism* put it:

> the Sabbath is to be sanctified by a holy resting all that day, even from such worldly employments and recreations as are lawful on other days; and spending the whole time in the publick and private exercises of God's worship, except so much as is to be taken up in the works of necessity and mercy.

But there are right and wrong ways of pursuing all goals, and the shrewdest among the teachers went out of their way to warn that both legalism, the negative habit of mind which stresses what one must *not* do on the Lord's Day and stops there, and pharisaism, the self-justifying habit of mind which is all too ready to censure others for real or fancied lapses in this matter, are both a violation of the spirit of the gospel. Baxter, as we should perhaps expect, has most to say about them, and he counters both with a constructive evangelical principle of judgement:

> I will first look at a man's positive duties on the Lord's Day, how he heareth and readeth and prayeth and spendeth his time, and how he instructeth and helpeth his family; and if he be diligent in seeking God, and ply his heavenly business, I shall be very backward to judge him for a word or action about worldly things that falls in on the by. . . .[28]

Here, surely, is Christian wisdom.

4

The above passages speak for themselves, and need no further comment. The issues of spiritual well-being that they raise must be left to each reader to consider. We close with a testimony and an admonition.

The testimony is that of Lord Chief Justice Sir Matthew Hale:

> I have found by a strict and diligent observation that a due observance of the duties of the Lord's Day hath ever had joined to it a blessing upon the

rest of my time, and the week that hath been so begun hath been blessed and prosperous to me; and on the other side, when I have been negligent of the duties of the day, the rest of the week has been unsuccessful and unhappy in my own secular employments. This I write, not lightly or inconsiderately, but upon long and sound observation and experience.[29]

The admonition is from Thomas Brooks:

For a close, remember this, that there are no Christians in all the world comparable for the power of godliness and heights of grace, holiness, and communion with God, to those who are more strict, serious, studious and conscientious in sanctifying the Lord's Day. . . . The true reason why the power of godliness is fallen to so low an ebb, both in this and in other countries also, is because the Sabbath is no more strictly and conscientiously observed. . . . And O that all these short hints might be so blessed from heaven as to work us all to a more strict seriousness and conscientious sanctifying of the Lord's Day. . . .[30]

CHAPTER FIFTEEN

The Puritan Approach to Worship

1

It is sometimes said that evangelicals are not interested in worship. If by worship one means the technicalities of liturgical study, this may be true. But I do not suppose that I am the only evangelical who finds that the actual exercise of worship, the deliberate lifting of one's eyes from man and his mistakes to contemplate God and his glory, grows increasingly precious as the years go by, and brings solace and refreshment to the spirit in a way that nothing else can do. Certainly, this was the experience of the great Puritans; and what I want to do now is to allow them to share it with us, and lead us deeper into the enjoyment of it for ourselves. Hence my choice of the word 'approach' in my title. We are to follow the Puritans in the *approach* to worship, which was, as we shall see, itself an *approach* to God. My main concern is thus not with the controversies about worship which divided the Puritans both from Anglican officialdom and from each other, but rather with the view of the nature of worship, and of the principles for practising it, on which in fact they were all agreed.

But their controversies about the formal and external aspects of worship were real and sustained, religiously motivated and passionately pursued, and to establish my right to pass them by in the body of my text I must first deal briefly with them now. I shall not trace their historical details, nor take sides (for I do not want to start them all over again!), but I shall try to bring into focus the problems which occasioned them, so that we see just how much—and at some points, how little—divided the conflicting parties. The problems themselves, as we shall see, remain living issues for us today.

Three main questions lay at the root of all the arguing. They were as follows:

1. *In what sense are the Scriptures authoritative for Christian worship?* It is usually said that, whereas Luther's rule in ordering public worship was to allow traditional things that were not contrary to Scripture and seemed helpful, it was Calvin's rule to admit nothing that the Bible did not directly prescribe; and that the Church of England officially followed Luther's principle, whereas the Puritans within its ranks espoused that of Calvin. This way of putting it gives the impression that Luther and the Reformed Church of England did not regard Holy Scripture as constituting an authoritative rule for worship at all—which was, of course, the constant Puritan accusation right up to the Civil War. It also gives the impression that the Puritan critique of Anglican public worship represented a reversion to the principles and practice of Calvin at Geneva—which, to be sure, the Puritans themselves thought it was. But both impressions are misleading.

A truer way of stating the issue would be to say that the authority and sufficiency of Scripture in all matters of Christian and church life was common ground to both sides, but that they were not agreed as to how this principle should be applied. In other words, their disagreement related to the interpretation and contents of Holy Scripture, rather than to the formal principle of the nature and extent of its authority. This is how it was that all parties to the debate could believe that their own position was a biblically proper one.

German, Swiss, and English Reformers held common basic principles about worship. They agreed that Christian worship must express man's reception of, and response to, evangelical truth, and they were substantially in agreement as to what that truth was. They agreed in analysing worship as an exercise of mind and heart in praise, thanksgiving, prayer, confession of sin, trust in God's promises, and the hearing of God's word, read and preached. They were in agreement also as to the nature and number of the gospel sacraments, and their place in the church's worship. They took the same view of the office of the Christian minister in leading the worship of the congregation. They agreed too that each church, or federation of churches ('every particular or national Church', as Article XXXIV puts it) is responsible for settling the details of its own worship in accordance with the apostolic principle that all must be done 'unto edifying' (1 Cor 14:26), and that as a means to that end everything must be done 'decently and in order' (v 40). Finally, they were all agreed that each church has liberty (the presupposition of its responsibility) to arrange its worship in the way best adapted to edify its own worshippers, in the light of their state, background, and needs; so that they all took it for granted that the worship of varied churches in varying pastoral situations would vary in detail. The only real differences regarding worship between any of the first generation of Reformers were differences of personal judgement as to what would edify and what would not—difference of the kind reflected in Calvin's judgement that the second Edwardian *Prayer Book* of 1552 contained *multas tolerabiles ineptias* ('many bearable pieces of foolishness'), or in the troubles at Frankfort in 1554, when the 'Coxian' group of exiles adhered to the 1552 *Prayer Book* as being sufficiently sound and edifying, while the 'Knoxians' felt obliged to abandon it in favour of an alternative order drawn up on the Geneva pattern.

The idea that direct biblical warrant, in the form of precept or precedent, is required to sanction every substantive item included in the public worship of God was in fact a Puritan innovation, which crystallised out in the course of the prolonged debates that followed the Elizabethan settlement. It is an idea distinct from the principle that tainted ceremonies, which hide the truth from worshippers and buttress superstitious error, should be dropped, as both dishonouring God and impeding edification. On this latter principle all the English Reformers were agreed from the start, as the 1549 *Prayer Book* Preface 'Of Ceremonies' shows; though they did not succeed in agreeing as to its application, which was why in 1550 Hooper clashed with the authorities over episcopal vesture, and why in the 1560s those who were first called Puritans felt obliged to campaign against the *Prayer Book* requirement of surplices, wedding-rings, baptising with the sign of the cross, and kneeling at Holy Communion. But this new principle went further, declaring that no justification of non-biblical rites and ceremonies in worship as convenient means to biblically prescribed ends could in the nature of the case be valid (in other words, that the line taken in the preface 'Of Ceremonies' was wrong); all ceremonies must have direct biblical warrant, or they were impious intrusions.

The same principle was applied to church government. The attempt to put the Puritan ideal of church life and worship on to this footing led to some curiosities of argument, such as the 'proof' that two services a Sunday were obligatory, from Numbers 28:9f, which prescribes two burnt offerings each Sabbath; or the 'proof' that catechising was a duty, from 'hold fast the form of sound words' (2 Tim 1:13); or the 'proof' that liturgical forms were unlawful, from Romans 8:26; or the 'proof' that the minister should stand in one place throughout the service from 'Peter stood up in the midst of the disciples' (Acts 1:15); or the 'proof' of the necessity of the controversial 'prophesyings' (area preaching meetings, at which several ministers spoke successively on the same passage of Scripture) from 1Corinthians 14:31 ('ye may all prophesy one by one, that all may learn and all may be comforted'). Much of this can be cogently defended, in terms of the principle that all things must be done unto edifying, but it is hard to regard these biblical arguments as anything like conclusive.

It should also be noticed that when the Puritans singled out some of the *ineptiae* of the *Prayer Book* as intolerable, when they challenged the principle that each church has liberty to ordain non-biblical ceremonies in worship where these seem conducive to edification and reverence, when they repudiated all set prayers, when they rejected kneeling in public worship, the Christian year, weekly Communion, and the practice of confirmation, they were not in fact reverting to Calvin, but departing from him, though, as Horton Davies says,[1] it is doubtful whether they realised this.

Even if they had realised it, however, it would not have affected their position; for their basic concern was not to secure Reformed solidarity as such (much though they made of this idea in controversy), but simply to obey God's authoritative word. But the question at issue was, how should the sufficiency of Scripture be understood in connection with worship? The Puritans thought the official Anglican view on this point lax and wrongheaded; Anglican spokesmen like Hooker criticised the developed Puritan view as legalistic and irrational. Which was right? The question still presses today. Do we agree with John Owen that 'God's worship hath no accidentals . . . all that is in it and belonging to it, and the manner of it, is false worship, if it have not a divine institution in particular'? The problem is not simple, and much can still be said on both sides.

2. *What regulations are proper for Christian worship?* There were, and are, three possible ways of ordering public worship: to have a set liturgy like the *Book of Common Prayer*, or a manual of general guidance like the *Westminster Directory*, or to leave it entirely to the individual minister or congregation to regulate its own worship at will. These alternatives are historically associated with Anglicans, Presbyterians, and Independents and Quakers respectively. Which now is preferable? How strong are the objections to each? Does liturgical worship necessarily breed formality and deadness? Is extempore prayer necessarily uneven in quality? Does it really make it harder for worship to be congregational than it is if a known form is being used? Does a regular order followed Sunday by Sunday quench the Spirit? Is it necessary, if a congregation would honour the Holy Spirit, for it to refuse to tie itself to an established pattern of worship, and simply at each meeting wait on the Spirit for a fresh leading? On these issues, evangelicals would differ now, as the Puritans differed in their day. Baxter, for instance, like Calvin and Knox, approved of a liturgy with room for extempore prayer at the minister's discretion; but Owen maintained that 'all liturgies, as such, are . . . false worship . . . used to defeat Christ's promise of gifts and God's Spirit'. Which was right? Here again is an issue which is not simple, and cannot be regarded as dead.

3. *What discipline is proper in connection with worship?* No doubt there would be general agreement that the attempts made under Elizabeth and the Stuarts to enforce strict national uniformity to the *Book of Common Prayer* were regrettable, and did more harm than good. Nobody, one

hopes, would wish to defend the kind of discipline administered upon non-conformists by the Courts of High Commission and Star Chamber before the Civil War, and by the judges and JPs of England during the years of the Clarendon Code. Yet a problem remains. Granted that the discipline we have mentioned was ungodly in its rigidity and disregard for tender consciences, is there to be no discipline in connection with public worship at all? Today, in some Protestant churches where set prayers are the rule, rituals and prayers from the Roman Mass are introduced, and in others where extempore prayer is practised, ministers are heard basing their public intercessions on the heresy that all human beings are God's redeemed children. In both these instances worship is spoiled through the doctrinal aberration of the minister. Is there not need for discipline in such cases? But of what sort? What steps are appropriate today in face of such disfigurements as these? The problem exercised the Puritans in their day, and it will be well if it continues to exercise us in ours.

2

But these problems concerned the forms and externals of worship only, and our present interest is rather in the inner reality of worship, as the Puritans understood it. Here, wherever else they differed, they were at one, and the written material they have left us is completely homogeneous, as we shall hope to show by a fairly wide range of quotations. What is worship? It is essentially doxology, a giving of glory, praise, honour, and homage to God. In the broadest sense of the word, all true piety is worship. 'Godliness is a worship,' wrote Swinnock:

> Worship comprehends all that respect which man oweth and giveth to his Maker. . . . It is the tribute which we pay to the King of Kings, whereby we acknowledge his sovereignty over us, and our dependence on him. . . . All that inward reverence and respect, and all that outward obedience and service to God, which the word [sc, godliness] enjoineth, is included in this one word worship.[2]

Usually, however, the Puritans used the word in its narrower and more common sense, to signify simply all our direct communion with God: invocation, adoration, meditation, faith, praise, prayer and the receiving of instruction from his word, both in public and in private.

Worship must be, as our Lord said, 'in spirit and in truth' (Jn 4:24). The Puritans understood this as meaning that, on the one hand, worship must be inward, a matter of 'heart-work', and, on the other, worship must be a response to the revealed reality of God's will and work, applied to the heart by the Holy Spirit. Therefore they insisted that worship must be simple and scriptural. Simplicity was to them the safeguard of inwardness, just as Scripture was the fountain-head of truth. The austere simplicity of Puritan worship has often been criticised as uncouth, but to the Puritans it was an essential part of the beauty of Christian worship. This comes out in two sermons by Owen on Ephesians 2:18, entitled 'The nature and beauty of gospel worship', in which the weightiest of all the Puritan theologians formulates to perfection the Puritan ideal of worship in scarcely veiled antithesis to the *Prayer Book* formalism of Laud ('the beauty of holiness' as Laud was pleased to call it).[3] It is worth quoting from this exposition at some length. Owen begins by making the point that the true 'decency', 'order', and 'beauty' of Christian worship lies in its trinitarian and evangelical character, as an exercise of faith on the worshippers' part.

> It is a principle deeply fixed in the minds of men that the worship of God ought to be orderly, comely, beautiful and glorious. . . . And indeed that worship may be well suspected not to be according to the mind of God which comes short in these properties. . . . I shall add unto this, only this reasonable assertion, . . . viz, That what is so in his worship and service, God himself is the most proper judge. If then we evince not that spiritual gospel worship, in its own naked simplicity, without any other external, adventitious helper or countenance, is most orderly, comely, beautiful, and glorious, the Holy Ghost in the Scripture being judge, we shall be content to seek for these things where else, as it is pretended, they may be found.
>
> . . . In the spiritual worship of the gospel, the whole blessed Trinity, and each person therein distinctly, do in that economy and dispensation, wherein they act severally and peculiarly in the work of our redemption, afford distinct communion with themselves unto the souls of the worshippers. [Owen shows how this is set forth in his text, which speaks of access to the Father through the Son by the Spirit.] This is the general order of gospel worship, the great *rubric* of our service. Here in general lieth its *decency*. . . . If either we come not unto it by Jesus Christ, or perform it not in the strength of the Holy Ghost, or in it go not unto God as a Father, we transgress all the rules of this worship. This is the great *canon*, which if it be neglected, there is no *decency* in whatever else is done in this way. And this in general is the *glory* of it. . . . Acting faith on Christ for admission, and on the Holy Ghost for his assistance, so going on in his strength; and on God, even the Father, for acceptance, is the work of the soul in this worship. That it hath anything more glorious to be conversant about, I am yet to learn. . . .[4]

In similar terms, Owen from his text gives theological substance to the idea of uniformity in worship:

> The saints . . . have all their access 'in one Spirit': and this is the spring of all the *uniformity* that God requires. So the apostle tells us, that as to the

gifts themselves [sc, abilities for leading the church in corporate worship] there are diversities of them, and difference in them; I Cor. xii. 4-6. But where then is uniformity? . . . The apostle answereth, verse 11. ('All these worketh that one and self-same Spirit'). Here lies the uniformity of gospel worship, that though the gifts bestowed on men for the public performance of it be various . . . yet it is *one Spirit*, that bestows them all among them . . . one and the same Spirit discovers the will and worship of God to them all; one and the same Spirit works the same graces for their king in the hearts of them all; one and the same Spirit bestows the gifts that are necessary for the carrying on of gospel worship in the public assemblies. . . . And what if he be pleased to give out his gifts . . . variously . . . 'dividing to every one severally, as he will'? yet this hindereth not, but that as to the saints mentioned, they all approach unto God by the one Spirit, and so have uniformity in their worship throughout the world. This is a *catholic uniformity*. . . .[5]

Finally, Owen scouts the idea that ornate buildings and rituals have, or can have, anything to do with the 'beauty' that God seeks and finds in the worship of his faithful people. He reminds us that Christians are themselves the temple and dwelling place of God, and that true worship, though done on earth in the body, is actually 'performed in heaven', inasmuch as 'those who have an access unto the immediate presence of God, and to the throne of grace, enter into heaven itself'. (Owen appeals for proof to Hebrews 5:20; 9:24; 10:19, 21; Revelation 4.) The idea that ritual pageantry in services and decoration of church buildings is of itself an enriching of worship thus appears as a ludicrous irreverence. 'What poor low thoughts have men of God and his ways, who think there lies an acceptable glory and beauty in a little paint and varnish!'[6]

Complementary to Owen's analysis is Charnock's anatomising of worship in his sermon entitled 'Spiritual Worship', on John 4:24.

Worship is an act of the understanding, applying itself to the knowledge of the excellency of God, and actual thoughts of his majesty. . . . It is also an act of the will, whereby the soul adores and reverenceth his majesty, is ravished with his amiableness, embraceth his goodness, enters itself into an intimate communion with this most lovely object, and pitcheth all his affections upon him.[7]

Only the regenerate can worship God acceptably, says Charnock, for only they have hearts that truly go out to him in adoration and self-subjection. Therefore 'we must find healing in Christ's wings, before God can find spirituality in our services. All worship issuing from a dead nature, is but a dead service.'[8]

Charnock goes on to show that spiritual worship is performed only by the Spirit's active help, since it requires sincerity and singleness of heart ('unitedness', Charnock calls it; 'concentration' would express his meaning). It involves acts of faith, love, humbling, and self-distrust, and must be an expression of the heart's desire for God. 'A spiritual worshipper actually aspires in every duty to know God. . . . To desire worship as an end, is carnal; to desire it as a means, and act desires in it for communion with God in it, is spiritual, and the fruit of a spiritual life. . . .'[9] Also, spiritual worship will be joyful:

> The evangelical worship is a spiritual worship, and praise, joy, and delight are prophesied of as great ingredients in attendance on gospel ordinances, Is. xii. 3-5. . . . The approach is to God as gracious, not to God as unpacified, as a son to a father, not as a criminal to a judge. . . . Delight in God is a gospel frame, therefore the more joyful, the more spiritual. . . .[10]

In worship we must seek to reflect back to God by our response the knowledge that we have received of him through his revelation.

> God is a Spirit infinitely happy, therefore we must approach him with cheerfulness; he is a Spirit of infinite majesty, therefore we must come before him with reverence; he is a Spirit infinitely high, therefore we must offer up our sacrifices with deepest humility; he is a Spirit infinitely holy, therefore we must address him with purity; he is a Spirit infinitely glorious, we therefore must acknowledge his excellency . . . he is a Spirit infinitely provoked by us, therefore we must offer up our worship in the name of a pacifying mediator and intercessor.[11]

'That all true believers whose minds are spiritually renewed have a singular delight in all the institutions and ordinances of divine worship is fully evident,' writes Owen, and quotes Psalms 42:1-4, 63:1-5, 84:1-4 to prove his point.[12] That the saints love public worship is a constant Puritan theme. Why their delight in it? Because in worship the saints do not merely seek God; they also find him. Worship is not only an expression of gratitude, but also a means of grace, whereby the hungry are fed, so that the empty are sent away rich. For 'there is in worship an approach of God to man.'[13] 'God's presence in his ordinances' is a reality; God is essentially present in the world, graciously present in his church. 'God delights to approach to men, and converse with them in the worship instituted in the gospel.'[14] And men honour God most when they come to worship hungry and expectant, conscious of need and looking to God to meet them and supply it.

The ordinances of Christian worship, declares Owen, are 'means of the communication of a sense of divine love, and supplies of divine grace unto the souls of them that do believe'. They are 'ways of our approaching unto God', and 'we are always to come unto God, as unto an eternal spring of goodness, grace, and mercy, of all that our souls do stand in need of.' 'To make a pretence of coming unto God, and not with expectation of receiving good and great things from him, is to despise God.' An aimless, careless, casual, routine habit of church-going is neither rational nor reverent. Asks Owen, with piercing rhetoric:

> What do men come to hear the Word of God for? What do they pray for? What do they expect to receive from him? Do they come unto God as the eternal fountain of living waters? As the God of all grace, peace and consolation? Or do they come unto his worship without any design as unto a dry and empty show? . . . Or do they think they bring something unto God, but receive nothing from him? . . . To receive anything from him they expect not, nor do ever examine themselves whether they have done so or no? . . . It is not for persons who walk in such ways, ever to attain a due delight in the ordinances of divine worship.[15]

Owen's application of this is uncomfortably searching:

> Many of the better sort of professors are too negligent in this matter. They do not long and pant in the inward man after renewed pledges of the love of God; they do not consider how much they have need of them . . .; they do not prepare their minds for their reception of them, nor come with the expectation of the communication unto them; they do not rightly fix their faith on this truth, namely that these holy administrations and duties are appointed of God in the first place, as the way and means of conveying his love and a sense of it unto our souls. From hence springs all that luke-warmness, coldness, and indifference unto the duties of holy worship, that are growing among us.[16]

This, surely, is a word for our times.

3

The Puritan lists of the parts and constituent activities of worship normally include the following: praise (especially the singing of psalms), prayer (confession, adoration, intercession), preaching, the sacraments ('ordinances'), and also catechising and the exercise of church discipline. In all these activities, the Puritans maintained, God comes to meet his people met together in his Son's name, but most of all in preaching. Preaching is the most solemn and exalted action, and therefore the supreme test, of a man's ministry: 'they [Puritans] hold that the highest and supreme office and authority of the Pastor is to preach the gospel solemnly and publicly to the Congregation by interpreting the written Word of God, and applying the

same by exhortation and reproof unto them.'[17] For preaching in the church
is supremely the ministration of the Spirit, in a way that (*pace* Richard
Hooker) the mere reading of the word to the Puritans' minds never could
be; therefore it is the supreme means of grace. So Thomas Goodwin writes:

> It is not the letter of the Word that ordinarily doth convert, but the spiritual
> meaning of it, as revealed and expounded. . . . There is the letter, the husk;
> and there is the spirit, the kernel, and when we by expounding the Word
> do open the husk, out drops the kernel. It is the meaning of the word which
> is the word indeed, it is the sense of it which is the soul. . . . Now, preaching
> in a more special manner reveals God's word. When an ointment box is
> once opened, then it casts its savour about; and when the juice of a medic-
> inal herb is once strained out and applied, then it heals. And so it is the spir-
> itual meaning of the Word let into the heart which converts it and turns it
> to God.[18]

For congregations, therefore, the hearing of sermons is the most momentous event of their lives, and the Puritans pleaded with worshippers to
appreciate this fact, and listen to the word preached with awe, attention,
and expectancy. Baxter put the point thus, in the course of his 'Directions
for Profitably Hearing the Word Preached' in the *Christian Directory*:

> Come not to hear with a careless heart, as if you were to hear a matter that
> little concerned you, but come with a sense of the unspeakable weight,
> necessity, and consequence of the holy word which you are to hear; and
> when you understand how much you are concerned in it, it will greatly help
> your understanding of every particular truth. . . .
>
> Make it your work with diligence to apply the word as you are hearing
> it. . . . Cast not all upon the minister, as those that will go no further than
> they are carried as by force. . . . You have work to do as well as the preacher,
> and should all the time be as busy as he . . . you must open your mouths,
> and digest it, for another cannot digest it for you . . . therefore be all the
> while at work, and abhor an idle heart in hearing, as well as an idle minister.
>
> Chew the cud, and call up all when you come home in secret, and by
> meditation preach it over to yourselves. If it were coldly delivered by the
> preacher, do you . . . preach it more earnestly over to your own hearts. . . .[19]

We complain today that ministers do not know how to preach; but is
it not equally true that our congregations do not know how to hear? An
instruction to remedy the first deficiency will surely be labour lost unless
the second is remedied too.

Not, however, that the hearing of sermons is an end in itself, or that
ardent sermon-tasting and preacher-hunting is the height of Christian devotion. Thomas Adams speaks sternly against the assumption that listening

to sermons is all that matters, reminding us that preaching must lead on to prayer and praise:

> Many come to these holy places, and are so transported with a desire of hearing, that they forget the fervency of praying and praising God . . . all our preaching is but to beget your praying; to instruct you to praise and worship God. . . . I complain not that our churches are auditories, but that they are not oratories; not that you come to sermons (for God's sake, come faster), but that you neglect public prayer: as if it were only God's part to bless you, not yours to bless God. . . . Beloved, mistake not. It is not the only exercise of a Christian to hear a sermon; nor is that Sabbath well spent that despatcheth no other business for heaven. . . . God's service is not to be narrowed up in hearing, it hath greater latitude; there must be prayer, praise, adoration. . . .[20]

Here, too, surely is a word for Christian people today.

4

There are, said the Puritans, three spheres of Christian worship: public, in the local church; domestic, in the family circle; private, in the closet. Of these three, public worship is the most important. David Clarkson was entirely typical when, preaching on Psalm 87:2 under the title 'Public Worship to be preferred before Private', he argued from Scripture that 'the Lord is more glorified by public worship', 'there is more of the Lord's presence in public worship', 'here are the clearest manifestations of God', 'there is more spiritual advantage to be got in the use of public ordinances', and 'public worship is more edifying.'[21] Strikingly, yet characteristically (for many others made the same point), he reminds us that public worship is 'the nearest resemblance of heaven' that earth knows: for 'in heaven, so far as the Scripture describes it to us . . . all the worship of that glorious company is public. . . . They make one glorious congregation and so jointly together sing the praises of him that sits on the throne, and the praises of the Lamb, and continue employed in this public worship to eternity.'[22] Similarly, Swinnock insists that on the Lord's Day church must come first, and everything else be built round it. 'Esteem the public ordinances the chief work of the day, and let thy secret and private duties be so managed that thy soul may be prepared for them, and profited by them.'[23]

But family worship was also, to the Puritans, vitally important. Every home should be a church, with the head of the house as its minister. Daily and indeed twice daily, the Puritans recommended, the family as a family should hear the word read, and pray to God. Sunday by Sunday, the family should seek to pool the profiting of its members from the public ordinances; day by day, its members should seek to encourage each other in the way of God. Parents must teach their children the Scriptures; all members of the household must be given time and a place to pray. Thus, informally, but conscientiously, the worship and service of God in the home must be carried on.

5

Incomplete though this survey has necessarily been (we have said nothing, for instance, of the sacraments), it has at least sketched in the main outline of Puritan ideals for worshippers—reverence, faith, boldness, eagerness, expectancy, delight, whole-heartedness, concentration, self-abasement, and above all a passion to meet and know God himself as a loving Father through the mediation of his Son. This ideal was common to them all—to those like Sibbes and Archbishop Usher, who conformed to the *Prayer Book* liturgy; to those like Owen, who thought all liturgies unlawful; and to those like Baxter, who were happy to alternate between 'free' and 'set' prayers, and were equally at home in either. Here, in their conception of what the worshipper's spirit and goal should be, the Puritans were at one; and perhaps we may venture the judgement that their agreements here were more significant than their differences, and that it is within the area of their agreements that their teaching can help us most today.

But still one question remains. How do we begin to get from where we are to where the Puritans show us that we ought to be in our own practice of worship? How can we, cold-hearted and formal as we so often are—to our shame—in church services, advance closer to the Puritan ideal? The Puritans would have met our question by asking us another. How do we *prepare* for worship? What do we do to rouse ourselves to seek God?

Here, perhaps, is our own chief weakness. The Puritans inculcated specific preparation for worship—not merely for the Lord's Supper, but for all services—as a regular part of the Christian's inner discipline of prayer and communion with God. Says the *Westminster Directory*: 'When the congregation is to meet for public worship, the people *(having before prepared their hearts thereunto)* ought all to come. . . .' But we neglect to prepare our hearts; for, as the Puritans would have been the first to tell us, thirty seconds of private prayer upon taking our seat in the church building is not time enough in which to do it. It is here that we need to take ourselves in hand. What we need at the present time to deepen our worship is not new liturgical forms or formulae, nor new hymns and tunes, but more preparatory 'heart-work' before we use the old ones. There is nothing wrong with new hymns, tunes, and worship styles—there may be very good reasons for them—but without 'heart-work' they will not make our worship more fruitful and God-honouring; they will only strengthen the syndrome that C.S. Lewis called 'the liturgical fidgets'. 'Heart-work' must have priority or spiritually our worship will get nowhere. So I close with an admonition from George Swinnock on preparation for the service of the Lord's Day, which for all its seeming quaintness is, I think, a word in season for very many of us:

> Prepare to meet thy God, O Christian! betake thyself to thy chamber on the Saturday night, confess and bewail thine unfaithfulness under the ordinances of God; shame and condemn thyself for thy sins, entreat God to prepare they heart for, and assist it in, thy religious performances; spend some time in consideration of the infinite majesty, holiness, jealousy, and goodness, of that God, with whom thou art to have to do in sacred duties; ponder the weight and importance of his holy ordinances . . .; meditate on the shortness of the time thou hast to enjoy Sabbaths in; and continue musing . . . till the fire burneth; thou canst not think the good thou mayest gain by such forethoughts, how pleasant and profitable a Lord's day would be to thee after such a preparation. The oven of thine heart thus baked in, as it were, overnight, would be easily heated the next morning; the fire so well raked up when thou wentest to bed, would be the sooner kindled when thou shouldst rise. If thou wouldst thus leave thy heart with God on the Saturday night, thou shouldst find it with him in the Lord's Day morning.[24]

CHAPTER SIXTEEN

Marriage and Family
in Puritan Thought

The common idea that typical English Puritans were solitary ascetics is as wrong as can be. The word 'ascetics' points to the Manichean mentality of despising physical pleasure and the body itself, and this certainly is something that two generations ago Puritans were often said to do. There is no reason to doubt that the following verse was written in full seriousness:

> The Puritan through life's sweet garden goes
> To pluck the thorn, and cast away the rose;
> And hopes to please, by this peculiar whim,
> The God who fashioned it and gave it him.[1]

But the picture is entirely mistaken: like Calvin before them, the Puritans affirmed the duty of appreciating the goodness and delights of the material creation, and forbade only such immoderate and disorderly enjoyment of these gifts as would steal one's heart from the Giver. Moreover, Puritans were not solitaries; they valued their friends, cultivated their friendships, wrote affectionate letters to each other, and held no brief whatever for choosing isolation when one could join with a group of believers. Finally, nothing shows the groundlessness of imagining Puritan people as solitary ascetics more clearly than does their ideal for marriage and family.

They did not invent this ideal; it is there in the original Reformers. But in teaching and enforcing it they gave it such strength, substance, and solidity as to warrant the verdict that in the same sense in which, under God, they were creators of the English Christian Sunday, so they were creators of the English Christian marriage, the English Christian family, and the English Christian home. Their ennobling purpose, described earlier, of sanctifying all the activities and relationships that living in the world involves found very thorough expression in their teaching on home life, and while it cannot be proved that they all lived up to the standard that they set for each other, it is beyond doubt that many of them did. (The evidence is in funeral sermons, in the many brief biographies that Puritans wrote about each other, and in Puritan diaries and volumes like Richard Baxter's *Breviate* [short account] *of the life of Mrs Margaret Baxter*, his deceased wife.) It is that standard that will occupy our attention in this chapter. In an era when marriage, even among Christians, is becoming brittle and unstable, and serial marriage through a sequence of divorces is modelled under limelight, so to speak, by top stars in the entertainment world, and casual sexual relations between adults raise no eyebrows, and teenage fornication is shrugged off as a universal and inevitable fact of life, and most children in most homes grow up in pagan ignorance of God and his law, there is much to be learned by tracking Puritan thought on marriage and the family.

1

The Puritans, like the Reformers, glorified marriage in conscious contradiction of the medieval idea that celibacy as practised by clergy, monks, and nuns is better—more virtuous, more Christlike, more pleasing to God—than marriage, procreation, and family life.

Thomas Aquinas gave teaching on womanhood that undergirded that opinion. He went so far as to opine that the birth of a girl is the result of a male embryo going wrong; that while a married man's wife is a convenience to him, in that she enables him to procreate and avoid concupiscence (roving passion, prompting promiscuity), in all other respects a man will always make him a better companion and helpmeet than his wife, or any woman, can ever be. Furthermore, affirmed Aquinas, women are mentally as well as physically weaker than men, and more prone to sin, and are always by their nature subject to some man. Husbands may correct their wives by corporal punishment if necessary, and children ought to love their father more than their mother.[2] It may be said without fear of contradiction that the great theologian's oracles about the second sex make distinctly dismal reading.

Thomas' negativism here was not, indeed, entirely his fault; not only did Aristotle, whose thought Thomas sought to claim for Christianity, take a very low view of women, but many of the orthodox Fathers, whose teaching Thomas' method required him to follow, had been just as negative and down-putting with regard to women, and even more so with regard to sexual relations in marriage. Chrysostom had denied that Adam and Eve could have had sexual relations before the Fall; Augustine allowed that procreation was lawful, but insisted that the passions accompanying intercourse were always sinful; Origen had inclined to the theory that had sin not entered the world the human race would have been propagated in an angelic manner, whatever that might be, rather than by sexual union; and Gregory of Nyssa was sure that Adam and Eve had been made without sexual desire, and that had there been no Fall mankind would have reproduced by means of what Leland Ryken gravely calls 'some harmless mode of vegetation'.[3] The Fathers' background was the decadent Graeco-Roman culture that had systematically debased marriage and sexual relations for centuries, so perhaps they, too, should not be blamed too much for views such as these. It is obvious, however, that so twisted a record urgently needed to be set straight, and this the Reformers, followed by the Puritans, forthrightly did.

Their first step was to celebrate marriage as a creation ordinance, a good gift of God to mankind, 'instituted . . . in the paradise and garden of pleasure,' as Miles Coverdale, the proto-Puritan Bible translator, makes Heinrich Bullinger say in his translation of Bullinger's *The Christian State of Matrimony* (1541).[4] Marriage, they said, is not a second-best; on the contrary, it belongs to the ideal human life as the Creator designed it.

Their second step was to define and describe marriage in biblical terms. Bullinger's statement seems to have been archetypal both for Cranmer's *Book of Common Prayer* (1549, 1552) and for later Puritan teachers as a body; it ran thus:

> Wedloke is the yoking together of one man and one woman whom God hath coupled together according to his worde with the consent of them both, from thenceforth to dwell together and to spend their life in an equall partakynge of all such things as God sendeth to the intent that they may bring forth children in the feare of him, that they may avoid whordom, and that (according to God's good pleasure) the one may helpe and comfort the other.[5]

Modern marriage theory, like Genesis 2:18 ('It is not good for the man to be alone'), stresses companionship as the fundamental value, and it is striking to see that a number of Puritans put this aspect of marriage first in line. Thomas Becon, the Reformer, whose mind-set was very much that of an early Puritan, had already done this in *The Boke of Matrimonye* (1564), specifying 'the avoidance of solitariness' as the first of God's three reasons for inventing marriage that Bullinger and the *Prayer Book* had listed in the order, children, chastity, and the comfort of companionship.

In due course the *Westminster Confession* endorsed this revised order, declaring in XXIV:ii: 'Marriage was ordained for the mutual help of husband and wife, for the increase of mankind with a legitimate issue, and of the church with a holy seed, and for preventing of uncleanness.' Puritan preachers are found pulling out the stops to proclaim the supreme blessing of togetherness in marriage, and declarations of it, quaint and quotable, abound. Here are some samples.

> The wife is ordained for man: like a little Zoar, a city of refuge to fly to in all his troubles: and there is no peace comparable unto her but the peace of conscience.[6]

> Women are creatures without which there is no comfortable Living for man. . . . They are a sort of Blasphemers then who despise and decry them, and call them *a necessary Evil*, for they are *a necessary Good*.[7]

> There is no society more near, more entire, more needful, more kindly, more delightful, more comfortable, more constant, more continual, than the society of man and wife, the main root, source, and original of all other societies.[8]

> A good wife being . . .
> The best Companion in Wealth;
> The fittest and readiest Assistant in worke;
> The greatest comfort in crosses and griefes; . . .
> And the greatest Grace and Honour that can be, to him that hath her.[9]

> There is no such fountain of comfort on earth, as marriage.[10]

> It is a mercy to have a faithful friend that loveth you entirely . . . to whom you may open your mind and communicate your affairs. . . . And it is a mercy to have so near a friend to be a helper to your soul and . . . to stir up in you the grace of God.[11]

> God the first Institutor of marriage, gave the wife unto the husband, to bee, not his servant, but his helper, counsellor and comforter.[12]

The third step was to set before marriage partners the ideal of wholehearted mutual love. Observed Matthew Henry, commenting on Genesis 2:22: 'The woman was *made of a rib out of the side of Adam*; not made out of his head to top him, nor out of his feet to be trampled upon by him, but out of his side to be equal with him, under his arm to be protected, and near his heart to be loved.' So the husband must constantly, conscientiously, and spontaneously practise love to his wife—which meant, for the Puritans, the erotic *agape* of a romantic marriage[13]—and the wife must love her husband in the same way. Richard Baxter spells this out beautifully in question and answer:

> I pray you, next tell me my duty to my wife and hers to me.
>
> The common duty of husband and wife is,
>
> 1. Entirely to love each other; and therefore choose one that is truly lovely. . . .; and avoid all things that tend to quench your love.
>
> 2. To dwell together, and enjoy each other, and faithfully join as helpers in the education of their children, the government of the family, and the management of their worldly business.
>
> 3. Especially to be helpers of each other's salvation: to stir up each other to faith, love, and obedience, and good works: to warn and help each other against sin, and all temptations; to join in God's worship in the family, and in private: to prepare each other for the approach of death, and comfort each other in the hopes of life eternal.
>
> 4. To avoid all dissensions, and to bear with those infirmities in each other which you cannot cure: to assuage, and not provoke, unruly passions; and, in lawful things, to please each other.
>
> 5. To keep conjugal chastity and fidelity, and to avoid all unseemly and immodest carriage [conduct] with another, which may stir up jealousy; and yet to avoid all jealousy which is unjust.
>
> 6. To help one another to bear their burdens (and not by impatience to make them greater). In poverty, crosses, sickness, dangers, to comfort and support each other. And to be delightful companions in holy love, and heavenly hopes and duties, when all other outward comforts fail.[14]

It should by now be clear that, in Edmund Morgan's words, 'the Puritans were neither prudes nor ascetics. They knew how to laugh, and they knew how to love.'[15] The realism of their affirmations of matrimonial affection stemmed from the fact that they went to the Bible for their understanding of the relationship—to Genesis for its institution, to Ephesians for its full meaning, to Leviticus for its hygiene, to Proverbs for its management, to several New Testament books for its ethic, and to Esther, Ruth, and the Song of Songs for illustrations and exhibitions of the ideal. Milton ceremoniously sets forth the fruit of their biblical researches, first in his differentiating of the two genders, then in his hymnic invocation of wedded love, and finally in his declaration of the spiritual good that such love can bring. Here, first, is the differentiation:

> Not equal, as their sex not equal seemed;
> For contemplation he and valour formed,
> For softness she, and sweet attractive grace,
> He for God only, she for God in him.

Now the invocation:

> Hail wedded love, mysterious law, true source
> Of human offspring, sole propriety
> In Paradise of all things common else.
> By thee adulterous lust was driven from men
>
> Among the bestial herds to rage, by thee
> Founded in reason, loyal, just, and pure,
> Relations dear, and all the charities
> Of father, son, and brother first were known.
>
> Far be it, that I should write thee sin or blame,
> Or think thee unbefitting holiest place,
> Perpetual fountain of domestic sweets,
> Whose bed is undefiled and chaste pronounced.

And finally the maturation:

> Love refines
> The thought, and heart enlarges, hath his seat
> In reason, and is judicious, is the scale
> By which to heavenly love thou mayest ascend.[16]

The Puritans understood wedded love very thoroughly; that is clear from such passages as this, in which Daniel Rogers, son of John Rogers of Dedham, depicts what today would be called falling in love:

> Marriage love is ofttime a secret worke of God, pitching the heart of one party upon another for no known cause; and therefore when this strong lodestone attracts each to the other, no further questions need to be made but such a man and such a woman's match were made in heaven, and God hath brought them together.[17]

Rogers recognises that this 'pitching' of the heart does not always happen, but stresses as all the Puritans do that steady affection on both sides is in every case a matter of divine command. Therefore, said the Puritans, in choosing a spouse one should look, not necessarily for one whom one *does* love, here and now, in Rogers' heart-pitched sense (such a person, if found, might still not be a suitable candidate for a life partnership), but for one whom one *can* love with steady affection on a permanent basis. Loving actions of all sorts, including physical mating, will ripen and deepen this affection, and lead to a warmth of conjugal love such as Thomas Hooker, the Cambridge Puritan who went to New England, pictures in his sermons when he wants to illustrate the covenant love of God for his people. Here, wishing to exhibit the sacraments of the gospel as love-tokens from the Lord, Hooker delineates the wife:

> As a wife deales with the letters of her husband that is in a farre Country; she finds many sweet inklings of his love, and shee will read these letters often, and daily; she would talke with her husband a farre off, and see him in the letters. Oh (saith she) thus and thus hee thought when he writ these lines, and then she thinkes he speaks to her againe; she reads these letters only, because she would be with her husband a little, and have a little parley with him in his pen, though not in his presence: so these ordinances are but the Lord's love-letters.[18]

And here, highlighting God's constant love and care for those who are his, Hooker delineates the husband:

> The man whose heart is endeared to the woman he loves, he dreams of her in the night, hath her in his eye and apprehension when he awakes, museth on her as he sits at table, walks with her when he travels and parlies with her in each place where he comes.[19]

> That the Husband tenders his Spouse with an indeared affection above al mortal creatures: This appeareth by the expressions of respect, that all he hath, is at her command, al he can do, is wholly improved for her content and comfort, she lies in his Bosom, and his heart trusts in her, which forceth al to confess, that the stream of his affection, like a mighty current, runs with full Tide and strength.[20]

While insisting that love for the Lord must come first, and that human loves are only in shape so long as they feed into it and do not divert us from it, the Puritans expected and indeed directed that wedded love should be ardent and robust. Though self-controlled, they were uninhibited people, and as they could be, and often were exuberant in expressing love for their God, so they believed that they should be with their spouses. William Gouge condemns

> the disposition of such husbands as have no heat, or heart of affection in them . . . a disposition no way warranted by the Word. The faithful saints of God . . . were no Stoicks, without all affection: nor did they think it a matter unbeseeming them, after a peculiar manner to delight in their wives (witness Isaaks sporting with his wife:) for this is a privilege which appertaineth to the estate of marriage.[21]

Puritan preachers made constant use of Proverbs 5:18-19: 'May you rejoice in the wife of your youth. A loving doe, a graceful deer—may her breasts satisfy you always, may you ever be captivated by her love.' The Puritans did not, indeed, equate wedded love with the ramifications of sexual desire, as is so commonly done today. Milton, who is consciously the mouthpiece for Puritan humanism throughout his poetry, states this very carefully through the angel Raphael, who thus admonishes new-created Adam as Adam seeks to bring into lucid focus his first overwhelming experience of loving Eve. Says Raphael:

> But, is the sense of touch, whereby mankind
> Is propagated, seem such dear delight
> Beyond all other, think the same vouchsafed
> To cattle and each beast; which would not be
>
> To them made common and divulged, if aught
> Therein enjoyed were worthy to subdue
> The soul of Man, or passion in him move.
> What higher in her society thou find'st
>
> Attractive, human, rational, love still:
> In loving thou dost well; in passion not,
>
> Wherein true Love consists not.[22]

Yet mating, though not the whole nor the heart of the matter, is a necessary and important expression of wedded love, which would be maimed and stunted without it. Accordingly, the preachers would stress that there must be no holding back on either side at this point.

2

It will not have escaped the reader that all the Puritan views noted thus far were mainly, if not wholly, thought out from the male standpoint. The reason for this was partly cultural: women in the sixteenth and seventeenth centuries had domestic roles and were neither emancipated nor in most cases educated beyond the minimum of being able to write and to use figures. Partly, too, the reason was historical: the low estimate of women that Aquinas and medieval theology as a whole shared, and the low estimate of marriage implied by the celibacy system for all the 'religious' (priests, monks, nuns), took some living down, and though it might seem sad it can hardly be thought strange that for some time after the Reformation women's perspectives on things were not seen as important by comparison with men's. From the Puritans' own point of view, however, the main reason for thinking out the ethics and spirituality of marriage in male-leadership terms was their belief that male leadership is in fact biblically prescribed, an exegetical conclusion that nearly everyone held from the second to the twentieth century. There were four arguments, all seen as confirming the rightness of male leadership as adumbrated in Milton's 'he for God only, she for God in him'.

The first argument was taken from the story of creation: the man was made first, then the woman, and the woman was made to benefit the man as a suitable helper for him.

The second argument was taken from the story of the Fall: the woman was first in the transgression, and God decreed in judgement that henceforth her husband should rule over her.

The third argument was taken from Paul's statement (1 Cor 11:3; Eph 5:23) that the man is the head whom the wife is to obey, as Christ is the Head whom the church is to obey.

The fourth argument was based on the words 'does not nature itself teach you?' (1 Cor 11:14); it was really an appeal to the hierarchical principle embedded in the then current cultural consensus, rather than to the Bible itself.

But the presupposition of functional subordination of wives, which for the Puritans was a closed issue, was their clear belief, also biblically based, that men and women are equal before God. Robert Bolton is strong on this.

> *Soules have no sexes*, as Ambrose saith. In the better part they [husband and wife] are both men. And if thy wives soule were freed from the frailty of her sexe, it were as manly, as noble, as understanding, and every way as excellent, as thine own. . . . Let the husband then be so farre from . . . contemning his wives worth . . . that out of consideration that her soule is naturally every as good as his own (*sic*); only the excellence of its native operations, something damped, as it were, and disabled by the frailty of that weaker body, with which God's wise providence hath clothed it upon purpose, for a more convenient and comfortable . . . serviceableness to his good; that I say, hee labour the more to entertaine and intreat her with all tendernesse and honour, to recompence, as it were, her suffering in this kinde for his sake.[23]

Sibbes observes:

> For the most part women have sweet affections to religion, and therein they oft go beyond men. The reason is, Religion is especially seated in the affections: And they have sweet and strong affections. Likewise they are subject to weakness, and God delights to show his strength in weakness.[24]

This is affirmation of a kind that women never receive in (for instance) Hindu and Islamic contexts.

When a man chooses a wife—and it is assumed that the man will do the choosing, or at least, if I may put in this way, the chasing—he needs to pray

much, and think hard, and get his value system very straight and clear. That
a Christian should only marry another Christian is axiomatic, but other
qualities, over and above a shared faith, will be needed for well-ordered
wedlock. Beauty of mind and character matter more than beauty of face
and body, and to marry where beauty of mind and character is lacking is
a sure recipe for disaster. A character estimate, therefore, ought to be the
first step in considering a possible life-partner, and such Scriptures as
Proverbs 31 and 1 Peter 3:1-7 will suggest the questions to ask. The Puritans would certainly have thought it hazardous to formulate one's hopes
as did the seminary student who a quarter of a century ago, in discussing
the Puritan position, declared: 'I want a Brigitte Bardot who can lead a
Bible class' (Bardot = Monroe = Madonna, etc). Looking for a sign, on the
model of what Abraham's servant did, is another spiritually stupid mistake.
Gataker knew a man who 'would test any woman on whom he had cast
his roving eye . . . by asking her, in sermon time, where the minister's text
was. If she not only told him the text, but offered him her Bible, she was
the woman who was to be his wife.'[25] To Gataker this seemed both irreverent and asinine,[26] and it is hard to quarrel with his verdict.

How should a character estimate be made? The wise way to form an
opinion about possible partners is to find out their reputation, watch how
they act in company, how they dress and talk, and note whom they select
as friends. ('The report, the looks, the speech, the apparel, and the companions . . . are like the pulses that show whether we be well or ill'—Henry
Smith.[27] 'Choose such a companion for thy life as hath chosen company
like thee before'—Robert Cleaver.[28]) For a realistic assessment, couples
wondering about matrimony need 'to see each other eating and walking,
working and playing, talking and laughing and chiding too; or else it may
be, the one shall have with the other lesse than he or she looked for, or more
than they wished for.'[29] Other things being equal, partners should be of
similar age, social position, wealth, and intellectual ability, and should have
secured their parents' goodwill towards the match. Also, they should be
able to see that an affectional bond is growing between them, based on the
conviction that God has given them to each other to glorify him by their
mutual love and service. The good sense of all this is obvious, and calls for
no comment save that this careful, prayerful blending of human and divine
wisdom, seeking the will of God through discernment of personal and circumstantial fitness in all its relevant forms, was the mark of Puritan deci-
sion-making in all matters of importance across the board.

The procedure in England for getting married consisted of (1) espousals,
a contract to marry corresponding to the modern engagement, but more
binding, inasmuch as sexual relations with a third party during the
espousal period were classed as adultery; (2) publication of the banns (an
announcement that the contract exists) on three successive Sundays in
church; (3) execution of the espousal contract by vows of entry into actual

marriage, taken before witnesses as part of a special service; (4) celebration of the event with feasting and fun, ordinarily at the home of the groom; (5) sexual intercourse. The Puritan pastors accepted this frame and sought to make the most of it in spiritual terms, preaching sermons of advice to the couple both at the espousals (which they structured as an act of worship, with psalm-singing and prayer) and also at the wedding itself, and putting into print manuals of various kinds that the partners could have with them for their future guidance.[30] Samples of the wisdom contained in these are the regular urging, prompted by Deuteronomy 24:5, that newly-weds avoid prolonged absences from each other for at least the first year of marriage while they work on their relationship, and the pleading of William Whateley (known as 'the Roaring Boy of Banbury') that couples starting out together should not be required to live in either of their parents' homes.[31]

Some marriages, even among Christians, unhappily break down; as they do today, so they did in the Puritan period. English law at that time recognised only declarations of nullity and judicial separation from bed and board, but Puritan thinkers generally agreed that divorce with right of remarriage was biblically permitted after adultery by one's spouse, and most Puritans followed Perkins in regarding desertion, broadly interpreted to cover all behaviour that nullified the matrimonial relationship in practice—'malicious desertion', when 'they require of each other intolerable conditions', 'long absence', cruelty, diseased conditions, and insanity are specified—as ground for the same grant, with equal rights for men and women.[32] Perkins' clearly articulated position was in fact that of Zwingli and Bucer, for which John Hooper had argued in 1550 and which Cranmer had incorporated into his never-enacted code of canon law, *Reformatio legum ecclesiasticarum*, in 1552. Luther, Calvin, and Beza did not commit themselves so far, merely allowing, unspecifically, that deliberate desertion could entitle the innocent party to divorce and remarry; and that was more than English law countenanced, as we saw, though Scottish and New England law embraced the principle of divorce for both adultery and desertion. But Perkins was at this point, as Knappen expresses it, 'a voice crying in the wilderness'.[33]

It should be noted, however, that no Puritan would have approved Knappen's phraseology; for Puritan pastors, a world of easy divorce would have been more, not less, a wilderness, morally and spiritually, than the world they knew. Chapter XXIV:ivi of the *Westminster Confession* reflects their perspective on divorce when it declares:

> Although the corruption of man be such as is apt to study arguments unduly to put asunder those whom God has joined together in marriage: yet, nothing but adultery, or such wilful desertion as can in no way be remedied by the church, or civil magistrate, is cause sufficient of dissolving the bond of

marriage: wherein a public and orderly course of proceeding is to be observed. . . .

In England, at any rate, no such course of proceeding existed, and it is clear that the Puritans did not see this as a bad thing. Their business, after all, was to help couples build marriages that would last, and all their efforts were directed to this end; and they did in fact offer a great deal of wisdom on maintaining love and goodwill, honour and respect, peace and contentment, common purposes and shared commitments, in the married state.

3

When the Puritans said 'family', they had in view not only parents and children, but also servants (all homes save the poorest had at least one live-in servant), elderly relatives being looked after (there were no retirement homes or geriatric hospitals in those days), and sometimes other residents too—in short, an extended as distinct from nuclear family. It was with reference to such human units that John Geree wrote, in his 1646 tract *The Character of an Old English Puritane, or Nonconformist*: 'His family he endeavoured to make a Church, both in regard of persons and exercises, admitting none into it but such as feared God; and labouring that those that were born in it, might be born again to God.'[34] To the Puritans, family life was enormously important, for 'a family is the seminary of church and state and if children be not well principled there, all miscarrieth.'[35] So 'keep up the government of God in your families: holy families must be the chief preservers of the interest of religion in the world.'[36]

The Puritans crusaded for a high view of the family, proclaiming it both the basic unit of society and a little church in itself, with the husband as its pastor and his wife as his assistant—subordinate indeed in the chain of command, but a key figure in the ongoing pastoral process nonetheless. As head of the family, the husband must be treated with respect before the children and guests. (That was why William Gouge directed that the wife should not call her husband 'ducks', 'chicks', 'sweet', or 'pigsnie', when others were present, but should address him as 'Master so-and-so', using his surname as his professional peers would do.) It was the husband's responsibility to channel the family into religion; to take them to church on the Lord's Day, and oversee the sanctifying of that entire day in the home; to catechise the children, and teach them the faith; to examine the whole family after each sermon, to see how much had been retained and understood, and to fill any gaps in understanding that might remain; to lead the family in worship daily, ideally twice a day; and to set an example of sober godliness at all times and in all matters. To this end he must be willing to take time out to learn the faith that he is charged to teach.

I do therefore desire, that all masters of families would first study well this work [the *Westminster* standards] themselves, and then teach it their children and servants, according to their several capacities. And, if they once understand these grounds of religion, they will be able to read other books more understandingly, and hear sermons more profitably, and confer more judiciously, and hold fast the doctrine of Christ more firmly, than ever you are like to do by any other course. First, let them read and learn the Shorter Catechism, and then the Larger, and lastly, read the Confession of Faith.[37]

Gaius Davies summarises Puritan ideals of child-rearing admirably.

The preachers stressed that love is the fountain of all parents' duties. But children should not be spoilt; parents must not, like apes, kill their young ones with hugging. The example of parents is the greatest stimulus to holiness, especially that of the mother, whose influence during the child's early years is greater.
... Education should begin as early as possible, and though it should be thorough, godliness is more important than learning, and schoolmasters must be chosen with this in mind. The aptness or gifts of children should be noted, that they might be trained for a suitable calling. The claims of the Christian ministry should be remembered, and where the ability exists, a son should be exhorted to enter it.
... The child's first instruction in religion should be adapted to its age, so that the child receives it with delight. Thus the seeds of godliness would be planted early. The Puritan attitude to children thus differed from that of some moderns, who expect a child's conversion to be a dramatic experience.[38]

And Davies' concluding comment on the preachers is just.

To these men godliness was to be shown in the daily round and the common task, more than anywhere else. Holiness was not to be sought by withdrawing from daily duties, whether to a spurious asceticism or in search of esoteric experiences. 'Pure religion breathing household laws' was with them not a poet's vision, but a practical programme and, in many cases, a realized ideal.[39]

The Puritans viewed all life-activities, whether deliberately chosen or circumstantially—which meant for them, providentially—imposed, as callings (vocations) from God: *particular* callings, as distinct from God's *general* calling of mankind to repentance in the gospel and his *effectual* calling of the elect to faith through the secret work of the Holy Spirit in and with the gospel. The concept of particular callings was basic to Puritan ethics, and on it, as on so many matters, the seminal writing was that of

Perkins. In *A Treatise of the Vocations* (1602), setting off from 1 Corinthians 7:20, where Paul directs Christians to stay in the calling wherein they were called, Perkins defines a particular calling as 'a certaine kind of life, ordained and imposed on man by God, for the common good' [40] and insists that Christians should each seek a lawful calling for which they are gifted by God and in which they may work to his praise. With this all later Puritans agreed.

Now, to the Puritan mind, marriage and family life constituted a calling in this sense: the domestic calling of the husband and father, and the entire calling of the wife and mother. Most people, declared the teachers, were called to marry, and were made aware of this by discovering the inconveniences and frustrations of living single; then the married were called to have children, as God's way of maintaining the race and, within the race, the church; and parents were called to teach their children obedience to God and to themselves (the Puritans did not expect to see the first without the second); while the children were called, and were to be taught that they were called, to learn this twofold obedience from their earliest days. Fulfilment of vocation was the formula for the sanctifying of home life, and this could prove to be a full-time job. 'The private vocations of a family and functions appertaining thereto, are such as Christians are called unto by God,' wrote William Gouge, and he continues:

> This is to be noted for satisfaction of certaine weake consciences, who thinke that if they have no publike calling, they have no calling at all . . . a conscionable performance of household duties in regard to the end and fruit thereof, may be accounted a publike worke. Yea, if domesticall duties be well and thoroughly performed, they will bee even enough to take up a man's whole time. . . . So a wife likewise, if she also be a mother and a mistris, and faithfully endeavour to doe what by virtue of those callings shee is bound to do, shall find enough to doe. As for children under the government of their parents and servants in a family, their whole calling is to be obedient to their parents and masters, and to doe what they command them in the Lord. Wherefore if they who have no publike calling, bee so much the more diligent in the functions of their private callings, they shall be as well accepted by the Lord, as if they had publike offices.[41]

Gouge is evidently speaking of, and to, those whom we might call ladies and gentlemen of leisure, who had learned the Puritan doctrine that for an able-bodied person not to have a 'publike calling', i.e., one that contributes to the well-being of the community, is sinful laziness. Concentrate on fulfilling your domestic calling properly, says Gouge, and you will find your hands full enough.

It is often thought that Puritan family life, both in principle and in practice, was harsh, regimented, legalistic, and tyrannical, but that is not true.

What is true, however, is, first, that the Puritans 'accounted religion an engagement to duty, that the best Christians should be the best husbands, best wives, best children, best Masters, best servants, best Magistrates, best subjects, that the doctrine of God might be adorned not blasphemed',[42] and, second, that Puritan teachers thought humane family life, in which Christian love and joy would find full and free expression, could not be achieved till the ordered pattern they envisaged—the regular authority-structure and daily routine—had been firmly established. Their passion to please God expressed itself in an ardour for order; their vision of the good and godly life was of a planned, well-thought-out flow of activities in which all obligations were recognised and met, and time was found for everything that mattered: for personal devotion, for family worship, for household tasks, for wage-earning employment, for intimacy with spouse and children, for Sabbath rest, and whatever else one's calling or callings required.

   The Puritan pastors knew that it is always hard to achieve a properly proportioned life-pattern of the kind described, and that many do not even try to achieve it, but live at random and haphazard, constantly intending to put their lives in order some day and never actually getting round to it. The preachers complained of this in their own era; they would find cause for much louder complaints could they inspect family life in the modern West. Facing situations in our secularised society in which parental careers disrupt the nuclear family so that children suffer, some of today's Christian teachers labour to reverse the priority, insisting that family concerns must have precedence over work in the world, not vice versa. But the Puritan way would be to recognise both public and domestic callings as God-given, and hence to seek a pattern of living that by shrewd and disciplined use of time meets both sets of claims. Is there not wisdom for us in the Puritan way? Surely the question bears thinking about.

THE PURITANS IN MINISTRY

CHAPTER SEVENTEEN

Puritan Preaching

1

Then said the *Interpreter*, Come in, I will shew thee that which will be profitable to thee . . . he had him into a private Room, and bid his Man open a Door: the which when he had done, *Christian* saw the Picture of a very grave Person hang up against the wall, and this was the fashion of it. *It had eyes lift up to Heaven, the best of Books in his hand, the Law of Truth was written upon his lips, the World was behind his back; it stood as if it pleaded with Men, and a Crown of Gold did hang over his head.*

Then said *Christian*, What means this?

Interpreter. The Man whose Picture this is, is one of a thousand; he can beget Children, travel [travail] in birth with Children, and nurse them himself when they are born. And whereas thous seest him with his eyes lift up to Heaven, the best of Books in his hand, and the Law of Truth writ on his lips: it is to shew thee, that his work is to know and unfold dark things to sinners; even as also thou seest him stand as if he pleaded with Men: And whereas thou seest the World as cast behind him, and that a crown hangs over his head; that is, to shew thee that slighting and despising the things that are present, for the love that he hath to his Master's service, he is sure in the world that comes next to have Glory for his Reward. Now, said the Interpreter, I have shewed thee this picture first, because the Man whose Picture this is, is the only Man, whom the Lord of the Place whither thou art going, hath authorized to be thy Guide in all difficult places thou mayest meet in the way.[1]

Thus Bunyan profiles the ideal Christian preacher.

The same ideal is projected in a complementary way by the *Westminster Directory for the Publick Worship of God*, in its section on the spirit and manner in which preaching must be done.

> Preaching of the Word, being the power of God unto salvation, and one of the greatest and most excellent works belonging to the ministry of the gospel, should be so performed, that the workman may not be ashamed, but may save himself and those who hear him. . . .
>
> The servant of Christ is to perform his whole ministry:
>
> 1. Painfully [i.e., taking pains], not doing the work of the Lord negligently.
>
> 2. Plainly, that the meanest may understand; delivering the truth not in the enticing words of man's wisdom, but in demonstration of the Spirit and of power, lest the cross of Christ should be made of none effect; abstaining also from an unprofitable use of unknown tongues, strange phrases, and cadences of sounds and words; sparingly citing sentences of ecclesiastical or other human writers, ancient or modern, be they never so elegant.
>
> 3. Faithfully, looking at the honour of Christ, the conversion, edification, and salvation of the people, not at his own gain or glory; keeping nothing back which may promote these holy ends, giving to every one his own portion, and bearing indifferent [equal] respect to all, without neglecting the meanest, or sparing the greatest, in their sins.
>
> 4. Wisely, framing all his doctrines, exhortations, and especially his reproofs, in such a manner as may be most likely to prevail; showing all due respect to each man's person and place, and not mixing his own passion or bitterness.
>
> 5. Gravely, as becometh the Word of God, shunning all such gesture, voice, and expression, as may occasion the corruptions of men to despise him and his ministry.
>
> 6. With loving affection, that the people may see all coming from his godly zeal, and hearty desire to do them good.
>
> 7. As taught by God, and persuaded in his own heart, that all he teacheth is the truth of Christ, and walking before his flock, as an example to them in it; earnestly, both in private and publick, recommending his labours to the blessing of God, and watchfully looking to himself, and the flock whereof the Lord hath made him overseer.
>
> So shall the doctrine of truth be preserved uncorrupt, many souls converted and built up, and himself receive manifold comforts of his labours even in this life, and afterward the crown of glory laid up for him in the world to come.[2]

A third projection of this ideal emerges when Richard Baxter speaks to his fellow-preachers about their preaching:

How few ministers do preach with all their might, or speak about everlasting joys and everlasting torments in such a manner as may make man believe that they are in good earnest! Alas, we speak so drowsily or gently, that sleepy sinners cannot hear. The blow falls so light that hard-hearted sinners cannot feel. The most of ministers will not so much as exert their voice, and stir up themselves to an earnest utterance. But if they do speak loud and earnestly,[3] how few do answer it with weight and earnestness of matter! And yet without this, the voice does little good; the people will esteem it but mere bawling, when the matter doth not correspond. It would grieve one to the heart to hear what excellent doctrine some ministers have in hand, while yet they let it die in their hands for want of close and lively application. . . .

O sirs, how plainly, how closely, how earnestly, should we deliver a message of such moment as ours. . . .In the name of God, brethren, labour to awaken your own hearts, before you go to the pulpit, that you may be fit to awaken the hearts of sinners. Remember they must be awakened or damned, and . . . a sleepy preacher will hardly awaken drowsy sinners. Though you give the holy things of God the highest praise in words, yet, if you do it coldly, you will seem by your manner to unsay what you said in the matter. . . . It is only here and there, even among good ministers, that we find one who has an earnest, persuasive, powerful way of speaking, that the people can feel him preach when they hear him. . . .

Though I move you not to constant loudness in your delivery (for that will make your fervency contemptible), yet see that you have a constant seriousness; and when the matter requireth it (as it should do, in the application at least), then lift up your voice, and spare not your spirits. Speak to your people as to men that must be awakened, either here or in hell. Look around upon them with the eye of faith, and with compassion, and think in what a state of joy or torment they must all be for ever; and then, methinks, it will make you earnest, and melt your heart to a sense of their condition. Oh, speak not one cold or careless word about so great a business as heaven or hell.

I confess I must speak it by lamentable experience, that I publish to my flock the distempers of my own soul. When I let my heart go cold, my preaching is cold; . . . and so I can oft observe also in the best of my hearers that when I have grown cold in preaching, they have grown cold too; and the next prayers which I have heard from them have been too like my preaching. . . . O brethren, watch therefore over your own hearts: keep out lusts and passions, and worldly inclinations; keep up the life of faith, and love, and zeal: be much at home, and much with God . . . a minister should take some special pains with his heart, before he is to go to the congregation: if it be then cold, how is he likely to warm the hearts of his hearers? Therefore, go then specially to God for life. . . .[4]

Puritan preaching has had a bad press in these latter days: the caricature is that Puritan sermons were regularly long, abstruse, and dull. In fact, one hour was the recognised length, practical biblical exposition was the actual substance, and liveliness was a regular mark of the style. Puritan preaching prolonged the down-to-earth raciness of presentation, with verbal pictures, narrative illustrations, and allusions to Bible stories scattered throughout in abundance, that the sermons of Hugh Latimer exhibit, and that probably represents a tradition, stylistically speaking, that goes back to the Lollards and the friars. What made Puritan preaching into the reality that it was, however, was less its style than its substance. Puritans preached the Bible systematically and thoroughly, with sustained application to personal life, preaching it as those who believed it, and who sought by their manner to make their matter credible and convincing, convicting and converting. Puritan rhetoric was servant to Puritan biblicism; Puritan pulpit passion was the product of a desire to be a transparent embodiment for the congregation of what it means to grasp, and be grasped by, God's revealed truth concerning grace and godliness, life and death, heaven and hell. 'In preaching there is a communion of souls, and a communication of somewhat from ours to theirs.'[5] If we are to understand Puritan preaching, it is with this Puritan perception of the preacher's task that we must start.

2

The ancestry of the Puritan sermon goes back at least to the day in 1519 when Huldreich Zwingli started to preach his way verse by verse through Matthew's Gospel in Zurich Minster; but Cambridge was its proper birthplace.

The Puritan tradition in preaching was created there at the turn of the sixteenth and seventeenth centuries by the leaders of the first great evangelical movement in that university—William Perkins, Paul Baynes, Richard Sibbes, John Cotton, John Preston, Thomas Goodwin and their fellows. The Puritanism which they had in common was not an ecclesiastical reform programme. Here, in fact they were not agreed at all; Perkins and Baynes dreamed with Cartwright of Presbyterianising the establishment, Cotton and Goodwin became Independents, Preston was a nonconforming Anglican, and Sibbes remained a meek conformist. Their Puritanism was rather the deep Calvinistic piety and urgent concern for vital religion that our previous chapters have described. Their principles in preaching, first formulated by Perkins in his *Arte of Prophecying*, found their best balanced expression in the Westminster Assembly's *Directory for the Publick Worship of God*, and reached perhaps their highest point of development in the pastoral and evangelistic sermons of Richard Baxter.

By the end of the seventeenth century sermon structure had been generally simplified from what it was in the Puritan heyday, and the modern 'three-pointer' had been born, but the heirs of the Puritans maintained in this new form the old practical thrust. In the eighteenth century Dissent claimed to uphold the letter of the Puritan tradition, but it was the Calvinistic Anglican evangelicals (who devoured Puritan theology almost as their staple diet) who best sustained its spirit. Charles Simeon restated its basic principles in a more precise and vigorous form in his edition of Claude's *Essay on the Composition of a Sermon* and illustrated them at length in the 2,536 skeletons which fill his 21-volume *Horae Homileticae*. C.H. Spurgeon, J.C. Ryle and Alexander Whyte, self-confessed heirs of the Puritans, maintained the tradition with distinction to the close of the nineteenth century; Dr Martyn Lloyd-Jones, almost alone, carried it on through the twentieth century. Today, other models and styles of pulpit work prevail, and Puritan preaching is in eclipse. It is hoped, however, that the following pages will commend the writer's conviction that the well-being of the church today depends in large measure on a revival of preaching in the Puritan vein.

3

Four axioms underlay all Puritan thought about preaching. We have met them already, but it is convenient to restate them here.

First, belief in *the primacy of the intellect*. It was a Puritan maxim that 'all grace enters by the understanding'. God does not move men to action by mere physical violence, but addresses their minds by his word, and calls for the response of deliberate consent and intelligent obedience. It follows that every man's first duty in relation to the word of God is to understand it; and every preacher's first duty is to explain it. The only way to the heart that he is authorised to take runs via the head. So the minister who does not make it his prime business, in season and out of season, to teach the word of God, does not do his job, and the sermon which, whatever else it may be, is not a didactic exposition of Scripture is not worthy of the name.

Second, belief in *the supreme importance of preaching*. To the Puritans, the sermon was the liturgical climax of public worship. Nothing, they said, honours God more than the faithful declaration and obedient hearing of his truth. Preaching, under any circumstances, is an act of worship, and must be performed as such. Moreover, preaching is the prime means of grace to the church. 'The most wonderful things that are now done on earth are wrought in the public ordinances,' declared David Clarkson in the course of a sermon entitled 'Public Worship to be Preferred before Private'.

Here the dead hear the voice of the Son of God and those that hear do live. . . . Here he cures diseased souls with a word. . . . Here he dispossess

Satan. . . . Wonders these are, and would be so counted were they not the common work of the public ministry. It is true indeed, the Lord hath not confined himself to work these wonderful things only in public; yet the public ministry is the only ordinary means whereby he works them.[6]

Preaching is thus a very solemn and momentous enterprise. Both minister and congregation should recognise that their Sunday sermons are the most important and significant events of the week. Whatever else is neglected, sermons must not be.

Therefore, the minister who knows his priorities will plan his week round the allotted time for sermon preparation. And he will take care not to skimp his preparation. One meets on occasion, among students who are starting to preach, the idea that, after a time, if they walk faithfully with God, sermons will begin to come naturally, and the need for special preparation will grow less and less. Preachers in the Puritan tradition have not thought so, nor found it so. There were plenty of mid-seventeenth-century zealots who thought it needless to prepare their sermons, but the Puritan leaders rejected this idea. 'Whereas some men are for preaching only extempore and without study,' says Thomas Goodwin, 'Paul bids Timothy meditate and study.'[7] Baxter states the principle positively:

If we give to reason, memory, study, books, methods, forms, etc., but their proper place, in subordination to Christ and to his Spirit, they are so far from being quenchers of the Spirit, that they are necessary in their places, and are such means as we must use, if ever we will expect the Spirit's help.[8]

Most of the Puritans were writing their sermons out in full to the end of their lives. Of Simeon's sermons, Bishop Daniel Wilson, in a posthumous tribute, wrote: 'Few cost him less than twelve hours of study—many twice that time: and some several days. He once told the writer that he had recomposed the plan of one discourse thirty times.'[9] To prepare good sermons may take a long time—but who are we, whom God has set apart for the ministry, to begrudge time for this purpose? We shall never perform a more important task than preaching. If we are not willing to give time to sermon preparation, we are not fit to preach, and have no business in the ministry at all.

Third, belief in *the life-giving power of Holy Scripture*. The Bible does not merely contain the word of God, as a cake contains currants; it *is* the word of God, the Creator's written testimony to himself. And, as such, it is light for the eyes and food for the soul. Recognising this, the Puritans insisted that the preachers' task is to *feed* their congregations with the contents of the Bible—not the dry husks of their own fancy, but the life-giving word of God. Better not preach at all, they would tell us, than preach beyond the Bible, or without utter and obvious confidence in the quickening, nourishing power of the biblical message. Reverence for revealed truth, and faith in its entire adequacy for human needs, should mark all preaching. How can we expect our preaching to beget such reverence and faith in others if it does not reflect this attitude in ourselves?

It is worth noting here that just because preaching is feeding men with the bread of life, the Puritans defined *pastoral* work in terms of *preaching* first and foremost. It is our habit to think of pastoral work as a matter of visiting and personal dealing only, and to oppose it to the public preaching of the word; a man, we say, may be a bad preacher yet a good pastor; but to the Puritan, faithful preaching was the basic ingredient in faithful pastoring. Since this point is important we may quote from John Owen's statement of it at some length:

> The first and principal duty of a pastor is to feed the flock by diligent preaching of the Word. It is a promise relating to the New Testament, that God 'would give unto his church pastors according to his own heart, which should feed them with knowledge and understanding' (Jer. iii.15). This is by preaching or teaching the word, and no otherwise. This feeding is of the essence of the office of a pastor. . . . The care of preaching the gospel was committed to Peter, and in him to all true pastors of the church under the name of 'feeding' (Jn. xxi.15, 16). According to the example of the apostles they are to free themselves from all encumbrances, that they may give themselves wholly unto to the word and prayer (Acts vi). Their work is to 'labour in the word and doctrine' (1 Tim. v.17), and thereby to feed the flock over which the Holy Ghost has made them overseers (Acts xx). . . . This work and duty, therefore, as was said, is essential unto the office of a pastor. . . . Nor is it required only that he preach now and then at his leisure; but that he lay aside all other employments, though lawful, all other duties in the church, as unto such a constant attendance on them as would divert him from this work, that he give himself unto it. . . . Without this, no man will be able to give a comfortable account of his pastoral office at the last day.[10]

The only pastor worthy of the name, in short, is the man whose chief concern is always to feed his people by means of his preaching with the enlivening truths of the word of God.

Fourth, belief in *the sovereignty of the Holy Spirit*. The Puritans insisted that the ultimate effectiveness of preaching is out of man's hands. Man's task is simply to be faithful in teaching the word; it is God's work to convince of its truth and write it in the heart. The Puritans would have criticised the modern evangelistic appeal, with its wheedling for 'decisions', as an unfortunate attempt by man to intrude into the Holy Spirit's province. It is for God, not man, to fix the time of conversion. 'God never laid it upon thee to convert those he sends thee to. No; to publish the gospel is thy duty. . . . God judgeth not of his servants' work by the success of their labour, but by their faithfulness to deliver his message'—so says Gurnall, and he speaks for them all.[11] When the preacher has finished instructing, applying and exhorting, his pulpit work is done. It is not his business to devise devices in order to extort 'decisions'. He would be wiser to go away and pray for God's blessing on what he has said. It is God's sovereign prerogative to make his word effective, and the preacher's behaviour in the pulpit should be governed by recognition of, and subjection to, divine sovereignty in this matter.

We now proceed to describe the type of preaching which these convictions produced.

1. It was *expository in its method*. The Puritan preacher regarded himself as the mouthpiece of God and the servant of his word. He must speak 'as the oracles of God'. His task, therefore, was not imposition, fastening on to Scripture texts meanings they do not bear; nor was it juxtaposition, using his text as a peg on which to hang some homily unrelated to it ('take it in the writer's meaning,' said Simeon, 'not as a motto'); the preacher's task was, precisely, exposition, extracting from his texts what God had encased within them. 'I never preach,' said Simeon, 'unless I feel satisfied that I have the mind of God as regards the sense of the passage.'[12] 'My endeavour is to bring out of Scripture *what is there* . . . I have a great jealousy on this head, never to speak more or less that I believe to be the mind of the Spirit in the passage I am expounding.' So, 'when you cannot get at the full and real meaning of a passage, leave it alone.'[13]

The Puritan method of 'opening' a text (their regular word, and a good one) was first to explain it in its context (they would have agreed with J.H. Jowett that 'a text without a context is a pretext'); next, to extract from the text one or more doctrinal observations embodying its substance; to amplify, illustrate and confirm from other scriptures the truths thus derived; and, finally, to draw out their practical implications for the hearers. The Puritans were devotees of continuous exposition, and have left behind them magnificent sets of expository sermons on complete chapters and books of the Bible, as well as on single texts. Most of Matthew Henry's wonderful *Commentary*, for instance, was first preached to his own flock at Chester.

2. Puritan preaching was *doctrinal in its content*. The Puritans received the Bible as a self-contained and self-interpreting revelation of God's mind. This revelation, the 'body of divinity' as they called it, is, they held, a unity, to which every part of 'the best of books' makes its own distinct contribution. It follows that the meaning of single texts cannot be properly discerned till they are seen in relation to the rest of the 'body'; and, conversely, that the better one's grasp of the whole, the more significance one will see in each part. To be a good expositor, therefore, one must first be a good theologian. Theology—truth about God and man—is what God has put

into the texts of Scripture, and theology is what preachers must draw out of them. To the question, 'Should one preach doctrine?', the Puritan answer would have been, 'Why, what else is there to preach?' Puritan preachers were not afraid to bring the profoundest theology into the pulpit if it bore on their hearers' salvation, nor to demand that men and women apply themselves to mastering it, nor to diagnose unwillingness to do so as a sign of insincerity. Doctrinal preaching certainly bores the hypocrites; but it is only doctrinal preaching that will save Christ's sheep. The preacher's job is to proclaim the faith, not to provide entertainment for unbelievers—in other words, to feed the sheep rather than amuse the goats.

3. Puritan preaching was *orderly in its arrangement*. The preachers knew the value of clear headings, and deliberately allowed the skeletons of their sermons to stick out. Peter Ramus, a Huguenot academic killed in the St Bartholomew's Day massacre of 1572, had formulated an educational theory in which analysis becomes the key to understanding, and the Puritans took his point at least to the extent of making sure that the layout and structure of their messages was as clear and logical as possible. The importance of this appears when we remember that the Puritans taught their congregations to memorise the sermons they heard, looking up references and taking notes if need be, so that they could 'repeat' the messages afterwards and meditate on them during the week. The ministry of the word was thus a co-operative activity, in which the laity were to labour to learn just as hard as the minister laboured to teach. A sermon that was needlessly hard to remember was for that very reason, of necessity, a bad sermon.

4. Puritan preaching, though profound in its content, was *popular in its style*. Learned pulpiteers vied with each other in stuffing their sermons with what Thomas Goodwin called 'the eminentist farrago of all sorts of flowers of wit that are found in any of the Fathers, poets, histories, similitudes, or whatever has the elegancy of wit in it'.[14] Preaching thus degenerated into a sophisticated entertainment for the cultured, and an occasion for the preacher's self-display. Baxter spoke for the Puritans generally when he condemned this 'witty' preaching as 'proud foolery which savoureth of levity, and tendeth to evaporate weighty truths', and complained that its practitioners 'deal liker to players than preachers in the pulpit'. Preaching that exalts the preacher, the Puritans said, is unedifying, sinful preaching. Baxter went on in the passage quoted to lay down the principle that determined the Puritans' own homiletic idiom: 'the plainest words are the profitablest oratory in the weightiest matters.'[15] To borrow Ryle's autobiographical phrase, they 'crucified their style'. They systematically eschewed any rhetorical display that might divert attention from God to themselves, and talked to their congregations in plain, straightforward, homely English. Not that their speaking was slipshod or vulgar. Dignified simplicity—'studied plainness', as one of their number once put it—was their

ideal. In fact, the 'studied plainness' of Puritan preaching often possesses a striking eloquence of its own—the natural eloquence that results when words are treated not at all as the orator's playthings, but entirely as the servants of a noble meaning. One thinks at once of Bunyan and Baxter here.

5. Puritan preaching was *Christ-centred in its orientation*. 'Young man,' said veteran Richard Sibbes to fledgling Thomas Goodwin, 'if ever you would do good, you must preach the gospel of the free grace of God in Christ Jesus.'[16] Puritan preaching revolved around 'Christ, and him crucified'—for this is the hub of the Bible. The preachers' commission is to declare the whole counsel of God; but the cross is the centre of that counsel, and the Puritans knew that the traveller through the Bible landscape misses his way as soon as he loses sight of the hill called Calvary. Simeon's sermons had three avowed aims—to humble the sinner, to exalt the Saviour, and to promote holiness; and it was the second aim that gave point to the first and meaning to the third. In this Simeon was as authentically Puritan as it is possible for a man to be.

6. Puritan preaching was *experimental in its interests*. The preachers' supreme concern was to bring men to know God. Their preaching was avowedly 'practical' and concerned with experience of God. Sin, the cross, Christ's heavenly ministry, the Holy Spirit, faith and hypocrisy, assurance and the lack of it, prayer, meditation, temptation, mortification, growth in grace, death, heaven were their constant themes. Bunyan's *Pilgrim's Progress* serves as a kind of gazetteer to the contents of their sermons. In their treatment of these matters they were deep, thorough, and authoritative. They spoke as holy experienced Christians who knew what they were talking about. Their rule was formulated by David Dickson when he charged a young minister at his ordination to study two books together: the Bible, and his own heart. The Puritans made it a matter of conscience to prove for themselves the saving power of the gospel they urged on others. They knew that, as John Owen put it, 'a man preacheth that sermon only well to others, which preacheth itself in his own soul. . . . If the word do not dwell with power *in* us, it will not pass with power *from* us.'[17] Robert Bolton was not the only one who 'never taught any godly point, but he first wrought it on his owne heart'.[18] Their strenuous exercise in meditation and prayer, their sensitiveness to sin, their utter humility, their passion for holiness, and their glowing devotion to Christ equipped them to be master-physicians of the soul. And deep called to deep when they preached, for they spoke of the black depths and high peaks of Christian experience first-hand. An old Christian who heard young Spurgeon, still in his teens, said of him, almost in awe, 'he was as experimental as if he were a hundred years old in faith.' That was a mark of all Puritan preaching.

7. Puritan preaching was *piercing in its applications*. Over and above

applicatory generalisations, the preachers trained their homiletical search-lights on specific states of spiritual need, and spoke to these in a precise and detailed way. Earlier we noted how Perkins in his *Arte of Prophecying* distinguished the different classes of people that the preacher could expect to be addressing in any ordinary congregation: the ignorant and unteach-able, who needed the equivalent of a bomb under their seats; the ignorant but teachable, who needed orderly instruction in what Christianity is all about; the knowledgeable but unhumbled, who needed to be given a sense of sin; the humbled and desperate, who needed to be grounded in the gospel; believers going on with God, who needed building up; and believers who had fallen into error, intellectual or moral, and needed correction. Other subcategories spring to mind, once one starts thinking of congrega-tions in these terms, such as the discouraged, the hurting, and the depressed (sufferers from 'melancholy', as the Puritans called it); perhaps Perkins had some of these in mind when, rather mysteriously, he identified as his final type 'a mixed people. A mixed people are the assemblies of our churches.'[19] (Could 'mixed' here mean 'mixed-up'?) To all of these different groups the word of God must be applied.

To Perkins' classification of types of people we must now add the list of types of application that the *Westminster Directory for Publick Worship*[20] gives. Having laid it down that the preacher, after establishing and clarifying a truth, must 'bring it home to special use, by application to his hearers', even though 'it prove a work of great difficulty to himself, requiring much prudence, zeal, and meditation, and to the natural and cor-rupt man will be very unpleasant', the *Directory* specifies application ('uses') of six kinds:

(1) instruction or information in the knowledge of some . . . consequence from his doctrine; (2) confutation of false doctrines; (3) exhorting to duties; (4) dehortation, reprehension, and publick admonition; (5) applying com-fort; (6) trial [self-examination], (which is very profitable . . .) whereby the hearers may be able to examine themselves . . . that accordingly they may be quickened and excited to duty, humbled for their wants and sins, affected with their danger, and strengthened with comfort [encouragement], as their condition, upon examination, shall require.

These types of application are all pastoral and evangelistic: the preacher should 'wisely make choice of such uses, as, by residence and conversing with his flock, he findeth most needful and seasonable; and, amongst these, such as may most draw their souls to Christ. . . .' In form they are infer-ential and logical, being structured thus: since this is true ('this' being the truth just taught), you must (1) be sure of the following further truths, which it implies; (2) abjure the following errors, which it contradicts; (3) do such-and-such good things, which it requires; (4) stop doing, or avoid doing, such-and-such bad things, which it forbids; (5) take to yourself the encouragement which it offers; (6) ask yourself where you stand spiritually in the light of it, and how far you are living by it. The quality of a preacher depended ultimately, in the Puritan estimate, on the clarity, wisdom, authority, and searchingness that hearers found in his application.

It was not, of course, possible for any preacher to make all six types of application to all seven types of listeners in any one sermon. Forty-two distinct applications would take all day! But Puritan pastoral preachers would spend half or more of their preaching time developing applications, and anyone making an inventory of their published sermons will soon find examples of all forty-two specific applications, often developed with very great rhetorical and moral force. Strength of application was, from one standpoint, the most striking feature of Puritan preaching, and it is arguable that the theory of discriminating application is the most valuable legacy that Puritan preachers have left to those who would preach the Bible and its gospel effectively today.

8. Puritan preaching was *powerful in its manner*. The Puritan coveted unction in the pulpit. He aspired to be what Baxter calls 'a plain and pressing downright preacher', speaking from a full heart 'in good sadness [good earnest]', 'with life, and light, and weight.' He sought to preach (as was once said of a Puritan minister) 'as if death were at his back'—in Baxter's words:

> As one that ne'er should preach again,
> And as a dying man to dying men.

And unless the Spirit was upon him, so that he felt what he spoke, it was to the Puritan mind hardly *preaching* at all. Later evangelicals were in agreement; Simeon said:

> It is easy for a minister to prate in the pulpit, but to preach is not easy—to carry his congregation on his shoulders, as it were, to heaven; to weep over them, pray for them, deliver the truth with a weeping praying heart; and if a minister has grace to do so now and then, he ought to be very thankful.[21]

That was why Baxter insisted, as we saw at the beginning, that

> a minister should take some special pains with his heart, before he is to go to the congregation; if he be then cold, how is he like to warm the hearts of the hearers? Therefore, go then specially to God for life; and read some rousing, awakening book, or meditate on the weight of the subject of which you are going to speak and on the great necessity of your people's souls, that you may go in the zeal of the Lord into his house.[22]

Such was Puritan preaching, and such was evangelical preaching generally till recent times. It was preaching of this kind that made evangelicalism great in the past, and there seems little likelihood that evangelicalism will be great again without a return to it. The churches of the West are currently in confusion about the way to make preaching spiritually significant for the modern congregation, and are treating the problem as primarily one of devising appropriate techniques. Technique is, of course, necessary in preaching, and it would not be false to say that the Puritan technique of exposition and application has been our theme in this chapter. But the Puritans themselves would be the first to insist that there is more to significant preaching than mere technique, even applicatory technique: and it seems appropriate to close by allowing Richard Baxter, 'Mr Reformed Pastor' as we may well call him, to speak once more, and make to his fellow-preachers the point—the cluster of points, rather—which today's church is too apt to forget.

All our work must be done spiritually, as by men possessed of the Holy Ghost. There is in some men's preaching a spiritual strain, which spiritual hearers can discern and relish. . . . Our evidence and illustrations of divine truth must also be spiritual, being drawn from the Holy Scriptures. . . . It is the sign of a distempered heart that loseth the relish of Scripture excellency. For there is in a spiritual heart a co-naturality to the Word of God, because this is the seed which did regenerate him. The Word is that seal which made all the holy impressions that are in the hearts of true believers, and stamped the image of God upon them; and, therefore, they must needs . . . highly esteem it as long as they live. . . .

Our whole work must be carried on under a deep sense of our own insufficiency, and of our entire dependence on Christ. We must go for light, and life, and strength to him, who sends us on the work. . . . Prayer must carry on our work as well as preaching; he preacheth not heartily to his people, that prayeth not earnestly for them. If we prevail not with God to give them faith and repentance we shall never prevail with them to believe and repent.[23]

CHAPTER EIGHTEEN

Puritan Evangelism

As long ago as 1918 an official Anglican committee defined evangelism thus: 'So to present Christ Jesus in the power of the Holy Spirit, that men shall come to put their trust in God through Him, to accept Him as their Saviour, and serve Him as their King in the fellowship of His Church.' With one word changed ('may' for 'shall', so that evangelism is defined in terms of purpose rather than results) this definition makes a good starting-point for the present study.[1]

Did the Puritans tackle the task of evangelism at all? At first sight, it might appear not. 'Evangelism' (a twentieth-century word) was not part of their vocabulary. They agreed with Calvin in regarding the 'evangelists' mentioned in the New Testament as an order of assistants to the apostles, now extinct, and as for 'missions', 'crusades', and 'campaigns', they knew neither the name nor the thing. But we must not be misled into supposing that evangelism was not one of their chief concerns. It was. Many of them were outstandingly successful as preachers to the unconverted. Richard Baxter, the apostle of Kidderminster, is perhaps the only one of these that is widely remembered today; but in seventeenth-century records it is common to read statements like this, of Hugh Clark: 'he begat many Sons and Daughters unto God'; or this, of John Cotton: 'the presence of the Lord . . . crowning his Labours with the Conversion of many Souls.'[2] Moreover, it was the Puritans who invented evangelistic literature. One has only to think here of Richard Baxter's *Call to the Unconverted*, and Joseph Alleine's *Alarm to the Unconverted*, both of them outstanding pioneer

291

works in this class of writing. And the elaborate practical 'handling' of the subject of conversion in Puritan books was regarded by the rest of the seventeenth-century Protestant world as something of unique value. Wrote two of the Puritan leaders:

> It hath been one of the glories of the Protestant religion that it revived the doctrine of *Saving Conversion*, and of the *New Creature* brought forth thereby.... But in a more eminent manner, God hath cast the honour hereof upon the Ministers and Preachers of this Nation, who are renowned abroad for their more accurate search into and discoveries hereof.[3]

The truth is that two distinct conceptions and types of evangelism have been developed in Protestant Christendom during the course of its history. We may call them the 'Puritan' and the 'modern' types. Today we are so accustomed to evangelism of the modern type that we scarcely recognise the other as evangelism at all. In order that we may fully grasp the character of the Puritan type of evangelism, I shall here set it in contrast with the modern type, which has so largely superseded it in our era.

1

Let us begin, then, by characterising evangelism of the modern type. It seems to presuppose a conception of the life of the local church as an alternating cycle of converting and consolidating. Evangelism almost acquires the character of a periodic recruiting campaign. It becomes an extraordinary and occasional activity, additional and auxiliary to the regular functioning of the local congregation. Special gatherings of a special sort are arranged, and special preachers are commonly secured to conduct them. Often they are called 'meetings' rather than 'services'; in some places they are called 'revivals'; in any case, they are viewed as separate and distinct from the regular worship of God. In the meetings, everything is directly aimed at securing from the unconverted an immediate, conscious, decisive act of faith in Jesus Christ. At the close, those who have responded or who wish to do so are asked to come to the front for counselling, or raise a hand, or fill up a card, or something similar, as an act of public testimony to their new resolutions. This, it is claimed, is good for those who do it, since it helps to make their 'decision' definite, and it has the further advantage of making them declare themselves for 'follow-up' purposes. Such persons will then be advised and drafted forthwith into local churches as converts.

This type of evangelism was invented by Charles G. Finney in the 1820s. He introduced the 'protracted meeting' (i.e., the intensive evangelistic campaign) and the 'anxious seat', forerunner of the counselling room, a front pew left vacant where at the meeting's end 'the anxious may come and be addressed particularly . . . and sometimes be conversed with individually'. In closing his mission sermons, Finney would say, 'There is the anxious seat; come out, and avow determination to be on the Lord's side.'[4] These were Finney's much opposed 'new measures'.

Finney, a one-time schoolmaster and lawyer, had come to faith at the age of twenty-nine, and had gone straight into evangelistic work. Brilliant and intense, articulate and commanding, zealous and independent, he held to Edwards' philosophy of revivals as cyclic visitations from God (see Chapter Nineteen below), while querying Edwards' assumption that man cannot precipitate revivals and jettisoning altogether Edwards' assertion of the Augustinian-Reformed-Puritan belief in total inability—the belief, that is, that fallen human beings are totally unable to repent, believe, or do anything spiritually good without renewing grace.

While acknowledging—indeed, insisting on—universal human depravity in the sense of a constant inclination to sin, he was a clear-headed and forthright Pelagian in his emphatic declarations that everyone is naturally able to turn whole-heartedly to God once he or she is convinced that that is the right, proper, and needful thing to do. Accordingly, Finney conceived the whole work of the Spirit in conversion in terms of moral persuasion, that is, of making vivid to our minds the reasons for laying down our rebel arms and surrendering to God. Man is always free to reject this persuasion—'Sinners can go to Hell in spite of God.' But the stronger the persuasion is, the more likely it is to succeed in breaking down resistance. Every means, therefore, of increasing the force with which truth impinges on the mind—the most frenzied excitement, the most harrowing emotionalism, the most nerve-racking commotion in evangelistic gatherings—is entirely in order. Finney expressed this in the first of his revival lectures:

> To expect to promote religion without excitements is unphilosophical and absurd . . . until there is sufficient religious principle in the world to put down irreligious excitements, it is vain to try to promote religion, except by counteracting excitements. . . . There must be excitement sufficient to wake up the dormant moral powers. . . .[5]

Moreover, since everyone, if he will only rouse up his 'dormant moral powers', can at any time yield to God and become a Christian, it is the evangelist's work and duty always to preach for immediate decision and commitment. 'I tried to shut them up,' Finney says of a typical mission sermon, 'to present faith and repentance, as the thing which God required of them . . . present and instant acceptance of Christ.'[6] It does not seem too much to say that for Finney evangelistic preaching was a battle of wills between himself and his hearers, in which his task was to bring them to breaking-point.

Now, if Finney's doctrine of the natural state of sinful man is right, then his evangelistic methods must be judged right also, for, as he often insisted, the 'new measures' were means well adapted to the end in view. 'It is in such practices that a Pelagian system naturally expresses itself if it seeks to become aggressively evangelistic,' observed B.B. Warfield.[7] But if Finney's view of man is wrong, then his methods must be called in question—which is an issue of importance at the present time: for it is Finney's methods, modified and adapted, that characterise a great deal of evangelism today. I do not suggest that all who use them are Pelagians; but I do raise the question whether the use of them is really consistent with any other doctrine than Finney's, and I shall try to show that, if Finney's doctrine is rejected, such methods are inappropriate to a degree, and actually detrimental to the real work of evangelism. It may be said that results justify their use; but the truth is that most of Finney's 'converts' backslid and fell away, as, so it seems, did the majority of those since Finney's day whose 'decision' was secured by these means. Most modern evangelists seem to have given up expecting more than a small percentage of their 'converts' to survive. So it is not obvious that results justify the methods that stem from Finney. I shall suggest later that these methods have a natural tendency to produce a crop of false converts, as evidently they have in fact done.

2

The Puritan type of evangelism, on the other hand, was and is the consistent expression in practice of the Puritans' conviction that *the conversion of a sinner is a gracious sovereign work of divine power*. Let me explain.

The Puritans did not use the picture-words 'conversion' and 'new birth'/'regeneration' as technical terms, and usage varies slightly from one to another; but most treated the words as synonyms for the process for which the technical name was *effectual calling*: *calling* being the biblical word for it in Romans 8:30; 2 Thessalonians 2:14; 2 Timothy 1:9, and the adjective *effectual* being added to distinguish it from the ineffectual external call mentioned in Matthew 20:16; 22:14. The *Westminster Confession* X:i puts 'calling' into its theological perspective by an interpretative paraphrase of Romans 8:30:

All those whom God hath predestinated unto life, and those only he is pleased, in his appointed and accepted time, effectually to call, by his Word and Spirit, out of that state of sin and death in which they are by nature, to grace and salvation by Jesus Christ.

The *Westminster Shorter Catechism*, answer 31, gives this analysis:

Effectual calling is the work of God's Spirit whereby, convincing us of our sin and misery, enlightening our minds in the knowledge of Christ, and renewing our wills, he doth persuade and enable us to embrace Jesus Christ, freely offered to us in the gospel.

Concerning this *effectual calling*, three things must be said if we are to grasp the Puritan view.

(1) It is *a work of divine grace*. It is not something a man can do for himself or for another. It is the first stage in the application of redemption to those for whom redemption was won; it is the event whereby, on the grounds of the eternal, federal, representative relation to Christ that election and redemption have established, the elect sinner is brought by the Holy Spirit into a real, vital, personal union with his covenant Head and Redeemer. It is thus a work of free mercy on God's part.

(2) It is *a work of divine power*. It is effected by the Spirit, who acts both *mediately*, by the word, in the mind, giving understanding and conviction, and also *immediately*, with the word, in the hidden depths of the heart, implanting new life and power, effectively dethroning sin and making the sinner both able and willing to respond to the gospel invitation. The Spirit's work is thus both *moral*, by *persuasion* (which Arminians and Pelagians affirm), and also *physical*, by *power* (which they deny). ('Physical' here means 'terminating on our personal being at a level below consciousness', not 'terminating on the body as distinct from the personal self [i.e., soul].') Writes Owen:

> There is not only a *moral*, but a *physical* immediate operation of the Spirit . . . upon the minds or souls of men in their regeneration. . . . The work of grace in conversion is constantly expressed by words denoting a real internal efficacy; such as creating, quickening, forming, giving a new heart. . . . Wherever the work is spoken of with respect unto an active efficacy, it is ascribed unto God. He *creates* us anew, he *quickens* us, he *begets* us of his own will; but when it is spoken of with respect to us, there it is passively expressed; we *are created* in Christ Jesus, we are *new creatures*, we are *born again*, and the like; *which one observation is sufficient to evert* [overthrow] *the whole hypothesis of Arminian grace*.[8]

'Ministers knock at the door of men's hearts, the Spirit comes with a key and opens the door.'[9] The Spirit's regenerating action, Owen goes on, is 'infallible, victorious, irresistible, or always efficacious'; it 'removeth all obstacles, overcomes all oppositions, and infallibly produces the effect intended'.[10] Grace is *irresistible*, not because it drags sinners to Christ against their will, but because it changes men's hearts so that they 'come most freely, being made willing by his grace.'[11]

The Puritans loved to dwell on the scriptural thought of divine power creatively put forth in effectual calling, which Goodwin regularly describes as the one 'standing miracle' in the church. They agreed that conversion was commonly not a spectacular affair; but Goodwin notes that sometimes it is precisely that, and affirms that hereby God shows us, in a paradigm case, so to speak, how great an exercise of power every Christian's effectual call involves. Goodwin writes:

> In the calling of some, there shoots up very suddenly an *election-conversion* (I used to call it so). You shall, as it were, see election take hold of a man, pull him out with a mighty power, stamp upon him the divine nature, stub up corrupt nature by the roots, root up self-love, put in a principle of love to God, and launch him forth a new creature the first day. . . . He did so with Paul, and it is not without example in others after him.[12]

Such dramatic conversions, says Goodwin, are

> visible tokens of election by such a work of calling, as all the powers in heaven and earth could not have wrought upon a man's soul so, nor changed a man so on a sudden, but only that divine power that created the world [and] raised Christ from the dead.[13]

The reason why the Puritans thus magnified the quickening power of God is plain from the passages quoted: it was because they took so seriously the Bible teaching that man is *dead* in sin (Eph 2:1, 5; Col 2:13), spiritually impotent (Jn 3:3, 5; 6:45; Rom 8:7; 1 Cor 2:14), radically depraved, sin's helpless slave (Rom 3:9; 6:20-22). Sin has such strength, they held, that only omnipotence can break its bond; only the author of life can raise the dead. Total inability requires total sovereignty for its overcoming.

(3) Effectual calling is *a work of divine freedom*. Only God can effect it, and he does so at his own pleasure. 'It is not of him that willeth, nor of him that runneth, but of God that showeth mercy' (Rom 9:16, KJV). Owen dwells on this in a sermon on Acts 16:9, 'A vision of unchangeable, free mercy in sending the means of grace to undeserving sinners.'[14] First he states the principle:

> All events and effects, especially concerning the propagation of the gospel, and the Church of Christ, are in their greatest variety regulated by the eternal purpose and counsel of God.

Then he illustrates. Some are sent the gospel, some not.

> In this chapter . . . the gospel is forbidden to be preached in Asia or Bithynia; which restraint, the Lord by his providence as yet continueth to many parts

of the world [while] to some nations the gospel is sent . . . as in my text, Macedonia; and England. . . .

Why this discrimination? asks Owen. Why do only some hear? And when the gospel is heard, why do we see

> various effects, some continuing in impenitency, others in sincerity closing with Jesus Christ? . . . In the effectual working of grace also for conversion and salvation . . . whence do you think it takes its rule and determination . . . that it should be directed to John, not Judas; Simon Peter, not Simon Magus? Why, only from this discriminating counsel of God from eternity. . . . The purpose of God's election, is the rule of dispensing saving grace.[15]

Jonathan Edwards, a Puritan evangelist born out of due time, often makes the same point. In a typical passage from a sermon on Romans 9:18, he lists the following ways in which God's sovereignty (defined as 'his absolute right of disposing of all creatures according to his own pleasure') appears in the dispensations of his grace:

> (1) In calling one nation or people, and giving them the means of grace, and leaving others without them. (2) . . . In the advantages he bestows upon particular persons' [e.g., a Christian home, a powerful ministry, direct spiritual influences, etc]. . . . . (3) In bestowing salvation on some who have had few advantages [e.g., children of ungodly parents, while the children of the godly are not always saved]; (4) . . . In calling some to salvation, who have been heinously wicked, and leaving others, who have been very moral and religious persons. . . . (6) In saving some of those who seek salvation and not others [i.e., bringing some convicted sinners to saving faith while others never attain to it].[16]

This display of sovereignty, maintains Edwards, is glorious: 'it is part of the glory of God's mercy that it is sovereign mercy.'

Perhaps no preacher in the Puritan tradition ever stressed the sovereignty of God as Edwards did. Yet his preaching was evangelistically fruitful. Revival swept through his church under his ministry, and in the revival, he says:

> I think I have found that no discourses have been more *remarkably blessed*, than those in which the doctrine of God's *absolute* sovereignty, with regard to the salvation of sinners, and his *just liberty*, with regard to answering prayer, and succeeding the plans, of natural men, continuing such, have been insisted on.[17]

Here, surely, is food for thought.

God's sovereign freedom appears also in the *time* of conversion. Scripture and experience show, writes Goodwin, that

> the great God for holy and glorious ends, but more especially . . . to make appear his love and kindness, his mercy and grace, hath ordained it so that many of his elect people should for some time remain in a condition of sin and wrath, and then he renews them to himself.[18]

It is never man, but always God, who determines when an elect sinner shall believe.

In the *manner* of conversion, too, God is sovereign. The Puritans taught that knowledge and conviction of one's sin, in its guilt, pollution, and ugliness, and of God's displeasure at it, must precede faith, since no one will come to Christ to be saved from sin till he or she knows from what sins salvation is needed. This is the Puritan 'preparation' for faith, often misunderstood as restricting access to Christ when in fact it alone opens the door of access to him. There must be, said the Puritans, *contrition* about one's sins, in the precise medieval sense of that word (i.e., sorrow for and hatred of one's sins, as God-dishonouring and self-defiling, so that one longs to be rescued from them); otherwise, one cannot genuinely, sincerely, and whole-heartedly come to Christ to be saved from sin's power as well as its penalty, which is what the gospel call to faith-and-repentance requires one to do. Wise preachers and counsellors, therefore, will not short-circuit the essential preparatory process, but will continue to press on the seeker's conscience the sinfulness of his sins and the depth of his need to be not just forgiven, but also led into holiness, until they can see that he has truly fallen out of love with sin; and then they will point him to the Saviour. This, said the Puritans, is the pastoral procedure that knowledge of the manner of God's work in conversion dictates. To their minds, it would be the worst advice possible to tell a troubled person to stop worrying about his sins and trust Christ at once when that person had not yet faced the specifics of his or her sinfulness and has not yet come to the point of clear-headedly desiring to leave all sinful ways behind and be made holy. To give this advice, they held, before the heart is weaned from sin would be the way to induce false peace and false hopes, and so to produce 'gospel-hypocrites', which is the last thing that a Christian counsellor should be willing to do.

But throughout the whole process of preparation God's free sovereignty has to be recognised. God converts no adults without preparation along the lines described, but within this formula there are any number of variations: 'God breaketh not all Men's hearts alike.'[19] Some conversions, as Goodwin said, are in every sense sudden; the preparation is done in a moment. Some are long-drawn-out affairs, with years passing before the seeker finds Christ and peace, as in Bunyan's case. No rule can be given as to how long, or how intensely, God will flay each sinner with the lash of conviction. There must be contrition before conversion can result. The work of effectual calling will proceed as fast as God wills, but no faster, and the counsellor's role is accordingly that of the midwife, whose task it is to see what is happening and give appropriate help at each stage, but who cannot foretell, let alone prearrange, how rapid the birth process will be.

3

The Puritan practitioners of evangelism were pastors with captive audiences (for church-going was part of national life in those days), and their evangelising of those who sat regularly in the pews was to the pastors no more, just as it was no less, than a main part of their larger task of building up the whole congregation in Christ. Their programme as evangelists was no more specialised than this: to teach and apply the Scriptures in a patient, thorough way, ranging wide in their declarations of the whole counsel of God but constantly returning to three themes. Theme one was the length, breadth, height and depth of everyone's need to be converted and saved. Theme two was the length, breadth, depth, and height of the love of God, who sent his Son to the cross for sinners, and of Christ, who from his throne calls burdened souls to himself for their salvation. Theme three was the ups, downs, blockages and pitfalls that face us as we travel the road from ignorant complacency about our spiritual state to informed, self-despairing, clear-headed and whole-hearted faith in Christ. The Puritan way of opening up this third theme was to keep ringing changes on four truths: the *duty* of receiving Jesus Christ as Saviour and Master; the *danger* of settling in religion for anything less; the *impossibility* of coming to Christ without renewing grace; and the *necessity* of seeking that grace from Christ's own hand. Formally from pulpits and informally in personal counselling, they highlighted the present duty of the unconverted to seek Christ; but they did not see this as implying a present capacity to receive Christ savingly, and so one does not find them commanding all the unconverted to 'decide for Christ' (the common modern phrase) on the spot, or making appeals in which they profess to be 'giving them an opportunity' to make this decision. Plainly, they did not believe that God sent them, or sends anyone else, to tell congregations that God requires everyone to receive Christ at the close of the sermon.

This is the point at which Pelagianism betrayed Finney, and Finney's example has betrayed many since his day. Believing that it is in everyone's power to accept Christ at any moment, Finney equated the immediate response that the gospel requires of all with instant conversion on the part of all. But by making this equation he made it impossible to avoid doing damage to some souls. If one tells people that they are under obligation to receive Christ on the spot, and calls in God's name for instant decision, some who are spiritually unprepared will come forward, accept directions, 'go through the motions', and go away thinking they have received Christ, when in reality they have not done so because they were not yet able to do so. So a crop of false conversions results from these tactics *in the nature of the case*. Bullying for 'decisions' can actually impede and thwart the work of the Holy Spirit in human hearts. When the evangelist takes it on himself to try to pick the fruit before it is ripe, the result is regularly false conversions and hardening. 'Quick sale' techniques in evangelism always tend to boomerang in this way; their long-term effect is regularly barrenness. Not for nothing was one of the areas where Finney first worked later labelled 'the burned-over district'. Finneyism, which seeks to break up the fallow ground, issues rather in a scorching of the earth, a state of diminished rather than enhanced responsiveness to the gospel.

Certainly, there have always been individuals—Finney himself, Richard Baxter, George Whitefield, John Wesley, D.L. Moody, Charles Spurgeon, John Sung, Billy Graham, Luis Palau are names that come at once to mind—whose gifts and personal qualities God uses in a special way to bring adults via the necessary preparation to conscious faith in Christ. Such men are properly called evangelists. But possession of an evangelistic gift does not oblige one to embrace false principles and flawed procedures in tackling the evangelistic task. It is not necessary to do all the things that Finney did just because Finney did them, nor to suppose that Finney's distinctive methods are the best option just because Finney thought they were. The work of evangelism has to be done afresh in every generation, and half the human race remains unevangelised today. While liberalism in the churches fades, evangelicalism steadily gains strength, and within evangelicalism evangelistic zeal is currently rising, for all of which we should thank God. But our increasing concern for evangelism makes it all the more important that careful thought be given to principles and procedures for future action. Facts to face as we think about this matter include the following.

During the past century, the headline-hitting Finneyan procedure—the 'spasm' evangelism of the big-scale, short-term, special-effort, hyped-up 'campaign' or 'crusade'—has been widely exported from America on what appears to be the evangelical equivalent of the secular slogan: 'What's good for General Motors is good for the world.' It has received a great deal of criticism of the kind expressed in this chapter, which has led some of its practitioners (not all) to take care lest they appear to have bought into the evangelical Pelagianism which the instant-commitment focus of the procedure naturally implies. Yet God, who graciously blesses truth even when error sits alongside it, has constantly used Finneyan ventures to bring to decisive and lasting commitment persons who have previously been touched by ministry of the word in church and/or the witness of Christian friends. Though the fallout of false conversions has been tragically and scandalously heavy, Finneyan 'protracted meetings' all round the world have brought sufficient spiritual gains, one way and another, to show they are not simply under God's curse, and Billy Graham, who uses a modified version of the Finneyan formula, has been one of the most significant figures on the world Christian stage in recent years. (One can say that without ceasing to suspect that better procedures might have been devised, just as one can thankfully acknowledge the many real conversions through mass evangelism without assuming that the parties concerned would never have been converted otherwise.) In the light of these facts, the following conclusions seem to suggest themselves:

First, modern evangelism will always depend for its fruitfulness, under ordinary circumstances, on the prior exposure of the audience it gathers to evangelism of the Puritan type—longer-term, broader-based, deeper-digging, church-, community- and friendship-centred, oriented more to worship and less to entertainment. Modern evangelism is only likely to reap where Puritan evangelism has first sowed.

Second, evangelism of the Puritan type, through faithful preaching and teaching of the gospel over a period of time, with applications that acknowledge the spread-out steps and stages via which a person's path to faith is likely to run, and sustained by confidence in God to give fruit in his own way at his own speed, is essential, always and everywhere; and modern evangelism must justify itself, if at all, as a rational supplement to Puritan evangelism rather than an alternative to it.

Third, practitioners of Puritan evangelism, who bow to the sovereignty of God in drawing people to faith, appear sometimes to lapse into unconcern about seeing conversions through their ministry, while practitioners of modern evangelism appear sometimes to imagine that no preachers seek conversions save themselves. Both states of mind are to be stigmatised as deplorable, and need to be renounced: the first because it is ungodly, and the second because it is unfounded.

Fourth, when ventures in 'spasm' evangelism are mounted, preachers and counsellors will be wisest if, while stressing the urgency of seeking Christ and becoming a true and thorough Christian, they funnel enquirers into catechetical classes, nurture groups, and church worship, highlighting these involvements as the proper way to express sincerity of contrition and commitment, rather than letting it seem that immediate 'decision', as an isolated act, is all that is needed to settle the issues of eternity for ever. That trust in Christ out of a changed heart does settle the issues of eternity for ever is not in question, but not all enquirers will have reached the point where they can exercise that truth in an authentic 'decision', even though they may think they can. So the provision of structures for further instruction and help towards conversion is a matter of necessity, just as 'follow-up' structures for establishing the converted are. But embrace of the

Pelagian mistake can blind people to this necessity, and there is no doubt that in circles where modern evangelism has been practised during the past century it has constantly done so.

4

Principles have more power with us when we see them embodied in persons whom we admire. Accordingly, I now round off my commendation of Puritan principles of evangelism by once more introducing the most distinguished and attractive, and happily also the most accessible, of Puritan evangelists, Richard Baxter, to whose Kidderminster ministry reference was made earlier.[20] Brilliant, passionate, eloquent, honest, open-hearted, sharp-sighted, and wholly devoted to the glory of God and the good of others, Baxter ranks with Augustine, Luther, Bunyan, Wesley and Finney (to look no further) in his flair for unselfconscious, self-revealing intimacy on paper. In the account of his Kidderminster days which, five or six years after he left the town, he put on paper 'to the Praise of my Redeemer' and 'for their sakes that would have the means of other Mens Experiments [experiences], in managing ignorant and sinful Parishes',[21] Baxter shares himself prodigally, as he also does in his classic on care for the congregation, *The Reformed Pastor*.[22] Let us meet him.

'BAXTER, Richard, gentleman; born 12 November 1615, at Rowton, Salop; educated at Donnington Free School, Wroxeter, and privately; ordained deacon by Bishop of Worcester, Advent 1639; head of Richard Foley's School, Dudley, 1639; curate of Bridgnorth, 1639-40; parish lecturer at Kidderminster, 1641-42; army chaplain at Coventry, 1642-45, and with Whalley's regiment (New Model Army), 1645-47; vicar of Kidderminster 1647-61; at Savoy Conference, 1661; lived privately in or near London, 1662-1691 (Moorfields, 1662-63, Acton 1663-69, Totteridge 1669-73, Bloomsbury 1673-85, Finsbury 1686-91); married Margaret Charlton (1636-81), 1662; imprisoned for one week at Clerkenwell, 1669, for twenty-one months at Southwark, 1685-86; died 8 December 1691; author of *The Saints' Everlasting Rest* (1650), *The Reformed Pastor* (1656), *A Call to the Unconverted* (1658), *A Christian Directory* (1673), and 131 other items printed in his lifetime, also of *Reliquiae Baxterianae* (autobiography, edited M. Sylvester, 1696), five other posthumous books and many unpublished treatises; special interests, pastoral care, Christian unity; hobbies, medicine, science, history.' Thus in *Who's Who* style I present Richard Baxter, the most outstanding pastor, evangelist and writer on practical and devotional themes that Puritanism produced.

Baxter was a big man, big enough to have large faults and make large errors. A brilliant cross-bencher, widely learned, with an astounding capacity for instant analysis, argument and appeal, he could run rings round anyone in debate, yet he could not always use his great gifts in the best way. In theology, for instance, as we saw earlier,[23] he devised an eclectic middle route between the Reformed, Arminian and Roman doctrines of grace: interpreting the kingdom of God in terms of contemporary political ideas, he explained Christ's death as an act of universal redemption (penal and vicarious, but not strictly substitutionary), in virtue of which God has made a new law offering pardon and amnesty to the penitent. Repentance and faith, being obedience to this law, are the believer's personal saving righteousness. Baxter, a Puritan conservative, saw this quaint legalistic construction as focusing both the essential Puritan and New Testament gospel and also the common ground with regard to God's grace that the warring trinitarian theologies of his day (Calvinist, Arminian, Lutheran, Roman Catholic) actually occupied.[24] Others, however, saw that 'Baxterianism' (or 'Neonomianism', as it was called because of the 'new law' idea at its heart) altered the content of the gospel, while its 'political method', if taken seriously, was objectionably rationalistic. Time proved them right; the fruit of the seeds which Baxter sowed was Neonomian Moderatism in Scotland and moralistic Unitarianism in England.[25]

Again, Baxter was a poor performer in public life. Though always respected for his godliness and pastoral prowess, and always honestly seeking doctrinal and ecclesiastical peace, his combative, judgemental, pedagogic way of proceeding with his peers made failure in his pacific purposes a foregone conclusion every time. For more than a quarter of a century after the ejections of 1662 he was the nonconformists' chief spokesman, and the comprehensivist ideal which he championed was undoubtedly statesmanlike,[26] yet Baxter can hardly be called a statesman himself. Granting that his habit of total and immediate outspokenness ('plain dealing') on all matters of theology and ministry was a compulsion of conscience and not just compensation for an inferiority complex (in fact, it was probably a bit of both), his lifelong inability to see that among equals a triumphalist manner is counter-productive was a strange blind spot. That (for instance) in 1669 he went to the great John Owen, with whom he had in the past crossed swords theologically and politically, in hope of achieving solidarity and co-operation with the independent leader in the ongoing church conflict, was typical and admirable. That on meeting Owen 'I told him that I must deal freely with him, that when I thought of what he had done formerly, I was much afraid lest one that had been so great a breaker would not be made an instrument of healing', though he was glad to see that in his most recent book Owen gave up 'two of the worst of the principles of popularity', was also typical, though perhaps less admirable. But that he was afterwards surprised, disappointed and hurt that Owen, while professing goodwill, took no action is surely remarkable![27] The plain fact is that Baxter insulted people, treating them as knaves or fools, and that has never been the way to win friends. Whether different behaviour or absence on Baxter's part could have altered any part of the wretched run of events (rejection, ejection, and persecution of Puritan pastors) between the Restoration (1660) and the Act of Toleration (1689) is doubtful, for passion, interest and distrust ran very high. The fact remains, however, that Baxter's well-meant but censorious interventions regularly deepened division, as when in 1690 he published *The Scripture Gospel Defended* to stop Tobias Crisp's sermons from causing trouble and thereby wrecked the 'Happy Union' between Presbyterians and Independents almost before it had begun.[28]

As a pastoral evangelist, however, Baxter was incomparable. His achievement at Kidderminster was amazing. England had not before seen a ministry like it, and by the late 1650s Baxter was a widely acclaimed role-model for pastors throughout Puritan England. Kidderminster parish contained about 800 homes and 2,000 adults, most of them in the town itself, and Baxter saw himself as spiritually responsible for them all. It appears that the majority came to a solid Christian faith under Baxter's ministrations. How did it happen? It has been said that there are three rules for success in the pastorate: the first is, teach; the second is, teach; and the third is, teach! Baxter is an outstanding instance of a man who observed these rules. A schoolmaster by instinct and prior experience, Baxter usually called himself his people's teacher, and teaching was to his mind the minister's main business. So, in a whole series of complementary ways, he gave himself to this task.[29]

In his regular sermons (one each Sunday and Thursday, each lasting an hour) he taught basic Christianity.

> The thing which I daily opened to them, and with greatest importunity laboured to imprint upon their minds, was the great fundamental principle of Christianity contained in their baptismal covenant, even a right knowledge, and belief of, and subjection and love to, God the Father, the Son, and the Holy Ghost, and love to all men, and concord with the church and one another. . . . The opening of the true and profitable method of the Creed (or doctrine of faith), the Lord's Prayer (or matter of our desires), and the Ten Commandments (or law of practice), which afford matter to add to the knowledge of most professors of religion, [takes] a long time. And when that is done they must be led on . . . but not so as to leave the weak behind; and so as shall still be truly subservient to the great points of faith, hope and love, holiness and unity, which must be still [always, constantly] inculcated, as the beginning and end of all.[30]

Such was Baxter's teaching programme in the pulpit.

In addition, he held a weekly pastor's forum for discussion and prayer;[31] he distributed Bibles and Christian books (one-fifteenth of each edition of his own books came to him free in lieu of royalties for him to give away);

and he taught individuals through personal counselling and catechising, giving an hour to the members of each of seven family units in his own home (seven hours altogether) on Monday and Tuesday afternoons and evenings, and so getting through nearly all the parish families once a year. (A few families refused to visit him for this purpose, but not many.) Christians, he urged, should regularly come to their pastor with their problems and let him check their spiritual health,[32] and ministers should regularly catechise their entire congregations.[33] To upgrade the practice of personal catechising from a preliminary discipline for children to a permanent ingredient in evangelism and pastoral care for all ages was Baxter's main contribution to the development of Puritan ideals for the ministry; and it was his concern for catechising that brought *The Reformed Pastor* to birth.

The members of the Worcestershire Association, the clerical fraternity of which Baxter was the moving spirit, had committed themselves to adopt the policy of systematic parochial catechising on Baxter's plan. They fixed a day of fasting and prayer, to seek God's blessing on the undertaking, and asked Baxter to preach. When the day come, however, Baxter was too ill to go; so he published the material he had prepared, a massive exposition and application of Acts 20:28. Because of his forthrightness in rebuking and exhorting his fellow-ministers, he called his work *Gildas Salvianus*, after two writers of the fifth and sixth centuries who also had not been mealy-mouthed about sin, and added *The Reformed Pastor* as subtitle. But on the title-page of the first edition[34] it is the word 'Reformed' in the subtitle that stands out, being printed in bigger and bolder type than anything else, and this is surely how Baxter wanted it. By 'Reformed' he does not mean Calvinistic in doctrine (through he was a sort of Calvinist, and wanted others to share his beliefs at this point); he means rather renewed and revived in practice. 'If God would but reform the ministry,' Baxter wrote, 'and set them on their duties zealously and faithfully, the people would certainly be reformed. All churches either rise or fall as the ministry doth rise or fall (not in riches or worldly grandeur) but in knowledge, zeal and ability for their work.'[35] It was the 'rise' of the ministry in this sense that Baxter sought.

The Reformed Pastor is the supreme transcript of Baxter's heart as a Puritan evangelist, and it is dynamite. Evangelism as an expression of Christian love through ministerial labour is what it is about, and its spiritual honesty, integrity, energy, and straightforwardness are almost unnerving. It is often said, quite fairly, that any Christian who seriously thinks that without Christ men are lost, and who seriously loves his neighbour, will not be able to rest for the thought that all around him people are going to hell, but will lay himself out unstintingly to convert others as his prime task in life; and any Christian who fails to behave this way undermines the credibility of his faith, for if he cannot himself take it seriously as setting priorities for his own living, why should anyone else take it seriously as a source of guidance for theirs? But *The Reformed Pastor* silences such thoughts: for here in the person of Richard Baxter we meet a terribly frank and earnest Christian who thinks, talks and behaves with perfect consistency at this point, being content to accept any degree of discomfort, poverty, overwork, and loss of material good, if only souls might be saved. When one knows one is going to be hanged in a fortnight, said Dr Johnson, it concentrates the mind wonderfully; and when, like Baxter from the time of his majority, one lives with one foot in the grave, it imparts an overwhelming clarity both to one's sense of proportion (what matters, and what does not), and also to one's perception of what is and what is not consistent with what one professes to believe.

'O sirs,' cries Baxter to his clerical colleagues (laymen will do well to listen, too),

> surely if you had all conversed with neighbour Death as oft as I have done, and as often received the sentence in yourselves, you would have an unquiet conscience, if not a reformed life, as to your ministerial diligence and fidelity: and you would have something within you that would frequently ask you such questions as these: 'Is this all thy compassion for lost sinners? Wilt thou do no more to seek and to save them? . . . Shall they die and be in hell before thou wilt speak to them one serious word to prevent it? Shall they there curse thee for ever that thou didst no more in time to save them?' Such cries of conscience are daily ringing in my ears, though, the Lord knows, I have too little obeyed them. . . . How can you choose, when you are laying a corpse in the grave, but think with yourselves, 'Here lieth the body; but where is the soul? and what have I done for it, before it departed? It was part of my charge; what account can I give of it?' O sirs, is it a small matter to you to answer such questions as these? It may seem so now, but the hour is coming when it will not seem so. . . .[36]

Nobody can say that Baxter was not real; and who will question our need of such reality today, and in the ministry most of all?

Then, again, as the book projects *reality*, so it is a model of *rationality* in relation to evangelism. Baxter is utterly thorough in working out means to his end. Like Whitefield and Spurgeon, he knew that men are blind, deaf and dead in sin, and only God can convert them; but, again like Whitefield and Spurgeon, he knew too that God works through means, and that rational men must be approached in rational fashion, and that grace enters by the understanding, and that unless all the evangelist does makes for credibility, his message is not likely to be used much to convince. So Baxter insisted that ministers must preach of eternal issues as men who feel what they say, and are as earnest as matters of life and death require; that they must practice church discipline, to show they are serious in saying that God will not accept sin; and that they must do 'personal work', and deal with individuals one by one, because preaching alone often fails to bring things home to ordinary people. Baxter was very frank on this.

> Let them that have taken most pains in public, examine their people, and try whether many of them are not nearly as ignorant and careless as if they had never heard the gospel. For my part, I study to speak as plainly and movingly as I can . . . and yet I frequently meet with those that have been my hearers eight or ten years, who know not whether Christ be God or man, and wonder when I tell them the history of his birth and life and death as if they had never heard it before. . . . But most of them have an ungrounded trust in Christ, hoping that he will pardon, justify and save them, while the world hath their hearts, and they live to the flesh. And this trust they take for justifying faith. I have found by experience, that some ignorant persons, who have been so long unprofitable hearers, have got more knowledge and remorse in half an hour's close discourse, than they did from ten years' public preaching. I know that preaching the gospel publicly is the most excellent means, because we speak to many at once. But it is usually far more effectual to preach it privately to a particular sinner. . . .[37]

Therefore personal catechising and counselling, over and above preaching, is every minister's duty: for this is the most rational course, the best means to the desired end. So it was in Baxter's day. Is it not so now?

One of the unhappy by-products of the institutionalising process that produced modern evangelism is the spread of the idea that evangelising is a special skill, confined to a minority. Granted, some pastors are used by God in the ministry of conversion more than others, but Baxter insists that every pastor must study the difficult art of winning souls. He writes:

> Alas! How few know how to deal with an ignorant, worldly man, for his conversion! To get within him and win upon him; to suit our speech to his condition and temper; to choose the meetest subjects, and follow them with a holy mixture of seriousness, and terror, and love and meekness, and evangelical allurement—oh! who is fit for such a thing? I profess seriously, it seems to me, by experience, as hard a matter to confer aright with such a carnal person, in order to his change, as to preach. . . . All these difficulties in ourselves should awaken us to holy resolution, preparation, and diligence. . . .[38]

Every pastor an evangelist, dealing with individuals about their souls, is Baxter's Puritan formula. Some will do it more fruitfully than others, but it is a ministry to which all are called and in which all must engage. This is the challenge of Puritan evangelism.

The Reformed Pastor faces the modern minister with at least these questions. (1) Do I believe the gospel Baxter believed (and Whitefield, and Spurgeon, and Paul), the historic biblical gospel of ruin, redemption and regeneration? (2) Do I then share Baxter's view of the vital necessity of conversion? (3) Am I then as real as I should be in letting this view of things shape my life and work? (4) Am I as rational as I should be in choosing means to the end that I desire, and am charged to seek, namely, the conversion of all the people whose pastor I am? Have I set myself, as Baxter set himself, to find the best way of creating situations in which I can talk to my people personally, on a regular basis, about their spiritual lives? How to do this today would have to be worked out in terms of present circumstances, which are very different from those Baxter knew and describes;[39] but Baxter's question to us is, should we not be attempting this, as a practice constantly and inescapably necessary? If he convinces us that we should, it will surely not be beyond us to find a method of doing it that suits our situation; where there's a will, there's a way!

Baxter's basic principle is that in the life of the church evangelism must be a matter of constant priority. He works this out within the clericalist frame of reference that the Puritans inherited from the Middle Ages and maintained against lay-led anarchy, as they saw it, during the Interregnum; so naturally he limits his discussion to the pastor's role, and represents evangelistic ministry to the captive congregation and its individual members as the pastor's exclusive responsibility. The evangelism Baxter envisages is catechetical and heavily didactic, and that emphasis reflects the deep doctrinal ignorance which at that time characterised the lay people of semi-rural Worcestershire, apart from some exceptional folk in his own congregation. Nowadays, things are different: the churches of the West are minority enclaves within secular communities; evangelism focuses on those who do not yet come to church; and knowledgeable laymen share in it, as they should.[40] In bringing Baxter's approach to bear on today's situation we must not lose sight of these differences. But the things that Baxter writes about—the need for pastors seriously to watch over themselves, and seriously to discover and minister to the spiritual needs of each member of their flock, taking pains to ensure first and foremost that these members are all thoroughly converted and truly regenerate—still apply; and this is where evangelism of the Puritan type finds its initial focus, in this or any age.

Said G.K. Chesterton: it is not that Christianity has been tried and found wanting, but that it has been found hard, and not tried. Are we not compelled in honesty to say the same about Puritan evangelism?

CHAPTER NINETEEN

Jonathan Edwards and Revival

1

Jonathan Edwards, saint, scholar, preacher, pastor, metaphysician, theologian, Calvinist, and revival leader, lived from 1703 to 1758. He was a tall, reserved, soft-spoken man, strong-minded and humble-hearted. In 1727, after five years in the ministry, he became co-pastor of the large and fashionable church at Northampton, New Hampshire, where his grandfather. Solomon Stoddard, the grand old man of ecclesiastical life in the Connecticut Valley, now a patriarchal eighty-three, had ministered since 1669. Northampton was a town of perhaps 2,000 inhabitants, and its church was the best known and most influential in New England outside Boston. Stoddard himself was almost idolised by the congregation, most of whom had grown up under his ministry. Two years later, in 1729, Stoddard's death brought his sixty-year pastorate to a close, and from then on Edwards was sole minister. In 1734-35 and 1740-42 he saw remarkable movements of the Spirit of God in his congregation and, in the latter case, throughout all New England. From 1743, however, Edwards was for various reasons in trouble with his church, and in 1750 he was dismissed from the pastorate because he insisted on restoring the demand, which Stoddard had dropped, for a personal confession of faith as the *sine qua non* of communicant church membership. Edwards then moved to a mission station in the frontier hamlet of Stockbridge, and it was here that he wrote his great treatises on *The Freedom of the Will* and *Original Sin*. In 1757 he was made President of Princeton College. He travelled to Princeton to take up his appointment in February, 1758. His first move was to be inoculated against smallpox; but the inoculation itself brought on fever, and in the following month he died.

2

Edwards was a Puritan born out of due time. It is hardly too much to say, with a recent writer, that Puritanism is what Edwards was. All his roots were in the theology and outlook of the founding fathers of New England, men like Hooker and Shepard, Cotton and Davenport. He was a true Puritan, first, in his *devotion to the Bible*. All his life he laboured, fearlessly and tirelessly, to understand and apply the Bible, and his written works (apart, perhaps, from those on prophecy) reveal an exegetical acumen comparable with that of Calvin, or Owen, or Hodge, or Warfield. All his life he fed his soul on the Bible; and all his life he fed his flock on the Bible.

Again, he was a true Puritan in his *doctrinal convictions*. In a day when, as in England, a rationalistic Latitudinarianism—the 'free and catholic' outlook of Charles Chauncy and his friends—was eating away the Puritan heritage, Edwards stood forth as an uncompromising and unashamed Calvinistic supernaturalist, diagnosing the fashionable view as Arminianism and opposing it, as the Puritans has opposed the Arminianism of their day, on the grounds of its religious implications. Edwards argued that Arminianism in any form—any form, that is, of the synergism which makes conviction of spiritual truth God's work, but conversion itself man's—undercuts true piety. It makes God less than God; it is three-quarters of the way to deism, and half-way to real atheism. It destroys due reverence for God, because it denies our complete dependence on him. It ministers to pride by representing the decisive act in our salvation as all our own work. Thus it introduces a principle of self-reliance into religion; which is in effect to render religion irreligious, and to base the form of godliness upon a denial of the matter of it. These were Puritan points, and in making them Edwards showed himself a true heir of the Puritan tradition in theology.

In the third place, Edwards was a true Puritan in his view of *the nature of Christian piety*. In essence, Edwards maintained, godliness is a matter of glorifying the Creator by humble dependence and a thankful obedience. In Christian terms, this means acknowledging our complete dependence upon God, as for life and health, so for grace and glory, and loving and praising and serving him for all that he has so freely given us through his Son. Edwards struck this note in 1731 in his first published sermon, a discourse on 1 Corinthians 1:29-31 entitled; 'God glorified in man's dependence.' The theme of the sermon is that 'God is glorified in the work of redemption in this, that there appears in it so absolute and universal a dependence of the redeemed on him'. And it concludes thus:

> Let us be exhorted to exalt God alone, and ascribe to him all the glory of redemption. Let us endeavour to obtain, and increase in, a sensibleness of our great dependence on God . . . to mortify a self-dependent and self-righteous disposition. Man is naturally exceeding prone to exalt himself, and depend on his own power of goodness. . . . But this doctrine should teach us to exalt God *alone*; as by trust and reliance, so by praise. *Let him that glorieth, glory in the Lord.* Hath any man hope that he is converted and sanctified . . . that his sins are forgiven, and he received into God's favour, and exalted to the honour and blessedness of being his child, and an heir of eternal life? let him give God all the glory; who alone makes him to differ from the worst of men in this world, or the most miserable of the damned in hell. . . . Is any man eminent in holiness, and abundant in good works, let him take nothing of the glory of it to himself, but ascribe it unto him whose 'workmanship we are, created in Christ Jesus unto good works'.[1]

The thought of man's complete dependence on a free omnipotent God controlled Edwards' whole religious outlook, and acted as the guiding principle of his entire theology.

To Edwards, therefore, true religion was much more than either orthodoxy, or ethics, or the two put together. Edwards held no brief for easy believism, or moralism, or formalism of any sort. True piety was to him a supernatural gift, dynamic in character and intensely experimental in its outworking. It was, in fact, a realised communion with God through Christ, brought into being by the Holy Spirit and expressed in responsive affections and activities.

The root of piety, Edwards maintained, is a hearty conviction (in his phrase, a 'cordial sense') of the reality and glory of the divine and heavenly things spoken of in the gospel. Such a conviction is more than an intellectual grasp of theological ideas, or a taking Christian truth for granted under the constraining pressure of community opinion; it is, rather, the result of direct divine illumination accompanying the written or spoken word of God, as Edwards explained in 1734 in his second published sermon, on Matthew 16:17, entitled, 'A divine and supernatural light, immediately imparted to the soul by the Spirit of God, shown to be both a Scriptural and rational doctrine'.

The divine enlightenment issues in conversions.

> This light is such as effectually influences the inclination, and changes the nature of the soul. It assimilates our nature to the divine Nature. . . . This knowledge will wean from the world, and raise the inclination to heavenly things. It will turn the heart to God as the fountain of good, and to choose

him for the only portion. This light, and this only, will bring the soul to a saving close with Christ. It conforms the heart to the gospel, mortifies its enmity and opposition against the scheme of salvation therein revealed: it causes the heart to embrace the joyful tidings, and entirely to adhere to, and acquiesce in, the revelation of Christ as our Saviour: it causes the whole soul to accord and symphonize with it . . . cleaving to it with full inclination and affection; and it effectually disposes the soul to give up itself entirely to Christ. . . . As it reaches the bottom of the heart, and changes the nature, so it will effectually dispose to a universal obedience. It shows God as worthy to be obeyed and served. It draws forth the heart in a sincere love of God . . . and it convinces of the reality of those glorious rewards that God has promised to them that obey him.[2]

From this inward renewal by vivifying light issue good works and changed basic attitudes.The scepticism of rationalists, and the delusions of 'enthusiasts', about authentically Christian frames of mind and heart forced Edwards to devote special attention to this subject, and in his *Treatise concerning Religious Affections* (published in 1746, first preached as a course of sermons in 1742-43) he gave the world the fruit of his study. He begins by arguing that, inasmuch as the affections are the fundamental functions of the will, the fount of action, it follows of necessity that 'true religion, in great part, consists in holy affections'. Edwards explains:

As the affections not only necessarily belong to the human nature, but are a very great part of it, so (inasmuch as by regeneration persons are renewed in the whole man) holy affections not only necessarily belong to true religion, but are a very great part of such religion. And as true religion is practical, and God hath so constituted the human nature, that the affections are very much the springs of men's actions, this also shows, that true religion must consist very much in the affections.[3]

Having established this, Edwards proceeds to characterise 'truly gracious and holy affections' with a pastoral and theological acumen that has secured for his book an unchallengeable place among the all-time classics of discipleship and devotion.

In all this, what Edwards is doing is clarifying and vindicating the Puritan conception of experiential religion against the cold moralism of the school of Tillotson. It is as the spiritual heir of Shepard, Flavel, and Stoddard, all of whom he constantly cites in his footnotes (the former especially), that Edwards is writing. With them, he is concerned to insist that true and vital Christianity is a religion of the heart as well as of the head, and to show as accurately as possible how the heart should be engaged in it. This, as we have seen, is a peculiarly Puritan interest, and Edwards shows his oneness with the Puritan outlook by pursuing it.

Fourthly, Edwards was a true Puritan in his *approach to preaching*. Like his seventeenth-century predecessors, he preached with a threefold aim: to make men understand, feel, and respond to gospel truth. Like them, he set out the matter of his sermons according to the threefold 'method' of proposition, proof, and application—'doctrine, reason, and use', as the Puritans called it. Like them, he studied plainness of style, concealing his learning beneath a deliberately bald clarity of statement. It is sometimes imagined that, because in the pulpit he read a manuscript in a steady, quiet, even tone, and avoided looking at his congregation as he spoke, he did not share the Puritan concern to preach with directness, authority, and felt power—the concern which Baxter voiced when he spoke of his desire to be 'a plain and pressing downright preacher', one who

> Preached as never sure to preach again,
> And as a dying man to dying men.

But this is a mistake. Edwards knew very well that 'the main benefit obtained by preaching is by impression made upon the mind at the time, and not by an effect that arises afterwards by a remembrance of what was delivered'.[4] And when the evangelistic earnestness and vehemence of Whitefield and the Tennents during the revival of 1740 came under fire from the Latitudinarians, who saw it as a regrettable lapse into 'enthusiasm', in the sense of fanatical fantasy, Edwards ran to their defence:

> I think an exceeding affectionate way of preaching about the great things of religion, has in itself no tendency to beget false apprehensions of them; but on the contrary, a much greater tendency to beget true apprehensions of them, than a moderate, dull, indifferent way of speaking of them. . . . If the subject be in its own nature worthy of very great affection, then speaking of it with great affection is most agreeable to the nature of that subject . . . and therefore has most of a tendency to beget true ideas of it. . . . I should think myself in the way of my duty, to raise the affections of my hearers as high as possibly I can, provided that they are affected with nothing but truth. . . . I know it has long been fashionable to despise a very earnest and pathetical way of preaching; and they only have been valued as preachers, who have shown the greatest extent of learning, strength of reason, and correctness of method and language. But I humbly conceive it has been for want of understanding or duly considering human nature, that such preaching has been thought to have the greatest tendency to answer the ends of preaching. . . . An increase in speculative knowledge in divinity is not what is so much needed by our people as something else. Men may abound in this sort of light, and have no heat. . . . Our people do not so much need to have their heads stored, as to have their hearts touched; and they stand

in the greatest need of that sort of preaching, which has the greatest tendency to do this.[5]

In fact, Edwards' own preaching was powerful in a high degree. Humanly speaking, he had a unique gift for making ideas live by the luminous precision with which he expounded them. He uncoils a length of reasoning with a slow, smooth exactness that is almost hypnotic in its power to rivet attention on the successive folds of truth sliding out into view. Had Edwards been no more than a pagan don teaching economics, he would without doubt have been a performer of 'Ancient Mariner' quality in the lecture-room. To this compelling expository power was added in the pulpit a terrible solemnity, expressive of the awe of God that was constantly on his spirit; and the result was preaching that congregations could neither resist nor forget. Edwards could make two hours seem like twenty minutes as he bore down on his listeners' consciences with the plain old truths of sin and salvation, and the calm majesty of his inexorable analysis was no less used of God to make men feel the force of truth than was the rhapsodic vehemence of George Whitefield. One of his hearers, asked whether Edwards was an eloquent preacher, replied:

> If you mean by eloquence, what is usually intended by it in our cities; he had no pretensions to it. He had no studied varieties of voice, and no strong emphasis. He scarcely gestured or even moved; and he made no attempt, by the eloquence of his style, or the beauty of his pictures, to gratify the taste, and fascinate the imagination. But, if you mean by eloquence the power of presenting an important truth before an audience, with overwhelming weight of argument, and with such intenseness of feeling that the whole soul of the speaker is thrown into every part of the conception and delivery, so that the solemn attention of the whole audience is riveted, from the beginning to the close, and impressions are left that cannot be effaced, Mr. Edwards was the most eloquent man I ever heard speak.[6]

'His words,' wrote his first biographer, Hopkins, 'often discovered a great deal of inward fervour, without much noise or external emotion, and fell with great weight on the minds of his hearers; and he spake so as to reveal the strong emotions of his own heart, which tended, in the most natural and effectual manner, to move and affect others.'[7] Such a feeling communication of felt truth was, in fact, precisely what the Puritans had had in mind when they spoke of 'powerful' preaching.

As a Bible-lover, a Calvinist, a teacher of heart-religion, a gospel preacher of unction and power, and, above all, a man who loved Christ, hated sin, and feared God, Edwards was a pure Puritan; indeed, one of the purest and greatest of all the Puritans. American historians of culture have recently rediscovered Edwards as a major contributor to the American philosophical and literary heritage. It is to be wished that evangelical Christians today might themselves rediscover the important contribution that this latter-day Puritan made to the elucidation of the biblical faith.

3

Last-century evangelicals, on the whole, admired Edwards, but nonetheless they did him a threefold disservice. First, they accused him of being unreadable. But one has only to make the experiment to find that this is not so at all. The levelling of this charge was in fact a case of the mote and the beam. It is true that Edwards does not go in for the flowery padding which the nineteenth century regarded as essential to good style, but this is to his credit rather than otherwise. He is today far more palatable as a writer than are many of his older critics. The most one can say against him is that on occasion his desire for a clinical precision of language leads him to write sentences that are too long and complex for easy assimilation on first reading. But this is his only stylistic fault, and that not a common one; most of the time he is admirably clear, exact, and pointed.

Then, in the second place, the last century treated Edwards as an essentially philosophical theologian, chiefly on the strength of *The Freedom of the Will*. Now, it is true that Edwards had a genius for abstract reasoning, and that he indulged it to the full in that particular treatise. But we need to remember what sort of a treatise *The Freedom of the Will* is. It is not a work of biblical theology, but an elaborate polemical essay directed against what is, as Edwards truly saw, an essentially speculative and philosophical position—that of rationalistic Arminianism, which builds everything on the axiom that divine control of human action is incompatible with man's moral responsibility, and cannot therefore be a fact. Edwards chose the most obviously crushing way to deal with this position—to turn its own weapons against itself; to give it points and a beating, so to speak, on its own home ground. But *The Freedom of the Will* was an occasional performance, and is not characteristic of the rest of Edwards' work. It is clear from his private notes and memoranda that metaphysical speculation fascinated him and was, indeed, his hobby, but he never let philosophy teach him his faith, or lead him away from the Bible. He philosophised *from* faith, not *to* it; he did not regard speculation as necessary to salvation, and no hint of his philosophical interests intrudes into his sermons. He took his convictions and concerns from the Bible, and it is as a scriptural theologian that his true stature is to be measured.

Finally—and this was the worst disservice of all—Edwards' last-century admirers quite overlooked Edwards' most original contribution to theology: namely, his pioneer elucidation of biblical teaching on the subject of revival. This oversight is, perhaps, pardonable, since Edwards' thoughts on this subject were put out piecemeal in five early works which he composed in his thirties: *A Narrative of a Surprising Work of God in the Conversion of many hundred souls in Northampton and the neighbouring Towns and Villages* (1735); *A History of the Work of Redemption* (sermons preached in 1739, published in 1744); *The Distinguishing Marks of a Work of the Spirit of God* (1741); *Thoughts on the Revival of Religion in New England in 1740* (1742); and the *Treatise on the Religious Affections* (1746). All these save the second are concerned, in one way or another, to vindicate the two revivals which Edwards had himself seen against the current charge that they were mere outbreaks of fanaticism. This immediate aim might seem to limit their interest for later generations of readers. Embedded in them, however, is a fairly complete account of revival as a work of God—in other words, a theology of revival—which is fuller than any produced before Edwards' time, and is of lasting value. It is, perhaps, the most important single contribution that Edwards has to make to evangelical thinking today.

It is a notable fact that interest in the subject of revival is increasing at the present time: witness the growth of revival fellowships of various kinds within the Protestant denominations. More and more the conviction is spreading that only a visitation from on high can touch the needs of the churches today. But most of us find ourselves uncertain as to what exactly revival is, and what might be expected to happen if revival came. And there are in particular two types of mistakes at this point to which we are all prone.

The first is the *antiquarian fallacy*. We fall victim to this mistake when we form a conception of revival from the history of a particular revival in the past, and then set up our conception, thus formed, as a norm and yardstick for any movement of revival in the future. To do this is to expose ourselves to a double danger.

On the one hand, we predispose ourselves to be too hasty in identifying with revival outbreaks of religious excitement which exhibit certain outward features that marked some revival of the past—prostrations, visions, spontaneous singing, or whatever the features are that have impressed us. We have to remember that the devil can produce the outward forms of religious excitement, as well as the Spirit of God, and that in fact Satan has often wrought havoc in the church through movements of self-deceived fanaticism which announced themselves, doubtless in all good faith, as movements of the Holy Spirit in revival. We need a criterion for telling the two apart; otherwise Satan will be free to fool us as he pleases by gratifying our hunger for revival with his own particular brand of 'enthusiastic' delusions. And precedent—'former observation', as Edwards calls it—is not of itself a sufficient criterion for this purpose. In Edwards' words, 'what the church has been used to, is not a rule by which we are to judge' in such cases, one way or the other.[8] We need a better touchstone than this for telling the spurious from the true.

Then, on the other hand, by conceiving of revival wholly in terms of some particular past revival, we make it harder for ourselves to recognise any future revival that God may send. For it is not God's habit to repeat himself. There is no ground for supposing that the externals of the next revival will be just like the externals of the last one, any more than there would be for expecting two people to pass through exactly the same sequence of experiences in their conversion. Those who will only allow that God is at work when they see him repeating exactly something that he has done before, Edwards tells us, 'limit God, where he has not limited himself. And this is especially unreasonable in this case [i.e., that of revival]'. He continues:

> For whosoever has well weighed the wonderful and mysterious methods of divine wisdom in carrying on the work of the new creation—or in the progress of the work of redemption, from the first promise to the seed of the woman to this time—may easily observe that it has all along been God's manner to open new scenes, and to bring forth to view things new and wonderful . . . to the astonishment of heaven and earth. . . .[9]

The second mistake that threatens us is the *romantic fallacy*. We fall into this when we let ourselves imagine that revival, once it came, would function as the last chapter in a detective story functions—solving all our problems, clearing up all the difficulties that have arisen in the church, and leaving us in a state of idyllic peace and contentment, with no troubles to perplex us any more.

A study of Jonathan Edwards on revival forewarns us against both these mistakes. In the first place, Edwards shields us from the antiquarian fallacy by teaching us the biblical principles for determining whether an outbreak of religious excitement is an outpouring of God's Spirit or not. 'We have a rule near at hand,' he claims, 'a sacred book that God himself has put into our hands, with clear and infallible marks, sufficient to resolve us in things of this nature.'[10] And he labours to show us in thorough detail just what these marks are.

Then, in the second place, Edwards shields us from the romantic fallacy by constantly directing our attention to the problems which revival brings in its train. Revival means renewal of life, and life means energy. It is true that revival delivers the church from the problems created by apathy and deadness, but it is equally true that revival plunges the church into a welter of new problems created by the torrential overflow of disordered and undisciplined spiritual vitality. In a revival, the saints are suddenly roused from a state of torpor and lethargy by a new and overwhelming awareness of the reality of spiritual things and of God. They are like sleepers shaken awake and now half blinded by the unaccustomed glare of the sun. They hardly know for the moment where they are; in one sense, they now see everything as they never saw it before, yet in another sense, because of the very brightness of the light, they can hardly see anything. They fall into pride, delusions, unbalance, censorious modes of speech, extravagant forms of action. Unconverted persons are caught up in what is going on; they feel the power of truth, though their hearts remain unrenewed; they become 'enthusiasts', deluded and self-confident, harsh and bitter, fierce and vainglorious, cranky and fanatical, quarrelsome and disruptive. Then, perhaps, they fall into spectacular sin, and apostatise altogether; or else remain in the church to scandalise the rest of men by maintaining, on dogmatic perfectionist grounds, that while what they do would be sin in others, it is not sin in them. Satan (who, as Edwards somewhere observes, was 'trained in the best divinity school in the universe') keeps step with God, actively perverting and caricaturing all that the Creator is doing.

A revival, accordingly, is always a *disfigured* work of God, and the more powerful the revival, the more scandalising disfigurements we may expect to see. Hence we cannot wonder if the revival comes to be bitterly opposed by respectable church members of limited spiritual insight, on account of the excesses linked with it; nor can we be surprised to find—as we regularly do—that many ministers stand aloof from the revival, and even preach against it and try to suppress it, on the grounds that it is not a spiritual phenomenon at all. Edwards had had to face all this in his own experience, and he makes us face it too. 'A work of God without stumbling-blocks is never to be expected,' he wrote grimly in 1741; '. . . we shall probably see more instances of apostasy and gross iniquity among professors. . . .'[11] No; revival, though in itself a purging and purifying work of God, is never free from attendant disfigurements. We need not read beyond the New Testament to appreciate that. Yet this must not blind us to the fact that revival is a real and glorious work of God, and a blessing much to be desired when the church's vitality is low. We proceed now to examine Edwards' theological account of it.

4

We shall expound his teaching under three main heads.

Principles Concerning the Nature of Revival

Here there are three propositions to consider, of which the first is the most important and fundamental, and will occupy us the longest.

First, *revival is an extraordinary work of God the Holy Spirit reinvigorating and propagating Christian piety in a community*. Revival is an *extraordinary* work, because it marks the abrupt reversal of an established trend and state of things among those who profess to be God's people. To envisage God *reviving* his church is to presuppose that the church has previously grown moribund and gone to sleep. To speak of God *pouring out his Spirit* in an *awakening*, as Edwards, following Scripture, does, is to imply that God does something sudden and decisive to change a state of affairs in which the Spirit's quickening influence, and a lively sense of spiritual realities, were conspicuous by their absence.

Revival is a work of *reinvigorating and propagating Christian piety*. Though it is through the knowledge of Bible truth that the Spirit effects his reviving work, revival is not merely, nor even primarily, a restoring of orthodoxy. It is essentially a restoring of *religion*. We have seen what Edwards conceived Christian religion to be: an experimental acquaintance with, and a hearty, practical response to, the divine realities set forth in the gospel. It is this that languishes during the time of sleep and barrenness before revival comes, and it is this that the outpouring of the Spirit renews. Hence the 'distinguishing marks of a work of the Spirit of God', i.e., of a revival, all have to do with a deepening of experimental piety. We may quote at length from Edwards' exposition of these marks, in the superb little treatise on 1 John 4:1 which bears the phrase just quoted as its title. All that is said is germane to our subject, and the passage as a whole is a fine example of Edwards' expository style.

I shall confine myself wholly to those marks which are given us by the apostle in the chapter wherein is my text, where this matter is particularly handled, and more plainly and fully than any where else in the Bible. And in speaking to these marks, I shall take them in the order in which I find them in the chapter.

1. When the operation is such as to raise their esteem of that Jesus who was born of the Virgin, and was crucified without the gates of Jerusalem; and seems more to confirm and establish their minds in the truth of what the gospel declares to us of his being the Son of God, and the Saviour of men; it is a sure sign that it is from the Spirit of God. This sign the apostle gives us in the 2d. and 3d. verses . . . [which speak of] a confessing not only that there was such a person who appeared in Palestine, and did and suffered those things that are recorded of him, but that he was Christ, i.e. the Son of God, anointed to be the Lord and Saviour, as the name Jesus Christ implies. . . .

The devil has the most bitter and implacable enmity against that person, especially in his character of the Saviour of men; he mortally hates the story and doctrine of his redemption; he would never go about to beget in men more honourable thoughts of him. . . .

2. When the Spirit that is at work operates against the interests of Satan's kingdom, which lies in encouraging and establishing sin, and cherishing men's worldly lusts; this is a sure sign that it is a true, and not a false, spirit. This sign we have given us in the 4th and 5th verses. . . . by the world . . . the apostle evidently means everything that appertains to the interest of sin, and

comprehends all the corruptions and lusts of men, and all those acts and objects by which they are gratified.

So that we may safely determine, from what the apostle says, that the spirit that is at work among a people, after such a manner, as to lessen men's esteem of the pleasure, profits, and honours of the world, and to take off their hearts from an eager pursuit after these things; and to engage them in a deep concern about a future state and eternal happiness . . . and the spirit that convinces them of the dreadfulness of sin, the guilt it brings, and the misery to which it exposes; must needs be the Spirit of God.

It is not to be supposed that Satan would convince men of sin, and awaken the conscience. . . .

3. The spirit that operates in such a manner, as to cause in men a greater regard to the Holy Scriptures, and establishes them more in their truth and divinity, is certainly the Spirit of God. This rule the apostle gives us in the 6th verse. . . . *We* are of God; that is, 'We the apostles are sent forth of God, and appointed by him to teach the world, and to deliver those doctrines and instructions, which are to be their rule; *he that knoweth God, heareth us,*' etc. The apostle's argument here equally reaches all that in the same sense are of *God*; that is, all those that God has appointed and inspired to deliver to his church its rule of faith and practice; all the prophets and apostles . . . in a word, all the penmen of the Holy Scriptures. The devil never would attempt to beget in persons a regard to that divine word. . . . A spirit of delusion will not incline persons to seek direction at the mouth of God. . . . Would the spirit of error, in order to deceive men, beget in them a high opinion of the infallible rule, and incline them to think much of it, and be very conversant with it? Would the prince of darkness, in order to promote his kingdom of darkness, lead men to the sun?

4. Another rule to judge of spirits may be drawn from . . . the 6th verse . . . if by observing the manner of operation of a spirit that is at work among a people, we see that it operates as a spirit of truth, leading persons to truth, convincing them of those things that are true . . . for instance if we observe that the spirit at work makes men more sensible than they used to be, that there is a God, and that he is a great and sin-hating God; that life is short, and very uncertain; and that there is another world; that they have immortal souls, and must give account of themselves to God; that they are exceeding sinful by nature and practice; that they are helpless in themselves; and confirms them in other things that are agreeable to some sound doctrine; the spirit that works thus, operates as a spirit of truth; he represents things as they truly are. . . . And therefore we may conclude, that it is not the spirit of darkness that doth thus discover and make manifest the truth. . . .

5. If the spirit that is at work among a people operates as a spirit of love to God and man, it is a sure sign that it is the Spirit of God. This sign the apostle insists upon from the 6th verse to the end of the chapter . . . and speaks expressly of both love to God and men; of *love to men* in

the 7th, 11th, and 12th verses; and of *love to God* in the 17th, 18th, and 19th verses; and of both together, in the last two verses. . . . The spirit that . . . works in them an admiring, delightful sense of the excellency of Jesus Christ . . . winning and drawing the heart with those motives and incitements to love, of which the apostle speaks . . . viz. the wonderful free love of God in giving his only-begotten Son to die for us, and the wonderful dying love of Christ to us, who had no love to him, but were his enemies; must needs be the Spirit of God. . . . The spirit that . . . makes the attributes of God as revealed in the gospel, and manifested in Christ, delightful objects of contemplation; and makes the soul to long after God and Christ—after Their presence and communion, acquaintance with Them, and conformity to Them—and to live so as to please and honour Them; the spirit that quells contentions among men, and gives a spirit of peace and good will, excites to acts of outward kindness, and earnest desires of the salvation of souls . . . there is the highest kind of evidence of the influence of a true and divine spirit.[12]

Edwards' case is that wherever these fruits are appearing, there the Spirit of God is at work; and, therefore, that these are the signs which infallibly indicate whether an outbreak of religious excitement, disorderly and in some ways distressing as it may be, is a work of revival or not. The criterion of revival is not the excitement and hullabaloo of the meetings, but the fruit of the Spirit—faith in, and love to, the Father and the Son and the Scriptures and their teaching, and good works to benefit other men. Where these fruits suddenly begin to appear in a church or community, after a time of barrenness, there revival, in some degree, has begun, whatever attendant disfigurements may appear at the same time.

The substance of religion, as Edwards conceived it (and he was a true Puritan to stress this), is conscious communion with God, and under the intense influence of the outpoured Spirit in a time of revival the individual's sense of God's presence, and absorption in the knowledge of him, and joy in the assurance of his love, might be raised to very remarkable heights. Edwards saw a good deal of this among his people, but no case seemed to him more outstanding than that of his own wife, whose experience he described at length (without saying whose it was) in *Thoughts on the Revival*, I:v (a section headed simply: 'The nature of the work in a particular instance'). The description should be read in full; we have space to quote only a few sentences. Sarah Edwards' experience, writes her husband, included the following elements:

A very frequent dwelling for some considerable time together, in views of the glory of the divine perfections and Christ's excellencies; so that the soul has been as it were perfectly overwhelmed, and swallowed up with light and love, a sweet solace, and a rest and joy of soul altogether unspeakable. . . . This great rejoicing has been with trembling, i.e. attended with a deep and lively sense of the greatness and majesty of God, and the person's own exceeding littleness and vileness. . . . The things already mentioned have been attended with . . . an extraordinary sense of the awful majesty, greatness, and holiness of God. . . . The strength of the body was very often taken away with a deep mourning for sin, as committed against so holy and good a God. . . . There has been a very great sense of the certain truth of the great things revealed in the gospel; an overwhelming sense of the glory of the work of redemption, and the way of salvation by Jesus Christ. . . . The person felt a great delight in singing praises to God and Jesus Christ, and longing that this present life may be, as it were, one continued song of praise to God. There was a longing, as the person expressed it, to sit and sing this life away; and an overcoming pleasure in the thoughts of spending an eternity in that exercise. . . .[13]

Such is the inward heart of the realised communion with God, the true, pure Christian piety, into which all the saints of God are led, more or less deeply, by the reviving work of the Holy Ghost. 'If such things are enthusiasm, and the fruits of a distempered brain,' writes Edwards with fine irony, 'let my brain be evermore possessed of that happy distemper!' Such experiences as these, he held (and, surely, with justice) were proof positive that the Holy Spirit of God was at work in the religious movements out of which the experiences came.

It should be stressed finally, under this head, that to Edwards revival meant the restoring of Christian piety *in a community*. The object of revival was the church, and the effect of the blessing was to spread the faith to the unconverted outside the church. Revival is a corporate affair. It was upon the company of disciples that the Spirit was poured out at Pentecost; it is to the church that God brings awakening (cf Is 51:17; 52:1). This is not, of course, to deny that an individual Christian may be spiritually vitalised while the church around remains dead, but simply to assert that the characteristic work of God which we are discussing at present under the name of revival is a work which in some sense has the church, and not just an individual Christian, as its object.

Second, *revivals have a central place in the revealed purposes of God.* 'The end of God's creating the world,' declares Edwards, 'was to prepare a kingdom for his Son (for he was appointed heir of the world).'[14] This end is to be realised, first through Christ's accomplishing of redemption on Calvary, and then through the triumphs of his kingdom. 'All the dispensations of God's providence henceforward (since Christ's ascension), even to the final consummation of all things, are to give Christ his reward, and fulfil his end in what he did and suffered upon earth.'[15] A universal dominion is pledged to Christ, and in the interim before the final consummation the Father implements this pledge in part by successive outpourings of the Spirit, which prove the reality of Christ's kingdom to a sceptical world and serve to extend its bounds among Christ's erst-while enemies.

> When God manifests himself with such glorious power, in a work of this nature [sc, such as the New England revival], he appears especially determined to put honour upon his Son, and to fulfil his oath that he has sworn to him, that he would make every knee to bow . . . to him. God hath had it much on his heart, from all eternity, to glorify his dear and only-begotten son; and there are some special seasons that he appoints to that end, wherein he comes forth with omnipotent power to fulfil his promise . . . to him. Now these are times of remarkable pouring out of his Spirit, to advance his kingdom; such is a day of his power. . . .[16]

And Edwards goes further. He claims:

> From the fall of man, to our day, the work of redemption in its effect has mainly been carried on by remarkable communications of the Spirit of God. Though there be a more constant influence of God's Spirit always in some degree attending his ordinances; yet the way in which the greatest things have been done towards carrying on this work, always have been by remarkable effusions, at special seasons of mercy. . . .[17]

On the assumption that every recorded renewal of vital piety among God's people indicates an outpouring of the Spirit, Edwards seeks to show that this generalisation holds with regard to Bible history, and that we have no reason to doubt that it holds still. Edwards, as a post-millennialist, looked forward to the conversion of the world; and he confidently predicted that this would be the direct consequence of a mighty revival throughout the whole church, leading to an unprecedented missionary offensive to every quarter of the globe.

Accordingly, when the church's life is ebbing out and God's judgements are falling on it, and missionary work is in decline, the Christian should hope for an outpouring of the Spirit that will reverse that state of affairs. And he has warrant for entertaining such a hope, and expressing it in his prayers: warrant, not in any worthiness on the church's part, but in the Father's eternal resolve to glorify the Son in his kingdom.

Third, *revivals are the most glorious of all God's works in the world.* Edwards insists on this, to shame those who professed no interest in the divine awakening that had come to New England, and insinuated by their attitude that a Christian's mind could more profitably be occupied with other matters.

> Such a work is, in its nature and kind, the most glorious of any work of God whatsoever [Edwards protests]. It is the work of redemption (the great

end of all the other works of God, and of which the work of creation was but a shadow) . . . it is the work of new creation, which is infinitely more glorious than the old. I am bold to say, that the work of God in the conversion of one soul . . . is a more glorious work of God than the creation of the whole material universe. . . .[18]

It follows, therefore, Edwards implies, that the theme of revival will be sweet and absorbing to the right-minded Christian man, whose heart rejoices when he sees the glory of God, and that the professed believer who can raise no interest in the subject must be spiritually in a very poor state.

Principles Concerning the Outward Form of Revival

We can be brief here, for we have already indicated how Edwards viewed this matter. He himself expounds all the points that fall under this head with particular application to the New England awakening, but we shall state them in a more generalised form.

Revival, Edwards tells us, is a *mixed* work. At each point Satan's tares intrude among God's wheat. From one standpoint, this makes the glory of God's work more apparent.

> The glory of divine power and grace are set off with the greater lustre by what appears at the same time of the weakness of the earthen vessel. It is God's pleasure to manifest the weakness and unworthiness of the subject, at the same time that he displays the excellency of his power and the riches of his grace.[19]

God is content to allow human weakness and sin to obtrude itself in times of revival, in order to make it evident beyond all peradventure that the spiritual fruits of the movement spring, not from any goodness in the persons concerned, but solely from his own work of grace. So Edwards writes again:

> It is very analogous to the manner of God's dealing with his people, to permit a great deal of error, and suffer the infirmity of his people to appear, in the beginning of a glorious work of his grace, for their felicity, to teach them what they are, to humble them, and fit them for that glorious prosperity to which he is about to advance them, and the more to secure to himself the honour of such a glorious work. For, by man's exceeding weakness appearing in the beginning of it, it is evident that God does not lay the foundation of it in man's strength or wisdom.[20]

Accordingly, Satan is not restrained from working in times of revival. And Satan has a characteristic strategy which he employs at such times.

> When he finds that he can keep men quiet and secure no longer, then he drives them to excesses and extravagances. He holds them back as long as

he can; but when he can do it no longer, then he will push them on, and, if possible, run them upon their heads.[21]

Thus, he seeks to carry away revived believers by exploiting the strength of their feelings, tempting them to pride, censoriousness, impatience with all established order in the church, and a persistent belief that the Spirit has more freedom to work when Christians leave themselves in a state of disorganisation, and when ministers preach without bothering to prepare their sermons; as if spur-of-the moment spontaneity is the supreme form or condition of spirituality. Satan further seeks to delude revived believers by immediate suggestions and inspirations, inviting them to conclude that all the thoughts and texts which come into their mind unbidden must be messages from God. By this and other means he seeks to lead them into imprudences of all sorts in the heat of their zeal. Such is his regular mode of procedure when a revival is in progress. Edwards delineates it very fully in the fourth part of his *Thoughts on the Revival*.

It is for this reason, Edwards insists, that it is so vitally important to judge spiritual movements, not by their immediate phenomena or by-products, but by their ultimate effects in the lives of those involved in them. If you concentrate on the phenomena, you can always find a great deal that is spurious, and ill-considered, and wrong-headed, and wild, and fanatical; and then you will be tempted to conclude that there is nothing of God in the movement at all. But, as we saw, the right way to assess what is happening is to see whether, amid all the tumult and disorder, the 'distinguishing marks of a work of the Spirit of God' are appearing. If they are, then we may know that it is God at work.

We shall be wise not to conclude too hastily that what Edwards is saying here has no message for us. We should be foolish to imagine that if God poured out his Spirit today, we should be able straightaway to recognise what was happening. Revival has always come in unexpected ways, through unexpected and often unwelcome people. We should not rule out the possibility that one day we shall ourselves stand nonplussed before an ebullient and uproarious spiritual movement, wondering whether it is of God, and finding ourselves strongly impelled by our instinctive distaste for its surface crudities and stupidities in theology, worship, and morals to look no further, but write if off at once. At such times, we shall need to bear in mind what Edwards has told us about the mixed character of revivals and the principles of judgement that should be applied in such a case.

Prayer For Revival
It is God's will, wrote Edwards,

> through his wonderful grace, that the prayers of his saints should be one great and principal means of carrying on the designs of Christ's kingdom

in the world. When God has something very great to accomplish for his church, it is his will that there should precede it the extraordinary prayers of his people; as is manifest by Ezek. xxxvi. 37, 'I will yet, for this, be enquired of by the house of Israel, to do it for them' [see the context]. And it is revealed that, when God is about to accomplish great things for his church, he will begin by remarkably pouring out the spirit of grace and supplications, Zech. xii. 10.[22]

This being so, Christians who desire revival have a strong incentive to pray for it. Nor is this all; Christians have a positive duty to pray for it. Edwards sought to prove this in *A humble attempt to promote Explicit Agreement and Visible Union of God's People in Extraordinary Prayer for the Revival of Religion*, a treatise which he wrote in support of a memorial circulated throughout English-speaking Christendom in 1746 by certain Scottish ministers, calling for special, 'extraordinary' prayer on Saturday evenings, Sunday mornings and the first Tuesday of each quarter, over a period of seven years, for the conversion of the world. Edwards argued the duty of making such prayers from the biblical predictions and promises of the extension of the church which showed it to accord with God's will that men should pray for worldwide revival, from the terms of the Lord's Prayer, and also from the undoubted need of revival in the world church of Edwards' own day. (The New England awakening had petered out in 1742.) We quote two thought-provoking passages:

> If we look through the whole Bible, and observe all the examples of prayer that we find there recorded, we shall not find so many prayers for any other mercy, as for the deliverance, restoration, and prosperity of the church, and the advancement of God's glory and kingdom of grace in the world . . . the greatest part of the book of Psalms is made up of prayers for this mercy, prophecies of it, and prophetical praises for it. . . .

> The Scripture does not only abundantly manifest it to be the duty of God's people to be much in prayer for this great mercy, but it also abounds with manifold considerations to encourage them in it. . . . There is perhaps no one thing that the Bible so much promises, in order to encourage the faith, hope, and prayers of the saints, as this; which affords to God's people the clearest evidence that it is their duty to be much in prayer for this mercy. For, undoubtedly, that which God abundantly makes the subject of his promises, God's people should abundantly make the subject of their prayers. . . .[23]

It is natural to wonder what resulted from the 1746 call to prayer. We cannot of course know how much praying was done during the seven years that followed, nor whether 'extraordinary' prayer continued after 1753 among those who had formed the habit. Certainly, nothing very startling happened at first. The evangelical revival in old England cooled somewhat after its first amazing decade, 1735-45, and New England was spiritually dry for a generation after the Great Awakening. But from the 1770s on Methodist preachers in Britain and North America saw great growth and occasionally renewed revival conditions; the Second Great Awakening blossomed in the 1790s; and the same decade saw revival in Norway under Hauge and in Finland under Ruotsalainen, plus the start of the Protestant missionary movement, which within a generation gave evangelical Christianity at least a toe-hold in all parts of the then known world. Was this fresh outburst of vital spiritual energy related to prayers that had been made decades earlier? Would it have occurred as it did without them? It is fascinating to guess—though guesswork remains guesswork, when all is said and done.

But however that may be, here is a task for all God's people in every age: to pray that God will build up Zion, and cause his glory to appear in her, by revival blessing. We shall do well to take Edwards' words to heart, and with them his closing remarks in this treatise, with which we close this chapter:

> And I hope, that such as are convinced it is their duty to comply with and encourage this design, will remember we ought not only to go speedily to pray before the Lord, and to seek his mercy, but also to go constantly. We should unite in our practice these two things, which our Saviour unites in his precept, Praying and Not Fainting. If we should continue some years, and nothing remarkable in providence should appear as though God heard and answered, we should act very unbecoming believers, if we should therefore begin to be disheartened, and grow dull and slack in seeking of God so great a mercy. It is very apparent from the word of God, that he is wont often to try the faith and patience of his people, when crying to him for some great and important mercy, by withholding the mercy sought, for a season; and not only so, but at first to cause an increase of dark appearances. And yet he, without fail, at last succeeds those who continue instant in prayer, with all perseverance, and 'will not let him go except he blesses. . . .' Whatever our hopes may be, we must be content to be ignorant of the times and seasons, which the Father hath put in his power: and must be willing that God should answer prayer, and fulfil his own glorious promises, in His own time.[24]

CHAPTER TWENTY

Afterword

The foregoing chapters have sought to appreciate the Puritans as men of God. They are, in other words, explorations in historical spirituality. They have aimed to look at aspects of Puritan belief and behaviour in ways that would enable us to see the grace of God in Puritans' lives and think to some purpose about what we might learn from them. I introduced the Puritans by comparing them to the California Redwoods, huge trees that are not handsome in any conventional sense but have very straight, strong, solid trunks. The evidence presented has, I believe, shown that the comparison is justified. Now we stand back from detailed evidence in order to take one last look at the Puritans and make sure that we see them steadily and whole. We shall reflect briefly on three final questions.

The first is the historical question: what, really and essentially, was a Puritan, and what, at deepest level, was Puritanism? To this disputed question, at which we glanced before, we can now give the following answer:

Puritans were Englishmen (some of whom eventually went to America) who embraced whole-heartedly a version of Christianity that paraded a particular blend of biblicist, pietist, churchly and worldly concerns. The blblicism was that of William Tyndale, the Bible translator; it led the Puritans to move with Tyndale into a reformational doctrine of justification by faith and to move beyond him, setting this doctrine in the frame of a sharply-etched Augustinian-Calvinist account of God's sovereign grace drawing faith, love, and holiness out of spiritually impotent sinners. The pietism was that of John Bradford, the Marian martyr, who pioneered the

Puritan discipline of keeping a journal as a kind of private confessional in order to spur himself on in the 'heart-work' of self-knowledge, self-watch, daily repentance for daily shortcomings, and methodical praise and prayer. The churchly concern was that of John Calvin, for whom the glory of God in his people's corporate life was always the goal, and the faith, form, and fidelity of churches at home and abroad was a matter of unending care. The worldly concern was that of John Knox, who saw the blessing of national reformation as entailing both God's call to model communal godliness for all to see and God's threat of judgement should this not be done. The essence of Puritanism was whole-heartedness in pursuing this fourfold concern by preaching and praying, by propaganda and pamphleteering, by programmes for changing the church, and by consciousness-raising education at every level, from the family and village school to the universities. All of this is reflected in the statement of an anonymous sixteenth-century tract, 'the hotter sort of Protestants are called Puritans.'

Puritans as a body shared all four concerns listed above, and viewed them holistically, as integral and inseparable elements in the social sanctification of which they dreamed—although within the spectrum of peers, squires, clergy, educators, lawyers, politicians, weavers, traders, and others, with womenfolk, who made up the Puritan constituency, specific aims and emphases on church and community questions varied from person to person. On matters of liturgy and order in the church, in particular, agreement on what needed to be abolished far outstripped agreement as to what should be brought in instead. But in seeking to honour and please God by the methodical holiness of mortifying sin, vivifying habits of grace, keeping the Sabbath, governing one's family, mastering the Bible, working hard in one's calling, practising purity, justice, and philanthropy in all relationships, and keeping up communion with God by regular, constant prayer, the Puritans were all at one, and all the more so because these were the things that their preachers most stressed. The sense of being called by God to practise and establish holiness wherever they went, and to crusade together for the moral and spiritual transformation of England, was strong in their hearts, and they valued the endless instruction on personal religion that the preachers gave as restoring their vision of God, renewing their grasp of his grace, and recharging their batteries for the tasks that lay ahead of them. They liked the loud, dramatic, uninhibited, down-to-earth, heart-to-heart, 'plain' expository preaching, ripping up consciences and lifting up Christ, that was a hallmark of the Puritan pulpit throughout; this seemed to them the only proper way for a man to speak when the issues of eternity were his subject. Love for such preaching was in fact as strong a bond among them as any, and that in itself tells us much about their habit of mind. As businesslike believers, unpretentiously serious, humble, sober, and confident in Christ, fair and just in all their dealings, wholly uncompromising when God's truth and glory were at stake, and willing to accept unpopularity and suffer for taking a stand, they were far and away the most impressive Englishmen of the era. In the short term, they lost their battles and failed in their reforming purposes; in the long term, however, they have done as much for English Christianity (not to mention that of America) as any group of would-be change agents has ever done, and their ministry to their successors shows no sign of ending yet.

Puritan piety can fairly be characterised as a reformed monasticism. Those who sought the desert and the cloister for a thousand years and more before the Puritans arrived did so because they wanted to be thorough-going for God (at least, this was the purpose of the best of them, and probably of most of them), and to that end they were willing to accept rigorously disciplined routines on a lifelong basis. The Puritans, whose minds were in some ways medieval just as they were in other ways modern, also accepted rigorously disciplined routines on a permanent basis, and for the same reason; but, like the Reformers, they believed that God calls his saints to serve him in the family, the church, and the world, rather than in any form of closed celibate society, and hence they thought and taught about the believer's life of 'duties' (a Puritan key word) in terms of these three spheres of relationship. Monasticism signified to them improper and entangling vows of celibacy and poverty, and they would have been horrified to think of their own path of devotion and duty as having any links with such perversions, but in fact their aim was to 'walk through the wilderness of this world' (Bunyan's phrase) with as rhythmical a routine for daily life as any monastic rule had ever required, and it is illuminating to observe the parallelism.

About the piety that was central to Puritanism we may generalise as follows. Four qualities stand out as showing its temper. The first is *humility*, the cultivated lowliness of a sinful creature who is always in the presence of a great and holy God, and can only live before him through being constantly pardoned. The second is *receptivity*, in the sense of openness to be taught, corrected, and directed by one's discoveries in Scripture; plus willingness to be disciplined by the darkness of disappointment and inward desertion, as well as encouraged by happy providences; plus readiness to believe that the good hand of a faithful and gracious God, who is ripening his children for future glory, shapes it all, the rough no less than the smooth. The third is *doxology*, the passion to turn everything into worship and so to glorify God by all one's words and deeds. The fourth is *energy*, the spiritual energy of the true Protestant work ethic whereby laziness and passivity are damned as irreligious, just because so much remains to be done before God's name is hallowed in his world as it should be. That all four qualities are formed by the Puritan view of God, who he is and what he does, is obvious; that, together, they constitute a mind- and heart-set which, once formed, nothing can daunt or destroy is surely no less obvious. In the combination of these four qualities lay the secret of the Puritans' indomitable and inexhaustible inner strength.

More can be said. For all the Puritans, the landscape of piety—that is, the spiritual topography of the ongoing life-situations in which each saint serves God—was determined by four realities, on all of which, as their books show, they laid out a great deal of expository effort. These were the sovereignty and sanctity of God, under whose eye we live, in whose hands we are, and whose purpose to have us holy, as he is holy, explains his way with our lives; the dignity and depravity of human beings, made for God but ruined by sin and now needing total renewal by grace; the love and Lordship of Christ, the Mediator, the Christian's Saviour-King; and the light and power of the Holy Spirit, who convicts, quickens, regenerates, witnesses, leads, and sanctifies.

Then, in mapping the path of piety, the Puritans focused on four areas of particular concern, to which in their preaching they constantly returned: the first steps (conviction and conversion through faith and repentance Christ-ward, leading to assurance); the fight (against the world, the flesh, and the devil, as one seeks to go forward with one's God); the fellowship (communion with God through prayer, and with other Christians by means of 'conference'—we would say, through talk and sharing); and the finish (dying well, in faith and hope, with all preparations made and a clear and quiet conscience as one moves into that final momentous meeting with the Father and the Son).

And four further emphases permeated all Puritan practical teaching: the need for Christians to see themselves as warrior-pilgrims, travelling home to God; the need for Christians to educate, sensitise, and heed their consciences on all matters of divinely specified duty; the need for Christians to sanctify all relationships, handling them all responsibly, benevolently, and creatively so as to please the God who calls for neighbour-love; and the need for Christians to delight in God and praise him joyfully at all times. Such was Puritan godliness: faithful, thoughtful, 'painful' (that meant, for the Puritans, taking pains, working hard), and joyful. We can now see why, for many evangelicals since the eighteenth century, to call persons 'Puritans' has been to pay them a compliment.

Now to our second question, which is evaluative and spiritual. I have compared the great Puritans to giant trees; I have implied throughout that they were saints of great stature, showing up the characteristic pigmyhood of present-day believers, at any rate in the West. What was so outstandingly grand-scale about them to merit this verdict? Here are four specifics, stated in generalised but not, I think, idealised terms.

First, these Puritans were great *thinkers*. The Puritan movement was led mainly by ministers, and most of the leaders among the ministers were brilliant and articulate polymaths from the universities. (Baxter and Bunyan are the significant exceptions, and Baxter became a polymath beyond most, even though he was not a university man.) The age was one of intellectual ferment in many areas, and Puritan teachers had to be abreast of many things—biblical exegesis, which was being practised at a much higher level of competence than is usually recognised; the ins and outs of Reformed theology as it was debated at home and abroad and written about, usually in Latin, in the large volumes that continental divines produced so prolifically; the Roman, Arminian, and Socinian controversies, plus in the Commonwealth period the aberrations of the sects; and, above all, the heritage of practical, pastoral, devotional theology that Greenham, Perkins and their followers had begun to develop, and that others were constantly augmenting throughout the Puritan era. The leading Puritan theologians—Owen, Baxter, Sibbes, Preston, Perkins himself, Charnock, Howe—all achieve a massive, adoring simplicity when speaking of God that argues intense reflective study, deep and prayerful Christian experience, and a sharp sense of responsibility to the church corporately, to their hearers and readers individually, and to the truth itself. This quality gives Puritan theological writing a flavour—you could call it an unction—that one rarely finds elsewhere. Luther's dictum that the three things that make the theologian are prayer, thinking in God's presence, and conflict, outward and inward (*oratio, meditatio, tentatio*), seems to find verification in the great Puritans; as you read, you feel a power of thought and a spiritual authenticity in their writings that is matched by very few. By comparison, a great deal of Christian communication in our own day is made to appear shallow, simplistic, and sloppy.

Second, these Puritans were great *worshippers*. The Puritans served a great God, the God of the Bible, unshrunk by any of the diminishing and demeaning lines of thought about him that press upon us today. The only forms of God-shrinking in the Protestant theology of the Puritan age were Arminianism, which limited God's sovereignty, and Socinianism, which in addition to doing that denied the Trinity and internal grace; and the Puritans repudiated both these views quite violently. For Scripture had given them a vision of the transcendent Creator who rules and speaks, the God from whom, and through whom, and for whom are all things, in whom we live and move and exist, the holy God who hates sin and judges it, and yet out of incomprehensible love has sent his Son to bear sin's curse on the cross so that guilty sinners might be justly justified and saved. Also, Scripture had shown them Christ the Mediator now glorified and reigning, and effectually calling blind, deaf, impotent, spiritually dead souls to himself by his Spirit's secret agency as God's human messengers—pastors and parents, friends and neighbours—laboured to instil into them the message of law and gospel. Finally, Scripture had told them of God's everlasting covenant relationship with believers—that total commitment on his part that guarantees blessing for eternity and entitles Christian to call on their Creator as '*my* God, *my* Father', just as each of them calls on Jesus as '*my* Saviour, *my* Lord, and *my* God.' The *Westminster Confession* is a Puritan statement of faith, and it is no accident that it is a classic embodiment of covenant theology. The Puritans' perception of the glory and greatness of God, of Christ, and of the covenant of grace thrilled their hearts, and produced in them an ardent, overflowing spirit of worship that on fast days at least, when time did not press, led pastors to pray extempore in their services for up to an hour at a time. It is a fact of Christian history that those who are consciously worshipping a great God do not find that worship services lasting two or three hours are a bore; on the contrary, they are experienced as a joy. That was true in the seventeenth century, as it is true today. By comparison, the modern Western passion for services lasting not more than sixty minutes raises the suspicion that both our God and our own spiritual statues are rather small.

Third, these Puritans were great *hopers*. One notable strength of the Puritans, setting them far apart from Western Christians today, was the firmness of their grip on the biblical teaching about the hope of heaven. Basic to their pastoral care was their understanding of the Christian's present life as a journey home, and they made much of encouraging God's people to look ahead and feast their hearts on what is to come. The classic works here are Richard Baxter's massive *Saints' Everlasting Rest*, written to show how the hope of glory, analysed by biblical study and internalised by meditation, should give believers energy and direction for present living, and Bunyan's *Pilgrim's Progress*, both parts of which reach their climax with triumphant passages through Jordan to the celestial city. The vividness of the vision of heaven in both Baxter and Bunyan is remarkable by any standards; sanctified imagination gives concreteness and colour to theological perception, resulting in extraordinary power to convey the flow of glory to the Christian heart. The Puritan point, which was first, of course, a New Testament point, was that Christians should know what their hope is and draw from it power to resist whatever discouragements and distractions present circumstances may produce. The unreadiness for pain and death that Western Christians too often reveal today contrasts unhappily with the realism and joyful hope that the Puritan masters inculcated in order to prepare the saints to leave this world in peace when their time came.

Fourth, these Puritans were great *warriors*. The Puritans saw the Christian calling as, from one standpoint, an unending fight against the world, the flesh, and the devil, and programmed themselves accordingly. 'His whole life he accounted a warfare,' said Geree of the old English Puritan, 'wherein Christ was his captain, his arms, praiers and tears.' One of the all-time classics of Puritan literature is William Gurnall's *The Christian in Complete Armour; A Treatise of the Saints' War against the Devil: Wherein a Discovery is made of that grand Enemy of God and his People, in his Policies, Power, Seat of his Empire, Wickedness, and chief design he hath against the Saints. A Magazine Opened, From whence the Christian is furnished with Spiritual Arms for the Battle, helped on with his Armour, and taught the use of his Weapon: together with the happy issue of the whole War*; it is a work of over 800,000 words, which C.H. Spurgeon described as 'peerless and priceless', and John Newton said he would choose it if he could only read one book beside the Bible. Bunyan's *Pilgrim's Progress* is a story of almost constant fighting, both verbal and physical, and the ideal Puritan pastor, Mr Great-heart, who acts as guide, instructor, and protector to Christiana's party, is cast for the role of giant-killer as well, fighting and destroying giants Grim, Maul, Slay-good and Despair as he goes along. When the pilgrim party meets another ideal Puritan figure, Mr Valiant-for-Truth, found 'with his Face all bloody', having just beaten off three thieves, Wildhead, Inconsiderate, and Pragmatick, the following exchange takes place:

> Then said Great-heart to Mr. Valiant-for-Truth, Thou hast worthily behaved thyself: let me see thy Sword. So he shewed it him.
>
> When he had taken it in his Hand, and looked thereon a while, he said, Ha! It is a right Jerusalem blade.
>
> *Valiant.* It is so. Let a man have one of these Blades, with a Hand to wield it, and skill to use it, and he may venture upon an Angel with it. He need not fear its holding, if he can but tell how to lay on. Its Edges will never blunt. It will cut Flesh, and Bones, and Soul, and Spirit, and all.
>
> *Greath.* But you fought a great while, I wonder you are not weary?
>
> *Valiant.* I fought till my Sword did cleave to my Hand: and when they were joined together, as if a Sword grew out of my Arm, and when the Blood run thorow my Fingers, then I fought with most Courage.
>
> *Greath.* Thou hast done well. Thou hast resisted unto Blood, striving against Sin.

In the margin alongside Valiant-for-Truth's second speech Bunyan inserted, 'The Word' (= the sword), 'The Faith' (= sword and hand joined together), and 'Blood' (= the cost of battling for God). The Puritans fought for truth against error, for personal holiness against temptations to sin, for ordered wisdom against chaotic folly, for church purity and national righteousness against corruption and hostility in both areas. One facet of their greatness was their principled hostility to all evils that stood in the way of godliness and true faith, and their willingness, much as they loved peace, to go out and fight those things, and to keep fighting as long as the evils were there.

The third question is practical: where do Christian people today fall short of the Puritans? and what ought we to learn from them for our own future?

It is said that the late Louis Armstrong, asked at the end of a performance what swing was, replied as follows: 'Lady, if you don't know by now, it's no use trying to explain.' In the light of all that I have said already,

I think it best to leave the thoughtful reader to answer my third question for himself or herself. I believe that in the providence of God some ages have special messages for other ages, and that as the New Testament era provides a model for the life of all churches and Christians everywhere, so the Puritan era has particular lessons to teach the Western Christian world at the end of the twentieth century. But that is something on which readers must make up their own minds. If my view of the Puritans as wise giants and ourselves as zany pigmies has not yet convinced you, it never will; if it has convinced you, you know already how my third question should be answered. So I leave the matter there.

Notes

Chapter 1: Introduction
1. John Owen, *Sin and Temptation*, abridged and edited by James M. Houston (Multnomah Press: Portland, 1983), introduction, pp xxv-xxix.
2. C. S. Lewis, *The Pilgrim's Regress*, 3rd edition (Geoffrey Bles: London, 1944), preface, pp 9f.

Chapter 2: Why We Need the Puritans
1. Cited from Gordon S. Wakefield, *Puritan Devotion* (Epworth Press: London, 1957), p x.
2. George Whitefield, *Works* (London, 1771), IV:306f.
3. Wakefield, *loc cit*. One cannot help thinking of the married lady who came to tell D.L. Moody that she thought she was called to be a preacher. 'Have you got any children at home?' Moody asked. 'Yes, six.' 'There's your congregation; off you go!'

Chapter 3: Puritanism as a Movement of Revival
1. See the citations in Basil Hall, 'Puritanism: the Problem of Definition, *Studies in Church History II*, ed E.J. Cuming (Nelson: London, 1965), pp 288ff.
2. The description of Puritans as 'rigid Calvinists' first appeared in print in M Antonius de Dominis, *The Cause of his Return, out of England* (Rome, 1623), p 31. The equation is already made, however, in a private document drawn up by John Overall, Regius Professor of Divinity at Cambridge, some time between 1610 and 1619, in which Overall contrasts the tenets of 'the Remonstrants or Arminians, and the counter-Remonstrants or Puritans'; see H.C. Porter, *Reformation and Reaction in Tudor Cambridge* (Cambridge University Press: Cambridge, 1958), p 410. William Perkins, the dominant Puritan theologian for the last two decades of Elizabeth's reign, and most if not all to whom the label 'Puritan' was fastened on other grounds during that period, had in fact maintained what de Dominis would call rigid Calvinism: see Porter, *op cit*, chap XII.
3. See C. Hill, *Society and Puritanism in Pre-Revolutionary England* (Mercury Books: London, 1966), pp 20-28, especially the extract from Lucy Hutchinson's *Memoirs of the Life of Colonel Hutchinson* on p 27.
4. C.H. and K. George, *The Protestant Mind of the English Reformation 1570-1640* (Princeton University Press: Princeton, 1961), p 6; cf pp 397-410.
5. Cf the comment in G.F. Nuttall, *Visible Saints: The Congregational Way, 1640-1660* (Basil Blackwell: Oxford, 1957), p 3, on the first Congregationalists: 'Underlying the seemingly disproportionate concern with forms of government there was, nevertheless, a passionate desire to recover the inner life of New Testament Christianity, which, it seemed reasonable to believe, would clothe and express itself in forms such as those in which it had first appeared.' B.R. White showed convincingly in *The English Separatist Tradition* (Oxford University Press: Oxford, 1971) that Separatism in England grew from the Puritan stock of ideas about the New Testament pattern of congregational life, and owed nothing decisive to Reformation Anabaptists; thus he justified another dictum of Dr Nuttall in *The Holy Spirit in Puritan Faith and Experience* (Basil Blackwell: Oxford, 1946), p 9: 'their taking

337

the final step of Separatism left undestroyed the greater part of those ideas and ideals which still, as hitherto, they had in common with the more conservative Puritans from among whom they came. In this wider sense Puritanism must be held to include Separatism'—though Separatists were not called Puritans in their own day.

6. Perry Miller, *Jonathan Edwards* (William Sloane Associates: New York, 1949), p 194; cf p 62: 'The simplest and most precise definition of Edwards' thought is that it was Puritanism recast in the idiom of empirical psychology.'

7. 'Jonathan Edwards and The Theology of Revival,' below, Chapter 19.

8. Irvonwy Morgan, *The Godly Preachers of the Elizabethan Church* (Epworth Press: London, 1965), p 11.

9. Cf e.g., William Haller, *The Rise of Puritanism* (Columbia University Press: New York, 1938); Nuttall, *The Holy Spirit* . . . ; G.S. Wakefield, *Puritan Devotion* (Epworth Press: London, 1957); N. Pettit, *The Heart Prepared* (Yale University Press: New Haven, 1966); books by the Georges and Morgan, already cited (nn 4, 8); O. Watkins, *The Puritan Experience* (Routledge and Kegan Paul: London, 1972); Peter Lewis, *The Genius of Puritanism* (Carey Publications: Hayward's Heath, 1977); C.E. Hambrick-Stowe, *The Practice of Piety* (University of North Carolina Press: Chapel Hill, 1982); C.L. Cohen, *God's Caress* (Oxford University Press: New York, 1986).

10. Compare the diametrically opposed interpretations of the theological relation between Puritanism and Anglicanism by the Georges, *op cit*, and J.F.H. New, *Anglican and Puritan. The Basis of their Opposition 1558-1640* (A. and C. Black: London, 1964). The former find Anglicans and Puritans in essential agreement everywhere, the latter speaks of 'two unities of principle . . . very different entities throughout' (p 111). What this extraordinary divergence shows is the comparatively undeveloped state of studies on the point in question: a fact reflected also by R.T. Kendall's paradoxical contention that Puritan theology, setting out to be Calvinistic, turned within half a century into Arminian legalism without anyone noticing (*Calvin and English Calvinism to 1649*; Oxford University Press: Oxford, 1979).

11. *Reliquiae Baxterianae*, ed M. Sylvester (London, 1696), first pagination, p 115.

12. Cf the documents (nos 14, 19-21) printed by H.C. Porter in *Puritanism in Tudor England* (Macmillan: London, 1970), pp 180 f, 217-227.

13. On the prophesyings, see Morgan, *op cit*, chap III, and *Elizabethan Puritanism*, ed L.J. Trinterud (Oxford University Press: New York, 1971), pp 191ff, where the Order of the Norwich Prophesying is printed.

14. On the feoffees, see I.M. Calder, *Activities of the Puritan Faction of the Church of England 1625-1633* (SPCK: London, 1957); Haller, *op cit*, pp 80ff; Irvonwy Morgan, *Prince Charles' Puritan Chaplain* (George Allen and Unwin: London, 1957), pp 174-183.

15. *Reliquiae Baxterianae, loc cit*.

16. Haller, *op cit*, pp 5, 173, etc.

17. Dering's sermon, which went through at least twelve editions in Elizabeth's lifetime, is printed in *Elizabethan Puritanism*, pp 138ff. The *Admonition* was reprinted in *Puritan Manifestoes*, ed W.H. Frere and C.E. Douglas (SPCK: London, 1907), pp 5ff.

18. Richard Baxter, *Practical Works of Richard Baxter* (George Virtue: London, 1838), I:731f, cf p 57.

19. John Downame, *A Guide to Godlynesse* (1622), Epistle Dedicatory.

20. Baxter, *Works*, II:501.

21. Edmund Calamy, *An Abridgement of Mr. Baxter's History . . . With an Account of many . . . Ministers who were ejected . . .* (London, 1702), p 315. 'No Book in

the English Tongue, (the Bible Excepted) can equal it for the Number that have been Dispersed.'

22. A representative selection of this material is printed in *William Perkins*, ed Ian Breward (Sutton Courtenay Press: Appleford, 1970). Breward discusses Perkins' casuistry, pp 58-80.

23. Haller, *op cit*, p ix.

24. *Reliquiae Baxterianae*, first pagination, pp 3f. Haller calls the *Bruised Reed* 'perhaps the most effective statement that any preacher accomplished of the dynamic element in Puritan morality' (*op cit*, p 160).

25. The main Puritan hagiographer was Baxter's friend Samuel Clarke, whose work and publications Haller describes, *op cit*, pp 102ff, 423ff.

26. William Brown's edition of *The Reformed Pastor* was reprinted, with an introduction by J.I. Packer, in 1974 (Banner of Truth: London).

27. Samuel Clarke, *Lives of Thirty-two English Divines* (3rd edition, 1677), pp 12f; citing from Henry Holland's preface 'To the Reader' prefixed to Richard Greenham, *Works* (1599). There are accounts of Greenham in M.M Knappen, *Tudor Puritanism* (University of Chicago Press: Chicago, 1939), pp 382-386, and in Porter, *Reformation and Reaction . . .*, pp 216-218.

28. *A Parte of a Register*, 1593, p 87.

29. Holland, 'To the Reader'.

30. Howe, *Works* (Frederick Westley and A.H. Davis: London, 1832), p 971. It is noteworthy that Fairclough's father Samuel, Vicar of Kedington, seventeen miles from Cambridge, from 1627 to 1662, exercised a ministry of just the same type, 'Preaching four times a Week: twice on the Lord's Day, a Thursday Lecture, (which was attended by all the Ministers for many Miles compass) and a Sermon on the Saturday Evening in his own House; and all the Country round flocked to him' (Calamy, *op cit*, p 254). His church was 'so thronged, that (though, for a village, very large and capacious, yet) there was no getting in, unless by some hours' attending before his exercise began; and then the outward walls were generally lined with shoals and multitudes of people, which came (many) from far, (some above twenty miles). . . .' (Clarke, *The Lives of Sundry Eminent Persons in This later Age*, 1683, p 187). He, too, was a man who, in Calamy's words, 'Catechiz'd Yound and Old; visited all in his Parish once a month, enquiring into the state of their Souls, and Counselling and Directing them as there was Occasion.'

31. *Reliquiae Baxterianae*, first pagination, pp 84f.

32. *Works*, IV:359 (= *Reformed Pastor*, ed W. Brown, p 43, with verbal changes).

33. *Reliquiae Baxterianae*, first pagination, p 86.

34. *Ibid*, p 85.

35. *Ibid*, pp 96f.

36. Because of Wesley's emphasis on the sovereignty of God in the new birth. Cf Charles Simeon's record of his conversation with Wesley on 20 December 1784 (date given in Wesley's *Journal*, in *Horae Homileticae* [Samuel Holdsworth: London, 1832]), cited in my own *Evangelism and the Sovereignty of God* (Inter-Varsity Fellowship: London, 1961), pp 13f, and see also G. Croft Cell, *The Rediscovery of John Wesley* (Henry Holt and Co: New York, 1935).

37. See Robert C. Monk, *John Wesley: His Puritan Heritage* (Abingdon Press: Nashville, 1966), and cf John Walsh, 'Origins of the Evangelical Revival' in *Essays in Modern English Church History*, ed G.V. Bennett and J.D. Walsh (A. and C. Black: London, 1966), pp 132ff, especially pp 154ff.

38. George Whitefield, *Works* (London, 1772), IV:306f.

39. *Ibid*, II:47.

40. Quoted from Robert Fleming, *The Fulfilling of the Scriptures*, by T. Hamilton, who narrates the Sixmilewater story in his *History of the Irish Presbyterian Church* (T.

and T. Clark: Edinburgh; nd), pp 42-44. See also John Gillies, *Historical Collections of Accounts of Revivals* (Banner of Truth: Edinburgh, 1981), pp 202ff.

41. Howe, *Works*, pp 1084f.
42. Cf Nuttall, *The Holy Spirit* . . . , especially chap. I, and this, from B.B. Warfield: 'The developed doctrine of the work of the Holy Spirit is an exclusively Reformation doctrine, and more particularly a Reformed doctrine, and more particularly still a Puritan doctrine.' 'It is only the truth to say that Puritan thought was almost entirely occupied with loving study of the work of the Holy Spirit, and found its highest expression in dogmatico-practical expositions of the several aspects of it' (introductory note prefixed to A. Kuyper, *The Work of the Holy Spirit* [Funk and Wagnalls: New York, 1900, pp xxxiii, xxviii]).
43. Cf Horton Davies, *The Worship of the English Puritans* (Dacre Press: London, 1948), and the *Westminster Directory for the Public Worship of God*. For an example of the 'fullness' and 'affection' in public prayer that was aimed at, see Richard Baxter's *Reformed Liturgy*, in *Works*, I:922ff. For Puritan ideals in preaching, see Perkins, *The Art of Prophesying*, in *William Perkins*, pp 325ff, and many passages in *The Reformed Pastor*.
44. Calamy, *op cit*, p 442.
45. *Ibid*, p 343.
46. *Ibid*, p 308, drawing on a life of Tregoss published in 1671, and summarised in Clarke's *Lives of Sundry Eminent Persons*. . . .
47. *Ibid*, p 214.
48. *Ibid*, pp 197f.

Chapter 4: The Practical Writings of the English Puritans

1. Richard Baxter, *Works*, editors' preface (1707), p xiii.
2. *Ibid*, I:4.
3. *Ibid*, I:731.
4. *Ibid*, I:732.
5. The authors and particular books in Baxter's list are: Richard Alleine; William Gurnall; John Preston; Richard Sibbes; Robert Bolton; William Whateley; Edward Reyner; William Scudder; Simon Ford; John Howe, *The Blessedness of the Righteous*; George Swinnock; William Gouge; Lewis Bayly, *The Practice of Piety*; Richard Allestree, *The Whole Duty of Man*; Henry Hammond, *A Practical Catechism*; John Pearson, *Exposition of the Creed*; George Downame, *A Treatise of Prayer* ('on the Lord's Prayer'); John Dod (and Thomas Cleaver), *The Ten Commandments*; Lancelot Andrewes, *The Ten Commandments*; John Brinsley, *The True Watch and Rule of Life*; Richard Greenham; Arthur Hildersam; Anthony Burgess; William Pink; John Downame, *The Christian Warfare*; Richard Rogers; John Rogers, *The Doctrine of Faith* and *A Treatise of Love*; John Stoughton; Thomas Taylor; Edward Elton; Daniel Dyke; Jeremiah Dyke; John Ball, *A Treatise of Faith* and *The Covenant of Grace*; Ezekiel Culverwell, *A Treatise of Faith*; Nathaniel Ranew; Faithful Teate; Samuel Shaw; John Rawlet; John Janeway; Thomas Vincent; Thomas Doolittle; Samuel Ward; William Fenner; Samuel Rutherford, *Letters*; Joseph Alleine, *The Life and Death of* (by his widow, Theodosia Alleine), and *An Alarm to the Unconverted*; Samuel Clark, *The Marrow of Ecclesiastical History* (2 parts) and *A General Martyrology* (both mainly biographical; Baxter refers to Clark's 'Lives' simply); *The Morning Exercise at (St. Giles) Cripplegate*; *The Morning Exercise at (St.) Giles in the Fields*; Benjamin Baxter; George Hopkins, *Salvation from Sin*; Edward Reynolds; Matthew Meade; Richard Vines; Henry Smith; Samuel Smith; Thomas Smith; William Strong; Joseph Symonds. Interestingly present are non-Puritan Anglicans (Allestree, Hammond, Andrewes, Pearson); surprisingly absent are John Owen, Thomas Goodwin,

Thomas Watson, and Thomas Brooks, each of whom was an established 'affectionate practical writer' when Baxter composed the *Christian Directory*. But clearly the list comes off the top of Baxter's head, and is not meant to be taken as exhaustive.

6. Baxter, *Works*, III:2.
7. *Ibid*, IV:797.
8. *Reliquiae Baxterianae*, first pagination, pp 3f.
9. See the Banner of Truth Trust catalogue, where the names of Owen, Sibbes, Goodwin, Gurnall, Baxter, Brooks, Flavel and others appear; also the publications list of Soli Deo Gloria (Ligionier, PA), which features Baxter, Burroughs, Bridge, and several more.
10. See the quotation from Whitefield above.
11. See above, pp. 35f.
12. *Reliquiae Baxterianae*, first pagination, p 2.
13. *Three Sixteenth-Century Chronicles*, ed J.M. Gairdner (Camden Society: London, 1880), p 143.
14. William Perkins, *Works* (1609), III:15.
15. R.T. Kendall, *Calvin and English Calvinism to 1649* (Oxford University Press: Oxford, 1979) pp 6-9.
16. G.W. Trevelyan, *England under the Stuarts* (Methuen: London, 1947), p 50. The statement is loose: separatists did not call themselves Puritans, nor were they so called in Elizabethan and Stuart days.
17. *Later Writings of John Hooper* (Parker Society: Cambridge, 1842), p 151.
18. Edward Dering, *Works* (1597), p 27; L.J. Trinterud, *Elizabethan Puritanism* (Oxford University Press: New York, 1971), p 159.
19. *Zurich Letters, 1558-1579* (Parker Society: Cambridge, 1842), p 236.
20. *Ibid*, pp 295f.
21. See above, Chapter 3, p.43
22. 'To the Reader' prefixed to Richard Greenham, *Works* (1599), np.
23. *Ibid*, p 204.
24. *Ibid*, p 1.
25. *A Parte of a Register* (1593), p 87. My italics.
26. *Ibid*, p 89.
27. *Ibid*, p 90.
28. Thomas Fuller, *The Worthies of England* (1662), p 117.
29. Stephen Egerton, 'To the Reader', prefixed to Richard Rogers, *Seven Treatises* (1603).
30. Cited from William Haller, *The Rise of Puritanism* (Columbia University: New York, 1938), p 75.
31. *The Seconde Parte of a Register*, ed Albert Peel (Cambridge University Press: Cambridge, 1915), II:185f.
32. *Reliquiae Baxterianae*, first pagination, p 85; see above.
33. Baxter, *Works*, II:885f.
34. *Ibid*, II:501.
35. He refers to *The Right Method for a Settled Peace of Conscience* (1653).
36. *Loc cit*.
37. *Ibid*, I:4.
38. 'The Printer to the Reader', prefixed to Perkins, *Works*, I (1608).
39. Baxter, *Works*, II:983.
40. *Richard Baxter's Penitent Confession* (1691), preface.
41. *Reliquiae Baxterianae*, first pagination, p 115.
42. Thomas Fuller, *The Holy and Profane State*, ed J. Nichols (Thomas Tegg: London, 1841), p 81.

43. John Owen, *Works*, ed William Goold (Johnstone and Hunter: Edinburgh, 1850-53), XVI:81f. The first sixteen volumes of this edition were reprinted photographically by the Banner of Truth Trust, 1965-68.

44. Perkins, *Works*, I:11.

45. *Reliquiae Baxterianae*, first pagination, p 5. 'Ursine' is Zacharias Ursinus, *The Summe of Christian Religion* (1587), a commentary on the *Heidelberg Catechism* of which he was one author. 'Amesius' is William Ames, *The Marrow of Sacred Divinity* (1643), a translation of *Medulla Theologiae* (1623).

46. William Tyndale, *Doctrinal Treatises* (Parker Society: Cambridge, 1848), pp 464f.

47. *Ibid*, p 399.

48. *Ibid*, p 463.

49. *Ibid*, p 320.

50. *Ibid*, p 484.

51. Perkins, *Works*, II:650f.

52. Cf, for instance, the answer to question 72 in the *Westminster Larger Catechism*: 'Justifying faith is a saving grace, wrought in the heart of a sinner by the Spirit and word of God, whereby he being convicted of his sin and misery, and of the disability in himself and all other creatures to recover him out of his lost condition, not only assenteth to the truth of the gospel, but *receiveth and resteth upon* Christ and his righteousness, therein held forth, for pardon of sin, and for the accepting and accounting of his person righteous in the sight of God for salvation.' My italics. Complementary is the definition in XIV:2 of the *Confession*: 'By . . . faith, a Christian believeth to be true whatsoever is revealed in the Word, for the authority of God himself speaking therein; and acteth differently upon that which each particular passage thereof containeth; yielding obedience to the commands, trembling at the threatenings, and embracing the promises of God for this life, and that which is to come. But the principal acts of saving faith are *accepting, receiving, and resting upon* Christ alone for justification, sanctification, and eternal life, by virtue of the covenant of grace.' My italics again.

53. Owen, *Works*, V:8. My italics.

54. Baxter, *Works*, II:481f.

55. *Ibid*, II:527.

56. Arthur Hildersam, *CLII Lectures upon Psalm LI* (1642), pp 55f.

57. Owen, *Works*, VI:7ff.

58. Baxter, *Works*, II:509.

59. Owen, *Works*, XXIV:218.

60. Perkins, *Works*, II:665ff.

61. Edward Bagshawe, 'Life and Death of Mr. Bolton' (bound with *M[r]. Bolton's Four Last Things*, 1632), p 13.

62. Thomas Goodwin, *Works*, ed J. Miller (James Nichol: London, 1861), II:lxivf.

63. Baxter, *Works*, II:399.

64. *The Works of John Flavel* (Banner of Truth: Edinburgh, 1968), VI:572.

65. Baxter, *Works*, II:400.

66. Richard Baxter, *The Reformed Pastor*, ed William Brown (Banner of Truth: Edinburgh, 1974), pp 53-64.

67. Owen, *Works*, XVI:76.

68. Cited from John Brown, *Puritan Preaching in England* (Hodder and Stoughton: London, 1900), p 66.

69. Cited from T.H.L. Parker, *The Oracles of God* (Lutterworth Press: London, 1947), p 60.

70. Owen, *Works*, V:4.

Chapter 5: John Owen on Communication from God

1. *Works*, IV:4ff; 118ff; XVI:281ff.

2. *Ibid*, III:128.
3. *Ibid*, III:197.
4. *Ibid*, III:130.
5. *Ibid*, IV:11.
6. *Ibid*, III:197; from an exposition of John 16:13-15.
7. *Ibid*, XVI:334.
8. *Ibid*, III:132f.
9. *Ibid*, III:144f.
10. *Ibid*, XVI:298.
11. *Ibid*, XVI:306.
12. *Ibid*, IV:15.
13. *Ibid*, XVI:308.
14. *Ibid*, IV:45.
15. *Ibid*, IV:102.
16. Owen cites Calvin's classic statement on the inner witness of the Spirit, *Institutes*, I:vii:5; IV:68f.
17. *Ibid*, IV:72f.
18. *Ibid*, XVI:307.
19. *Ibid*, XVI:320.
20. *Ibid*, XVI:328.
21. *Ibid*, XVI:318; cf viii:537: 'We believe it [Scripture] not because men have ministerially led us to receive it, or told us that is of God; but because we ourselves have heard and felt him speaking in it. The Spirit shines into our mind by the light of the word, and speaks loudly to our hearts by the power of it, and plainly tells us whose word it is; and so makes us yield to God's authority.'
22. *Ibid*, XVI:328.
23. *Ibid*, IV:107.
24. *Ibid*, XVI:327.
25. *Ibid*, IV:64.
26. *Ibid*, IV:60.
27. *Ibid*, IV:103.
28. *Ibid*, IV:13.
29. 'Causes, Ways, and Means', chap 7; IV:199-209.
30. *Ibid*, IV:188.
31. *Ibid*, IV:188-190.
32. 'The end of the Word itself, is to instruct us in the knowledge of God in Christ' (I:65). 'Then do we find food for our souls in the Word of truth, then do we taste how gracious the Lord is therein, then is the Scripture full of refreshment unto us as a spring of living water,—when we are taken into blessed views of the glory of Christ therein' (I:316). Owen's interpretation of Scripture is rigorously and resolutely Christ-centered (though in Calvin's way rather than Barth's); for Owen views Christ as ontologically the only Saviour and epistemologically the only full disclosure to us of the glory of God, and he wants all whom he instructs to see and honour Christ as he himself does.

Chapter 6: The Puritans as Interpreters of Scripture

1. John Howe, *Works*, pp 1084f.
2. Thomas Goodwin, *Works*, IX:28.
3. Thomas Watson, *A Body of Divinity* (Banner of Truth: London, 1958), p 25.
4. John Owen, *Works* (see Chapter Four n. 43), IV:205.
5. Goodwin, *Works*, V:537.
6. Owen, *Works*, VI:69.
7. Goodwin, *Works*, IV:302.

8. Owen, *Works*, IV:203.
9. Richard Baxter, *Works*, I:478.
10. Owen, *Works*, IV:206.
11. William Bridge, *Works* (Thomas Tegg: London, 1845), I:454.
12. Owen, *Works*, IV:215.
13. James Durham, *Exposition of the Song of Solomon* (George King: Aberdeen, 1840), p 28.
14. Bridge, *Works*, I:459.
15. *Westminster Confession*, I:ix.
16. Owen, *Works*, IV:197.
17. Richard Bernard, *The Faithful Shepherd* (1607), p 28.
18. Bridge, *Works*, I:411.
19. Thomas Adams, *Works* (James Nichol: Edinburgh, 1861-62), III:224.
20. Isaac Ambrose, *Works* (1701), p 201.
21. Owen, *Works*, V:8.
22. Thomas Manton, *Works* (James Nisbet: London, 1871), V:103.
23. *Westminster Directory for the Publick Worship of God* (1645), 'Of the Preaching of the Word', in *The Confession of Faith* . . . (Free Presbyterian Publications: Glasgow, 1973), p 380.

Chapter 7: The Puritan Conscience

1. William Ames, *Conscience with the Power and Cases thereof* (1643), p 2.
2. David Dickson, *Therapeutica Sacra . . . The Method of Healing the Diseases of the Conscience Concerning Regeneration* (1664), p 3.
3. Thomas Goodwin, *Works*, VI:272.
4. Dickson, *op cit*, p 4.
5. Ames, *op cit*, p 3.
6. Richard Sibbes, *Works* (James Nichol: Edinburgh, 1862), III:209; Thomas Brooks, *Works* (James Nichol: Edinburgh, 1867), V:281; William Gurnall, *The Christian in Complete Armour* (Banner of Truth: Edinburgh, 1964), p 5.
7. Sibbes, *Works*, III:210f.
8. John Bunyan, *The Holy War* in *Works*, ed G. Offor (Glasgow: Blackie and Son, 1859) III:260ff.
9. William Fenner, *A Treatise of Conscience* in *Works* (ed 1651) second pagination, p 24.
10. D. Clarkson, *Works* (James Nichol: Edinburgh, 1864), II:475. 'God alone is Lord of the conscience, and hath left it free from the doctrines and commandments of men, which are in any thing contrary to his Word' (*Westminster Confession*, XX:2).
11. Richard Baxter, *Works* (George Virtue: London, 1838), I:116.
12. *Ibid*, I:115f.
13. *Ibid*, I:116.
14. Fenner, *op cit*, pp 108f.
15. Sibbes, *Works*, VII:490.
16. Fenner, *op cit*, p 79f.
17. John Bunyan, *Pilgrim's Progress* in *Works*, III:242.
18. Ames, *op cit*, p 20.
19. Fenner, *op cit*, pp 143f.
20. John Owen, *The True Nature of a Gospel Church* in *Works*, XVI:76.

Chapter 8: 'Saved by His Precious Blood': An Introduction to John Owen's 'The Death of Death in the Death of Christ'

1. John Owen, *Works*, X:6.
2. Jon 2:9.

3. Plus any others who, though they had not heard the gospel, lived up to the light they had—though this point need not concern us here.
4. *Westminster Confession*, X:1.
5. Granted, it was Charles Wesley who wrote this, but it is one of the many passages in his hymns which make one ask, with 'Rabbi' Duncan, 'Where's your Arminianism now, friend?'
6. Gal 6:14.
7. C.H. Spurgeon was thus abundantly right when he declared:

> I have my own private opinion that there is no such thing as preaching Christ and Him crucified, unless we preach what is nowadays called Calvinism. It is a nickname to call it Calvinism; Calvinism is the gospel, and nothing else. I do not believe we can preach the gospel . . . unless we preach the sovereignty of God in His dispensation of grace; nor unless we exalt the electing, unchangeable, eternal, immutable, conquering love of Jehovah; nor do I think we can preach the gospel unless we base it upon the special and particular redemption of His elect and chosen people which Christ wrought out upon the Cross; nor can I comprehend a gospel which lets saints fall away after they are called.'

> C.H. Spurgeon, *The Early Years*, Autobiography, vol I (Banner of Truth: London, 1962), p 172.

8. Owen, *Works*, X:159.
9. *Ibid*.
10. Eph 2:9.
11. 'Life of John Owen' in Owen, *Works*, I:38.
12. Compare this, from C.H. Spurgeon:

> We are often told that we limit the atonement of Christ, because we say that Christ has not made a satisfaction for all men, or all men would be saved. Now, our reply to this is, that, on the other hand, our opponents limit it: we do not. The Arminians say, Christ died for all men. Ask them what they mean by it. Did Christ die so as to secure the salvation of all men? They say, 'No, certainly not.' We ask them the next question—Did Christ die so as to secure the salvation of any man in particular? They answer 'No.' They are obliged to admit this, if they are consistent. They say 'No. Christ has died that any man may be saved if'—and then follow certain conditions of salvation. Now, who is it that limits the death of Christ? Why, you. You say that Christ did not die so as infallibly to secure the salvation of anybody. We beg your pardon, when you say we limit Christ's death; we say, 'No, my dear sir, it is you that do it.' We say Christ so died that he infallibly secured the salvation of a multitude that no man can number, who through Christ's death not only may be saved, but are saved, must be saved and cannot by any possibility run the hazard of being anything but saved. You are welcome to your atonement; you may keep it. We will never renounce ours for the sake of it.

13. See Owen, *Works*, X:311-316, 404-410.
14. 'What, I pray, is it according to Scripture, for a man to be assured that Christ died for him in particular? Is it not the very highest improvement of faith? doth it not include a sense of the spiritual love of God shed abroad in our hearts? Is it not the top of the apostle's consolation, Rom. viii. 34, and the bottom of all his joyful assurance, Gal. ii. 20?' (*Ibid*, X:409.)
15. *Ibid*, X:315.
16. *Ibid*, X:407f.
17. *Loc cit*.
18. *Ibid*, I:422.
19. Jer 6:16.
20. Opening words, 'To the Reader', Owen, *Works*, X:149.
21. *Loc cit*.

22. *Ibid*, X:156.
23. Owen indicates more than once that for a complete statement of the case against universal redemption he would need to write a further book, dealing with 'the other part of this controversy, concerning the cause of sending Christ' (pp 245, 295). Its main thesis, apparently, would have been that 'the fountain and cause of God's sending Christ, is his eternal love to his elect, and to them alone' (p 131), and it would have contained 'a more large explication of God's purpose of election and reprobation, showing how the death of Christ was a means set apart and appointed for the saving of his elect, and not at all undergone or suffered for those which, in his eternal counsel, he did determine should perish for their sins' (p 245). It looks, therefore, as if it would have included the 'clearing of our doctrine of reprobation, and of the administration of God's providence towards the reprobates, and over all their actions', which Owen promised in the epistle prefixed to *A Display of Arminianism* (*Works*, X:9), but never wrote. However, we can understand his concluding that it was really needless to slaughter the same adversary twice.
24. Davenant's *Duae Dissertationes*, one of which defends universal redemption on Amyraldean lines, came out posthumously in 1650. Owen was not impressed and wrote of it: 'I undertake to demonstrate that the main foundation of his whole dissertation about the death of Christ, with many inferences from thence, are neither formed in, nor founded on the word; but that the several parts therein are mutually conflicting and destructive of each other' (*Works*, X:433, 1650).

    Baxter wrote a formal disputation defending universal redemption but never printed it; it was published after his death, however, in 1694.
25. 'Prefatory Note' in *Works*, X:140.
26. *Gangraena* (1646), II:86.
27. Richard Baxter, *Reliquiae Baxterianae*, i:50.
28. *Loc cit*.

Chapter 9: The Doctrine of Justification in Development and Decline Among the Puritans

1. G.C. Berkouwer, *Faith and Justification* (Eerdmans: Grand Rapids, 1954), p 17.
2. *The Works of Robert Traill* (Banner of Truth: Edinburgh, 1975), I:313.
3. *Ibid*, p 332.
4. 'The forsaking of the doctrine of justification by faith in Christ's righteousness, hath been the first step of apostasy in many, who have not stopped till they revolted from Christianity itself' (*ibid*, p 333).
5. *Ibid*, p 332.
6. John Owen, *Works*, V:4.
7. Traill, *op cit*, pp 313f.
8. *Ibid*, pp 321, 329.
9. *Decrees of the Council of Trent*, VI:vii, cf V:v; both translated in C.F. Allison, *The Rise of Moralism* (SPCK: London, 1966), pp 213f, a book in which much thought-provoking material about the doctrine of justification in the seventeenth century is assembled.
10. Among the Anglicans were Richard Hooker; Bishops George Downame, John Davenant, James Usher, Robert Hall, Thomas Barlow, John Bramhall, William Beveridge; and Thomas Tully. Among the Presbyterians and later nonconformists were Anthony Burgess, John Owen, and Robert Traill. I celebrate Traill's excellent discussion in the chapter text; and John Owen's treatise, *The Doctrine of Justification by Faith through the Imputation of the Righteousness of Christ; Explained, Confirmed, and Vindicated* (1677; *Works*, V) is justly described as a 'great work' by the editor, William Goold (V:3).

11. 'It is entirely by the intervention of Christ's righteousness that we obtain justification before God. This is equivalent to saying that man is not just in himself, but that the righteousness of Christ is communicated to him by imputation, while he is strictly deserving of punishment. Thus vanishes the absurd dogma, that man is justified by faith inasmuch as faith brings him under the influence of the Spirit of God, by whom he is rendered righteous' (*Institutes* III:xi:23). See also Calvin's discussion of Session VI of the Council of Trent, *Tracts and Treatises* (Eerdmans: Grand Rapids, 1958), III:108ff, especially pp 114-121.

12. George Smeaton, *The Doctrine of the Holy Spirit* (Banner of Truth: London, 1958), pp 327f.

13. In the *Westminster Confession* Chapter X ('Of Effectual Calling') precedes Chapter XI ('Of Justification'). The first two sections of Chapter X read as follows:

    All those whom God hath predestinated unto life, and those only, he is pleased, in his appointed and accepted time, effectually to call, by his word and Spirit out of that state of sin and death in which they are by nature, to grace and salvation by Jesus Christ; enlightening their minds spiritually and savingly to understand the things of God; taking away their heart of stone, and giving unto them an heart of flesh; renewing their wills, and by his almighty power determining them to that which is good; and effectually drawing them to Jesus Christ; yet so as they come most freely, being made willing by his grace.

    This effectual call is of God's free and special grace alone, not from any thing at all foreseen in man; who is altogether passive therein, until, being quickened and renewed by the Holy Spirit, he is thereby enabled to answer this call, and to embrace the grace offered and conveyed in it.

14. A clear if unsympathetic summary of Antinomian tenets, viewed as so many deviations from Reformed orthodoxy, is given in James Buchanan, *The Doctrine of Justification* (Banner of Truth: London, 1961), pp 171ff. The main Antinomian authors were John Eaton, Henry Denne, Robert Towne, John Saltmarsh, and (in the view of some) Tobias Crisp.

15. From a hymn by A.M. Toplady, entitled 'Faith Reviving', which mirrors most strikingly in devotional response the particularistic efficacy, i.e., the genuinely substitutionary character of Christ's atoning death. This hymn, as Toplady wrote it (verbal smoothings in modern printings sometimes smudge the theology), brilliantly focuses the Reformed recognition of what Jesus and the apostolic writers meant by saying that the death at Calvary was 'for' people (Greek, *huper* and *anti*), and as such merits full quotation (from *Diary and Selection of Hymns of Augustus Toplady*, Gospel Standard Baptist Trust: Harpenden, 1969, p 193).

> From whence this fear and unbelief?
> Hath not the Father put to grief
>   His spotless Son for me?
> And will the righteous Judge of men
> Condemn me for that debt sin
>   Which, Lord, was charged on thee?
>
> Complete atonement thou hast made,
> And to the utmost farthing paid
>   Whate'er they people owed;
> How then can wrath on me take place
> If sheltered in thy righteousness,
>   And sprinkled with thy blood?

If thou hast my discharge procured,
And freely in my room endured
    The whole of wrath divine,
Payment God cannot twice demand—
First at my bleeding Surety's hand,
    And then again at mine.

Turn then, my soul, unto thy rest!
The merits of thy great High Priest
    Have bought thy liberty;
Trust in his efficacious blood,
Nor fear thy banishment from God,
    Since Jesus died for thee.

16. *Harmonia Apostolica* (Library of Anglo-Catholic Theology, J.H. Parker: Oxford, 1844 I:58); quoted in Allison, *op cit*, chap 6, 'The Theology of George Bull.'
17. A.W. Harrison, *Arminianism* (Duckworth: London, 1937), p 111. Amyraldism is evaluated (under the name 'Post-redemptionism') in B.B. Warfield, *The Plan of Salvation* (Eerdmans: Grand Rapids, 1984), pp 90-96.
18. After Baxter's death in 1691 his position was championed by Daniel Williams (*Gospel-Truth Stated and Vindicated*, 1692) and Samuel Clark (*Scripture Justification*, 1698), and controverted by (among others) the Baptist Benjamin Keach, in a series of five books published between 1692 and 1698 that follow closely in Owen's footsteps.
19. Cf Peter Toon, *The Emergence of Hyper-Calvinism in English Nonconformity, 1698-1765* (Olive Tree: London, 1967), chap 3, for details of the story.
20. *Sermons on Important Subjects; by the Rev. George Whitefield, A.M.* (1832) pp 207ff.

Chapter 10: The Puritan View of Preaching the Gospel
1. Richard Baxter, *Works*, II:482.
2. Robert Bolton, *Instructions for a Right Comforting Afflicted Consciences* (3rd edition, 1640), p 185.
3. Thomas Manton, *Works*, II:102f.
4. Thomas Goodwin, *Works*, III:483.
5. John Owen, *Works*, XI:227.
6. Baxter, *Works*, II:589f.
7. Thomas Shepard, *The Sound Believer* (1849 edition), p 217.
8. Bolton, *op cit*, p 186.
9. *Sermons by Rev. C.H. Spurgeon*, ed W. Robertson Nicoll, p 112.
10. *Reliquiae Baxterianae*, I:7.
11. Goodwin, *Works*, IV:346.
12. Firmin, *The Real Christian* (1670), p 2.
13. John Rogers, *The Doctrine of Faith* (1627), p 502.
14. Shepard, *op cit*, p 238f.
15. Owen, *Works*, I:422.
16. *Westminster Confession*, XV:i,ii,iii,v.
17. Zachary Crofton, 'Repentance . . . plainly asserted, and practically explained', in *The Morning Exercises* (1660; reprinted as *Puritan Sermons, 1659–89*, Richard Owen Roberts: Wheaton, 1981).
18. Crofton, *op cit*, V:376-390.
19. *Ibid*, V:373f.
20. *Ibid*, V:395.
21. *Ibid*, V:420-425.

Chapter 11: The Witness of the Spirit in Puritan Thought

1. Thomas Goodwin, *Works*, ed J. Miller (James Nichol: London, 1861), VIII:260.
2. Thomas Watson, *A Body of Divinity*, p 151.
3. Thomas Brooks, *Works*, II:359.
4. *Ibid*, II:335, 316f, 371.
5. Goodwin, *Works*, VIII:346.
6. Brooks, *Works*, II:371.
7. Goodwin, *Works*, VIII:346, 352; I:236.
8. Brooks, *Works*, II:316.
9. Goodwin, *Works*, I:233.
10. Richard Sibbes, *Works*, III:456.
11. Goodwin, *Works*, I:257.
12. *Ibid*, VIII:355.
13. *Ibid*, VIII:379.
14. Sibbes, *Works*, V:442.
15. Goodwin, *Works*, I:250.
16. Brooks, *Works*, II:522.
17. Goodwin, *Works*, I:250.
18. Brooks, *Works*, II:515f.
19. Goodwin, *Works*, VI:27.
20. *Ibid*, I:306.
21. *Ibid*, VIII:366f.
22. John Goodwin, *A being filled with the Spirit* (James Nichol: Edinburgh, 1867), p 449; so also Watson, *op cit*, p 174, Thomas Manton, *Works*, XII:129, and others.
23. Sibbes, *Works*, V:440.
24. Goodwin, *Works*, 1:233.
25. *Ibid*, I:250.
26. *Ibid*, I:260.
27. *Ibid*, I:260.
28. See Sinclair B. Ferguson, *John Owen on the Christian Life* (Banner of Truth: Edinburgh, 1987), pp 117-121. Calvin had construed the phrase 'the Holy Spirit of promise' in Ephesians 1:13 as meaning that the Holy Spirit 'verifies and confirms the promises in and to the hearts of believers' (Matthew Pool, *Annotations*, 1685, *ad loc*). Perkins then explained the confirming of God's promise in terms of the Spirit bestowing assurance of personal salvation: 'When God by his spirit is said to seale the promise in the heart of every particular believer, it signifieth that he gives unto them evident assurance that the promise of life belongs unto them' (cited from Ferguson, *op cit*, p 117). Finally, Sibbes and Preston introduced the thought that this assuring activity of the Spirit is temporally subsequent to, and thus distinct from, the dawning of personal faith. Preston preached it thus: 'You will say, what is the *seale or witness* of the Spirit? My beloved, it is a thing that we cannot express . . . a certain secret manifestation, that *God* hath received us, and put away our sinnes: I say, it is such a thing, that no man knowes, but they that have it' (*The New Covenant*, London, 1634, pp 400f; my italics). The 'seal' of the Spirit (i.e., the Spirit in his role as God's seal, set upon us to mark us out as his possession) is here equated with a particular form of witnessing activity that takes place subsequent to conversion ('after that ye believed', Eph 1:13, KJV).
29. Goodwin, *Works*, I:248.
30. *Ibid*, VIII:264.
31. *Ibid*, I:248.
32. *Ibid*, I:245.
33. *Ibid*, I:249.
34. Owen, *Works*, IV:401.

35. *Ibid*, I:400. 'When we seal a deed or grant to any one, we do not say the man is sealed, but the deed or grant', I:243.
36. *Ibid*, I:242.
37. *Ibid*, I:243.
38. *Ibid*, IV:399-406.
39. *Ibid*, IV:404.
40. *Ibid*, IV:405.
41. *Ibid*, I:253. This is the first of two ways whereby the Spirit brings joy to the Christian heart, namely that whereby 'he doth it *immediately* by himself; without the consideration of any other acts or works of his, or the interposition of any reasonings or deductions and conclusions' (p 252). The other way is by blessing our 'consideration' (deliberate thoughts) of God's mercy so that they issue in rejoicing.

Chapter 12: The Spirituality of John Owen
1. For details on Owen's Life, see Peter Toon, *God's Statesman* (Paternoster Press: Exeter, 1971); A. Thomson, 'Life of Dr. Owen' in Owen, *Works*, I:xxi-cxii.
2. The Latin text is in Owen, *Works* I:cxiii f. The 'translation' offered there and reproduced in Toon, *op cit*, pp 182f, is not a translation in the ordinary present-day sense, but a loose explanatory amplification. 24 August, St Bartholomew's Day, had been made 'dreadful' by the Hugnenot massacre of 1572 and the Puritan ejections of 1662.
3. David Clarkson, *A Funeral Sermon on the Much Lamented Death of the Late Reverend and Learned Divine John Owen D.D.* (London, 1720); cited from Toon, *op cit*, p 173.
4. Owen, *Works*, VI:200.
5. *Ibid*, VI:201.
6. *Ibid*, XVI:76.
7. *Ibid*, X:488.
8. *Ibid*, I:lxxvi.
9. C.H. Spurgeon, *Commenting and Commentaries* (Banner of Truth: London, 1969), p 103.
10. Owen, *Works*, VI:213, 216.
11. *Ibid*, VI:254.
12. *Ibid*, VII:397.
13. *Loc cit*.
14. A phrase from Anglican Article XX.
15. Owen, *Works*, VI:173.
16. *Ibid*, VI:178.
17. *Ibid*, VI:157.
18. *Ibid*, VI:181.
19. *Ibid*, VII:532f.
20. *Ibid*, I:166f.
21. *Ibid*, III:324.
22. *Ibid*, III:320.
23. *Ibid*, VI:8.
24. *Ibid*, VI:11.
25. *Ibid*, VI:192f.
26. *Ibid*, IV:204.
27. *Ibid*, III:386.
28. *Ibid*, III:370.
29. *Ibid*, III:470.
30. *Ibid*, III:385.
31. *Ibid*, III:389.

32. *Ibid*, III:529.
33. *Ibid*, III:364.
34. *Ibid*, III:545.
35. *Ibid*, VI:8.
36. *Ibid*, III:545.
37. *Ibid*, III:543.
38. *Ibid*, III:552f.
39. *Ibid*, III:554.
40. *Ibid*, III:560.
41. *Ibid*, VI:85.
42. *Ibid*, III:563f.
43. *Ibid*, VI:86.
44. *Westminster Shorter Catechism*, answer to question 1.
45. Owen, *Works*, II:78.
46. *Ibid*, II:22.
47. *Ibid*, II:8f.
48. *Ibid*, II:19.
49. *Ibid*, II:22f.
50. *Ibid*, II:24.
51. *Ibid*, II:52.
52. *Ibid*, II:58f.
53. *Ibid*, II:194.
54. *Ibid*, II:205f.
55. *Ibid*, II:249.
56. Thomas Goodwin, *Works*, VIII:376ff. Goodwin refers to John 14:21-33.
57. *Ibid*, VII:193.
58. *Ibid*, VII:197ff.
59. Owen, *Works*, II:118.
60. *Ibid*, II:119f.
61. *Ibid*, II:124f.
62. *The Banner of Truth* 194 (November 1979): pp 10-15. See also Sinclair Ferguson's *John Owen on the Christian Life*, pp 79-86. This book is a thorough survey of its subject, ranging much wider than the present chapter.
63. Owen, *Works*, VII:338f.
64. Cited from Ferguson, *op cit*, p 18. Owen's last letter, dictated the day before, had said: 'I am going to him whom my soul hath loved, or rather who hath loved me with an everlasting love; which is the whole ground of all my consolation' (*loc cit*).
65. Robert Bruce, *Sermons on the Sacrament*, ed T.F. Torrance (James Clarke: London, 1958), p 64.
66. Richard Baxter, *Works*, III:816.
67. Owen, *Works*, IX:517-622.
68. *Ibid*, IX:622.
69. Ferguson, *op cit*, pp 221-224.
70. Owen, *Works*, IX:566.
71. Ferguson, *op cit*, p 224.
72. John Bunyan, *Grace Abounding to the Chief of Sinners*, ed Roger Sharrock (Oxford University Press: London, 1966), p 16. It is worth noting that Owen admired Bunyan's preaching, and arranged for his own publisher to print the first edition of *The Pilgrim's Progress*: see Ferguson, *op cit*, pp 3,16; Toon, *op cit*, pp 161ff.
73. Owen, *Works*, II:7.
74. On Puritan spiritual autobiography, see Owen Watkins, *The Puritan Experience* (Routledge and Kegan Paul: London, 1972; Schocken Books: New York, 1972).

75. Owen, *Works*, XII:52.
76. *Loc cit.*

Chapter 13: John Owen on Spiritual Gifts

1. In his *Inquiry concerning . . . Evangelical Churches,* written after the publication of Stillingfleet's sermon *On the Mischief of Separation* (preached 2 May 1680) and before Stillingfleet's larger work, *The Unreasonableness of Separation,* appeared in the following year (Owen, *Works,* XV:221f, 375). Owen refers to his *Discourse of Spiritual Gifts* as already written (p 249). In the preface to *The Work of the Spirit in Prayer,* published in 1682, he mentions a treatise on spiritual gifts as something he proposes to write (IV:246). This indicates that *The Work of the Spirit in Prayer,* which follows *Causes, Ways and Means of Understanding the Mind of God* (published 1678) in the sequence of Owen's treatises on the Holy Spirit, was written perhaps three years before it was published, since by 1680 its promised successor had already been completed. The *Discourse of Spiritual Gifts* is in IV:420-520.
2. The only Protestant tongue-speakers in the seventeenth century appear to have been the Camisards, Huguenot refugees who fled to the Cevennes after the Edict of Nantes was revoked in 1685. In other ways the Camisard movement was unquestionably fanatical; see *Oxford Dictionary of the Christian Church* (1957), sv, and literature there cited.
3. 'The air was thick with reports of prophecies and miracles, and there were men of all parties who lived on the border land between sanity and insanity' (R. Barclay, *The Inner Life of the Religious Societies of the Commonwealth,* Hodder and Stoughton: London, 1876, p 216). Barclay gives a number of instances.
4. Owen, *Works,* IV:518.
5. See B.B. Warfield, *Miracles Yesterday and Today* (Banner of Truth: London, 1967), chap I.
6. Matthew Henry calls tongues 'the most useless and insignificant of all these gifts' (on 1 Cor 12:28). It is unlikely that Owen would have quarrelled with this verdict.
7. The book is dated 1644, but Owen elsewhere states that this was the printer's deliberate mistake (*Works,* XIII:222).
8. *Ibid,* XIII:44f.
9. *Ibid,* p 47.
10. *Ibid,* IV:518.
11. *Ibid,* p 420f.
12. *Ibid,* p 432.
13. *Ibid,* p 421.
14. *Loc cit.*
15. *Ibid,* p 428.
16. *Loc cit.*
17. *Ibid,* p 479f.
18. *Ibid,* p 426.
19. *Ibid,* p 471.
20. *Ibid,* p 421.
21. *Ibid,* p 423.
22. *Ibid,* p 421f.
23. *Ibid,* p 507.
24. *Ibid,* p 482.
25. *Ibid,* p 423.
26. *Ibid,* p 242.
27. *Ibid,* p 437.
28. 'Helps' and 'governments' were not identified with certainty by any Puritan

exegete. Matthew Pool (*Annotations*, 1685 *ad loc*) confessed it 'very hard to determine' who they were—'whether he meaneth deacons, or widows . . . as helpful in the case of the poor, or some that assisted the pastors in the government of the church, or some that were extraordinary helps to the apostles in the first plantation of the church.' Matthew Henry thought 'helps' were sick visitors, and 'governments' were, in effect, deacons, or 'poor stewards' in the old Methodist sense, distributing the church's charitable gifts to the needy. Richard Baxter thought 'helps' were 'eminent Helpers of the Churches by Charity and special Care, especially for Ministers and the Poor; Governments to arbitrate Differences and keep Order' (*Paraphrase of the New Testament, ad loc*). None of these writers, however, nor any other Puritan so far as I know, thought of a gift of helping and governing.

29. Owen, *Works*, IV:438.
30. *Ibid*, p 442.
31. Owen's remarks on prophets in the New Testament are worth noticing:

The names of *prophet* and prophecy are used variously in the New Testament: for, 1. Sometimes an extraordinary office and extraordinary gifts are signified by them; and, 2. Sometimes extraordinary gifts only; and, 3. Sometimes an ordinary office with ordinary gifts, and sometimes ordinary gifts only. And unto one of these heads may the use of the word be everywhere reduced.

1. In the places mentioned (Eph 4:11; 1 Cor 12:28) extraordinary officers endued with extraordinary gifts are intended. . . . And two things are ascribed unto them: (1) that they received immediate revelations and directions for the Holy Ghost' [Owen cites Acts 13:2]; (2) They foretold things to come (Acts 11:28ff; 21:10f.

2. Sometimes an extraordinary gift without office is intended (Acts 21:9; 19:6; 1 Cor 14:29-33).

3. Again, an ordinary office with ordinary gifts is intended by this expression (Romans 12:6—prophecy here can intend nothing but teaching or preaching, in the exposition and application of the word; for the external rule is given unto it, that it must be done according to the 'proportion of faith', or the sound doctrine of faith revealed in the Scriptures). Hence also those who are not called unto office, who have yet received a gift enabling them to declare the mind of God in the Scripture unto the edification of others, may be said to 'prophesy' (*Works*, 451f).

32. *Ibid*, p 494.
33. *Ibid*, p 495.
34. *Ibid*, p 505.
35. *Ibid*, p 509.
36. *Ibid*, p 510.
37. *Ibid*, p 510f.
38. *Ibid*, p 512.
39. *Ibid*, p 512f.
40. *Ibid*, p 438.

Chapter 14: The Puritans and the Lord's Day

1. See particularly W.B. Whitaker, *Sunday in Tudor and Stuart Times* (Houghton Publishing Co: London, 1933), and James T. Dennison, Jr, *The Market Day of the Soul: The Puritan Doctrine of the Sabbath in England, 1532-1700* (University Press of America: Lanham, 1983).
2. Richard Baxter, *Works*, III:906.
3. Philip Stubbes, *Anatomie of Abuses in England* (1583).
4. *Early Writings of John Hooper* (Parker Society: Cambridge, 1843), p 342: 'This Sunday that we observe is not the commandment of man . . . but it is by express

words commanded, that we should observe this day for our sabbath, as the words of St. Paul declareth, I Cor. xvi. . . .'

5. *Sermons by Hugh Latimer* (Parker Society: Cambridge, 1844), pp 471-473: 'This day was appointed of God, that we should hear his word, and learn his laws, and so serve him. . . . God hateth the disallowing of the sabbath as well now as then [under the Old Testament] . . . he will have us to keep his sabbath, as well now as then. . . .'

6. Edmund Bunny, *The Whole Summe of Christian Religion* (1576), p 47: the Fourth Commandment requires Christians 'to spend the whole Sabboth day, eyther in Publique exercise, as in ordinary service, or sermons; or in private meditation'.

7. Gervase Babington, *A very fruitfull Exposition of the Commandments* (1583): 'the first unambiguous statement of what history knows as the Puritan doctrine of the Sabbath . . . the Sabbath commandment is perpetually binding upon all men. To hallow the Sabbath day is to: (1) rest from the labors of our calling; (2) assemble for worship; (3) rest from sin. . . .' (Dennison, *op cit*, p 29).

8. Whitaker, *op cit*, p 95.

9. Baxter, *Works*, III:904; from *The Divine Appointment of the Lord's day, Proved* (1671).

10. *Reliquiae Baxterianae*, first pagination, p 84.

11. John Calvin, *Institutes of the Christian Religion*, II:viii:29.

12. *Ibid*, II:viii:34.

13. Patrick Fairbairn, *The Typology of Scripture* (Smith and English: Philadelphia, 1854), II:142; see Appendix A, pp 514ff, for the evidence.

14. Jonathan Edwards, sermon II on 'The Perpetuity and Change of the Sabbath', a fine statement of the Puritan position; in *Works*, II:95. The definitive Puritan statement is in *Westminster Confession*, XXI:vii:

As it is the law of nature that in general, a due proportion of time be set apart for the worship of God; so, in his Word, by a positive, moral, and perpetual commandment binding all men in all ages, he hath particularly appointed one day in seven for a Sabbath, to be kept holy unto him: which, from the beginning of the world to the resurrection of Christ was the last day of the week, and from the resurrection of Christ, was changed into the first day of the week, which, in Scripture, is called the Lord's Day, and is to be continued to the end of the world, as the Christian Sabbath.

15. *Ibid*, II:96.

16. John Dod and Robert Cleaver, *A Plaine and Familiar Exposition of the Ten Commandments* (London, 1628), p 143.

17. George Swinnock, *Works* (James Nichol: Edinburgh, 1868), I:239.

18. Thomas Brooks, *Works*, VI:299.

19. Edwards, *Works*, II:102.

20. Swinnock, *Works*, I:258.

21. Dod and Cleaver, *op cit*, pp 138f.

22. Baxter, *Works*, I:470.

23. Swinnock, *Works*, I:230.

24. Baxter, *Works*, I:472.

25. Richard Greenham, *Works*, (1611 edition), p 208.

26. Dod and Cleaver, *op cit*, p 145.

27. Baxter, *Works*, III:905.

28. *Ibid*, III:908.

29. *Works of Sir Matthew Hale*, ed T. Thirlwall (1805), I:196.

30. Brooks, *Works*, VI:305f.

Chapter 15: The Puritan Approach to Worship

1. Horton Davies, *The Worship of the English Puritans* (Dacre Press: London, 1948), p 48.

2. George Swinnock, *Works*, I:31.
3. John Owen, *Works*, IX:53-84.
4. *Ibid*, IX:56f.
5. *Ibid*, IX:76f.
6. *Ibid*, IX:77f.
7. Stephen Charnock (James Nichol: Edinburgh, 1864), *Works*, I:298.
8. *Ibid*, I:299.
9. *Ibid*, I:307.
10. *Ibid*, I:308.
11. *Ibid*, I:315.
12. Owen, *Works*, VII:430f.
13. Charnock, *Works*, I:319.
14. *Ibid*.
15. Owen, *Works*, I:319.
16. *Ibid*, VII:439.
17. William Bradshaw, *English Puritanisme* (1605), p 17.
18. Thomas Goodwin, *Works*, XI:364.
19. Richard Baxter, *Works*, I:473, 475.
20. Thomas Adams, *Works*, I:103.
21. David Clarkson, *Works*, III:190ff.
22. *Ibid*, III:194.
23. Swinnock, *Works*, I:234.
24. *Ibid*, I:229f.

Chapter 16: Marriage and Family in Puritan Thought

1. Kenneth Hare, 'The Puritan' cited from Gordon S. Wakefield, *Puritan Devotion* (Epworth Press: London, 1957), p 1.
2. The evidence for Thomas' views is collected and summarised by C.H. and K. George, *The Protestant Mind of the English Reformation 1570-1640* (Princeton University Press: Princeton, 1961), pp 261-264, 280-283.
3. Leland Ryken, *Worldly Saints: the Puritans as They Really Were* (Zondervan: Grand Rapids, 1986), p 41.
4. Bullinger, *op cit*, fol. 1.
5. *Op cit*, fol. 3.
6. John Dod and Robert Cleaver, *A Godly Forme of Householde Government* (1598), p 125.
7. John Cotton, *A Meet Help* (1694), p 15.
8. Thomas Gataker, *A Wife Indeed*; cited from Ryken, *op cit*, p 42.
9. Thomas Gataker, *A Good Wife God's Gift* (1637), p 166.
10. Thomas Adams; cited from C.H. and K. George, *op cit*, p 268.
11. Richard Baxter, *A Christian Directory*; cited from Ryken, *op cit*, p 43.
12. John Downame, *The Plea of the Poor* (1616), p 119.
13. 'The rise of romantic marriage and its validation by the Puritans . . . represents a major innovation within the Christian tradition' (Herbert W. Richardson, *Nun, Witch, Playmate: the Americanization of Sex*, Harper and Row: New York, 1971, p 69). 'The conversion of courtly love into romantic monogamous love was . . . largely the work of . . . Puritan poets' (C.S. Lewis, 'Donne and Love Poetry in the Seventeenth Century,' in *Seventeenth Century Studies Presented to Sir Herbert Grierson* (Oxford University Press: Oxford, 1938, p 75).
14. Richard Baxter, *Works*, IV:234 (*The Poor Man's Family Book*, 1674).
15. Edmund S. Morgan, *The Puritan Family* (Harper and Row: New York, 1966), p 64. See further Ryken, *op cit*, chap 3 'Marriage and Sex', pp 39-54.

16. John Milton, *Paradise Lost*, IV:296-299, 750-761; VIII:589-592. 'Scale' means 'ladder'.
17. Daniel Rogers, *Matrimoniall Honour* (1642), p 148. L.L. Schücking, *The Puritan Family* (Schocken Books: New York, 1970), p 25, describes Rogers as 'one of the most generous-minded writers that has ever treated the problems of marriage, and one endowed with quite exceptional delicacy of feeling.'
18. Thomas Hooker, *The Soules Humiliation* (1638), pp 73f.
19. Thomas Hooker, *The Application of Redemption* (1659), p 137.
20. Thomas Hooker, *A Comment upon Christ's Last Prayer* (1656), p 187.
21. William Gouge, *Of Domesticall Duties* (1634), p 366.
22. John Milton, *Paradise Lost*, VIII:579-589.
23. Robert Bolton, *Works* (1631-41), IV:245f.
24. Richard Sibbes, *Works*, VI:520.
25. Gaius Davies, 'The Puritan Teaching on Marriage and the Family', *Evangelical Quarterly*, XXVII.1 (January 1955), p 19.
26. Thomas Gataker, *A Marriage Praier* (1624), p 16.
27. Henry Smith, *Works* (James Nichol: Edinburgh, 1866-67), I:15.
28. Cited from Davies, *art cit*, p 20.
29. Dod and Cleaver, *op cit*, p G:6.
30. Examples, over and above printed espousal and wedding sermons, include Dod and Cleaver, *op cit*; William Perkins, *Christian Oeconomie* (1590); Matthew Griffith, *Bethel: or, a Forme for Families* (1634); William Whateley, *Care-cloth: A Treatise of the Cumbers and Troubles of Marriage* (1624); William Gouge, *Of Domesticall Duties* (1634); Richard Baxter, *A Christian Directory* (1673), Part II: Christian Economics (*Works*, I:394-546).
31. 'As the young Bees do seek unto themselves another Hive so let the young couple another house . . . that whatsoever come, they may never fall into that unhappiest of all unhappinesses, of either being tormentors of their parents or tormented by them' (Whately, *Care-cloth*, preface, p x).
32. Perkins, *Works* (1616-18), III:690, 688, 683-684.
33. M.M. Knappen, *Tudor Puritanism* (Chicago University Press: Chicago, 1939), p 461. In England prior to the Matrimonial Causes Act of 1857 there was no legal procedure for divorce and remarriage save the passing of a special Act of Parliament in each case, a device that was first used in 1669.
34. Wakefield, *op cit*, p x.
35. 'Mr. Thomas Manton's Epistle to the Reader', *The [Westminster] Confession of Faith* (Free Presbyterian Publications: Glasgow, 1973), p 8. The Geneva Bible's note on Genesis 17:23 says: 'Masters in their houses ought to be as preachers to their families, that from the highest to the lowest they may obey the will of God.' The thought of the husband and father as spiritual instructor to the household recurs constantly.
36. Baxter, *Works*, IV:229. Baxter wrote *The Poor Man's Family Book* (1674) and *The Catechising of Families* (1683) as resources for the instructional side of family government.
37. Richard Baxter, cited anonymously in 'Mr. Thomas Manton's Epistle to the Reader', *op cit*, pp 9f.
38. Davies, *art cit*, p 29.
39. *Ibid*, p 30.
40. Perkins, *Works*, I:750.
41. Gouge, *op cit*, pp 10f.
42. Geree, *loc cit*.

Chapter 17: Puritan Preaching

1. John Bunyan, *The Pilgrim's Progress* (Oxford University Press: Oxford, Oxford Standard Authors series, 1904), pp 36f.
2. *The Westminster Directory* is currently in print in *The [Westminster] Confession of Faith* (Free Presbyterian Publications: Glasgow, Banner of Truth: Edinburgh). The section 'Of the Preaching of the Word' is pp 379-381. The quotation in the text is from p 381.
3. Loudness marked a number of Puritan preachers: Thomas Hooker was once (at least) referred to as 'bawling Hooker', and William Whateley was known as 'the Roaring Boy of Banbury'.
4. Richard Baxter, *The Reformed Pastor* (Banner of Truth: London, 1974), pp 174f, 61f.
5. *Ibid*, p 149.
6. David Clarkson, *Works*, pp. 193f.
7. Thomas Goodwin, *Works*, IX:378f.
8. Baxter, *Works*, (George Virtue: London 1838), I:726.
9. W. Carus, *Memoirs of . . . the Rev. Charles Simeon* (3rd edition, 1848), p 595.
10. John Owen, *Works*, XVI:74f.
11. William Gurnall, *The Christian in Complete Armour* (Banner of Truth: London, 1964), second pagination, p 574.
12. A.W. Brown, *Reflections of the Conversation Parties of the Rev. Chas. Simeon* (1862), p 177.
13. *Ibid*, p 183.
14. Goodwin, *Works*, II:lxivf; cited above.
15. Baxter, *Works*, II:399; cited above.
16. Goodwin, *Works*, II:lxxi.
17. Owen, *Works*, XVI:76.
18. Edward Bapshawe, 'Life and Death of Mr. Bolton' (bound with *M(r). Bolton's Four Last things*, 1632), p 13.
19. William Perkins, *Works*, II:665f.
20. *Ibid*, pp 380f.
21. Brown, *op cit*, pp 105f.
22. Baxter, *The Reformed Pastor*, p 62f.
23. *Ibid*, pp 120-23.

Chapter 18: Puritan Evangelism

1. I discuss this definition, and the necessary change, in *Evangelism and the Sovereignty of God* (Inter-Varsity Press: London and Downers Grove, 1961), pp 37-41.
2. Samuel Clarke, *Lives of Fifty-Two . . . Divines* (1677), pp 131, 222, etc.
3. Thomas Goodwin and Philip Nye, preface to Thomas Hooker, *The Application of Redemption*, 1956.
4. Charles G. Finney, *Revivals of Religion* (Oliphants: London, 1928), chap XIV, p 304.
5. *Ibid*, chap I, p 3.
6. Finney, *Autobiography* (Salvation Army Book Dept, nd), p 64.
7. B.B. Warfield, *Perfectionism, Works of B.B. Warfield*, vol VIII (reprinted Baker Book House: Grand Rapids, 1981), II:34.
8. John Owen, *Works* (see Chapter Four n 43), III:316f.
9. Thomas Watson, *A Body of Divinity*, p 154.
10. Owen, *Works*, III:317f.
11. *Westminster Confession*, X:i.
12. Thomas Goodwin, *Works*, IX:279.

13. *Ibid.*
14. Owen, *Works*, VIII:5-41.
15. *Ibid*, VIII:14-16.
16. Jonathan Edwards, *Works*, II:849f.
17. *Ibid*, I:353.
18. Goodwin, *Works*, VI:85.
19. *Reliquiae Baxterianae*, first pagination, p 7.
20. Above, Chapter Three.
21. *Reliquiae Baxterianae*, first pagination, pp 83, 86.
22. Richard Baxter, *The Reformed Pastor* (Banner of Truth: London, 1974).
23. Above, Chapter Nine.
24. See *Richard Baxter's Catholick Theologie: Plain, Pure, Peaceable: for the Pacification of the Dogmatical Word-Warriours* (1675).
25. See above, Chapter Nine.
26. On Baxter's ecclesiastical ideals, see Irvonwy Morgan, *The Nonconformity of Richard Baxter* (Epworth Press: London, 1946), and A. Harold Wood, *Church Unity without Uniformity* (Epworth Press: London, 1963).
27. *Reliquiae Baxterianae*, second pagination, pp 61-69.
28. Cf Peter Toon, *The Emergence of Hyper-Calvinism in English Non-conformity 1689-1765* (The Olive Tree: London, 1967), chap 3; 'Puritans and Calvinism' (Reiner: Swengel, 1973), chap 6.
29. '. . . the minister is in the church, as the schoolmaster in his school, to teach, and take an account of everyone in particular; and . . . all Christians, ordinarily, must be disciples or scholars in some such school' (*The Reformed Pastor*, pp 180f).
30. *Reliquiae Baxterianae*, first pagination, pp 93f.
31. 'Every *Thursday* Evening my Neighbours . . . met at my House, and there one of them repeated the Sermon, and afterwards they proposed what Doubts they had about the Sermon, or any other Case of Conscience, and I resolved their Doubts; And last of all I caused sometimes one, and sometimes another of them to Pray' (*ibid*, p 83).
32. Baxter, *The Reformed Pastor*, pp 86ff, 170ff.
33. Baxter describes his practice in detail in *The Reformed Pastor*, pp 162ff.
34. Reproduced opposite p 51 of J.T. Wilkinson's edition of *The Reformed Pastor* (Epworth Press: London, 1939).
35. *Reliquiae Baxterianae*, first pagination, p 115.
36. *The Reformed Pastor*, pp 194f.
37. *Ibid*, pp 186f.
38. *Ibid*, p 193.
39. *Ibid*, pp 173ff, 221-246.
40. Lay involvement did in fact emerge spontaneously in Kidderminster: 'Another Advantage which I had was, by the *Zeal* and *Diligence* of the Godly People . . . who thirsted after the Salvation of their Neighbours, and were in private my Assistants, and being dispersed throughout the Town, were ready in almost all Companies to repress seducing Words, and to justify godliness, and convince, reprove, exhort Men according to their needs; as also to teach them how to pray; and to help them to sanctifie the Lord's Day; For those People that had none in their Families who could pray, or repeat the Sermons, went to their next neighbour's house who could do it, and joined with them; so that *some Houses* (of the ablest Men) in each Street were filled with them that could do nothing, or little on their own' (*Reliquiae Baxterianae*, first pagination, p 87).

Chapter 19: Jonathan Edwards and Revival

1. Jonathan Edwards, *Works*, II:7; the sermon starts on p 3.

2. *Ibid*, II:17; the sermons starts on p 12.
3. *Ibid*, I:237, 238.
4. *Ibid*, I:394.
5. *Ibid*, I:391.
6. *Ibid*, I:ccxxxii (from Dwight's *Memoirs* of Edwards).
7. *Loc cit*.
8. *Ibid*, II:261.
9. *Ibid*, I:369.
10. *Ibid*, I:375.
11. *Ibid*, II:273.
12. *Ibid*, II:266-269.
13. *Ibid*, I:376f.
14. *Ibid*, I:584.
15. *Ibid*, I:583.
16. *Ibid*, I:380. Edwards refers in the context to Psalms 2 and 110.
17. *Ibid*, I:539.
18. *Ibid*, I:379.
19. *Ibid*, I:380.
20. *Ibid*, I:374.
21. *Ibid*, I:397.
22. *Ibid*, I:426.
23. *Ibid*, II:291.
24. *Ibid*, II:312.

Index

Abraham, 85, 268
Act of Uniformity, 23, 119, 120, 121
Adam, 82, 83, 85, 261, 266
Adams, Thomas, 254
'Admonition to the Parliament' (John Field and Thomas Wilcocks), 35, 53
Aggravation of Sin (Thomas Goodwin), 166
Alarme to the Unconverted, An (Joseph Alleine), 40, 166, 291, 340
Alleine, Joseph, 40, 166, 291, 340
Alleine, Richard, 166, 340
Alleine, Theodosia, 340
Allestree, Richard, 340
The Almost Christian (Matthew Meade), 40, 166
Ambrose, 267
Ames, William, 32, 68, 109, 110, 117, 118
Amyraldism, 12, 146, 157, 158, 346
Amyraut (Amyraldus), Moise, 146, 157
Andrewes, Lancelot, 340
Anglican church, 13, 14, 15, 21, 23, 28, 35, 36, 51, 53, 60, 119, 120, 245, 246, 248, 280, 281, 291, 338, 346
Annesley, Samual, 48
Anselm, 117
Antinomianism, 28, 108, 155, 158, 347
Application of Redemption, The (Thomas Hooker), 40, 166
'Application' of Scripture, 15, 39, 66, 70, 71, 72, 73, 98, 104, 105, 114, 116, 117, 119, 143, 165, 227, 233, 234, 279, 284, 286, 287, 288, 289, 313
Aquinas, Thomas, 109, 260, 261, 266
Aristotle, 260
Arminianism, 31, 46, 68, 127, 128, 129, 130, 131, 132, 133, 134, 137, 142, 146, 151, 152, 153, 154, 155, 156, 157, 158, 160, 165, 192, 295, 303, 310, 315, 333, 337, 338, 345
Arminius, 156
Armstrong, Louis, 16, 335
Arte of Prophecying (William Perkins), 70, 219, 280, 287
Augsburg Confession, 108
Augustine, Augustinian thought, 13, 68, 69, 99, 236, 237, 261, 293, 302, 329

Babington, Gervase, 235
Ball, John, 166, 340

Banner of Justification Displayed, The (John Goodwin), 157
Baptism, 36, 77, 153, 174, 186, 187, 188, 304
Barlow, Thomas, 346
Barth, Karl, Barthians, 15, 84, 95, 204, 343
Baxter, Benjamin, 340
Baxter, Richard, 13, 14, 15, 16, 26, 28, 29, 32, 35, 36, 38, 39, 40, 41, 42, 43, 44, 45, 46, 47, 49, 50, 54, 59, 60, 61, 62, 63, 65, 69, 71, 74, 75, 100, 112, 113, 118, 119, 121, 146, 152, 156, 157, 158, 159, 160, 164, 166, 168, 169, 171, 172, 175, 181, 193, 203, 213, 214, 216, 235, 236, 241, 242, 248, 254, 260, 263, 278, 280, 282, 285, 286, 288, 289, 291, 300, 302, 303, 304, 305, 306, 307, 308, 313, 332, 333, 334, 341, 346, 353
Bayly, Lewis, 59, 340
Baynes, Paul, 57, 280
Becon, Thomas, 261
Berkouwer, G.C., 149
Bernard, 12, 69, 209
Beveridge, William, 346
Beza, 269
Blair, Robert, 47
Blessedness of the Righteous, The (John Howe), 340
Blondel, 146
Boke of Matrimonye, The (Thomas Becon), 261
Bolton, Robert, 56, 61, 166, 169, 203, 267, 286, 340
Bondage of the Will (Martin Luther), 13
Book of Common Prayer (Thomas Cranmer), 261
Bound, Nicholas, 235
Bradford, John, 28, 329
Bramhall, John, 346
Breviate (Richard Baxter), 260
Bridge, 102
Brinsley, John, 340
Brooks, Thomas, 29, 75, 179, 182, 184, 240, 243, 341
Bruce, Robert, 213
Bruised Reed (Richard Sibbes), 40, 42, 50
Bucer, 269
Bull, Bishop, 157
Bullinger, Heinrich, 53, 261

Bunny, Dean Edmund, 235
Bunyan, John, 14, 16, 22, 23, 28, 29, 42, 60, 75, 95, 111, 114, 116, 142, 166, 216, 278, 286, 298, 302, 331, 332, 334, 335, 351
Burgess, Anthony, 340, 346
Burgess, Daniel, 202
Burroughs, Jeremiah, 166

Calamy, 40, 121, 339
Call to the Unconverted, A (Richard Baxter), 39, 40, 62, 63, 71, 166, 291, 302
Calling of the Ministerie, The (William Perkins), 219
Calvin, John, Calvinism, 15, 26, 28, 31, 35, 36, 38, 46, 76, 81, 82, 83, 86, 90, 108, 127, 128, 129, 130, 131, 132, 133, 134, 136, 137, 138, 142, 153, 157, 165, 180, 193, 198, 201, 222, 226, 227, 237, 246, 247, 248, 259, 269, 280, 281, 291, 303, 305, 309, 310, 314, 329, 330, 337, 338, 343, 345, 347, 349
Cameron, John, 146, 157
Cartwright, Thomas, 28, 35, 53, 280
Caryl, Joseph, 73
A Case of Conscience (William Perkins), 58
Catechism, Puritans' use of, 27, 45, 72, 241, 253, 270, 271, 305, 307, 308
Catechizing of Families, The (Richard Baxter), 62
Catholic Unity (Richard Baxter), 62
Cause of God and Truth, The (John Gill), 134
Causes Ways, and Means of Understanding the Mind of God (John Owen), 83
Chaderton, Laurence, 56, 57
Character of an Old English Puritane or Nonconformist, The (John Geree), 22, 270
Charnock, Stephen, 60, 251, 252, 333
Chauncy, Charles, 310
Chesterton, G.K., 308
Christ a Complete Saviour (John Bunyan), 166
Christian Directions Shewing how to Walk with God All the day Long (Thomas Gouge), 118, 203
Christian Directory (Richard Baxter), 28, 39, 41, 49, 62, 118, 254, 302, 341
Christian in Complete Armour, The (William Gurnall), 73, 334
Christian State of Matrimony, The (Bullinger), 261
Christian's Great Interest, The (William Guthrie), 42
Christian Warfare, The (John Downame), 58, 340
Christ Is All (Philip Henry), 166

Christ set Forth (Thomas Goodwin), 166
Chrysostom, 261
Church of England see Anglican church
Clark, Hugh, 291
Clark, Samuel, 340
Clarkson, David, 193, 255, 281
Claude, 281
Cleaver, Robert, 59, 268
Cleaver, Thomas, 41, 340
Collinges, 203
Conscience, 12, 15, 23, 28, 29, 41, 48, 56, 66, 68, 69, 75, 76, 104, 107 (Chapter 7 passim), 150, 151, 159, 173, 183, 193, 234, 236, 249, 298, 320, 330, 332, 344
Conversion, 14, 27, 40, 41, 74, 132, 143, 168, 169, 174, 175, 197, 217, 271, 278, 283, 292, 293, 294, 295, 296, 297, 298, 299, 301, 306, 307, 308, 311, 332
Cotton, John, 57, 280, 291, 310
Council of Trent, 153, 347
Covenant of Grace, The (John Ball), 340
Covenant theology, divine covenants, 66, 68, 88, 91, 132, 154, 155, 156, 167, 168, 198, 202, 211, 212, 217, 229, 295, 333, 334
Coverdale, Miles, 261
Cowper, William, 138
Cox, Bishop, 53, 56
Cranmer, Thomas, 14, 261, 269
Crisp, Tobias, 158, 304, 347
Crofton, Zachary, 174
Cromwell, 25, 27, 59, 60
Crucifying the World by the Cross of Christ (Richard Baxter), 62
Culverwell, Ezekiel, 40, 42, 166, 340
Curcellaeus, 156

Daillé, 146
Davenant, John, 146, 346
Davenport, 310
Davies, Gaius, 271
Davies, Horton, 248
Death of Death in the Death of Christ, The (John Owen), 12, 125 (Chapter 8 passim)
Denne, Henry, 347
Doctrine of Faith, The (John Rogers), 40
de Groot, Hugo see Grotius
Dennison, 235
Dent, Arthur, 59, 118
Dering, Edward, 28, 38, 52, 53, 57, 58
Des Marets (Maresius), 146
Dickson, David, 109, 286
Directions and Persuasions to a Sound Conversion (Richard Baxter), 62, 166
Directions for Weak, Distempered Christians (Richard Baxter), 62
Discourse concerning the Holy Spirit (John Owen), 194

Discourse of Spiritual Gifts (John Owen), 219, 222, 224, 225, 226
Display of Arminianism, A (John Owen), 145, 346
Divine Life, The (Richard Baxter), 62, 203
Doctrine of Faith, The (John Rogers), 166, 172, 340
Doctrine of Justification by Faith, The (John Owen), 68, 150, 346
Dod, John, 41, 59, 340
Doolittle, Thomas, 340
Downame, George, 340, 346
Downame, John, 39, 58, 340
Duncan, Rabbi, 194
Durham, James, 101, 203
Duties of Pastors and People Distinguished, The (John Owen), 221
Dying Thoughts (Richard Baxter), 39
Dyke, Daniel, 40, 166, 340
Dyke, Jeremiah, 340

Eaton, John, 347
Edwards, Jonathan, 21, 37, 46, 239, 293, 297, 309 (Chapter 19 *passim*)
Edwards, Sarah, 321
Edwards, Thomas, 146
Election, 126, 128, 129, 130, 131, 132, 155, 157, 165, 271, 296, 298, 345, 346
Elton, Edward, 340
Episcopius, 156
Essay on the Composition of a Sermon (Claude), 281
Evangelism, 26, 28, 51, 141, 142, 143, 163, 164, 165, 166, 171, 175, 176, 234, 283, 287, 291 (Chapter 18 *passim*)
Eve, 261, 266
Evil of Evils, The (Jeremiah Burroughs), 166
Exposition of Romans 9, An (John Goodwin), 157
Exposition of the Creed (John Pearson), 340

Fairclough, Richard, 43, 45
Faith, 15, 32, 66, 67, 68, 69, 84, 85, 88, 89, 90, 91, 108, 115, 117, 130, 131, 134, 139, 140, 143, 144, 145, 149, 152, 154, 155, 163, 164, 167, 170, 171, 172, 173, 174, 180, 181, 182, 185, 188, 197, 200, 204, 205, 212, 213, 229, 250, 252, 271, 279, 283, 289, 298, 300, 301, 303, 321, 327, 332, 335, 342, 347, 349
Family, the, 25, 26, 29, 41, 241, 255, 259 (Chapter 16 *passim*), 330, 331, 356
Fenner, William, 112, 114, 115, 117, 340
Ferguson, Sinclair, 209, 212, 214
Field, John, 53
Finney, Charles G., 292, 293, 294, 299, 300, 301, 302
Firmin, Giles, 166, 172

Fisher, E., 166
Flavel, John, 29, 40, 75, 166, 312
Fleming, Robert, 47
Ford, Simon, 340
Freedom of the Will, The (Jonathan Edwards), 309, 315
Fuller, Thomas, 35, 57, 63, 240

Gataker, 268
General Martyrology, A (Samuel Clark), 340
Geree, John, 22, 26, 270, 334
Gildas Salvianus (Richard Baxter), 305
Gill, John, 134
Glendinning, James, 47
Glory of Christ, The (John Owen), 166
God, Christ, love of, 12, 13, 15, 24, 33, 115, 132, 139, 142, 173, 183, 184, 189, 200, 201, 205, 209, 212, 213, 215, 299, 321, 332, 333, 345 sovereignty of, 12, 29, 36, 89, 126, 127, 128, 129, 130, 134, 138, 140, 141, 143, 145, 184, 249, 284, 294, 297, 298, 301, 332, 333, 339, 345
Godliness, 12, 28, 54, 81, 93, 107, 114, 119, 192, 243, 249, 271, 310, 332, 335
Godly Preachers of the Elizabethan Church, The (Irvonwy Morgan), 46
Golden Chain, A (William Perkins), 58
Goodwin, John, 184
Goodwin, Thomas, 29, 40, 47, 57, 60, 73, 74, 75, 97, 100, 103, 109, 152, 157, 166, 167, 172, 179, 182, 183, 184, 185, 186, 187, 188, 196, 203, 207, 208, 254, 280, 282, 285, 286, 296, 298, 340
Goold, William, 146, 147, 346
Gospel, the, 28, 36, 37, 40, 48, 65, 69, 72, 74, 105, 118, 126, 134, 136, 138, 139, 140, 142, 143, 149, 163 (Chapter 10 *passim*), 180, 181, 182, 185, 193, 196, 200, 209, 218, 234, 271, 278, 295, 296, 297, 300, 301, 307, 311, 313, 319, 333, 342, 345
Gouge, Thomas, 118, 203
Gouge, William, 57, 265, 270, 272, 340
Grace, 27, 30, 31, 33, 36, 66, 69, 71, 74, 75, 93, 108, 114, 118, 126, 130, 132, 133, 134, 138, 142, 144, 145, 149, 152, 167, 170, 171, 172, 173, 175, 182, 195, 196, 197, 198, 199, 200, 202, 204, 205, 206, 209, 212, 215, 216, 217, 223, 225, 228, 229, 230, 239, 240, 243, 252, 253, 254, 281, 286, 293, 295, 296, 297, 298, 299, 303, 306, 324, 330, 332, 334, 342, 347
Grace Abounding, 216
Grace and Duty of Being Spiritually Minded, The (John Owen), 199
Graham, Billy, 300, 301
Great Awakening, the, 27, 327
Greenham, Richard, 28, 43, 44, 48, 54, 55, 57, 58, 59, 235, 333, 340

Gregory of Nyssa, 261
Grotius, 156, 158
Gurnall,William, 29, 73, 75, 121, 284, 334, 340
Guthrie, William, 42

Hale, Matthew, 242
Hall, Robert, 346
Haller, William, 22, 28, 38, 42
Hammond, Henry, 340
Harrison, A.W., 157
Heart of Christ in Heaven towards Sinners on Earth, The (Thomas Goodwin), 166
'Heart-work,' 32, 48, 215, 241, 249, 256, 257, 329
Heaven on Earth (Thomas Brooks), 179
Heaven Opened (Richard Alleine), 166
Henry, Matthew, 98, 238, 239, 262, 284, 353
Henry, Philip, 166
Hermandzoon, Jacob see Arminius
Hildersam, Arthur, 57, 71, 73, 340
History of the Puritans (Daniel Neal), 37
History of the Word of Redemption, A (Jonathan Edwards), 316
Hodge, 310
Hoggart, Richard, 107
Holiness, 11, 23, 24, 26, 29, 32, 33, 39, 183, 188, 193, 198, 200, 243, 271, 286, 298, 330, 332, 335
Holland, Henry, 43, 55, 69
Holy Spirit, the, 12, 31, 32, 36, 48, 60, 66, 68, 70, 75, 76, 83, 84, 85, 86, 87, 89, 90, 91, 92, 93, 94, 95, 96, 99, 100, 108, 113, 128, 131, 144, 154, 163, 164, 168, 174, 179 (Chapter 11 passim), 193, 198, 201, 206, 207, 209, 211, 212, 217, 220, 221, 222, 225, 227, 229, 234, 248, 249, 250, 271, 282, 283, 284, 289, 291, 293, 295, 300, 309, 311, 317, 318, 319, 320, 321, 322, 323, 325, 332, 333, 340, 342, 343, 347, 349, 350
Holy War (John Bunyan), 111
Hooker, Richard, 254, 346
Hooker, Thomas, 40, 135, 166, 171, 172, 248, 264, 265, 310, 357
Hooper, Bishop, 51, 235, 247
Hopkins, George, 340
Hooper, John, 28, 269
Hopkins, 314
Horae Homileticae (Charles Simeon), 281
Howe, John, 29, 43, 45, 47, 60, 97, 340
Howe, Obadiah, 147, 333
Humble attempt to promote Explicit Agreement and Visible Union of God's People in Extraordinary Prayer for the Revival of Religion, A (Jonathan Edwards), 326

Humility, 15, 24, 31, 138, 193, 196, 200, 252, 286, 331

Imputatio Fidei (John Goodwin), 157
Indwelling Sin (John Owen), 194
Institutes (John Calvin), 90, 108, 226
Interpreting Scripture, 83, 84, 93, 96, 98, 99, 101, 102, 103, 104, 105, 128, 246

Janeway, John, 340
Johnson, Dr., 14, 306
Jowett, J.H., 284
Justification, 66, 67, 76, 104, 108, 149 (Chapter 9 passim), 202, 333, 342, 346, 347

Kendall, R.T., 51
Knappen, Marshall, 22, 28, 269
Knowledge of God the Father and His Son Jesus Christ, The (Thomas Goodwin), 166
Knox, John, 28, 38, 248, 330

Laodiceanism, 14, 21, 77, 122
Latimer, Bishop Hugh, 235, 280
Laud, Chancellor, 38, 118, 192, 250
Lawrence, D.H., 107, 108
Laws of Ecclesiastical Polity (Thomas Hooker), 135
Leighton, 121
Letters (Samuel Rutherford), 340
Lewis, C. S., 14, 15, 16, 257
The Life and Death of Joseph Alleine (Theodosia Alleine), 340
Life of Faith, The (Richard Baxter), 39, 62
Limborch, 156
Livingstone, John, 47
Lloyd-Jones, Martyn, 69, 281
Luther, Martin, 13, 15, 28, 67, 107, 108, 149, 151, 152, 160, 246, 269, 302, 333
Lye, Thomas, 48

Manton, Thomas, 29, 75, 167
Marrow of Ecclesiastical History, The (Samuel Clark), 340
Marrow of Modern Divinity, The (E. Fisher), 166
Meade, Matthew, 40, 166, 340
Meditation on the Word, 13, 24, 30, 32, 94, 116, 183, 199, 207, 215, 237, 249, 257, 282, 286
Meditations and Discourses of the Glory of Christ (John Owen), 213
Methodism, 27, 327
Method of Grace (John Flavel), 40, 166
Mildmay, Sir Walter, 57
Miller, Perry, 22, 28, 37
Milton, John, 266, 267

Mischiefs of Self-ignorance, The (Richard Baxter), 62

Moffatt, James, 207

Moody, D.L., 300

More, Thomas, 146, 147

Morgan, Edmund, 22, 263

Morgan, Dr Irvonwy, 37, 46

Morning Exercise at (St.) Giles Cripplegate, The, 340

Morning Exercise at (St.) Giles in the Fields, The, 340

Mortification, 12, 199, 200, 236, 330

Mortification of Sin (John Owen), 194

Mystery of Selfe-Deceiving (Daniel Dyke), 40, 166

Narrative of a Surprising Word of God, A (Jonathan Edwards), 316

Neal, Daniel, 37

Neonomianism, 156, 157, 303

Neo-orthodox thought, 83

New Birth, The (William Whateley), 40, 166

New Covenant, The (John Preston), 166

New England Mind Vol I; The Seventeenth Century, The (Perry Miller), 28

Newton, John, 335

Nonconformists, 35, 51, 56, 60, 108, 121, 160, 236, 249, 303, 346

Nye, Philip, 40

Oasland, Henry, 48

Object and Acts of Justifying Faith, The (Thomas Goodwin), 203

Of Christ the Mediator (Thomas Goodwin), 166

Of Communion with God the Father, Son and Holy Ghost (John Owen), 202, 204

Of the Divine Originall, Authority, Self-evidencing Light and Power of the Scriptures (John Owen), 83

Of the Object and the Acts of Justifying Faith (Thomas Goodwin), 179

Origen, 261

Original Sin (Jonathan Edwards), 309

Orthodoxy, 14, 26, 27, 31, 81, 84, 311, 347

Owen, John, 12, 16, 29, 42, 60, 64, 68, 71, 72, 73, 75, 76, 81 (Chapter 5 *passim*), 100, 102, 103, 104, 117, 125 (Chapter 8 *passim*), 150, 152, 166, 168, 173, 179, 180, 188, 189, 191 (Chapter 12 *passim*), 219 (Chapter 13 *passim*), 250, 252, 253, 256, 283, 286, 295, 296, 297, 303, 310, 333, 340, 343, 346, 351, 353

Palau, Luis, 300

Parable of the Ten Virgins (Thomas Shepard), 40, 166

Payne, William, 213

Pearson, John, 340

Pelagianism, semi-Pelagianism, 127, 133, 151, 293, 294, 295, 299, 300, 302

Perkins, William, 28, 29, 32, 36, 40, 41, 42, 50, 56, 57, 58, 59, 63, 64, 67, 68, 70, 72, 73, 75, 76, 109, 118, 152, 186, 219, 269, 272, 280, 287, 333, 337, 349

Piety, 25, 28, 35, 117, 152, 212, 236, 249, 280, 310, 311, 318, 319, 322, 323, 331, 332

Pilgrim's Progress (John Bunyan), 30, 42, 95, 103, 286, 334, 335, 351

Pilgrim's Regress, The (C. S.Lewis), 15

Pink, William, 340

Plaine and Familiar Exposition of the Ten Commandments (John Dod and Thomas Cleaver), 41

Plain Man's Pathway to Heaven, The (Arthur Dent), 59, 118

Pneumatologia: A Discourse Concerning the Holy Spirit (John Owen), 83

Pool, Matthew, 353

Poor Man's Family Book (Richard Baxter), 62

Practical Catechism, A (Henry Hammond), 340

Practice of Christianity, The (Richard Rogers), 58

Practice of Piety, The (Lewis Bayly), 59, 63, 340

Prayer, 13, 24, 25, 26, 30, 48, 71, 94, 96, 100, 144, 175, 183, 198, 199, 200, 207, 215, 221, 225, 227, 230, 237, 240, 241, 242, 246, 248, 249, 253, 255, 256, 268, 283, 284, 286, 288, 289, 297, 304, 305, 323, 325, 326, 327, 330, 332, 333, 334

Preaching, Puritan, 37, 60, 65, 71, 72, 73, 74, 75, 76, 77, 95, 108, 116, 117, 126, 127, 137, 138, 139, 140, 141, 142, 145, 149, 163 (Chapter 10 *passim*), 193, 195, 253, 254, 273, 277 (Chapter 17 passim), 301, 307, 313, 314, 330, 332, 353, 357

Preston, John, 57, 61, 166, 186, 280, 333, 340, 349

Promises, God's, 24, 67, 68, 87, 139, 185, 198, 211, 212, 246, 323, 349

'Public Worship to be preferred before Private' (David Clarkson), 255, 281

Puritanism and Liberty (A.S.P. Woodhouse), 28

Quakers, the, 27, 60, 86, 248

Ramus, Peter, 73, 285

Ranew, Nathaniel, 340

Rawlet, John, 340

Real Christian, The (Giles Firmin), 166, 172

Reason of Faith, The (John Owen), 83

Redemption, 74, 125, 129, 130, 131, 135, 155, 165, 167, 168, 170, 202, 295, 311, 323, 345

Redemption Redeemed (John Goodwin), 157, 196

Reformation, the, Reformed thought, 12, 13, 25, 28, 37, 40, 41, 51, 52, 62, 64, 66, 68, 69, 81, 82, 83, 84, 86, 90, 136, 149, 151, 152, 159, 165, 186, 193, 222, 226, 235, 248, 293, 303, 333, 340, 347

Reformed Pastor (Richard Baxter), 13, 26, 38, 43, 45, 75, 302, 305, 306, 307

Refutation ... of Thomas More, A (Thomas Whitefield), 147

Reliquiae Baxteriane (Richard Baxter, 302

Repentance, 32, 36, 77, 138, 141, 144, 152, 167, 171, 172, 173, 174, 175, 197, 215, 229, 289, 293, 298, 303, 332

Restoration, the, 21, 29, 42, 46, 47, 51, 121, 157, 304

Revival, 27, 28, 36, 37, 38, 39, 42, 46, 47, 48, 51, 293, 297, 309 (Chapter 19 *passim*)

Reyner, Edward, 340

Reynolds, Edward, 121, 166, 340

Rise of Puritanism, The (William Haller), 28

Rivet, 146

Robinson, John, 99

Rogers, Daniel, 264

Rogers, John, 40, 47, 97, 98, 166, 171, 172, 173, 264, 340

Rogers, Richard, 57, 58, 59, 114, 118, 340

Rutherford, Samuel, 196, 340

Ryken, Leland, 261

Ryle, J. C., 14, 281, 285

Saints' Everlasting Rest, The (Richard Baxter), 36, 39, 49, 61, 302, 334

Saltmarsh, John, 347

Salvation, 27, 33, 39, 84, 126, 130, 131, 132, 133, 134, 138, 142, 143, 145, 152, 165, 171, 185, 204, 207, 297, 298, 299, 342, 349 assurance of, 180, 181, 182, 183, 184, 185, 186, 188, 189, 332, 345

Salvation from Sin (George Hopkins), 340

Sanctification, 24, 39, 153, 155, 198, 199, 201, 225, 236, 332, 342

Sandys, Edwin, 53, 54

Savoy Confession, 193

Scholes, Percy, 22

Scripture Gospel Defended, The (Richard Baxter), 158, 304

Scudder, William, 340

Self-Denial (Richard Baxter), 62

Senhouse, Dr, 73

Seven Treatises (Richard Rogers), 58, 118

Shaw, Samuel, 340

Shepard, Thomas, 40, 166, 171, 173, 310, 312

Sibbes, Richard, 29, 40, 42, 50, 56, 57, 61, 75, 103, 110, 115, 179, 184, 186, 203, 256, 267, 280, 286, 333, 340, 349

Simeon, Charles, 281, 282, 284, 286, 288

Sinfulnesse of Sin, The (Edward Reynolds), 166

Smeaton, George, 154

Smith, Henry, 340

Smith, Samuel, 340

Smith, Thomas, 340

Some General Directions for a Comfortable Walking with God (Robert Bolton), 203

Soul's Preparation for Christ, The (Thomas Hooker), 172

Sound Believer, The (Thomas Shepard), 166

Spanheim, 146

Spiritual Desertions (William Perkins), 58

'Spiritual Worship' (Stephen Charnock), 251

Spirituality, 12, 15, 16, 151, 191 (Chapter 12 *passim*), 251

Spurgeon, C. H., 12, 30, 69, 142, 171, 172, 191, 194, 281, 286, 300, 306, 307, 335, 345

Stalham, John, 147

Stoddard, Solomon, 309, 312

Stoughton, John, 340

Stowe, John, 50

Strong, William, 340

Sung, John, 300

Swinnock, George, 239, 241, 249, 255, 257, 340

Sylvester, M., 302

Symonds, Joseph, 340

Synod of Dort, 35, 128, 130, 134, 135, 138

Taylor, Thomas, 340

Teate, Faithful, 340

Temptation (John Owen), 194

Ten Commandments, The (Lancelot Andrewes), 340

Ten Commandments, The (John Dod and Robert Cleaver), 59, 340

Testard, 146

Thomas, Thomistic thought see *Aquinas*

Thomson, Andrew, 136, 147, 194

Thoughts on the Revival of Religion in New England in 1740 (Jonathan Edwards), 316, 321, 325

Tillotson, 312

Toplady, 12, 347

Towne, Robert, 347

Traill, Robert, 150, 151, 158, 160, 346

Trapp, 121

Treatise concerning Religious Affections (Jonathan Edwards), 312, 316

Treatise of Conscience, A (William Fenner), 112

Treatise of Conversion, A (Richard Baxter), 62, 74, 166

Treatise of Faith (John Ball), 166, 340

Treatise of Faith (Ezekiel Culverwell), 40, 42, 166, 340

Treatise of Love, A (John Rogers), 340

Treatise of Prayer, A (George Downame), 340

Treatise of the Nature and Practice of Repentance (William Perkins), 40

Treatise of the Sabbath (Richard Greenham), 235

Treatise of the Vocations, A (William Perkins), 272

Treatise Tending unto a Declaration whether a man be in the estate of Damnation or in the estate of Grace (William Perkins), 41, 58

Tregoss, Thomas, 48

Trevelyan, G.M., 51

True Doctrine of the Sabbath (Dr Nicholas Bound), 235

Tudor Puritanism (M.M. Knappen), 28

Tully, Thomas, 346

Twisse, William, 155

Two treatises (William Perkins), 58

Tyndale, William, 28, 66, 67, 329

Unction, 23, 43, 75, 92, 227, 314, 333

Universalist Examined and Convicted, The (Obadiah Howe), 147

Universality of God's Free Grace in Christ to Mankind, The (Thomas More), 147

Unregenerate Man's Guiltiness before God, An (Thomas Goodwin), 166

Usher, James, 61, 62, 146, 256, 346

Vain Religion of the Formal Hypocrite Detected, The (Richard Baxter), 62

Vincent, Thomas, 340

Vindication of the Protestant Doctrine concerning Justification (Robert Traill), 150, 158

Vindiciae Redemptionis (John Stalham), 147

Vines, Richard, 340

Wales, Elkanah, 48

Ward, Samuel, 340

Warfield, B.B., 13, 220, 294, 310

'Warrant of Faith, The', (C.H. Spurgeon), 171

Watch and Rule of Life, The (John Brinsley), 340

Watson, Thomas, 29, 75, 99, 341

Wesley, Charles, 345

Wesley, John, 46, 48, 142, 300, 302, 339

Westminster Confession, 95, 153, 154, 155, 173, 193, 238, 262, 269, 294, 333, 342, 344, 347, 354

Westminster Directory, 117, 248, 256, 278, 280, 287

Westminster Larger Catechism, 95, 241, 342

Westminster Shorter Catechism, 45, 99, 242, 271, 294

Whateley, William, 40, 166, 269, 340, 357

Whitefield, George, 23, 30, 46, 142, 161, 300, 306, 307, 313, 314

Whitfield, Thomas, 147

Whole Duty of Man, The (Richard Allestree), 340

Whyte, Alexander, 72, 179, 198, 281

Wilcocks, Thomas, 53

Williams, Charles, 14, 16

Wilson, Daniel, 282

Woodhouse, A.S.P., 28

Work of Christ as an Advocate, The (John Bunyan), 166

Worship, 24, 25, 26, 28, 31, 36, 48, 94, 126, 134, 144, 152, 202, 208, 211, 213, 221, 224, 235, 237, 238, 239, 241, 242, 245 (Chapter 15 *passim*), 269, 270, 273, 281, 325, 333, 334, 354

Zwingli, Huldreich, 269, 280